The Political Economy of Regional Cooperation in the Middle East

The Middle East has been seen as one of the most volatile regions in the world. It appears to be the exception in the general global trend of peaceful cooperation, economic liberalisation, and relative democratisation. Is it destined to remain characterised by violent conflicts, authoritarian regimes and closed, inefficient economies?

Political Economy of Regional Cooperation in the Middle East explores the current anatomy of regional cooperation and why it has often failed to take hold. It argues that focusing on international and regional factors alone is insufficient in explaining the prevailing instability in the region. Instead the authors highlight domestic factors as crucial to understanding conflict and cooperation in the Middle East. Based on the literature on domestic sources of foreign policy, this study develops its own original conceptual model and demonstrates why it is essential to mobilise domestic support for cooperation amongst countries of the Middle East. Without such support from economic and social groups, inter-governmental cooperation is less likely to last.

This study offers an alternative view of politics and international relations in the Middle East. The findings show that cooperation among the relatively more open regimes, such as Israel, Jordan, Egypt, Palestine and Turkey can pave the way to increased stability in the region.

Ali Çarkoğlu is Assistant Professor of Political Science at Boğaziçi University, Istanbul. **Mine Eder** is Assistant Professor of International Affairs at Lewis and Clark College, Portland. **Kemal Kirişci** is Professor of International Relations at Boğaziçi University, Istanbul.

Routledge Advances in International Relations and Politics

1 **Foreign policy and discourse analysis**
Henrik Larsen

2 **Agency, structure and international politics**
From ontology to empirical enquiry
Gil Friedman and Harvey Starr

3 **The political economy of regional cooperation in the Middle East**
Ali Çarkoğlu, Mine Eder, Kemal Kirişci

4 **Peace maintenance**
The evolution of international political authority
Jarat Chopra

5 **International relations and historical sociology**
Breaking down boundaries
Stephen Hobden

6 **Equivalence in comparative politics**
Edited by *Jan W. van Deth*

The Political Economy of Regional Cooperation in the Middle East

Ali Çarkoğlu, Mine Eder and Kemal Kirişci

ROUTLEDGE

London and New York

First published 1998
by Routledge
11 New Fetter Lane, London EC4P 4EE

Simultaneously published in the USA and Canada
by Routledge
29 West 35th Street, New York, NY 10001

Typeset in Baskerville by
Ponting–Green Publishing Services, Chesham, Bucks
Printed and bound in Great Britain by
Clays Ltd, St. Ives PLC

British Library Cataloguing in Publication Data
A catalogue record for this book is available from the British Library

Library of Congress Cataloguing in Publication Data
Çarkoğlu, Ali, 1963–
The political economy of regional cooperation in the Middle East / Ali Çarkoğlu, Mine Eder & Kemal Kirişci.
p. cm.
Includes bibliographical references and index.
1. Middle East – Economic integration. 2. Middle East – Economic conditions–1979– 3. Middle East – Foreign economic relations. 4. Arab cooperation. I. Eder, Mine, 1965– . II. Kirişci, Kemal, 1954– . III. Title.
HC415.15.C37 1998
337.56–dc21 98–17666

ISBN 0–415–19445–8

Contents

List of figures and tables vi
Acknowledgements viii
List of abbreviations ix

1 Introduction 1

2 New regionalism and the Middle East 16

3 Political economy of regional cooperation: towards a model 36

4 The economic map of the Middle East 56

5 Potential for regional economic cooperation 112

6 Dynamics of political change in the Middle East 139

7 Potential for regional political cooperation 165

8 Regional cooperation and the 'like-minded' states: the case of Turkey from a two-level-game perspective 192

9 Conclusion 227

Notes 233
Bibliography 236
Bibliography of journals and newspapers 251
Index 252

Figures and tables

Figures

3.1	Sequential and simultaneous two-level games	44
3.2a	Level I: Game between international negotiators	45
3.2b	Level II: Game between relevant domestic constituencies	45
3.3	Game between international negotiators (further detail)	46

Tables

2.1	Various degrees of regional cooperation	17
4.1	Perennial rivers in the Middle East	58
4.2	Basic environmental indicators	59
4.3	Population figures in the Middle East	60
4.4	Regional labour force	62
4.5	Population and labour force	64
4.6	Access to safe drinking water and sanitation	65
4.7	Agriculture and food in the Middle East	68
4.8	World economic growth	71
4.9	Commodity prices	72
4.10	Value of exports and imports in the Middle East	73
4.11	Export shares of various products in the Middle East	74
4.12	Import shares of various products in the Middle East	76
4.13	Export and import price indices in the Middle East	77
4.14	Terms-of-trade index in the Middle East	78
4.15	Workers' remittances received in the Middle East	79
4.16a	Direction of trade in the Middle East: exports	80–1
4.16b	Direction of trade in the Middle East: imports	82–3
4.17	Exports to OECD markets of dynamic products from Middle Eastern countries	85
4.18	Trade intensity index for selected Middle Eastern countries' exports	87
4.19	Revealed comparative advantage indices	90
4.20	Military expenditure in the Middle East	100

4.21	Macroeconomic indicators	104
4.22	Real GDP per capita and changes in real GDP per capita	106
4.23	Percentage share of income or consumption	107
4.24	Real consumption, real investment and real government share of GDP	108
4.25	Inflation	109
5.1	Non-residential capital stock per worker	127
	Capital stock per worker in producer durables	127
	Capital stock per worker in transportation equipment	127
8.1	Turkey's foreign trade with the Middle East	201
8.2	Imports of Turkish crude oil and natural gas	203
8.3	Turkey's primary energy consumption	204

Acknowledgements

We have accumulated a large number of debts in the lengthy process of writing this book, and we would like to acknowledge them here. First, we want to thank the Turkish Economic and Social Studies Foundation who supported our project under their Dr Nejat F. Eczacıbaşı Research Grants Program. Without their support, we would have never reached the point in our thinking on the peace process and regional cooperation in the Middle East. Ali Çarkoğlu and Mine Eder also received partial funding from a Middle East Research Competition Grant from the Ford Foundation. Our interview with Şerif Egeli was an early and very significant influence on our conception of the problem and led us towards the work of Robert Putnam whose influence on our work is most certainly recognisable. Soli Özel read an earlier version of the manuscript and acted as our discussant in our panel at the Middle East Studies Association's 1997 meetings in San Francisco. His criticisms and corrections acted as an early warning mechanism for us and helped us better present our views in many respects. Mehmet Arda of UNCTAD helped us in finding and processing our data, only some of which have found their way into our final manuscript. Many others have helped us during the course of writing this book. Space precludes us from naming them all individually but we would like to thank the Egyptian, Jordanian, Palestinian and Turkish academics, business people and officials who gave their time to answering our endless questions. A number of assistants have spent long hours in shaping our tables, reading, correcting and translating our earlier versions of the manuscript. These include Kemal Bodur of the Department of Economics at Boğaziçi University, Emre Erdoğan, Serkan Tanka and Yüksel Taşkın of the Department of Political Science and International Relations. Foremost, we would like to express our appreciation to Boğaziçi University, Istanbul, Lewis and Clark College, Portland and the University of Michigan, Ann Arbor which provided facilities during the completion of this book. We would also like to thank Routledge for their excellent editorial work and two anonymous reviewers for their valuable inputs.

Finally, this project had to be completed while we were all at three different institutions on two different continents. Short visits to our base at Boğaziçi University thus had to suffer from even shorter times allocated for our families and loved ones, to all of whom we owe our greatest thanks. We dedicate this book to them, Gül, Can, Gökhan, Gülsen, Candan, and Eda.

List of abbreviations

ACM	Arab Common Market
ACRS	Arms Control and Regional Security (Working Group)
ANAP	Motherland Party
ANZCERTA	Australia–New Zealand Closer Economic Relations Trade Agreement
AOPEC	Arab Organisation of Petroleum Exporting Countries
APEC	Asia–Pacific Economic Cooperation Group
ASEAN	Association of South-East Asian Nations
CACM	Central American Common Market
CARICOM	Caribbean Community
CARIFTA	Caribbean Free Trade Area
CCT	Common Customs Tariff
CEAO	Economic Community of West Africa
CENTO	Central Treaty Organisation
CET	Common External Tariff
CHP	Republican People's Party
COMECON	Council for Mutual Economic Assistance
CSCE	Conference on Security and Cooperation in Europe
DEP	Democracy Party
DOP	Israeli–PLO Declaration of Principles
DYP	True Path Party
ECLA	Economic Commission for Latin America
ECOWAS	Economic Community of West African States
ECSC	European Coal and Steel Community
EEC	European Economic Community
EFTA	European Free Trade Area
EU	European Union
FIS	Islamic Salvation Front
GAP	Southeastern Anatolia Development Project
GATT	General Agreement on Tariffs and Trade
GCC	Gulf Cooperation Council
GSP	Generalised System of Preferences
HEP	People's Labour Party

IMF	International Monetary Fund
INC	Iraqi National Congress
LAFTA	Latin American Free Trade Area
MEBRD	Middle Eastern Bank for Reconstruction and Development
MEDB	Middle East and North Africa Development Bank
MEMTTA	Middle East Mediterranean Travel and Tourism Association
MENA	Middle East North Africa
MERCOSUR	Southern Cone Common Market
MFA	Multi-Fibre Arrangement
MHP	Nationalist Action Party
MUSIAD	Independent Association of Industrialists and Businessmen
NAFTA	North American Free Trade Agreement
NATO	North Atlantic Treaty Organisation
NGO	Non-Governmental Organisation
NTM	Non-Tariff measure
OECD	Organisation of Economic Cooperation and Development
OIC	Islamic Conference Organisation
PKK	Workers' Party of Kurdistan
PLO	Palestine Liberation Organisation
PNC	Palestine National Council
PTP	Preferential Tariff Protocol
RCA	Revealed Comparative Advantage
RP	Welfare Party
SACU	Southern African Customs Union
SITC	Standard International Trade Classification
TII	Trade intensity index
TUSIAD	Turkish Industrialist and Businessmen Association
UDEAC	Central African Customs and Economic Union
UNICEF	United Nations Education Fund
UNSCOM	United Nations Special Commission
UR	Uruguay Round
WEU	Western European Union
WHO	World Health Organisation

1 Introduction

> 'The Middle East is a visionary's paradise: An area whose most famous city is the City of Peace, but whose most common characteristic so often seems to be its perpetual war.'
>
> Roberts (1995: 11)

No other region in the world offers as contradictory a picture as the Middle East. Home of three religions, the region has an unparalleled diversity of culture and history. With its rich oil reserves, it is the host of one of the world's most precious natural resources. Yet it has also been an ongoing host to historic conflicts between the Arab countries and Israel, between conservative and radical regimes, between Iran and Iraq, between Iraq and the Gulf-War coalition, between the oil-rich and non-oil states, between secularists and Islamic fundamentalists.

The 1980s and early 1990s witnessed developments that may indeed transform this land of political turbulence and conflicts. Can the Middle East become an 'economically prospering', 'democratising' region like most regions in the world and finally begin to fulfil its potential? Or is the region bound to remain 'exceptional', plagued with violent conflict, slow growth, relative isolation, and closed and inefficient economies? Can the existing barriers to political and economic cooperation be overcome in the region? If so, how can the Middle East join in the global trend of regional cooperation? What are the new opportunities and prospects emerging in the region that make such cooperation more likely? What are the conditions of successful economic and political cooperation in the Middle East? Do these conditions exist in the region? What role can states with democratic and open regimes with fewer inter-state conflicts, or what may be called 'like-minded' states, play in fostering cooperation in the region? What kind of a role can one of these 'like-minded' states, namely Turkey, play in order to enhance cooperation and peace in the Middle East? This study explores the answers to these questions by analysing the constraints and prospects of regional cooperation in the Middle East. In answering these questions, we observe that exploring the prospects of economic and political cooperation in the Middle East is a highly urgent and crucial issue. Such a focus is likely to have important repercussions not only for peace and development in the region but also for the world. The Gulf War has clearly shown that few conflicts in the Middle East can actually remain regional. Given the geo-strategic and economic significance of the region, ensuring stability through regional cooperation, is indeed a priority.

Five main arguments are developed throughout this study. First, we suggest that recent trends both in global economy, international politics as well as changes in regional politics have created an environment in the Middle East that is conducive to cooperation in the region. Indeed, the end of the Cold War, the Arab–Israeli peace process – fragile though it might be – the decline of Arab radicalism and the fragmentation of Pan-Arabism have opened new paths for cooperation. Furthermore, changes in global economy such as increasing globalization, expansion of trade and the increased participation of the former Soviet republics and Eastern Europe into the world markets, have all created new economic pressures for the region to engage in economic cooperation. Most importantly, rapidly declining oil prices, which meant declining revenues and income for the oil-rich states, suggest that economic cooperation may well become inevitable. The need to find new sources of revenue may indeed help enhance cooperation in the region.

The second argument is that peace and economic cooperation in the region are mutually reinforcing processes, crucial in initiating and sustaining stability as well as economic growth. Both peace and economic cooperation are necessary but insufficient conditions for one another. Clearly, while the resolution of Arab–Israeli conflict and reduction of hostilities in the region is necessary for effective economic cooperation, so are the changes in regional and domestic economic structures for maintaining peace and stability in the Middle East. There are, however, significant barriers to such a restructuring often embedded in state bureaucracies and significant rent-seeking activities. State spending in the Middle East, particularly in the 1970s thanks largely to oil revenues, has in fact formed large entitlement groups (Anderson 1987). The size and composition of these entitlement groups varied significantly and began to change in the 1980s. As Chaudhry (1994: 45) summarises, '(w)here the so-called "laissez-faire" regimes created large, dependent, and protected private sectors, the so-called socialist regimes cultivated large bases of support in society by directly setting prices and wages while systematically destroying the traditional private sector'. Either way, such state–society networks often created significant barriers to both peace and inter-state cooperation. Any study on the political economy of cooperation, in the Middle East, has to focus simultaneously on the dynamics of peacemaking and economic restructuring while analysing such domestic barriers. Meanwhile, even though economic conditions such as trade complementarity might not exist to any significant degree in the Middle East, these barriers can be overcome through political will. That is why coordination and increased harmony among domestic political and economic structures of the Middle East countries are crucial for regional cooperation.

Our third argument is that countries that had relatively fewer conflicts with more open economies, moderate and democratic regimes, or what we call 'like-minded' states, which include Jordan, Israel, Egypt, Palestine and Turkey, are more likely to initiate collaboration and can play a pivotal role in fostering overall cooperation in the region. Based on the extensive literature on 'democratic peace', we suggest that, despite its significant challenges and possible reverse effects, democratisation among Middle East governments is likely to improve chances of peace and cooperation in the region. For various reasons there are growing pressures for democratisation. Indeed, high levels of impoverishment, the increasing gap between the rich and the poor, persisting clientelistic ties and corruption in public policy and in resource allocation, along with the absence of legitimate channels to convey discontent on the part of the public, have all increased pressures for democratisation (Tessler and Grobschmidt 1995: 136–137). As Norton and Wright argue,

> the next phase of Middle East upheaval will centre on a more fundamental – but also more explosive – challenge. Instead of countries fighting each other, conflict will mainly occur within countries, often pitting societies against governments. And while it may take diverse and disparate forms over the next decade or more, these new conflicts will often be dominated by the same issue: economic, social and political empowerment.
>
> (Norton and Wright 1995: 7)

Nevertheless, relative democratisation in Middle Eastern states is a necessary though not sufficient condition for eventual regional cooperation and peace in the region. As the 'democratic peace' argument suggests, democracies tend to resort to violence less frequently even though they often fight non-democracies. The reasons as to why democracies are less war-prone than others lie in factors such as democratic norms which enhance non-violent forms of conflict resolution, institutional factors and the necessity to mobilise popular support. There are, however, several threats to the prospects of democratisation in the Middle East such as fundamentalism and intolerance as well as existing economic problems.

Furthermore, in many of the Middle East countries, economic cooperation has remained rather limited while political cooperation has developed only recently. The reason lies in the absence of sufficiently developed civil society and democratisation in most Middle Eastern states. These states lack elaborate domestic economic groups, associations and civil organisations that have developed a degree of transnational ties and that have a stake in the economic growth and political stability in the region.

Our fourth argument then is that in the absence of such domestic constituencies, which push their governments toward cooperation, mere intra-governmental agreements, with little or no reference to demands of respective societies leaving the domestic economic and political structures intact, are less likely to last. Any project for cooperation must thus include mobilisation of economic and social groups and most importantly support for democratisation. As Solingen (1996a) argues, however, democratisation without economic liberalisation might not be long lasting. Export-oriented groups that aim to liberalise their economy and increase cross-boundary interaction are indeed crucial for regional cooperation. In contrast, closed, nationalist and authoritarian regimes tend to become one of the major barriers to cooperation mainly because, Solingen argues,

> the prospects of cooperation undermine the viability of the state agencies and enterprises associated with military functions and production, threaten with extinction the state's ability (erstwhile justified in state building and national security terms) to disburse unlimited resources among rent-seeking groups, and deprive populist leaders of a rich fountain of myths.
>
> (Solingen 1996a: 96)

In short, regional cooperation will clearly threaten the interests of those that reap the benefits of the existing regime. They will vehemently oppose any attempt to change the political and economic status quo.

Our fifth and final argument focuses on Turkey and Turkey's role in the Middle East as one of the 'like-minded' states, and addresses how this country can potentially help build economic and political bridges in the region. From the Kurdish problem to its urgent energy needs, Turkey's security and economic interests are closely linked to that of the Middle East. The country has much to lose if the region drifts into violence and instability and much to gain if a new Middle East based on cooperation, peace and democracy can be established. That is why Turkey offers a compelling case study in discussing barriers and prospects of regional cooperation in the region. Clearly, a foreign policy that focuses on domestic groups' interaction while demonstrating the political will at the governmental level through increased interactions among 'like-minded' states both at a bilateral and multilateral basis, can go a long way in enhancing cooperation in the Middle East.

This study is, in effect, an attempt to evaluate the emerging definition of a 'new' Middle East and the role of 'like-minded' states in this process. A new Middle East – not defined, as is usually done, through conflicts, mutual suspicion, military build-up, authoritarian and closed societies, but one based on open regimes and mutual trust where trade replaces arms and cooperation replaces conflict – might at first sight appear naive or too utopian. Clearly as Quandt suggests,

> [the] twentieth century has not been kind to the peoples of the Middle East. Far too many have died in wars; far too many have lived in poverty and ill health; far too many have been deprived of their human rights … far too many may still die in future wars in which weapons of mass destruction may very well be used; and far too many still live under repressive, unaccountable political regimes. For a region rich in resources, this is not a record of which to be proud.
>
> (Quandt 1996: 10)

But as he also adds later:

> Without being pollyannish, one can imagine the emergence of a zone of peace in the Eastern Mediterranean in the coming decade that would allow for a flourishing of democratic politics and economic growth in Israel, Palestine, Jordan and Lebanon, with beneficial spill-over effects in Syria and Egypt as well.

> If this corner of the Middle East, possibly along with North Africa and Turkey, enters into the next century in conditions of improved governance, greater economic prosperity, and peace, a genuine revolution will have taken place. The region could become one in which real national independence might be achieved, cultural life would recover from the dead hand of bureaucratic control, diversity might be seen as a source of strength, individual rights would not be considered a threat to collective identities, and wasteful spending on arms might be reduced.
>
> Needless to say, this vision is far from becoming a reality, but it is a vision that is not foreign to the aspirations of the people in the region, who, after all, are not so different from people elsewhere.
>
> (Quandt 1996: 17)

Identifying the barriers to the establishment of this alternative vision of the Middle East, offering ways of eliminating such barriers and evaluating the role of 'like-minded' states – particularly the role of Turkey in this transformation – are the main aims of this study. If democracy, economic liberalisation, normalisation of Arab–Israeli relations and regional cooperation are indeed intricately intertwined, how can these three goals be achieved in the Middle East? What role, if any, can Turkey and the 'like-minded' states play in achieving these goals?

Methodology of the study

In underlining the importance of domestic actors and, more importantly, how domestic actors interact with international ones, and how they both in turn influence foreign policy outcomes as well as domestic configurations in respective states, this study uses Putnam's (1988) two-level game framework. Using this framework as a heuristic tool, it elaborates on how the metaphor of a 'two-level game' might be useful in understanding prospects of regional cooperation in the Middle East. Putnam's framework notes that in a given inter-state negotiation, two games are simultaneously at work at two different levels. One game is played at Level I, which refers to negotiators at inter-state level. The other game refers to the interaction between the negotiators and their respective domestic constituencies or Level II actors. In any given international negotiation, the statesmen strategically bargain on 'two tables', trying to achieve an international agreement at Level I and its ratification at Level II. The two-level-game framework suggests that both the bargaining phase at Level I and ratification at Level II in reaching an international agreement are intrinsically intertwined and strategically interactive. The two-level game approach, in short, allows for simultaneous analysis of the domestic game that is at work between the negotiators and their domestic constituencies, as well as the international game among the negotiators (Evans, Jacobson and Putnam 1993).

This emphasis on the interactive nature of domestic and international dynamics in the foreign-policy process is what gives the two-level game framework an advantage over the existing explanations of foreign policy. The international (or 'systemic') explanations of foreign policy, for instance, focus almost exclusively on how the changes in the international system – such as the end of the Cold War or changes in overall balance of power – affect foreign-policy outcomes. Domestic explanations, on the other hand, focus on the nature of state institutions, pressures from domestic groups and overall state–society relations, tending to see foreign policy as an outcome of these domestic constraints. The metaphor of 'two-level game', on the other hand, suggests that a mere understanding of conflicts and agreements at the governmental level (Level I), nor an exclusive focus on domestic factors (Level II) can be sufficient in evaluating foreign policy. As Moravcsik (1993: 15) aptly puts it, 'the image of the executive as "Janus-faced" – forced to balance international and domestic concerns in a process of "double-edged" diplomacy – stands in sharp contrast to the images that privilege either the demands of domestic political constituents or the systemic logic of national interest.'

This conception of diplomacy as a strategic and simultaneous interaction between domestic and international factors provides a fertile ground for assessing the prospects and constraints of regional cooperation in the Middle East. A 'systemic' look at the region would focus on factors such as the Arab–Israeli peace process, the post-Cold War dynamics as well as the new international economic realities. There is no doubt that these factors have induced a reassessment of the possibilities of cooperation in the region. However, an exclusive focus on international and regional factors is insufficient in addressing some of the persisting problems as well as the new prospects in transforming this region from one of continued hostilities to one of cooperation and peace. An analysis of domestic factors, and how these domestic factors interact with patterns of inter-governmental ties and vice versa in the Middle East, is crucial in understanding the prospects of regional cooperation.

As such, the metaphor of the 'two-level game' leads to fruitful questions such as 'what are the linkages between economic liberalisation, strengthening of civil society, democratisation and peace in the region', 'how do the existing Middle East governments use the status quo at the international level for domestic purposes, and how do the domestic factors in return reinforce or undermine inter-state ties in the region', 'what kind of domestic constituencies in the Middle East would support cooperative schemes' and, finally, 'how can these domestic constituencies be mobilised'. An attempt to answer these questions requires a simultaneous look at the relationship between Middle Eastern governments and their respective domestic constituencies (Level II), along with the international factors.

The use of the 'two-level game' framework also leads to the argument that mobilisation of domestic constituencies for various cooperative schemes can play a crucial and determinant role in pushing both for democracy and peace in the Middle East. That is why successful cooperation among such 'like-minded' states with relatively more open and democratic regimes can well have a demonstrative effect both at Level I and Level II. This could also form an initial step for gradual evolution towards a 'democratic peace' and cooperation in the Middle East.

Finally, this study utilises the political-economy approach and suggests that economic issues of the region such as oil, population, trade and water cannot be discussed separately from issues of political transformation and regime types. Thus, apart from exploring theoretical linkages between international, regional and domestic levels in the foreign policy-making process, this study also focuses on how economic and political issues are intrinsically intertwined at the nexus of economic liberalisation, democratisation and peace in the context of the Middle East.

In exploring the political economy of regional cooperation, we simultaneously analyse the political dynamics behind economic events and economic logic of political changes. At the domestic level we discuss, for instance, how political dynamics such as the nature of the regime, the nature of state institutions and the degree of the influence of various interest groups can help explain the patterns of economic policies. At the international level we raise such questions as how the security concerns inhibit trade relations and distort priorities in the economic policy-making process in the region, or what the possible economic consequences of a prospective Arab–Israeli peace process are.

Similarly, a political-economy approach also suggests how the economic changes and developments relate to political dynamics. We discuss, for instance, how the changing economic realities in the world as well as the region can push for gradual political transformation in the region. Clearly, the drying up of oil revenues will make it increasingly difficult for most regimes in the region to find new ways of containing rising economic discontent. Meanwhile, increasing globalisation and regionalism in the world economy, coupled with increased pressures for democratisation, can induce significant transformation of the existing authoritarian regimes.

In the end, the main aim of this study is understanding how the complex web of relations between economic and political dynamics – both at the domestic and international level – shape the prospects and barriers to regional cooperation in the Middle East.

Defining the Middle East

Before elaborating on how we aim to respond to the above questions, a definition of the Middle East and a diagnosis of the main problems in the region must first be offered. As Peretz (1994: 2) notes, there is not a generally agreed geographical definition of the Middle East. Yet it is possible to identify roughly three variants of the Middle East. The most commonly employed definition of the Middle East is the one that embraces an area fringed by five seas: the Mediterranean, Black, Caspian and the Red seas and the Persian or Arabian Gulf, 'to include Turkey in the north-west, Iran in the east, and Egypt and the northern Sudan in the west' (Rowley 1984: xvii). A broader definition of the Middle East covers the area from Morocco across Arab North Africa to Afghanistan and Pakistan and from Turkey on the Black Sea southwards through to the Sudan (Bill and Springborg 1994). A third and even broader definition of the Middle East is one that has been favoured by Lewis (1994: 21) covering the areas which in earlier days 'belonged to the great Arab, Persian, and Turkic empires of Islam, of which such great Muslim cities of Samarkand and Bukhara were as essential a part as Baghdad or Cairo, Isfahan or Istanbul'. In today's post-Soviet era this would mean the re-inclusion of Central Asia and parts of the Caucasus into the narrower definition of the Middle East that was more appropriate during the Cold War.

For the purposes of this study, the 'Middle East' is regarded as including the area covered by Turkey, Iran and Israel, and the Arab states from Egypt eastwards. An important factor that has influenced our definition of the Middle East is our interest in examining the prospects of greater cooperation in the region as a result of the Arab–Israeli peace process from the perspective of Turkey. Our definition includes those Arab countries that are in relative geographical proximity to Turkey and that had relatively high levels of trade with Turkey prior to Iraq's invasion of Kuwait. These are also those very countries in which internal economic and political developments have traditionally had important consequences for Turkey. When surveying the economic situation of the Middle East, we will include the Arab countries from North Africa in our analysis. However, as the analysis itself will reveal, these are countries that have had relatively little direct economic ties with the Middle East let alone with Turkey. These are countries that are economically much more closely integrated with Europe even though there is a general recognition that they do also have a potential role to play in the Arab–Israeli peace process. However, their role remains secondary in terms of greater security, stability and prosperity in the Middle East, it is relations between Israel and her immediate Arab neighbours that count most.

A number of factors have also led us to include Iran in our definition. The size of its population, its natural resources and potential for economic growth, and its geographical location as a transit country for Central Asian oil and natural gas put Iran in a position of considerable influence in terms of developments in the Middle East. Traditionally, Iran, both before and after Khomeini, has always had an interest in Middle Eastern politics. It would be difficult to see how one can analyse the prospects of cooperation in the Middle East without including Iran's role.

The Middle East as defined above faces a number of significant problems that appear to go against the overall trends in global economic and international political developments, particularly in the aftermath of the Cold War. Indeed, in a number of ways, the Middle East appears to be an exception to the general trend of peaceful cooperation, economic liberalisation and relative democratisation in the world. Instead, the region has been plagued with wars, conflicts and protected, inefficient markets as well as often authoritarian and militaristic regimes. From protracted conflicts such as the stop–go Arab–Israeli wars, to the long Iran–Iraq war, and from internal wars to the most recent Gulf War, the region has been host to numerous inter- and intra-state conflicts. These armed conflicts have taken a high toll both in human and economic terms. As a result of the armed conflicts in the region during the 1948–92 period, 13.6 million people were displaced and 1.85 million people were dead. Furthermore, given the rapid expansion of both nuclear and chemical weapons of mass destruction in the region, the cost of wars in the region is bound to be even higher and more catastrophic (Ibrahim 1995: 35).

A high degree of political turbulence and instability also explain the ongoing arms race, and consequent war economies. As is to be expected in a region that has witnessed continuous wars, the Middle Eastern governments have very high military expenditures. The region is first in buying and consuming lethal weapons in the developing world. Middle Eastern governments have spent an average of

US$100 billion annually on weapons during the last two decades (Ibrahim 1995: 35). While the ratio of military spending to GNP was 6.6 in 1995, for instance, this ratio was only 5.5 in the developing countries and 5.4 in the industrialised world. Fischer (1995: 419) calculates that if the military spending ratios in the Middle East can be pulled down to world levels, new resources as high as US$50 billion could be freed up for other types of investment.

To the devastating economic effects of war and conflict in the region is added what Richards and Waterbury (1996: 45) calls 'the three simple facts of the political economy of Middle East: much oil, little rain, and rapidly growing (therefore young) population'. These three facts give the region an aura of exceptionalism. Oil is finite and non-renewable. Oil reserves in Saudi Arabia, which holds 25 per cent of the world's total oil reserves is expected to last, for instance, for 83 years at the current rate of pumping. Iraq has 110 years while Iran has 69 years of reserves left at current rates (*The Economist* 2 August 1997: 84). Clearly, the Middle Eastern economies cannot continue to rely on oil revenues. Declining oil prices since 1986 have already changed the economic landscape of the region, slowing down oil exports and, most importantly, growth. For most of the countries in the region, except for Israel, 1973–80 was a period of exceptional growth based on rising oil prices. Declining oil prices immediately reversed this trend. While the average GDP per capita income for Middle East and North Africa for 1986 was US$2,490, for instance, this figure dropped to US$1,580 by 1994. In the same period, the world GNP per capita has jumped from US$2,780 to US$4,470 (World Development Report, 1996). The entire region, particularly Libya, Saudi Arabia and United Arab Emirates, actually experienced negative growth during the 1980–89 period. Slow rate of growth in the region sets a sharp contrast to the overall positive rate in the world economy, which averaged at about 3.9 per cent in 1996.

Water and high population also remain as serious regional problems. While scarcity of water puts natural limits to agricultural growth in the region, rising population poses a major threat to the prospects of economic development. Not surprisingly, the problem of scarce water resources has led to serious disputes in the region. While Syria, Turkey and Iraq dispute over the Euphrates–Tigris basin, Israel and Jordan have similar disputes over the Jordan river. Sudan and Egypt disagree on the use of the Nile. In no other region in the world does water become such a source of conflict and interdependence at the same time. The need for water increases with increased demand for more agricultural production and industrial growth. But the rates at which services, investments and jobs grow in the region fall well below the rates of growth in the increasingly young population, creating what Richards (1995a: 60) called a 'demographic time bomb'. Rapid urbanisation and high unemployment have created a significant army of migrant workers, leading to very high-labour dependency ratios.

The region's economic problems, however, are not limited to the prospective depletion of oil reserves, water and high population. The Middle East is also very much isolated from world trade and investment flows. The region's total exports accounted for only 3.9 per cent of world trade in 1992. Foreign direct investment flows remained limited particularly in comparison to investment flows to East Asia

(Stallings 1995: 26, 74). To this unfavourable international economic outlook is added the difficulty of undertaking economic reforms at the domestic level. Ineffective and inefficient governments, and a state-dependent private sector that continuously feed off the state-rents, lie at the core of economic problems in the Middle East. The same is true for most of the military elite in the Middle Eastern states which have entrenched interests and direct ties in the economy. The difficulties of introducing significant fiscal reforms and discipline in government expenditures are underscored by the dominance of war-prone economies and the readiness of domestic elites to play the so-called 'security card' whenever an alternative private sector and interest groups emerge.

One of the main reasons as to why these economies remained so state-dominated and why such attempts in Egypt and Syria such as *infitah* (an Arabic term used to refer to economic opening) have had relatively limited success, was that economic liberalisation brought fears of political opening-up which the governments might not be able to control. A burgeoning private sector that is independent of the state might also mean mobilisation of domestic constituencies for policies that may not be favoured by the state elite. Furthermore, too much economic liberalisation might also mean a change of rents for a significant number of interest groups. Hence, the main barrier to economic liberalisation can be identified as the absence of a civil society that has grown autonomous from state pressures. The limited structural economic reforms that started in the 1980s did not have much of a 'spillover' effect on the political arena. Indeed, the persistence of authoritarian regimes such as the ones in Syria and Iraq, at a time when successful transitions to democratic regimes (particularly in Latin America and Eastern Europe) have occurred, constitutes yet another problem in the Middle East. The limited success of economic liberalisation with the well-guarded, entrenched interests of the domestic private sectors that are dependent on state resources were closely intertwined with the presence of repressive and militaristic regimes. Hence, absence of significant structural reforms coupled with repressive political regimes in the Middle East has created a vicious cycle.

Civil society, democratisation and peace in the Middle East

How can this vicious cycle be transformed into a cycle of simultaneous economic liberalisation, political reforms and ultimately peace, thus creating a virtuous cycle instead?

There are several trends in the Middle East, which suggest that days of authoritarian regimes with inefficient governments unable to manage their economies may fast be coming to an end. Indeed, there are significant side effects to a war-prone economy. Especially with rapidly changing technology, keeping up with the arms race in the region has become increasingly costly. Similarly, overemphasis on food self-sufficiency instead of food security has also become a very expensive strategy for Middle Eastern governments. Declining oil revenues and shrinking economies have created significant pressures for reform, particularly the reform of the state's involvement in the economy. Excessive statism and centralisation of power in the hands of the state came to be regarded as highly inefficient. Only a 'decentralised political economy' can begin to address the problems of the Middle East (Richards 1995a: 73).

Can these increasing pressures for economic opening-up necessarily lead to political reforms and democratisation? Although the link is clearly not automatic, political reforms are becoming increasingly important, not only for long-term economic growth but also for peace in the region. In fact, it is this very process of 'incipient democratisation', as Solingen (1996b) called it, that is likely to play a pivotal role in the long-term viability of the peace process. While peace in the region is clearly the precondition for political restructuring and reforms, such opening-up of societies and the development of civil society are, in turn, fundamental for the consolidation of stability and peace in the region. In short, a study of regional cooperation in the Middle East has to take into account the complex web of relations between democratisation and peace.

From economic restructuring to small steps towards the creation of civil society, to the incremental peace process, the Middle East is undergoing significant transformation. One such trend is that economic and political cooperation in the region is increasingly becoming a necessity. The changes both in the international environment and regional inter-state relations have created new prospects for cooperation in the region. However, the key to successful regional cooperation does not lie in international and regional dynamics only. The harmonisation of both political and economic structures as well as government policies in the region would be necessary. Keys to successful cooperation also revolve around the nexus of economic liberalisation and democratisation at the domestic level. Only when sufficiently powerful and independent private sectors and civil organisations are mobilised for cooperation, we suggest, can a sustainable, long-term peace be achieved in the region. Only then, perhaps, can peace stop being a mirage for the region, but a reality.

'Like-minded' states, Turkey and the Middle East

In fostering cooperation in the region, relatively open and democratic countries – or what we call 'like-minded' states – can play a leading role. Analysing one of these 'like-minded' states, i.e., Turkey, and reviewing major problems and prospects that this country faces with regards to its ties with the Middle East, offer an important opportunity to explore patterns of cooperation and conflict in the region. We argue that Turkey faces an unprecedented opportunity in the aftermath of the Cold War to assume a constructive and engaging role in building a new Middle East. Such a role is important for Turkey as well. In the aftermath of the Cold War and especially the Gulf War, the Middle East has already become a significant region for Turkey's strategic, political and economic interests. With the Gulf War, Turkey has emerged as a key player in the Middle East, particularly in the context of Western security and US foreign policy. Turkey also had to assume further responsibility in terms of providing support for the moderate regimes in the region and bearing the costs of holding radical regimes at bay.

A second major issue that became even more important in the post-Cold War era – and where Turkey's role in the region will make a crucial difference – is the Kurdish problem. The human and economic costs of dealing with this problem coupled with the challenges of the rising Kurdish ethnic identity clearly renders Turkey vulnerable against its neighbouring countries. The Kurdish issue is as much a transnational one as it is domestic. Despite denials, Turkey's accusations of Syrian and Iranian support for the activities of the Workers' Party of Kurdistan (PKK), for instance, have seriously damaged mutual trust and prospects of cooperation. Turkey's and its neighbours' inability to address this problem aggravates the situation.

Furthermore, from the Kerkük–Yumurtalık oil pipeline, to Turkey's rising demand for electricity and natural gas, from the need to revitalise the border trade (to help develop the Southeastern Anatolian region) to the need to find new markets, the Middle East is also vital for Turkey's economic needs. Reducing the income disparities between the Southeastern Anatolian region and the rest of the country, and achieving overall development of the region are also important goals for Turkey in terms of addressing the economic aspects of the Kurdish problem. Unless a cooperative scheme – based on establishing confidence-building measures which will remove 'the tit for tat' mentality that exists between Turkey and its neighbours – is found, the resolution of both the Kurdish and the regional developmental problems will indeed be difficult.

Water is another major issue that concerns Turkey in terms of its relations with the Middle East. Turkey, Syria and Iraq have serious disagreements over what constitutes an 'equitable' distribution of water in the Euphrates–Tigris rivers. While Turkey stresses its rights as an upstream country, both Iraq and Syria insist on the riparian rights calling both rivers 'international waters'. In the light of Syria's tendency to use support for PKK activities as a bargaining chip against Turkey, and the regional development goals that Turkey has targeted in the context of the Southeastern Anatolia Development Project (GAP), the resolution of this water problem is particularly important for Turkey.

All of these issues that Turkey faces with regards to its ties with the Middle East constitute a good case study for analysing both the difficulties and the prospects of cooperation in the region. First, the study of a country such as Turkey, that has increasingly faced new challenges in the aftermath of the Cold War and that experienced significant shifts in its geopolitical and economic status in the region, offers an opportunity for analysing how the changing international dynamics can reconfigure regional issues. The fact that Turkey has a series of significant political and economic linkages in the region also allows for a closer look.

Furthermore, in congruence with the two-level-game framework, exploring domestic pressures in Turkey and how they shape Turkey's foreign policy towards the Middle East also offers an opportunity to uncover the interdependence of domestic and international factors in foreign-policy making. How various domestic actors, political parties in particular, persistently use the foreign-policy issues towards the Middle East in order to appeal to their respective constituencies in Turkey, and how these domestic constituencies shape the foreign-policy outcomes in return, underscore the necessity of at least minimal harmonisation of domestic structures and regime types among Middle Eastern governments for regional cooperation. Hence, by using the Turkish case, an argument based on the importance of 'like-minded' states in establishing the initial steps towards cooperation in the region can be developed.

Organisation of the study

Chapter 2 of this book introduces different types of regionalism and schemes of regional cooperation. It aims to provide an overview of different trends of regionalism in the global economy, and to discuss why some regional schemes have been more successful than others. Based on this global review, this chapter raises some of the preliminary questions as to why the Middle East remains an exception to the overall global trend of regionalism and regional cooperation. Offering a wide ranging spectrum of cooperation schemes ranging from détente to economic and political union, this chapter also sets up some of the parameters of regional cooperation. Defining 'deep integration' as harmonisation of political and economic systems, the chapter elaborates on the increasing requirements of regionalism. While suggesting that EU- or NAFTA-like regional cooperation schemes for the Middle East are highly unlikely and unrealistic, the chapter underscores the importance of transforming the existing policy structures and patterns of policy-making on the domestic front for successful regional cooperation.

Chapter 3 reviews the literature on international cooperation and focuses on the two-level-game framework of Robert Putnam. The main theoretical argument elaborated in this chapter is that the existing literature on cooperation is limited, as it focuses almost exclusively on government-to-government relations largely overlooking the interaction between domestic dynamics and how the domestic constituencies influence the decision makers. Putnam's two-level framework remedies this problem to a large extent by addressing how the Level II actors (domestic constituencies) interact and influence the patterns of negotiations at Level I decision making. This chapter also develops a number of arguments regarding the regional and domestic dynamics in the Middle East, which are discussed at some length throughout the work.

Chapter 4 offers an economic map of the region and analyses closely both regional and domestic-level economic dynamics of the Middle East. From the issue of food security to agricultural trends, from climatic conditions to the issue of population, the chapter offers an explanation of why the Middle East is economically a unique region. This chapter also identifies the major economic barriers to cooperation, such as inefficient and/or ineffective economic policy-making largely due to war-ready economies, income distribution problems, population growth, and absence of economic deepening and macroeconomic instabilities. This chapter also evaluates the existing trade data in the region and analyses the degree of trade compatibility in the Middle East.

Chapter 5 elaborates on how the economic barriers to cooperation can be overcome. Using the two-level-game framework, this chapter underscores how cooperation at Level II is crucial for effective cooperation in the region. The main argument of this chapter is that, although there is currently limited cooperation and trade in the region largely due to political conflicts and hostilities, these barriers can indeed be overcome through functional cooperation (such as water and energy sharing arrangements). These functional cooperation schemes, it is argued, are instrumental in fostering both peace and democratisation in the Middle East. By comparing two different areas of potential cooperation, namely water and energy sharing arrangements, this chapter underscores how different functional cooperation schemes can be used to mobilise domestic constituencies, which can form preliminary pressures for democratisation.

Chapter 6 is an evaluation of the political dynamics of the Middle East. The chapter offers an overview of the political dynamics both at the international and regional level throughout the Cold War and post-Cold War period. It demonstrates how the Cold-War dynamics and requirements of bipolarity coupled with Pan-Arabism and the Arab–Israeli conflicts closed the channels of political and economic cooperation in the region throughout the Cold War years. The immediate internationalisation of the conflicts coupled with the polarisation of Middle Eastern politics along moderate and radical regimes have impeded the development of a region-wide cooperation. The chapter also explains how the end of the Cold War, the Gulf crisis, and domestic developments helped create an environment for the Arab–Israeli peace process to start.

Chapter 7, on the other hand, evaluates the potential for political cooperation in the region. Focusing on the Madrid process and the post-Cold War dynamics, the chapter analyses how issues, such as the end of bipolarity and relative decline in the ideological polarisation in the region coupled with initial steps towards the normalisation of Arab–Israeli relations, appear to create an opportunity for region-wide cooperation. Based on the argument of 'democratic peace', the chapter underlines the necessity of opening-up the existing regimes in most of the Middle Eastern countries. Finally, the chapter elaborates on the concept of 'like-minded' states and argues how cooperation among countries such as Jordan, Israel, Palestine, Egypt and Turkey might take the first steps towards region-wide cooperation and set an example through interaction both at Level I and Level II.

Chapter 8 focuses specifically on the role of Turkey as one of the 'like-minded' states and elaborates on major issues that this country faces in its relations with the rest of the Middle East. Reviewing why and how the Middle East is becoming ever more important for Turkey's interests, and how Turkey's international and regional position have changed in the aftermath of the Cold War, this chapter discusses a range of issues and challenges that Turkey has in the region. These challenges include the geopolitical and economic effects of the Gulf War, the Kurdish problem, the water problem, the economic interests and needs of Turkey in the Middle East, as well as the impact of the customs-union agreement with the EU on Turkey–Middle East ties. In congruence with the logic of the two-level game framework, a discussion of how the domestic dynamics in Turkey have influenced its foreign policy towards the Middle East and the implications of this linkage between domestic politics and foreign politics are also discussed.

Finally, in our conclusion (Chapter 9) we underscore the importance of a political-economy approach in studying the dynamics of cooperation in the region. We conclude that only through an approach that takes into account both the region's unique economic factors – such as oil, water, energy, population issues – and political factors – such as regime transformation, democratisation and the opening-up of political systems – can we best explore the prospects and constraints of cooperation in the region. Secondly, we suggest that cooperation in the region cannot be understood only at inter-governmental level or, what we will call throughout this study, Level I dynamics. We suggest instead that a multiple-level game framework that simultaneously looks at the domestic, regional and international dynamics and interactions can serve to disentangle the complex patterns of cooperation and conflict in the region. Finally, economic liberalisation and increased political participation are two important paths, we suggest, towards peaceful cooperation in the region. Democratisation coupled with economic reform, and fostering domestic constituencies that favour cooperation and interdependence might indeed hold the key for long-term stability in the region.

2 New regionalism and the Middle East

From Colbert's customs-union plan to integrate all the provinces of France, to Prussia's Zollverein, from the British Commonwealth to Jean Monnet's project of a unified Europe, regional economic cooperation was the subject and goal of many statesmen, historians, economists, as well as political scientists. Increasing globalisation in the world economy coupled with new geopolitical and strategic dynamics emerging in the aftermath of the Cold War has made regional economic cooperation schemes particularly attractive in recent years. From the typical example of the European Union (EU), to the Asia–Pacific Economic Cooperation Group (APEC) to the Southern Cone Common Market (MERCOSUR), regional economic cooperation is flourishing in many regions around the world.

In an era when the benefits of increased economic cooperation through regionalism are increasingly acknowledged, the Middle East appears to be an exception to this overall trend. The region accounts for a minimal portion of world trade and foreign direct-investment flows (Stallings 1995) and is, with the exception of oil flows, one of the regions least integrated into the global economy. This chapter first looks at the emerging dynamics of regionalism in the global economy and the reasons behind it. It briefly defines the possible forms of regional cooperation and discusses how regional cooperation schemes have evolved in the aftermath of the Second World War. The middle part of the chapter discusses the unique trend in the contemporary international political and economic scene and identifies how 'new' regionalism differs from old ones. Based on the framework developed up to this point, the final part is reserved for a preliminary assessment of the potential for regionalism in the Middle East and addresses the prospects and constraints of cooperation in the region.

Different forms of regional cooperation

Most economists agree that the last decade has witnessed a significant level of trade liberalisation. What is interesting with the patterns of trade liberalisation, however, is that it was pursued simultaneously by regional and multilateral agreements. While the last round of the General Agreement on Tariffs and Trade (GATT) talks continued between 1986 and 1993, leading to global trade liberalisation among more than one hundred members, many regional agreements have also been negotiated. For instance, European countries deepened their integration through the Single European Act of 1985, and the United States, Canada and Mexico got together to form the North American Free Trade Agreement (NAFTA). While there are 17 such agreements in Europe, 14 agreements in Africa and 7 in Asia, the Middle East has concluded 5 regional agreements. GATT records indicate that about 90 per cent of all GATT members are signatories to such agreements (Lawrence 1996: 1).

It is misleading, however, to evaluate these regional arrangements within the same framework. Regional cooperation might vary from a simple reduction of tariffs in a certain sector – as was the case in the European Coal and Steel Community (ECSC) established in 1952, or the 1981 Preferential Trade Area for Eastern and Southern Africa – to economic union, which establishes functioning supranational institutions and presupposes significant harmonisation of fiscal, monetary and trade policies among its members. A breakdown of various degrees of regional cooperation has been laid out in Table 2.1.

Table 2.1 Various degrees of regional cooperation

Type of agreement	*Removal of internal quotas and tariffs*	*Common external customs tariff*	*Free movements of labour, capital and services*	*Harmonization of economic policies and creation of supranational institutions*	*Unification of political supranational institutions*
Free trade agreement	X				
Customs union	X	X			
Common market	X	X	X		
Economic union	X	X	X	X	
Political union	X	X	X	X	X

Source: Adapted from Gibbs and Michalak (1994: 24)

A free trade agreement eliminates barriers to trade but does not require a common external policy such as the adoption of a common customs tariff or factor mobility, i.e., free movement of capital and labour. Thus, a textbook example of a free trade agreement actually covers a narrow range of issues and allows each member country to follow its own external economic and commercial policies independently. Among well-known free trade agreements are the Latin American Free Trade Area (LAFTA) created in 1961, the European Free Trade Area (EFTA) formed the same year among the Western European countries, the Caribbean Free Trade Area (CARIFTA), the Australia–New Zealand Closer Economic Relations Trade Agreement (ANZCERTA) and the more recent NAFTA, which came into effect in 1994. Several ongoing attempts to liberalise trade among the East Asian and Pacific countries, such as ASEAN and APEC, can also be evaluated in this category.

A customs union, on the other hand, eliminates intra-regional barriers to trade and establishes common external policies – a common customs tariff (CCT) or a common external tariff (CET) – but does not require factor mobility. This type of economic integration would require harmonisation of a wide range of issues and policies among the member countries. These issues include the harmonisation of commercial laws and laws on the protection of intellectual and industrial property rights. By implication, a customs union also brings significant limitations on subsidies or regulations that might have a distorting effect on trade. The earliest example of a customs union is Prussia's Zollverein established in 1834. The Ouchy Agreement signed in 1932 between Belgium, Netherlands and Luxembourg (Benelux) constitutes the first example of a twentieth century economic integration scheme in Western Europe. This agreement was a prelude to the first customs union agreement that the Benelux countries signed in 1944. The best-known and the most successful example, the European Customs Union, was initially formed between the Benelux countries, France, Germany and Italy and was formally established by article 9 of the Treaty of Rome in 1958. The Treaty of Rome formed the basis of the European Economic Community (EEC) which later became the European Union (EU). Other such agreements include the Southern African Customs Union (SACU), which is the oldest customs union in Africa formed in 1910, the Economic Community of West Africa (CEAO), which came into effect in 1976 and later became a part of ECOWAS (Economic Community of West African States), and the Central African Customs and Economic Union (UDEAC), which was signed in 1964; none of these fully materialised.

A common market is the most extensive and encompassing of all the economic regional-integration schemes. Along with elimination of all tariffs and quantitative restrictions on trade between member countries, a common market allows factor mobility, free flow of labour, capital and goods, and establishes a common external trade policy against the non-member countries. The freedom of establishment – namely, the right of each citizen of the member country to apply for employment and establish business in another member country – is also included in the concept of a common market and was clearly envisioned in the Treaty of Rome establishing the EEC. Apart from the EEC, other regional cooperation schemes that aimed to create a common market but were relatively less successful were the Central American Common Market (CACM), the Caribbean Community (CARICOM), the more recent MERCOSUR between Argentina, Brazil, Uruguay and Paraguay, and the Arab Common Market (ACM) which essentially failed to establish the free mobility of goods and services except for some agricultural products.

Economic union adds the harmonisation of fiscal, monetary policies to the already coordinated commercial policies. Supranational institutions in such a union begin to play an important role. The Single European Act of 1985 and the Maastricht Treaty of 1992 essentially created such a union and the name of the European Economic Community was changed to the European Union. The Single European Act and Maastricht targeted the creation of a single regional market, introduction of uniform standards throughout the EU, lowering costs of business in EU countries. But perhaps the most important and the most controversial target is European Monetary Union in which member states agreed to bring their monetary policies and inflation rates in line with one another. This target also envisions the creation of a European Central Bank (currently known as the European Monetary Institute). Clearly the European Union sets the most ambitious example of an economic union. Whether such a union is possible (especially in the monetary field), however, remains to be seen.

Finally, political union signifies the harmonisation of defence and foreign-policy issues and the further transfer of sovereignty by member states to supranational institutions which would acquire political responsibility. Such a political union was also one of the targets in Maastricht which increased the powers of the European Commission, Council of Ministers as well as the European Parliament. The agreement encouraged member states to cooperate on foreign policy and defence issues with the ultimate goal of political federation. The treaty designated the Western European Union (WEU), which was formed as early as 1948, as the major organ to formulate and implement common EU foreign and defence policies. The failure of the member countries to come up with a common foreign policy over Bosnia coupled with the inability of WEU to differentiate itself from the North Atlantic Treaty Organisation (NATO) are some of the indications of how difficult political union will be in Europe.

Short of a complete political union, however, several forms of political cooperation are indeed possible. As Wolfers has pointed out in his classic text, *Discord and Collaboration* (1962), a variety of political relations between states that range from the pole of enmity to the pole of amity is possible in international relations. The transition from war-like relations to mutual cooperation might indeed involve different stages. The first diplomatic step, largely based on the US–Soviet relations during the Cold War is called 'détente' which refers to relaxation of acute tensions and the reduction of hostile behaviour. Détente is clearly a long way from political cooperation as the sides are far from settling their disagreements but simply agree not to heighten tensions. The US–Soviet détente in the 1970s provides a good example as two countries with wide political, economic and ideological differences took steps toward the reduction of hostilities. Both sides avoid making irredentist claims and tone down their ideological rhetoric. The next step toward the pole of amity is 'rapprochement'. Here, one of two sides expresses a desire to search for areas of agreement. Whether such an agreement can be found is a different matter. The important step is that the sides express willingness to try to find an agreement and eliminate the sources of conflict.

'Entente' is yet another step towards political cooperation and involves the recognition on all sides that there are common interests and similarities of views. Diplomatic historians point out how France and Great Britain formed an entente, for instance, in the aftermath of the Fashoda War of 1898, not only seeking an agreement (rapprochement) but also realising that continuing with the colonial wars could be detrimental for the long-term interests of both countries (Craig and George 1990: 253). Another step towards political cooperation is 'appeasement', which refers to the methodological removal of the sources of conflict by the sides involved. Although this term is often equated with Neville Chamberlain's ill-fated policy of giving up Sudetenland in order to appease Hitler, appeasement can indeed be a constructive step towards peace making and stability. The important aspect of appeasement is the systematic attempt to solve problems and advance relations. Willy Brandt's *Ostpolitik* is a good example of appeasement.

Finally, alliance is yet another stage towards cooperation. Alliance involves an agreement to coordinate foreign policies of the involved states towards other states and acknowledgement that these states have similar ideological and political goals. All sides agree to cooperate on issues and act together in the international arena. Military alliances such as NATO and Central Treaty Organisation (CENTO) are examples of such organisations. How long alliances last without major modificaion will depend on the nature of perceived threat or the common enemy (the Soviet Union in the case of NATO) or how common the interests of the allied states are. Alliances also suggest that the relations between the involved states do not involve a zero-sum game, rather a positive-sum game where cooperation benefits all the parties.

What are some of the barriers that need to be overcome in transition from détente to alliance and political union? First, regimes with aggressive foreign policy and expansionist claims are also incompatible with political cooperation for which an international security environment is a necessity. As John Herz (1950) has pointed out, for cooperation to be possible the states should overcome the 'security dilemma' – the fact that the increase of security of one state can have the unintended effect of decreasing the security of others. As Thucycides wrote in *Peloponnesian War* (trans. 1954), for instance, what made war inevitable was the growth of Athenian power and the fear which this caused in Sparta. This dilemma, has been a stumbling block for cooperation.

Setting aside the evident barriers such as ideological differences, wide discrepancy in regime types also constitutes a significant obstacle to political cooperation. Closed authoritarian regimes usually have difficulty cooperating with open democratic regimes and vice versa. The burgeoning literature on the causes of war, for instance, increasingly links domestic factors to international disputes and conflicts as well as the changes in the international arena to the domestic changes (Bueno de Mesquita 1981; Bueno de Mesquita and Lalman 1992; Desch 1996; Doyle 1983; Gaubatz 1996; Siverson and Emmons 1991; Thompson 1996). As Thompson indicates:

> States heavily involved in the pursuit of regional primacy and coercive expansion, have been the least likely to develop liberal republican/democratic forms of government. Such states, rather, were most likely to develop into authoritarian, highly bureaucratised, war making machines. If war made states, then the states most involved in aggressively making and preparing for war (as implied by the pursuit of a coercive regional primacy strategy) were most likely to be shaped by their foreign policy ambitions and battlefield experiences. ... Some level of peace, especially as indicated by the abandonment of expansionist foreign policies, made the historical development of liberal institutions and democratisation feasible.
>
> (Thompson 1996: 146)

The severity and longevity of regional or bilateral conflicts are also crucial impediments to cooperation. If there has been violation and abuse of trust in interstate ties, the transition to détente let alone alliance can be very difficult. Long-term stable alliances are possible only after sustained effort to establish mutual trust and credible commitments.

There is no doubt that establishing such a security environment and trust is intricately intertwined with prospective economic ties and interdependence. While political convergence of goals is necessary for effective cooperation, economic ties and necessities can also help create an environment conducive for political cooperation. That is why processes of economic cooperation that range from free trade agreements to full economic integration, and processes of political cooperation that range from détente to political union, need to be analysed simultaneously when accounting for regionalism in global political economy.

The development of regionalism

At first sight, regionalism does not appear to develop naturally in contemporary-world political economy. On the contrary, rapid decline in the cost of transportation, the gradual replacement of wood ships with iron and steel and the possibility of sailing by steam all made extra-regional trade possible. Animosities and rivalry particularly among the European countries actually made extra-regional trade more attractive than intra-regional trade. It was no wonder that patterns in international trade throughout the nineteenth century and the early twentieth century were based on colonial ties rather than geographic proximity. However, regional economic cooperation and intra-regional trade gradually began to dismantle these extra-regional ties in the aftermath of the Second World War. Regional cooperation and integration indeed became very popular concepts in Europe in the 1950s. The Paris Treaty in 1951 on steel and coal, which formed the European Steel and Coal Community, the signing of the Treaty of Rome, by the six European countries (Benelux, Germany, France and Italy) creating the EEC, and the creation of EFTA all became the early signs of regionalism in Western Europe. What is interesting in this first wave of regional cooperation is that they were largely motivated by political and ideological concerns. The Cold War starting in the immediate aftermath of the Second World War, led to the creation of two important economic blocs in Europe: the EEC and the Council for Mutual Economic Assistance (COMECON) designed to improve cooperation among the Eastern European countries. Meanwhile, several free-trade areas emerged: EFTA in Europe in 1961, LAFTA in Latin America in 1960, CARIFTA in the Caribbean in 1965, as well as the Arab Common Market in the Middle East in 1965.

An important element in these early regional arrangements is that they took place either among North–North or South–South countries. The motivations and reasons behind the Northern cooperation schemes differed from the developing countries. As already indicated, economic cooperation and integration in Western Europe were largely based on political motivations from the beginning. As Jean Monnet stated:

> The need for [a Common Market] was political as well as economic. The Europeans had to overcome the mistrust born of centuries of feuds and wars.

> The governments and peoples of Europe still thought in the old terms of victors and vanquished. Yet, if a basis for peace in the world was to be established, these notions had to be eliminated. Here again, one had to go beyond the nation and the conception of national interest as an end in itself. ... We thought that both of these objectives could be reached in time if conditions were created enabling these countries to increase their resources by merging them in a large and dynamic common market; if these same countries could be made to consider that their problems were no longer solely of national concern, but were mutual European responsibilities.
>
> (Monnet 1964: 43)

It is no wonder that the early theorists of regional cooperation and integration, the so-called early functionalists, as found in the writings of Mitrany (1946), argued that cooperation in non-political spheres is likely to have significant spill-over effects in the political arena. While these theories included a significant normative bias in terms of pushing for world-wide peace, they were the first to point the relationship between economic and political cooperation. Concepts such as 'low politics' (issues of bread and butter) and 'high politics' (issues of national security), and transferability of cooperation from one area to another, became important tools in theorising about regional integration. Neofunctionalists such as Haas (1958), and Lindberg and Scheingold (1970) also explained increasing political cooperation from this perspective of 'spillover effects'.

The main problem with the early functionalists as well as neofunctionalists was that they were based on the successful European example and had little to say about success and failure of other regional cooperation schemes in the rest of the world. The question of whether such a 'spillover effect' could be created elsewhere remained unanswered. Secondly, neofunctionalists were so focused on political integration that they saw economic cooperation only as a means not as an end. In most regional agreements, particularly those signed in recent years, however, economic cooperation is as important as (if not more important than) political cooperation. Regional agreements among developing countries, for instance, are largely based on welfare concerns that are intertwined intermittently with security concerns. In short, such a distinction between low and high politics is often irrelevant if not misleading in the context of developing countries. The pursuit of power is closely associated with the pursuit of plenty (Viner 1987). Finally, although neofunctionalists offered a mechanism through which further integration could be achieved, it had little to say about how long such an integration is likely to take. It offered little in terms of concrete policies and development strategies.

It was the development economists, dominating the debates on regional economic cooperation and trade throughout the sixties, who began to remedy the selective bias of the functionalist theories. As the structural approaches became popular in development economics, regional integration schemes appeared as important tools not for liberalising trade but for creating import substitution zones. Many countries, particularly those in Latin America and Africa, came together throughout the 1960s in order to protect themselves from the competition of the advanced industrialised countries. The Economic Commission for Latin America (ECLA) within the UN and its chief economist, Raul Prebisch, advocated that regional integration would lead to further economies of scale, to the development of infant industries and to an increase in productivity. Regional arrangements such as CACM, CARIFTA, and the Andean Group all stemmed as a result of these expectations (Hirschman 1981). The dependency school, which soon came to dominate the field, also emphasised the self-reliance of the southern countries. The argument was one of emphasising the necessity to reduce trade ties with the advanced industrialised countries because of unequal terms of trade. (On variations of these themes see Cardoso and Faletto 1979; Frank 1967; Wallerstein 1983.)

Relative failure of regionalism in the developing world

Most of these regional integration schemes among the developing countries failed to achieve their targets. By the 1970s most of these agreements were either suspended, or went into effect but did not create an expansion in trade. Some even did worse by diverting trade, thus having unintended reverse effects. The reasons behind these failures varied considerably from region to region. Nevertheless, several observations are possible. First, one of the main problems with these cooperation schemes was that the member countries were very different in terms of their income, Gross Domestic Product (GDP), resources and development. This created unwillingness on the part of better-off countries to carry the burden of trade liberalisation and led to the temptation of worse-off countries to free-ride without liberalising their own trade. Such a problem was common, for instance, in CACM where the relatively more rapid industrial development of Guatemala and El Salvador created a problem. Similarly, the economic gap in MERCOSUR between Uruguay and Paraguay on the one hand and Argentina and Brazil on the other was the major impediment to further integration in Latin America. The relative success of the EU in economic integration is largely attributed to relative similarity of the levels of development in member countries or the availability of social funds that can offset the initial side effects of membership. Even in the case of Greece, Portugal and Spain where the economic discrepancy between these economies and the rest of the region was most evident, the regional funds of the EU have helped reduce the gap. Similarly, although the wide economic discrepancy between Mexico and the United States calls the success of NAFTA into question, the level of trade and financial interdependence between these countries suggests that NAFTA might not share the same fate that most regional arrangements had throughout the seventies.

A corollary problem emerged with the equal distribution of benefits from economic integration. The creation of the Andean Group, for instance, in 1969 brought together the weaker members of LAFTA – Bolivia, Colombia, Ecuador, Peru and Chile – against the stronger members – Argentina, Brazil and Mexico. Similar problems emerged with CARICOM and ECOWAS. The issues of relative gains and asymmetric payoffs were indeed barriers to cooperation (Vaitsos 1978).

Although the wide discrepancy in terms of economic development constitutes a significant obstacle for cooperation, too much similarity in the member economies can also prove problematic. The advanced industrialised countries could trade well within the same industry thanks to high-value content, diversification and transformation of products (hence intra-industry trade). At high levels of income, demand for different products is higher thus leading to gains from intra-industry specialisation. However, developing countries require complementarity of economies in order to trade with other countries (De Melo and Panagariya 1992). Since the trade and industry potential of the member countries was mostly limited, intra-regional trade did not increase significantly in the aftermath of the agreements. Lack of resources, very similar economies and low trade potential thus became main reasons behind the failure of these agreements.

Similarly, as most dependency theorists and world-system theorists would argue, it is very difficult, if not impossible, for the developing countries to generate significant trade among each other since the source of original and up-to-date technology remains in the hands of the advanced industrialised countries. The developing countries, regardless of how much they may trade with one another, are bound to be tied to a crucial trade partner such as the United States, Germany, France or Japan in order to acquire valuable foreign currency, advanced technology and know-how. Indeed, even in the case of East Asian trade patterns, and despite recent diversification of destinations, Japan still remains the 'hub' country. As such, regional arrangements among the developing countries might not be as determinant (hence not successful) as the 'pole' country to which a given developing country is economically linked (Stallings 1995).

In the collective comparative work on the Andean group, CARICOM, South Pacific Forum and ASEAN, Axline and others conclude that,

> the strategies in the negotiation of regional policies are based on the calculation of the perceived opportunity costs of participation in regional cooperation, and one of the main determinants of the costs and benefits is whether a country is a more advantaged or less advantaged member of the regional organisation. Support of particular policies will be based on a consideration of alternative ways of achieving the national goals of a member country, e.g., autonomously, closely associated with non-regional partner (often a metropolitan country), or through regional cooperation. In all the case studies examined here, bilateral relationships with external partners played an important role in member countries' support for regional policies.
>
> (Axline 1994: 201–202)

An intervention by a 'metropolitan' country might also take a political form and impede cooperation. One of the main reasons as to why CARICOM failed, for instance, was the intervention by the United States through President George Bush's Caribbean Basin Initiative which rewarded more free-market oriented regimes in the region and hindered regional cooperation.

Perhaps the most important barrier to successful regional cooperation has been the absence of political trust and harmony among the prospective members. As we already indicated, the initial motivation behind the European integration schemes was political, i.e., the avoiding of the recurrence of the hostilities between France and Germany. It had taken a widespread war for the long-time feuds to be replaced by trade agreements. Similar problems prevailed in most of the regional agreements where consistent commitment to harmonisation of economic policies is necessary. The wide differences in domestic political regimes, and regional disputes created major problems. Jamaica, for instance, supported the CARICOM during the socialist-oriented regime of Manley but lost interest during the free-market oriented regime of Seaga. Similarly, the overthrow of Allende by Pinochet was a major blow to the regional movement and was one of the major reasons behind the failure of the Andean group. MERCOSUR began to gain some success only in the 1990s when democratic regimes, especially in Argentina and Brazil, had been well established. In fact, MERCOSUR is increasingly seen as a guarantor of democracy in the continent.[1] Existing regional arrangements, particularly the European Union, include rigorous standards in terms of accountability of democratic institutions, respect for human rights and the implementation of the rule of law. Those members who do not fulfil these requirements face the risk of being marginalised and isolated. The credibility of commitments, the stability and similarity of regimes in member states, and the similarities in foreign-policy goals are thus becoming increasingly important for effective regionalism.

Why regionalism now?

The dependency theories began to lose their analytical and empirical appeal in the eighties, largely due to the failure of import substitution policies, the unprecedented success of the East Asian countries, and the changing dynamics in the world political economy. The early 1980s actually became the heyday of multilateral trade negotiations and the ongoing Uruguay Round of GATT talks became the arena for worldwide and non-discriminatory trade liberalisation. The results were significant. The average tariff levels fell from approximately 40 per cent in 1948 to around 5 per cent in 1987 (Gibbs and Michalak 1994). In the meantime, however, from NAFTA to MERCOSUR and from APEC to numerous preferential trade agreements, there was a simultaneous stampede towards regionalism.

In the aftermath of the Second World War, regionalism was largely seen as complementary to multilateralism. Recently, however, regionalism is increasingly seen as a barrier to GATT and multilateral liberalisation of trade. Although customs unions and preferential trade agreements are allowed in GATT according to its article XXIV, the creation of trade blocs essentially along continental lines, particularly in Europe, Asia and the Americas, indicate that 'new' regionalism might indeed impede the further liberalisation of global trade (Bhagwati 1991). This view is particularly common among the multilateralists who see the emerging regional agreements as steps towards the creation of trade blocs or 'fortresses' centred on Europe, North America and Asia.

Regardless of what the overall impact of regionalism on world trade might be, regional economic cooperation schemes are being increasingly preferred in recent years. The World Trade Organisation lists 76 free trade areas or customs unions set up or modified since 1948. Of these, more than half came into being in the 1990s (*The Economist* 7 December 1997: 23). Why has regional economic cooperation become such a fashionable and desirable goal in recent years? Among the many reasons behind this eminent surge of regionalism, three stand out as most significant. These are (1) the changing rules of competition in the global economy, (2) the end of the Cold War and (3) trends towards economic and political liberalisation especially in the developing world.

Changing global economy

First, the rules and patterns of competition in the global economy have changed significantly in recent years. The decades following the Second World War were marked by US dominance in the global economy. The US accounted for almost half of the world GDP and had all the interest in maintaining a free trade system. The subsequent liberalisation of trade during the 1950s and 1960s under the GATT system was in fact an anomaly to the overall mercantilist bias in trade policies. As economists and public choice theorists remind us, free trade, though beneficial to all parties in aggregate, is generally accepted as a public good and thus creates significant free-riding problems (Axelrod and Keohane 1985; Olson 1971). The US was willing and interested in providing this 'public good' so long as it benefited from it. Indeed, as Gowa (1994) indicates, the security as well as the economic payoffs of the free trade system was most beneficial for the US.

The unprecedented rapid growth in Japan and East Asia, coupled with the strengthening of the EC, however, increasingly began to challenge the so-called hegemonic leadership of the US. With it came the questions and concerns over multilateral liberalisation of trade and the GATT system. Both the advanced industrialised economies and the developing countries complained about insufficient access to one another's markets (Baldwin 1993). The rising cost of the free trade system, which began to increase particularly for EC countries and the US largely due to the significant market penetration of East Asian goods, led these countries to adopt the so-called 'grey-area measures'. These measures purposefully designed to manage trade included such bilateral agreements as 'Orderly Market Arrangements', 'Voluntary Exchange Restraints' and 'Anti-dumping provisions'. The aim was to protect the failing domestic industries and meet the emerging Asian challenge.

However, the 'grey-area measures' were in fact clear violations of GATT principles based on nondiscrimination and nonexclusivity. These measures also marked a significant change toward trade policies particularly in the US. 'The main driving force for regionalism today', Bhagwati notes,

> is the conversion of the US. … As the key defender of multilateralism through the postwar years, its decision now to travel the regional route (in the geographical and the preferential sense simultaneously) tilts the balance of forces at the margin away from multilateralism to regionalism.
>
> (Bhagwati 1995: 29)

Indeed, first the free trade agreement with Canada and later NAFTA were clear signs of regionalism in North America.

Exploring the reasons behind the US shift towards regionalism – whether it was the changing production paradigms at the micro level or the end of mass production; whether it was the failure of GATT and other cooperation attempts, etc. – is beyond the scope of this book. However, the intellectual appeal of the strategic trade theory for the policy makers in the US was also a sign of changing times. In the US, where limited government and non-intervention have been a historical norm, concepts such as 'managed trade' began to shatter the false dichotomy of free trade versus protectionism. The partial legitimisation of government intervention and policies in order to promote the country's market power and competitiveness (provided that there were sufficient externalities and excess profits) was a significant change in the US political economy (Cohen and Zysman 1987; Krugman 1986; Lipsey and Dopson 1987; Richardson 1990). The wide range of corporate and industry demands as well as the policy options for the government were acknowledged (Aggarwal *et al.* 1987; Milner 1988; Milner and Yoffie 1989). Regionalism then became one of the effective tools among the policy makers in order to adapt the US to changing conditions of the world economy.

Changing international political scene

The incentives for regionalism in recent years are not limited to economic factors and the changes in the global political economy. International political changes and the end of the Cold War in particular have also created new impetus for regionalism. Mansfield tested the argument, for instance, that there is an inverted U-shaped relationship between the concentration of resources and capabilities, restraints on trade and tensions leading to interstate hostilities. In *Power, Trade and War*, he convincingly demonstrated that during periods when resources and capabilities are dispersed among half a dozen countries, the states' concern over their relative positions and relative gains would rise which would then increase the tendency towards regionalism (Mansfield 1993; 1994). Multi-polar international systems are thus more likely to resort to regionalism than bipolar systems which have a higher degree of power concentration. If Mansfield's argument is accepted, given the end of bipolar system thanks to the end of the Cold War, more regionalism is to be expected.

Despite its lucidity, however, Mansfield's argument sees regionalism as a mechanism that will fragment the world economy and eventually reduce the likelihood of global peace. Regionalism is thus seen as a sign of increased interstate hostilities. When considered from a different angle, however, a more benevolent reading of the post-Cold War situation and regionalism is possible. Based on Gowa and Mansfield's argument that allies tend to trade more with one another than with adversaries, one can argue that with the tensions of the Cold War reduced, more cross-cutting alliances and military-political cooperation schemes are possible. Recent trends with the expansion of NATO and the cooperation on the resolution of the Bosnian crisis are the early signs of new options and 'new' types of military-political cooperation. These new alliances thus open new doors for types of regional economic and social cooperation which would not have been possible during the Cold War years. As will be elaborated in the following chapters, in sharp contrast to the Cold War years, when regional and bilateral disputes often gained international status thanks to the superpower rivalry (as was the case in Angola, Congo, Afghanistan and Arab–Israeli conflicts), the end of the Cold War opened prospects for regional settlements of disputes and long-time adversities.

Furthermore, with the end of bipolarity and the collapse of the Soviet Union, the economic rationale behind regionalism appears to take over. Indeed, economic policy makers now have a freer hand and economic concerns begin to overshadow political and strategic ones. Would the European Union's progress towards a single borderless Europe have been as easy with a Europe preoccupied with the threat of the Soviet Union? Would not the United States have hesitated to enter NAFTA with the concerns of alienating other strategically important Latin American partners at the height of the Cold War? Clearly, the so-called 'new world order' after the Cold War opens new opportunities for economic and commercial cooperation which partly explains the boom in regionalism.

Trends towards economic and political liberalisation in the developing world

The 1980s and 1990s have also witnessed an unprecedented degree of economic and political liberalisation particularly in the developing world. By economic liberalisation we refer to the right of each individual to engage in private economic activity constrained only by the rights of others. This trend involved a series of reforms such as privatisation, incentives for the private sector as well as laissez-faire policies on trade and investment. Political liberalisation, on the other hand, broadly refers to the establishment of individual liberty under the law. For the purposes of our discussion, we assume that the establishment of democratic institutions in a given country is a significant step towards political liberalisation.

As we indicated above, except for a few Asian countries, most developing economies were characterised by import substitution policies and closed trade regimes up until the 1980s. During the 1980s and 1990s, however, there was a pervasive shift towards the opening-up of markets in Latin America and Eastern Europe as well as in Africa. The failed import substitution policies, the collapse of communism and the subsequent distaste for government intervention in the economy largely led to the dramatic shifts towards export-led and private sector-led growth (Lawrence 1996). What is interesting is that these policy shifts transformed the developing countries' markets for the multinationals into attractive sites for foreign direct investment. While increased global competition pushed the multinationals to the farthest corners of the world, widely acknowledged mobility of goods and capital across national barriers left most of the developing countries competing for foreign investment. Hence the developing countries increasingly felt the pressure to enter into the loop of globalisation. The entry of foreign investment created further impetus for economic liberalisation and privatisation. Meanwhile, international monetary institutions have long tied the availability of funds and credits to the 'rolling-back' of the state and adoption of economic liberalisation. The International Monetary Fund (IMF) and the World Bank more than ever demanded free private enterprise and integration into the world economy. Regional economic cooperation with advanced industrialised countries became an effective tool for the developing countries to attract new foreign investment. Elimination of tariffs and other trade and non-trade barriers between these countries made these countries, at least on paper, more attractive for foreign investment.

Pressures for economic liberalisation were also coupled with pressures for political liberalisation and democratisation in these countries. Cultural and domestic political developments in the developing world began to draw new attention as advanced industrialised countries struggled to define new sources of instability and threats in the new security environment in the aftermath of the Cold War. From 'clash of civilisations' to the study of human rights, normative, cultural and domestic political issues began to dominate the international relations literature. The emerging security threats were found not so much in the nuclear arsenals of the Soviet republics (though these were still an issue) but in the rising threat of Islamic fundamentalism, authoritarianism and violation of human rights (Huntington 1993; 1996). In short, domestic political structures particularly in the developing world were increasingly linked to prospects of international stability.

The emphasis on political reform and democratisation was also evident in foreign assistance programs. Good governance and democracy became increasingly included as conditions of eligibility for financial assistance. Indeed the 1980s and 1990s have witnessed an unprecedented degree of democratisation in the developing world. From the re-democratisation attempts in Latin America to political revolutions in Eastern Europe and the former Soviet Union, this 'Third Wave' of democratisation, as Huntington called it, led to significant liberalisation of political structure, restructuring of the state and mobilisation of domestic constituents. There is still a lot to be done in terms of political reforms, particularly in changing the role of the state and bureaucracy. Clearly not all the developing countries were included in this wave nor was the degree of liberalisation the same. But this wave of democratisation was crucial in establishing some rule of law and institutional reforms across the Third World (Huntington 1993).

What is 'new' in new regionalism?: Towards 'deep integration'

Why are trends towards economic and political liberalisation as well as democratisation important in evaluating prospects of regional cooperation? Why are these domestic factors so relevant in discussing regionalism? Most economists agree that new regionalism is no longer defined as simple mutual liberalisation of trade but as 'harmonization and possibly coordination of economic policies and domestic law and institutions' (Brookings Institution Project 1995). Hence regional cooperation is no longer equated with reduction of tariffs and increase of trade in goods, services and capital. 'Deep integration' focuses on eliminating barriers to investment as well as trade; the emerging regional arrangements include the development of regional production systems.

> Almost by definition, any regional arrangement worth its name entails the imposition of some common rules of conduct on the countries entering the arrangement and a set of reciprocal commitments and obligations. Regional integration thereby enforces a certain degree of arbitrage among national institutions, just as it brings about arbitrage in markets for goods and services.
> (Rodrik 1995: 176)

This kind of arbitrage involves institutional adjustments that range from reaching common labour and environmental standards to harmonising competition rules and investment incentives as well as policy objectives.

Achieving common rules of conduct and entering into reciprocal commitments and obligations, however, assumes some degree of 'like-mindedness' on the part of governments. Convergence of policy goals, domestic policy change toward outer orientation, improved administrative capacity for compliance to the terms agreed and most importantly, political resources to sustain the necessary policy changes are preconditions for successful 'deep integration'.

Although the strictly economic benefits of cooperation and integration might not sometimes be obvious, these political and institutional changes are likely to outweigh the costs of adjustment. As Rodrik points out,

> The harmonization in domestic laws and institutions entailed by deep integration presents an opportunity for reformist governments in developing countries to 'lock in' their reforms and render them irreversible. It is no secret that Carlos Salinas wanted NAFTA at least as badly for its potential role in cementing Mexico's institutional reforms since 1986 as for its market-access provisions. Arguably, the EU's greatest contribution to the long-run prosperity and stability of Spain, Portugal, and Greece resides in its having made a return to the military rule in these countries virtually impossible.
> (Rodrik 1995: 110)

Regional cooperation can also increase the credibility of commitments via signalling (Rodrik 1989). Entering regional commitments might alleviate the problem of the credibility gap that often plagues the governments of the developing countries willing to undertake reform. Regional cooperation schemes can signal to the private sectors in these countries that 'the rules of the game are now changing for good' (Rodrik 1995: 111).

Regional cooperation might also create structures to prevent rent-seeking behaviour. Rent seeking, as argued by Krueger (1974), refers to all activities in which incumbents engage in order to benefit themselves and their supporters. The incumbents might distribute state resources directly through subsidies, loans, contracts and services, or use their authority through laws to create rents to their own groups. Such high returns from the state discourage investment in productive sectors thus creating enormous inefficiency and distortion in the market. Such states are 'predatory', to use Evans' terminology, and 'have no more regard for their societies than a predator does for its prey' (Evans 1992: 122). These states are unable to allocate their resources effectively and constitute a significant barrier to the establishment of market logic and market signals in the economy. By resolving the credibility problem through signalling, and by setting up institutional standards and procedures of policy making, regional cooperation might indeed help reduce the rent-seeking behaviour and indeed help restructure the role of the state in the economy.

Finally, regional cooperation is also an effective path for securing access to foreign markets, capital, investments and technology. As Solingen argues,

> cooperative arrangements erode risk considerations and enable foreign investment, avoid potential sanctions and penalties from international private and public actors and reinforce (liberal) the coalition's ties to economic institutions (IMF, World Bank), to which they endear themselves by virtue of their reform programs. … New regional cooperative and (potentially integrative) regimes emerge that serve both the purpose of strengthening the liberalising model at home, and of lubricating external ties to the global political economy.
> (Solingen 1996a: 89)

Indeed, regional cooperative schemes can be an effective tool for integrating into the world economy while strengthening the domestic constituencies that support liberal reforms.

Exploring prospects and constraints of regionalism in the Middle East

Despite all these expected benefits from cooperation schemes, the Middle East remains a peculiar exception to the overall trend of regionalism. Among various regions, the Middle East is not only the least integrated into the world economy but is also characterised by the lowest degree of regional economic cooperation. During an era when the benefits of schemes of regional economic cooperation are increasingly acknowledged, why is the Middle East relatively left behind? And what are the emerging prospects for cooperation in the region?

First and foremost, most analysts agree that the absence of a viable regional security environment in the Middle East has constituted the major impediment for economic cooperation (Anderson 1995; Solingen 1996a; 1996b). Throughout the Cold War, the region was an arena of superpower competition which significantly decreased the costs of wars for the countries in the region (Brown 1984). By the end of the 1967 Arab–Israeli war, for instance, the Soviet Union had replaced 80 per cent of the war losses incurred by all the Arab states (Anderson 1995: 39). The end of the Cold War has reduced some of the economic, political and ideological differences in the region. Even though some of the strategies of the Middle Eastern governments might still stem from an incentive to tap into foreign economic resources, the international pressures have clearly shifted from being an inducement for a proxy war to peace in the region.

There is no doubt that the severity of conflicts in the region coupled with disputes ranging from territorial issues to water rights have been, and still are, fundamental barriers to cooperation. An overall reduction of the threat to the external security environment, however, is likely to have important repercussions on economic and social cooperation in the region. The potential economic benefits of peace range from a 'peace dividend' that can be used for productive investment and greater macroeconomic stability, to increased foreign capital in the region as investors will be more inclined to invest in a stable environment and expanding markets.

On the face of it, the reduction in security threats will lead to more economic cooperation. However, as Diwan and Papandreou (1993) remind us, given the domestic political instability in many of the Middle Eastern countries, elimination of the external threat might actually reduce the capacity of the governments to contain this instability, and might induce the governments to maintain or recreate this 'external threat' in order to play the 'security card' on the domestic front. The absence of significant schemes of economic cooperation in the Middle East then can be linked both to the continuing security concerns in the region as well as the willingness of the governments to play the security card in order to control domestic political instability. Peace, then, is a necessary but insufficient condition for effective economic cooperation in the region.

Nevertheless, the absence of peace also explains yet another barrier to regional cooperation in the region, namely the ineffective economic policies. The region has the highest military spending, wastes valuable resources on agricultural self-sufficiency which leads to enormously ineffective use of precious water in the region. The best example, of course, is Saudi Arabia becoming a wheat exporter by using the non-replaceable and soon-to-be-depleted underwater resources. Only when the security concerns of the Middle Eastern governments are addressed and a minimal trust is established, can we expect a reversal of ineffective and economically irrational policy making.

Apart from increased prospects of peace in the region, increasing regionalism in the world economy, particularly in the aftermath of the Cold War, is also having significant repercussions for the Middle East. The trends for regionalism increasingly suggest that if similar schemes of regional cooperation are not designed for the region, the Middle East will increasingly become marginalised in the world economy. More importantly, declining oil revenues, which started in the 1980s, had already begun pushing the Middle Eastern governments to undertake significant economic reforms. The end of the Cold War has also opened up new oil reserves in the former Soviet Republics to the world markets, which means, provided a reasonable route of carrying this oil from the region is found, the West will become increasingly less dependent on Middle Eastern oil. The oil crisis has already speeded up the shift to alternative oil resources. The crisis of the Gulf War has further fuelled this change.

Meanwhile, the shift towards 'new' regionalism and deeper integration in the world economy suggests that even the simplest trade agreement (let alone a customs union or economic union) requires significant harmonisation of the domestic policies and coordination amongst states. Such a harmonisation would simply require significant overhaul of the existing institutional economic and political structure of the Middle Eastern states and redefinition of the state–society relationships.

Reforming both the economic and political domestic structures is clearly a daunting task particularly when most Middle Eastern governments are characterised by closed regimes and heavy state involvement in the economy. State spending in the Middle East, particularly in the 1970s thanks largely to oil revenues, has in fact formed large entitlement groups (Anderson 1987). It is indeed no wonder that the Middle Eastern states have been the subject of the burgeoning literature on the 'rentier state' (for examples of such studies, see Anderson 1987; Beblawi and Luciani 1987; Chaudhry 1993; 1994; 1997; Mahvadi 1970). The size and composition of these entitlement groups have varied significantly, and began to change in the 1980s as the massive inflow of capital into the oil exporters in the region began to dry up. The nature of the so-called exogenous rents (whether it is foreign aid, oil revenues or labour remittance) and the historical legacy of colonial experience clearly shape the patterns of state making and market creation in the Middle Eastern countries (Chaudhry 1989). Understanding the institutional barriers that stand in the way of significant political and economic reforms including economic liberalisation is thus necessary. That is why complementarity and increased harmony among domestic political and economic structures of the Middle Eastern countries are crucial for regional cooperation.

Similarly, in the absence of such domestic constituencies, which would push their governments toward cooperation, mere intra-governmental agreements or harmonisation of institutions with little or no reference to demands of domestic constituencies are less likely to last. Any project for cooperation must therefore include mobilisation of economic and social groups and most importantly support for democratisation. Once again, one of the significant barriers to democratisation in the region is embedded in the region's political economy, namely what Anderson calls, 'soft-budget constraints' (Anderson 1995). As she explains:

> The availability of exogenous revenues releases governments from their reliance on domestic taxes for significant (if variable) components of their income and, therefore, from many of the ordinary obligations of domestic accountability. ... Resource distribution through subsidies and patronage militates against political democratization and liberalization not only because it releases governments from marginal reliance on domestic taxpayers but also because it creates citizenry that is financially dependent on the state.
>
> (Anderson 1995: 32–33)

In short, soft-budget financing leads to the failure and the reluctance on the part of governments to undertake political reforms that might indeed mobilise constituencies that will challenge the existing state policies.

Most states, particularly the oil exporting ones, are also known as 'predatory' states subject to pressures from dominant economic groups on the domestic front (Evans 1992). In the meantime, however, the development of a private sector through the state and exogenous rents have also made it extremely difficult for the Middle Eastern states to undertake significant economic reforms at a later stage (Chaudhry 1994). The discussion of whether the ineffective state stemmed from the autonomous, overly powerful entrenched elite that resisted economic reforms and did not want to lose its privileges or whether it rose from a weak administrative state or even from a weak, underdeveloped private sector is beyond the scope of this book. The resulting ineffective and often inefficient state, however, – either unable to undertake reforms as is the case in Saudi Arabia or where the state directly intervened in the economy as in the case of Yemen and Iraq – can seriously affect prospects of cooperation in the region. Since such inefficiencies are embedded in very institutional and state–society relationships, understanding regional cooperation in the Middle East will essentially depend on untying the existing state–business relationships.

In short, absence of comprehensive peace coupled with lack of significant economic reforms, largely due to ineffective government policies, has blocked the prospects of cooperation in the region (Solingen 1996a; Chaudhry 1994). The fear that economic and political liberalisation might indeed mobilise social forces and interest groups that these governments might not be able to control essentially hindered the possibility of significant reform. Strengthening of the civil society was simply too big a risk to take for these governments already plagued by immense problems of unemployment, rapid urbanisation and repressive political activity.

That is why the Middle East is also one of the regions that has benefited least from the global trends towards economic and political liberalisation. *Infitah* (an Arabic term used to refer to economic opening), which several Middle Eastern countries undertook in the 1980s, has had limited effect particularly in changing the role of the state in these countries (Richards and Waterbury 1996). As in most late developers, dictatorial regimes, inefficient and corrupt bureaucratic structure, and the excesses of state involvement in the economy were significant barriers to the development of private domestic and foreign investment in these countries. The uncertainty of the Arab–Israeli conflict, excessive military expenditures, consequent budget deficits and macroeconomic instabilities all made economic and political liberalisation very difficult (Fischer, Rodrik and Tuma 1993).

Perhaps the most fundamental barrier to political and economic liberalisation and hence regional cooperation remain, however, the credibility of commitments made by Middle Eastern governments. As will be elaborated further in the next chapter, the issue of credibility, particularly the credibility of the governments at the domestic and international level, is crucial for regional cooperation. Largely due to weak opposition and the absence of a sufficiently developed civil society, the pressure on the Middle Eastern governments to carry out their commitments has been minimal. It is precisely the absence of such domestic obligations (hence the arbitrariness and the reversibility of commitments) that have raised significant questions on a durable cooperation scheme in the Middle East.

Most analysts agree that the high number of failed economic and political unions in the region create a serious problem of credibility (Fischer 1995: 440). As we note in Chapter 7, there have been several attempts in the region to create regional cooperation. Even the least ambitious of those efforts – the League of Arab States – has largely been unable to foster significant economic cooperation and exert independent political influence.

Similarly, as discussed above, regional cooperation schemes are not likely to be successful when there is wide discrepancy in terms of economic development in the region. Unfortunately, the Middle East suffers severely from this problem. The economic discrepancy, as will be discussed in Chapter 4, between the oil exporters and the non-oil states in the region has helped raise concerns over the distribution of benefits from regional cooperation.

Can the Middle Eastern governments undertake such political and economic reforms, overcome the barriers described above, and achieve both politically and economically feasible cooperation? As already indicated, the existing political and economic structures do not, at first glance, portray an optimistic picture. Significant economic discrepancies, lack of complementarity of the existing economies and the continuation of protectionist and inefficient policies all suggest that creating such cooperative structures is indeed difficult. 'There is no realistic prospect of Middle-East wide regional integration on either the NAFTA or EC models in the near future' (Fischer 1995: 426). Cooperation in the Middle East is neither a simple cessation of conflicts nor is it the signing of a free trade agreement. From energy issues to trade and from agriculture to water, all aspects of policy making, as in all the late developers, are highly political processes.

Nevertheless, limited moves towards economic cooperation may indeed be possible. Potential gains from such cooperation range from increased peace dividends, and collaboration on water use and management to meeting regional infrastructure and transportation needs, and increased efficiency of the Middle Eastern economies. Given these potential gains, exploring the barriers to cooperation and how they can be overcome in the region is an urgent necessity. Clearly, regional cooperation is not a panacea that will cure all the political and economic problems of the Middle East. Establishing political will to enhance cooperation, however, might be a step in the right direction and might put an end to the so-called Middle East exceptionalism.

3 Political economy of regional cooperation

Towards a model

This study is based on the argument that there is a complex set of domestic political factors that affect the extent and nature of cooperation in the Middle East which will in turn affect the respective domestic constituencies in each country of the region. The composition and articulation of interests by different groups in the countries of the Middle East are not only affected by the developments in the international environment but are also moulded by changes in their economies and political structures. Any move by decision-makers of the Middle Eastern countries to change the existing set of economic and political relationships towards more or less cooperative milieux will have to be approved by the relevant domestic constituencies and other political forces. The interaction between the domestic and international actors must be understood in order to explain the character and prospects of political and economic cooperation in the region.

We specifically focus on the following set of questions: Under what conditions is regional economic and political cooperation meaningful and possible? What determines the prospects and constraints of regional cooperation? Who are the main actors involved? What level of analysis should be used to locate the main actors? How do they influence the policy outcomes? These questions constitute the core issues for social scientists from a wide variety of fields including international relations, political economy and trade theory. This study aims to respond to these questions through analysing the prospects of economic and political cooperation in the Middle East. While we explore international, regional and domestic political and economic factors that shape the dynamics of regional cooperation in the Middle East, we also try to address several theoretical issues on regionalism. These issues include:

1 To what extent are the existing theories of international relations sufficient in understanding the problem of regional cooperation?
2 What is the role of the state and state institutions in explaining foreign-policy outcomes (both political and economic)? What kind of a state/regime is necessary for effective regional cooperation? How relevant are the 'state-centric' arguments and theories based on the role of the state in understanding regional cooperation?

3 How effective is a society-centred approach in explaining foreign-policy outputs? How significant is the ongoing struggle for influence among domestic political and social forces? And most importantly, how do they interact with state and international actors?

We base our analysis below on the concept of the two-level games in international politics suggested by Putnam (1988). Framing the analysis of the Middle East within a wider literature concerning the region's socio-economic structure, various armed conflicts and impinging developments in the world markets, we demonstrate that such an analysis can explain the hurdles as well as latent sources of leverage in regional cooperation in general.

Putnam's (1988) theoretical framework is focused on international negotiations in which governments represent constituencies that must ratify a negotiated agreement before it can be implemented. We argue that the slowly moving experiment of creating a regional cooperative environment is essentially undergoing a similar negotiation and ratification process. Each actor – governments in this case – not only has concerns shaped by the international political and economic environment but also a domestic environment composed of different interest groups with various conflicting incentives and political leverage upon the government. This chapter focuses on the character of the interaction within the Middle Eastern context between the governments' international level interactions as they are shaped by, and as they affect, the domestic political and economic structure. Below, we first briefly present the theoretical approaches to international and regional cooperation, lay down the basic tenets of the two-level game approach and try to underline its explanatory power within the Middle Eastern context in comparison to alternative approaches.

International cooperation: Theoretical basis

Having observed the devastating consequences of two world wars, contemporary theorists on international relations have long explored the prospects and possibilities of international cooperation. This extensive literature also offers interesting insights to the issue of regional cooperation. Realism, which dominated the field of international relations since the Second World War offered a rather pessimistic analysis of the prospects for international cooperation.[1] Realist theorists argued that states are the main actors in the international system, and that they are unitary, rational actors that try to maintain their power and security in an increasingly anarchic international environment. That is why states are more likely to face competition and conflict than cooperation even though they may have common interests (Grieco 1988). The main challenge to the realists came from the so-called liberal institutionalists. These theorists refuted the realist conception that states are the only main actors in international politics and emphasised instead the role of international institutions. While the early functionalist international theory underlined the role of specialised international agents such as the World Health Organisation (WHO) and the United Nations Education Fund (UNICEF), the neo-functionalists came to focus on supranational institutions such as the European Community (Haas, B.E. 1958; 1964; Mitrany 1975).

The main argument of the neo-liberals was that international or supranational institutions may help overcome problems of collective (cooperative) action among the states since states try to maximise their absolute gain and are indifferent to the gains by other states. The realists, on the other hand, argue that states are also concerned with relative gains and will refuse cooperation when and if benefits of cooperation to one state are more than to the other. Since the intentions and capabilities of states are constantly changing in an anarchic international system, cooperation on a relative gain basis is highly unlikely and cheating is common (Grieco 1988, 1990; Mastanduno 1991). Both the realists and neo-institutionalists agree that balanced or reciprocal (or Axelrod's tit-for-tat) agreements are the key for successful cooperation (Axelrod 1984; Keohane 1986a; Snidal 1991a; 1991b).

A similar debate on international cooperation continued throughout the 1970s. This time the neo-institutionalists began to emphasise increasing economic interdependence and globalisation in the world economy, which they claimed opened new avenues for cooperation. Coming to accept the states as rational actors in the international system, these theorists used game theory and the prisoner's dilemma as a key tool of analysis. The game of prisoner's dilemma, where rational actors choose sub-optimal outcomes and 'defect' to their own detriment rather than mutually cooperate, was used to demonstrate how barriers to information and communication can impede cooperation in world politics. The proponents of this literature argued that states could overcome such information and communication problems through international and multilateral institutions (Axelrod 1984; Lipson 1984; Stein 1982). As Haas explains 'the need for collaboration arises from the recognition that the costs of national self-reliance are usually excessive' (Haas, E.B. 1980: 357). As Milner (1992: 467) points out, the strength of this literature lies in the acceptance of a common definition of cooperation. Accordingly, international cooperation occurs 'when actors adjust their behavior to the actual and anticipated preferences of others, through a policy coordination' (Keohane 1984: 51–52).

The ensuing 'regime' literature in international relations theory introduced the idea that states can indeed agree on certain norms, rules and procedures in order to regulate an issue area (Haas, E.B. 1980; Krasner 1983). What was new in the regime literature was that it combined, for the first time, the importance of positional power of a state with the possibility of rule-governed behaviour on certain issues. Another advantage of the regime literature was that it explored the linkages between relative political powers of states and issues of economic cooperation in the international arena. In effect it combined some elements of realism with that of neo-liberalism (Keohane 1984; 1986b). A variant of the regime theorists explained cooperation through the creation of the so-called 'epistemic communities', i.e. transnational groups with shared values, causal models and validation criteria as well as a common project (Haas, M.P. 1989: 55; 1992). Such epistemic communities reduce uncertainty, provide expert information and enhance the value of negotiation.

The problem with both the regime theorists as well as the epistemic community hypothesis is that both can explain how cooperation can be deepened and rendered more durable rather than how it is initiated. Both literatures assume that there is a prior agreement to cooperate which is what actually needs to be explained (Milner 1992: 479). The best known offspring of the regime theories was the so-called hegemonic stability theory which explored the relationship between the existence of a hegemonic power in the international system and free trade/economic cooperation. Defining international free trade as a public good, the hegemonic stability theorists argued that for the world economy to be stable there needs to be a stabiliser (Kindleberger 1973). They argued that cooperation in the world economy thus relies heavily on the existence of a hegemon, which was the US in the aftermath of the Second World War. The hegemonic stability theory was heavily criticised and left many questions unanswered. Why a hegemon but not a small group? Is free trade a public good? Why does the hegemon accept free trade when optimal tariff levels are economically more rational? (Gowa 1994; Conybeare 1983).

Nevertheless, hegemonic stability theory was used as a theoretical tool to explore the international political dynamics necessary for effective economic cooperation, in this case the issue of free trade. Gowa (1994) succinctly argued, for instance, that free trade is more likely among allies than with adversaries. She argued that,

> because trade produces security externalities, it should not be any less vulnerable to the play of great-power politics than any other type of state interaction. Trade with an ally produces a positive externality, trade with an adversary creates security diseconomy. As a result, ceteris paribus, free trade is more likely within than across political-military alliances.
>
> (Gowa 1994: 120)

Similarly Mansfield explored the relationship between the distribution of power in the international system and the possibilities of regionalism in international trade (Mansfield 1994). He, too, reaches the conclusion that alliance helps internalise the security externalities of trade and increases the trade flows while a state trading freely with its adversary is likely to augment the political power of its trading partner and undermine, in effect, its own security. He even goes so far as to suggest that trade and peace go hand in hand (Mansfield 1994).

The level-of-analysis problem

Although the system-level theories of international relations summarised above shed some light on the international conditions under which regional cooperation is possible, it has the major deficiency of looking at the states as black-boxes and of overlooking the domestic dynamics that play a crucial role in inter-state relations. Apart from being limited to one level of analysis, they also fail to provide a dynamic picture. Change is only possible, according to this perspective, through significant transformation of the international distribution of power or a 'systemic' shift. Clearly, international dynamics are far from being sufficient in explaining why states behave the way they do (Singer 1961).

Domestic factors, both economic and political, play a crucial role in shaping state policies and inter-state relations as well. Extensive research has been done exploring the domestic sources of international effects. In *Man, State and War* for instance, Waltz (1959) called these domestic factors the 'second image' in explaining the causes of war. Frieden (1988a), Gourevitch (1978; 1986), Katzenstein (1985), Lake (1988), Rogowski (1989) and others reversed this 'second image' and focused on international sources of domestic politics applying this framework in various empirical contexts such as domestic responses to the Great Depression and to the debt crisis in the 1980s. Allison's (1971) bureaucratic-politics approach to international relations also explored the relations between bureaucratic interests in the foreign policy process but did not go beyond acknowledging that bureaucratic interests matter. In fact, these studies, as Putnam (1988) rightly points out, only provided a partial picture and failed to show precisely how the domestic politics of several countries get precisely intertwined with international dynamics and vice versa.

A valuable contribution to the domestic level of analysis came from the state-centric arguments which focused on the role and strength of the state. Rediscovery of state as a fruitful analytical tool within the last fifteen years has led to a burgeoning literature that included exploring the role of the state in foreign economic policy-making (Evans, Rueschemeyer and Skocpol 1985; Katzenstein 1978). Whether defined as an organisational structure focusing on domestic decision-making structures (neo-institutionalism) or as an actor consisting of politicians and bureaucrats, state-centric arguments were soon criticised for seeing the state as a monolithic entity. The critiques then led to arguments centring on state–society relations. Weak–strong state distinction emerged where the strength of the state was defined in terms of the range of policy tools available to the state and the centralisation of decision-making. The weak states, for which the US was a good example, were characterised by excessive penetration of special interests in policy-making and fragmentation of power along bureaucratic and institutional lines (Krasner 1978). The weak–strong state distinction, however, misses the contextual factors in which state decisions are made and the influences and preferences that go into this decision-making. Clearly, the domestic political institutions may condition the preferences and the capacity of the state in the policy-making (Ikenberry, Mastanduno and Lake 1988).

Nevertheless, domestic political institutions are clearly not the only factors that influence policy-making. Parties and interest groups that will be, either positively or negatively, affected from the policy outcomes will also shape the state's preferences to the degree that they have access to the policy-making institutions.

That is why society-centred explanations focus on the struggle for influence among domestic social and political groups. Here the preferences of various interest groups and the dynamics of the party systems are most crucial in accounting for policy outcomes. Thus, preferences of interest groups, civil organisations and how their interests are aggregated and organised are all crucial. As Epstein and O'Halloran point out, '(p)olitical preferences are not immediately translated into policy, outcomes also reflect the method by which interests are aggregated. Thus, understanding political outcomes requires an analysis of both preference and institutions' (Epstein and O'Halloran 1996: 302). This approach has been particularly used in analysing US foreign economy policy, for instance, where competing interest groups and corporate demands were analysed (Aggarwal, Keohane and Yoffie 1987; Ferguson 1984; Milner 1987, 1988). Students of development also elaborated their own version where 'rent-seeking' effects on the state and markets were explored (Krueger 1974).

Although both state-centric and the society-centred explanations are crucial steps towards understanding how and why the negotiators (the states) behave the way they do and the kind of tactics they employ at the negotiation table, neither the state-centric nor the society-centred arguments explore how these domestic dynamics are specifically linked to the 'first image', i.e. system level factors. In short, while rightfully criticising the system-level theorists for leaving out the domestic factors, domestic-level analyses leave out the analysis of how domestic factors play out in the international arena. To put it in game-theoretic terms, these arguments see the game constrained to the domestic arena and fail to see concomitant games that are at work simultaneously entangled, influencing and being influenced by the international dynamics. To argue that domestic politics matters, should not suggest that the outcome of foreign policy depends only on an individual state's own policy process. Whether a given state adopts the 'preference-driven' models or 'institutional models', policy outcomes in that state will surely affect and be affected by the policies of other states.

Putnam's work on two-level games offers a better alternative both to the system-level and state-and-society-centred theories as he is able to explore the linkages between all these factors and offer a dynamic picture. By offering the metaphor of two-level games, Putnam avoids an aggregate construction of the state and can reject the unitary conception of the state so common among the system-level theorists. Below, we lay down the logic of the two-level-game approach to international negotiations and adapt it to a framework of analysis for regional economic and political cooperation in the Middle East.

The two-level game: A theory of interdependence between domestic and international forces

Many times in politics, one faces a situation where a conclusion that seems only logical at first sight is never realised. A reaction to an action that is all too expected is never observed. Series of events that seem very illogical and too costly by most, however, never seem to end. Numerous examples illustrate these characteristics. Take for instance, the trade negotiations between France and the United States over the reduction of agricultural subsidies and liberalisation of agricultural trade. Both states use such subsidies in order to support their own agricultural sectors. France has consistently refused to reduce such subsidies and liberalise its trade which, when analysed at the international level, would appear illogical. The agricultural prices in France are well above world levels, indicating absence of economies of scale and inefficiency. The country could get access to much cheaper food and dairy products if it agrees to import and liberalise its trade. This would also mean reduced food prices at home along with all other associated benefits.

Putnam (1988) and Tsebelis (1990) offer a simple explanation to problems faced in situations similar to the ones depicted above. Their answer is simply that when decision-makers play more than one game at the same time, and when the strategies to be followed in each of these games depend on each other, then a peculiar situation can arise. It is possible to reach a situation in these interconnected 'games' where the outcome may seem 'irrational' unless the full range of interconnections between the different games played are taken into account. In other words, the position of the French government can be understood only if the demands of the agricultural elite and domestic power of the farmers are taken into account. The violent demonstrations of the French farmers during the US–EU trade negotiations is a reminder of the simultaneous two games at work: one at inter-state level (Level I) and another at the level of the negotiator's domestic constituencies (Level II).

Putnam's (1988) starting point is the simple observation that a negotiator typically has to simultaneously satisfy these two interdependent imperatives. The outcome of any such negotiation thus depends critically on simultaneous acceptance and approval of both competing negotiators as well as each and every one of their own domestic constituencies. Approval or refusal by the negotiators at Level I (trade negotiations) depend on whether or not the terms agreed upon by the negotiators are acceptable to their domestic constituencies (French and US farmers, respectively). At Level II domestic constituencies' decisions depend on the terms agreed upon by their negotiators at Level I, as well as some domestic concerns which need not depend on any decision at Level I.

Defining the 'win set' as a set of Level I agreements that will be acceptable to the Level II constituency, Putnam develops three main hypotheses: (1) that larger winning sets will make Level I agreement (regional cooperation in this case) more likely, (2) that credibility at Level I is enhanced by the negotiator's demonstrated ability to deliver at Level II and (3) that the relative size of the win sets at Level II will affect the distribution of the joint gains from the international bargain. A smaller win set at home might actually give the negotiator effective bargaining power since then the negotiator can credibly claim at Level I that the terms of agreement at the bargaining table are not acceptable for its domestic constituency unless some of its domestic concerns are reflected to Level I. We will return to these arguments below in the context of regional cooperation in the Middle East.

What determines the size of the win set? Here Putnam also offers three factors. First is the combination of the power and preferences of possible domestic coalitions. The cost of 'no agreement' for the domestic constituents, the degree of heterogeneity of the constituents, and degree of politicisation of the issue at hand (how exactly will the constituents be affected) all shape the patterns of domestic coalitions and their role in negotiations. Second, the nature of domestic institutions is also important. Ratification procedures can change the size of the win set. The party discipline, for example, can influence the win set: strong discipline in the governing party, for instance, increases the win set. The two-level analysis actually offers an interesting twist on strong–weak state distinctions based on the 'autonomy' of the central government from domestic pressures. In sharp contrast to the existing literature which sees such pressures as highly inefficient and wasteful, Putnam suggests that the greater the autonomy of the decision-makers from the constituents, the larger is the win set. However, the negotiator also loses a significant bargaining leverage since it does not have any domestic pressures which could be manipulated to demand more concessions at the table.

Third, by pointing out that there are two games simultaneously going on in negotiations mutually affecting each other, Putnam captures how international negotiations create opportunities for the negotiators to pursue synergistic strategies aiming to shape domestic politics both of their own and of their counterparts in order to reach an agreement (Schoppa 1993). Employing transnational linkages whenever there is significant opposition at the domestic level, offering side payments to domestic constituents of both one's own and the counterpart, or targeting swing voters are some of the innovative strategies which are open to the negotiators and which transform the game at Level II.

Most importantly, the two-level-game framework offers a better conceptual framework for cooperation. The negotiations are no longer viewed as a binary game based on cooperation or defection, but as a continuum where many tactics and bargaining tools are employed (Jervis 1988). By utilising a two-level-game framework, variations in policy outcomes across various issues – even when the domestic and international factors do not vary – can be explained. By avoiding the binary two-by-two game-theoretic model, Putnam opens the path towards explaining suboptimal cooperation. So the two-level-game framework acknowledges that 'cooperation below the Pareto frontier' to use Krasner's term (1991), is possible and indeed very common, thanks to the domestic game that is simultaneously at work. Playing into the hands of the domestic constituencies at Level II might indeed prove for the Level I actors to be much more important than achieving the optimal agreement at Level I. The two-level-game framework avoids the binary conception of international cooperation and can better account for the various cooperative outcomes.

Following a similar logic in a more generalised context, Tsebelis (1990) tries to account for certain anomalies in the literature on comparative politics. The full implication of Tsebelis's work for our purposes is that when there is a game within a game, one has to assume that players will remain rational at each relevant step until the full game takes its course. If the game is played sequentially then, from the first stage to the last, players will have to proceed in a rational way. If, as Putnam seems to argue, all games are played simultaneously then, however complex, rationality in each cannot be compromised.

Implications of this multi-level-game approach for our objectives can be illustrated with a generic game of cooperation. Consider the dilemma of a stylised state and its relations with another country, possibly but not necessarily its neighbour or one other regional country. At any given time these two countries will be negotiating an existing conflict. During these negotiations the critical decision is whether to offer concessions or impose severe demands on the other party. Any such decision by one party typically leaves the other party with two options: either to retaliate by similar severe demands or to compromise. Clearly, each decision depends on the other and, typically, decision-makers will have to reveal their decisions simultaneously which of course complicates the decision even further.

Two basic types of interrelationship exist within the multi-level-game approach. First is a sequential interaction where negotiations at Level I lead to a new game of ratification at Level II. Second is a more complicated simultaneous negotiation at Level I and ratification at Level II. Figure 3.1 depicts these two forms of interaction. Within each of the boxes denoting different levels of the game there are many players interacting to shape decisions. Figures 3.2a and 3.2b open up these two boxes and expose the nature of interaction at each level in more detail. Solid lines denote the direction of the sequence of the game. Those actors playing at two different levels that are connected with a dotted line choose their actions simultaneously and thus do not observe each other's actions.

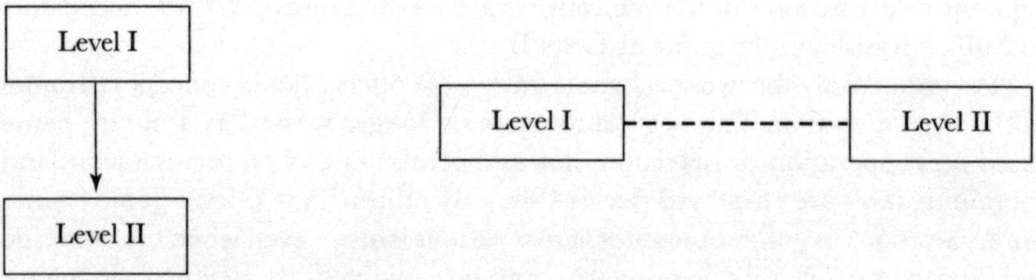

Figure 3.1 Sequential and simultaneous two-level games

The extensive form representation of this game is given in Figures 3.2a and 3.2b. For simplicity, it is assumed that the sequence of the game can be differentiated into sequential moves. At each level, however, the relevant players (i.e., negotiator or constituency) play simultaneously and choose their moves from only two options. The game at each level is assumed to be started by player 1, but since at each level the game is played simultaneously, the identity of the starting player is irrelevant and can be chosen arbitrarily.

All constituencies here belong to one or other of the negotiators at Level I. We assume that no constituency interacts with others across different players. In other words, domestic constituencies are assumed to be in contact with each other across different states only through the representation of negotiators at Level I. All relevant constituencies at Level II make their moves simultaneously.

Going back to Figure 3.1, to solve the sequential interaction across different levels one can proceed with an extension of simple backwards induction and apply the subgame perfection principle. Accordingly, each part of the proper subgame of the two-level interaction should be solved by keeping to the rationality principle in each case. By a 'proper subgame' we mean 'parts of a game that can be treated as games in their own right'; see Morrow (1994: 128) for a clear exposition of subgame

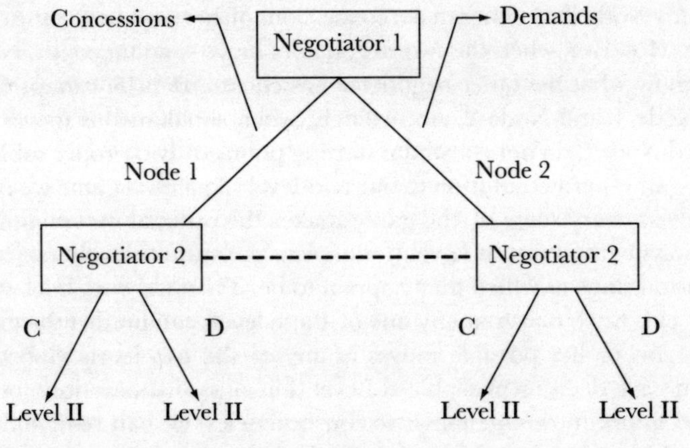

Figure 3.2a Level I: Game between international negotiators
Note: Only two Level I negotiators are assumed here

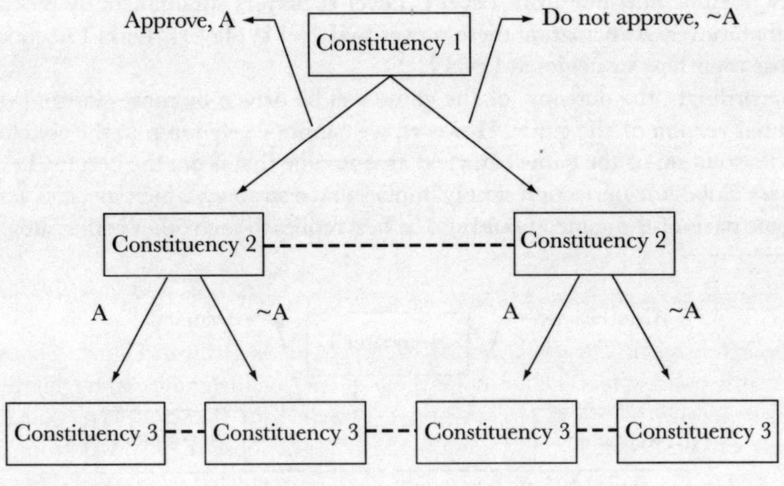

Figure 3.2b Level II: Game between relevant domestic constituencies

perfection. It is clear from Putman's treatment of the two-level approach to international interactions that each level constitutes a proper subgame. In other words, all actions at Level I are clearly observed by constituents at Level II. However, within each level the existence of simultaneous moves limits the existence of proper subgames. Take for instance the situation of Negotiator 2 at Level I. If Negotiator 2 could observe the move by Negotiator 1, or in other words if they did not move simultaneously, then each move at the two nodes available to her (or him) would have constituted a proper subgame. With sequential moves within Level I Negotiator 2 would then observe the other's move of either making concessions or demands. If a concession (or demand) were made, Negotiator 2 would have to decide in her proper subgame at Node 1 (or Node 2) to either make concessions of her own or to raise demands as a response. However, when the two negotiators move simultaneously, Negotiator 2 does not know what the other negotiator has chosen, thus he cannot differentiate between Node 1 and Node 2. Accordingly, when simultaneous moves are made, Node 1 and Node 2 do not constitute starting points of two proper subgames.

In a subgame-perfect solution to our two-level sequential game we require that each player at every stage of the game makes the optimal moves and thus stays rational. Solving the game at Level II, domestic constituencies choose optimally at every decision stage at which they happen to be. Then we work backwards to the earlier Level I. Each player at any one of these levels can predict the exact consequences of his or her possible moves at any of the two levels. Substituting the outcome of each decision available at Level II in all available actions for Level I (as anticipated future moves of domestic constituencies) we can resolve the decision of the Level I negotiator. Within each level or proper subgame, players need not know the actions of each other. In fact, since within each level the players move simultaneously, they do now know what each other player is doing. For each and every possible outcome from Level I, Level II players simultaneously pick their optimal moves. Anticipating these moves by Level II players, Level I negotiators choose their best strategies at Level I.

Accordingly, the outcome of the game will be driven by moves last in this sequential version of the game. However, we cannot easily jump to the conclusion that no solution of the game can yield an outcome that is not the best for Level II players. Subgame perfection simply implies that a strategy, which specifies actions in some parts of the game, should also be best replies to each other in that subgame.

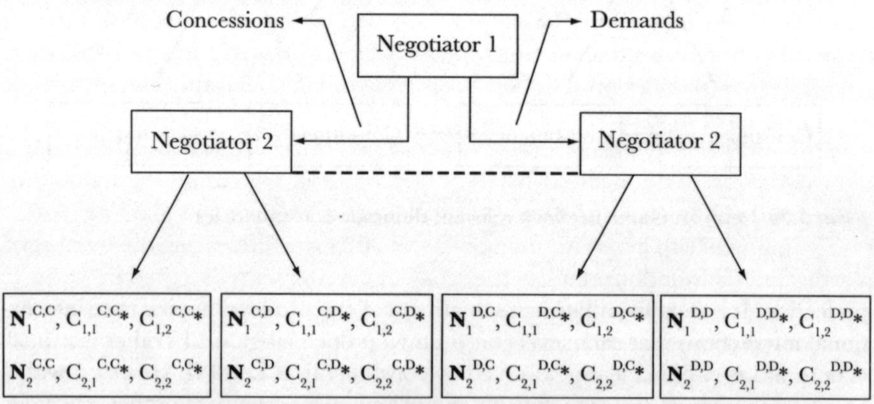

Figure 3.3 Level I: Game between international negotiators (further detail)

Notes: **N**: Negotiator; C: Concessions; D: Demands; $\mathbf{N}_i^{C,C}$: payoff for Negotiator 1 when both negotiators make concessions and the domestic constituency choose their best reply to the Level I game; e.g., $C_{1,1}^{C,C*}$, $C_{1,2}^{C,C*}$. The superscripts denote the move of Negotiator 1 and then Negotiator 2; for example, $\mathbf{N}_i^{C,D}$ denotes the payoff for Negotiator 1 when Negotiator 1 played concessions while Negotiator 2 played increasing demands. The starred payoffs for domestic constituencies denote those payoffs associated with playing the optimal choice at Level II.

Only strategies that satisfy this principle are subgame perfect. In a subgame-perfect strategy, all players credibly commit themselves to sticking to their moves in that particular strategy.

Consider the following detailed exposition of the two-level game as shown in Figure 3.3. At Level I negotiators simultaneously pick their moves either making concessions or demands. The pay-offs at Level I are given not only for the negotiators but also for each one of their constituencies. Constituency pay-offs are starred to indicate that they represent the optimal choice by the domestic players given the outcome of the previous Level I game. So, if any one of these Level I decision nodes are reached, Level II moves are given by the starred strategies. The critical point to note here is that negotiators' payoffs are all functions of the subsequent Level II optimal strategies. If this were not so, choices by the negotiators would be independent of their own domestic constituencies'. In other words, what happens at the domestic level affects the pay-offs at Level I. However, as we will discuss in greater detail below, there is nothing in this framework guaranteeing that the optimal move by the negotiator will also provide the highest payoff for the domestic constituencies. However, no matter what the outcome of Level I, the resulting moves at Level II will be the best reply.

Some conceptual and theoretical problems of two-level games

The above-depicted framework is consciously kept simple to clarify the structure of the argument. By doing so, we also hope to illustrate the limitations of the model. First and most obvious is the implausible nature of a sequential game across the two levels. A more realistic but disproportionately more complex version is the one where both international negotiations as well as domestic interactions take place in a simultaneous fashion. The negotiators are never free from being affected by their domestic constituencies. And in no instance can we assume that Level I negotiations do actually end. A relatively minor simplification is the assumption of only two parties at each level. Equally restrictive is also the assumption that every party involved has only two options. Increasing the number of parties and options open to each clearly makes the model more plausible. However, combined with inherent simultaneity of all moves, increasing the number of players and their options renders the model more and more intractable.

Another problem with this framework is that it remains silent on the initial preferences or the preference orderings of the states at the outset. As Cohen points out,

> [g]ame models are only as good as the assumptions on which they are built. They provide insights into the strategic choices that can be expected of individual players once the ordering of all the actor's preferences are fully detailed. However, ... there is nothing in the essential logic of game theory that tells us how the configurations of preferences get to be determined in the first place.
>
> (Cohen 1990: 276–277)

Since in two-level game, both the domestic and international preferences are subject to constant change, it becomes very hard to define the initial context within which the negotiations take place.

This initial context is clearly important, however, in understanding in what way the states evaluate their payoffs, that is, the costs and benefits of each outcome on the table. This issue is particularly salient on the question of how the distribution of gains from cooperation is distributed. While some states might be prone to accept an absolute gain regardless of its distribution, others might be concerned with the issue of relative gains (Grieco 1990; Oye 1986; Powell 1991). The sensitivity of the negotiator to the distributive terms of an accord will rely heavily on whether these states are initially allies or adversaries. One of the main problems in the Middle East, for instance, has been the emphasis of relative gains which has systematically hindered prospects of cooperation.

Clearly, whether the bargaining at hand is perceived as 'integrative' (win-win), or distributive (win-lose), to use Walton and McKersie's (1965) distinction, it will differ significantly if the states are allies than if they are adversaries. Hence, as Knopf (1993) proposes, a conceptualisation of a three-level game, where intra-alliance and inter-alliance negotiations are differentiated, can partly solve this problem.

Another problem with the two-level game is the assumption of rationality of all the actors involved. Although this framework goes a long way in terms of explaining outcomes that may appear irrational and suboptimal by pointing out the 'nested' games that are simultaneously at work, it still assumes that the actors involved at least agree on the rules of the game. As Tsebelis argues,

> rational choice is a better approach to situations in which actors' identity and goals are established and the rules of interaction are precise and known to the interacting agents. As the actors' goals become fuzzy, or as the rules of the interaction become more fluid, and imprecise, rational-choice explanations will become less applicable.
>
> (Tsebelis 1990: 33–34)

That the actors will agree on the rules of the game might indeed be too unrealistic an assumption to make, particularly in the context of the Middle East where the rules of the game are periodically called into question.

Similarly, the two-level-game framework does not sufficiently distinguish among different contexts within which the domestic–international interactions take place. Knopf (1993) argues for instance, that three distinct types of interaction can be observed: transgovernmental, transnational and cross-level.

> *Transgovernmental processes* come into play when officials on one or both sides are internally divided and one or both seek to bolster the influence of the like-minded faction in the other government. The *transnational pathway* involves links between domestic actors, by which I mean actors outside the executive branch or its equivalent, on both sides, where each seeks to add to the like-minded coalition on the other side. Finally, *cross-level processes* involve commu-

> nication between leaders on one side and domestic constituents on the other, regardless of which side initiates the connection.
>
> (Knopf 1993: 606, italics added)

The assumption in the two-level-game analysis that domestic constituencies do not affect each other across different states (transnational pathway) is indeed problematic. As we shall see in the following chapters, such an assumption is particularly troubling within the context of the Middle East. The existence of a common Arab identity has had some impact upon the decisions of several states. Dynamics of Arab identity and the pressures it creates upon different states is not under the control of any particular agent or country. However, both the negotiators as well as different constituencies within each state are known to use Arab identity as a tool to affect the domestic level decisions in other regional countries.

The distinctions among the variety of domestic–international ties, are crucial since each type of domestic–international interaction can lead to a different outcome. The two-level-game framework fails to identify which one of the bargaining tactics are most effective and when and why each can be employed. Such a distinction of domestic–international interaction is a step toward identifying which types of states might be more effective.

Finally, the two-level-game framework fails to specifically define what is meant by the bargaining leverage or bargaining power at the negotiating table. Although it introduces the much-needed domestic dimension, it does not adequately specify how specifically the bargaining power of a given state increases. Bargaining power clearly need not be defined solely in terms of military potency or the ability to withstand losses or financial resources. As Schelling (1960: 22) points out, these factors may in fact have contrary value. Is the bargaining power the ability to determine who plays the game? Is it the ability to define the rules or is it the ability to change the values within the payoff matrix? Is it the ability to change the perception of payoffs of your counterpart? Does it underestimate your win set to receive the maximum concessions? Clearly, the definition of bargaining power will have to include all of these factors. Bargaining power does not correspond to the systemic or regional power of a given state. In a region where even the smallest powers might play a crucial role at the negotiating table, such a distinction is indeed crucial.

None of these shortcomings invalidate the central argument of the two-level-game approach: interactions in the international arena have an integral reflection in the domestic politics of each involved state. Any decision at the international level has to be viewed within the framework of its implications for the domestic constituents to which international negotiators are being held accountable. Accordingly, the two-level game approach serves best as a heuristic metaphor. Even the main argument is analytically quite complicated to formalise. However, insights gathered from this informal metaphorical treatment are very useful in order to understand the dynamics of Middle Eastern negotiations.

Cooperation in the Middle East: the use of two-level-game perspective

As reviewed above, scholars of international relations and analysts of comparative politics, amongst others, have offered various answers as to why, when and how international cooperation is possible. In what follows, we discuss how some of the theoretical arguments that we have reviewed can be applied to the study of regional cooperation in the Middle East. We will specifically focus on the utility of the two-level games in analysing this issue and present several hypotheses and arguments that will be elaborated and examined in the following chapters.

As already indicated, one of the main contributions of the realist perspective in international relations has been the emphasis on the security dilemma and how economic ties cannot be effectively developed in the absence of a functioning security environment. That is why, at Level I, one of the arguments that is explored in this book is that economic ties cannot be effectively developed in the absence of a functioning security environment. Indeed, our first hypothesis is that the so-called security–trade dilemma – namely, that trading with your adversary might augment the enemy's political power and might in effect undermine one's own security – has been a crucial barrier to effective regional cooperation in the Middle East. The distribution of economic and political power among the Middle Eastern countries – the so-called systemic position of each country in the region (i.e., the power of these states against one and other) – is clearly taken into account in choosing trade partners. The concern that an existing enemy might increase their power vis-à-vis a given country and might pose a security threat seriously limits the patterns and prospects of cooperation in the region.

The absence of an international security regime in the region torn between the two major blocs was indeed a significant barrier to regional cooperation. As will be discussed in Chapter 6, such an environment clearly brought the problem of relative gains in trade relations and limited the potential for extensive economic ties. This also constrained the development of regional institutions, and reduced rule-governed behaviour and the creation of interdependence. Meanwhile, the tendency of the Middle Eastern countries to draw international actors – particularly the US and the Soviet Union throughout the Cold-War years – into the regional conflicts has also made cooperation very difficult. The ease with which the regional conflicts in the Middle East could escalate into a bilateral, and even a global conflict, was very evident, for instance, during the 1973 Arab–Israeli war when the two superpowers came to the brink of a nuclear war.

A corollary to the above hypothesis is that potential for regional cooperation will be greatly advanced when international and regional sources of conflict and insecurity are eliminated in the region. As elaborated in chapter 2, regional cooperation schemes increasingly rely on coordination of foreign economic and political strategies. Elimination of inter-state hostilities is crucial for preliminary steps towards regionalism. The establishment of a secure environment might even lead to 'deeper integration', as relaxation of tensions (détente) might lend itself to rapprochement and entente.

However, such 'system-level' explanations that focus on changes in bipolar dynamics and transformation in the global economy fail to capture the totality of reality in the Middle East. State- and society-centred explanations also offer several hypotheses based on domestic factors in analysing prospects of regional cooperation in the Middle East. Clearly, regime types, the domestic political institutions and how the state–society relations are structured will have important repercussions in the foreign-policy-making process in the region. As suggested in Chapter 7, the evaluation of the prospects of 'democratic peace' in the region – namely, how democratisation might affect the prospects of peace and cooperation in the Middle East – underline the importance of such domestic factors.

The two-level-game framework goes beyond both the exclusively 'systemic' and 'domestic' explanations by offering an 'interactive' model and focusing on how domestic factors affect and are affected simultaneously by international dynamics. Here, as Putnam states in his original article (1988), game theory is only used as a metaphor, and propositions are not really derived through choice-theoretic analysis. Instead, the two-level game is used as a framework to raise a set of questions. This type of theorising constitutes what Stanley Hoffmann once called 'theory as a set of questions', as opposed to 'theory as a set of answers' (Hoffmann 1960: 7–8).

The utility of the two-level-game framework in the context of regional cooperation in the Middle East stems precisely from the compelling questions it raises. Rather than dismissing the case of the Middle East as an exception, which appears to be the case when analysed from a purely 'systemic' perspective, the two-level-game metaphor allows for a better understanding of why Middle Eastern states behave the way they do. What kind of domestic constraints, along with international ones, do the Middle Eastern governments face in transforming this region from one of continuous hostilities to one of democratisation, peace and cooperation. How do Middle Eastern governments use external threats at home? What kind of side-payments do the governments offer to their domestic constituencies, if any, in shaping their inter-state ties in the region? Are there ways of expanding the 'win-set' during international exchanges? If so, how?

A good example of the use of the two-level-game framework is how national-security issues can be purposefully exaggerated or continuously kept on the public agenda for domestic purposes. Norton and Wright give an example of how the Arab–Israeli conflict has been used for domestic purposes by the Arab governments. They argue that

> [t]he legitimacy of many Arab governments has been eroding since the 1960s. The in-built failure of these Arab systems has, however, long been hidden behind the facade of national security. Under the cover of the Arab–Israeli dispute, many Arab governments of both right and left developed praetorian behemoths in the form of military, paramilitary and police forces that became more active – and more effective – in controlling the activities of real or perceived domestic opposition than in defeating Israel. The systematic

> expansion of defence and internal security budgets, often in the name of Arab honour, allowed many regimes to secure and perpetuate their rule.
>
> (Norton and Wright 1995: 8)

A similar argument can also be made for the Israeli government where the discussion of the Arab–Israeli peace process played a determining role in the outcome of the recent elections.

This discussion of how external security issues can be used for domestic purposes demonstrate the utility of the two-level-game analysis and leads to the argument that barriers to, as well as prospects for, regional cooperation in the Middle East should not only be sought in positional power of the states in the region or in macroeconomic compatibility, but also in domestic political and economic dynamics and their link to international factors. The two-level-game framework, adds that the approval and implementation of regional agreements rely heavily on the domestic pressures (or the lack thereof) bearing on the negotiator.

That is why, for regional cooperation to be effective in the Middle East, similarity or at least compatibility of economic and political institutions is necessary. This is necessitated not only by the recent trends of 'new regionalism' based on deep integration but also by the recognition that foreign-policy outcomes are clearly affected by domestic constituencies and vice versa. Indeed, one of the barriers to regional cooperation in the Middle East has been the wide discrepancy of economic structures and political regimes. The absence of democratic regimes and open societies has indeed constituted a major problem that has so far proved very difficult to overcome. How can a degree of economic and political convergence based on economic liberalisation and democratisation be achieved in the Middle East? In what ways should the domestic economic and political structures be reformed in order to foster cooperation in the region?

In seeking answers to these questions, the following argument forms the core of this study. We suggest that regional cooperation schemes are more likely to be successful in the Middle East if and when there are sufficiently large domestic constituencies that will approve such arrangements. In the absence of such domestic constituencies of Level II actors supporting Level I agreements, regional cooperation schemes cannot be sustained in the long run. That is why an initial cooperation between 'like-minded' states that have relatively open regimes, credible and responsible governments with sufficient economic liberalisation are more likely to be successful. As proposed in Chapter 7, an initial cooperation scheme among Israel, Jordan, Egypt, Palestine and Turkey in the Middle East can form the initial nucleus of region-wide cooperation.

Linked to the issue of democracy and 'like-minded' states, which is also a focus of the two-level-game framework, is the issue of credibility, particularly the credibility of the governments at the domestic and international level. To the question of how we get international cooperation, Gourevitch responds:

> In two ways, first through a convergence of policy objectives – agreement on the substance of what is sought in trade, security and other issues; second by

> credible commitment to institutions that manage policy disputes. Put in negative, nations conflict when they cannot agree on policy or when they are unable to sustain commitment to agreements that they may make. For nations to cooperate, they must agree to the regime (convergence of policy preference) and they must agree that they will not cheat and will adhere to the regime and to the process of resolving disputes that may occur (credibility of commitment).
> (Gourevitch 1986: 249)

Schelling had demonstrated long ago in his *Strategy of Conflict* (1960) how important the credibility of one's commitments, threats and promises in the anarchic international system is for the resolution of conflict. The two-level game carries this issue of credibility to the domestic arena as well. Credibility of a negotiator is clearly advanced in his or her status at the domestic level. One of the fundamental problems in the case of the Middle East is the relatively low level of legitimacy of the governments at the domestic level which has also reduced the credibility in international commitments undertaken by the Middle Eastern governments. Clearly, democratic governments and open regimes will be more pressured to give an account of their actions, explain their policy rationale to their constituencies and most importantly keep their commitments both at the domestic and international levels. That is why, the mobilisation of Level II actors is absolutely crucial in establishing a 'democratic peace' in the Middle East.

A corollary argument is that the reason why such cooperative schemes have failed is also due to the low cost of cheating (particularly political costs) for the Middle Eastern governments at the domestic level. When a non-democratic regime fails to comply to Level I commitments, either there are no domestic reactions that will have political costs for the administration or such reactions can easily be suppressed. Accordingly, such regimes have very little, if any, restrictions upon them to follow a consistent pattern of policy-making or a predictable policy environment bound by domestic restrictions. The fact that the state did not depend on taxation, and hence the domestic constituencies, for its revenues, also explains the case of oil exporting states (Anderson 1995; Glasser 1995). In fact, an argument parallel to the use of external security threats for domestic political gains can be developed here. The availability of oil rents, or 'soft-budget constraints' to use Anderson's terminology (1987), has largely postponed the need for domestic political and economic reforms and has often been used to appease domestic demands. Given the declining oil rents, to what extent the existing governments can postpone these reforms, however, remains to be seen.

Another related problem is the level of uncertainty on the benefits and costs of regional cooperation. In most cases, the uncertainty in the Middle East also arises from the changing power calculations of the negotiators both at home and abroad which may emerge as a result of such agreements. Who will gain more from cooperation? Will the benefits be distributed evenly? It is precisely these questions that have hindered cooperation in the region despite its widely acknowledged political and economic benefits. A certain level of uncertainty both in terms of the expected outcome of the agreement as well as the size of the win-set can enhance the chances of cooperation. Some level of uncertainty about the outcome of the agreement, for instance, can increase the bargaining leverage on both sides and gives the statesmen more flexibility to manoeuvre through playing on public perceptions both internationally and domestically.

However, too much uncertainty, which is often the case in the Middle East, may also create fears of involuntary or voluntary defection. In such cases, even if there are domestic constituencies that might benefit from the outcome of an international negotiation, they might choose not to act. The absence, or relatively low level, of mobilisation of those domestic constituencies which will benefit extensively from increased trade and peace in the Middle East can also be partly explained by the excessive uncertainty and quick reversibility of international agreements.

The issues of uncertainty, credibility of commitments and low cost of cheating are crucial in applying the two-level-game framework in the Middle East. More often than not, the governments play the 'security card' and fail to concede. The uncertainty of the game because of its simultaneity increases the likelihood of the players to avoid compromise. Indeed, most Middle Eastern governments facing a very uncertain game have long avoided the first move of compromise, preferring a status quo based on hostilities and increased demands rather than concession and compromise. The absence of credibility of commitments, largely fuelled by minimal political constraints at home and/or easy appeasement of domestic opposition through side payments, have made a radical revision of the status quo in the Middle East very difficult.

Using the two-level game, we also suggest that cooperation and peace in the Middle East can best be achieved through the mobilisation of the Level II actors and by improving collaboration and interaction among domestic constituencies across countries. In the absence of such transnational ties, we argue that sustaining cooperation and peace in the region will indeed be difficult.[2] Creating business ties, and improving communication and functional cooperation among the societies are indeed keys for creating peace in the region. As will be elaborated in Chapters 5 and 7, only through exploring avenues for establishing such Level II ties can a lasting solution to the problems and conflicts of the Middle East be found.

Finally, in light of the above discussion of the two-level-game framework, an additional perspective also arises which helps us to draw a link between public opinion and foreign-policy-making. Although the conceptual framework that the two-level-game approach offers is a fruitful basis, analysis of specific negotiations or policy areas remains largely without a clear methodological guideline. So far, the applications of the two-level-game framework have been limited to interpretative and largely descriptive analyses of specific negotiations (see Mayer 1992, Schoppa 1993 and Friman 1993). In Chapter 8 we offer a preliminary alternative. Our analysis is based on the question of how regional cooperation is perceived by the public opinion at Level II. Clearly, public opinion is not a homogenous entity. We offer accordingly differences in public opinion on the basis of different party supporters. If the perception of policy options differs across party supporters, these differences should form the boundaries of Level II bargaining. In addition, the relative power of these party supporters in the parliament allows us to determine, in general terms, the direction of the effects that Level II has on Level I administrators. Accordingly, specific policy decisions taken by Level I leaders can be traced back to specific coalitions and differentiations across opinions held by different party supporters. As such, a new interpretation of the linkage between public opinion and foreign policy can be offered within the framework of two-level games.

4 The economic map of the Middle East

Recent developments in the Middle East have led many to argue that economic necessities underlie many of the hopes of a stable and peaceful region. Clawson (1995: 317) argues rightfully that 'economic cooperation is a field that attracts optimists, not to say dreamers'. Although it is clear that a close relationship exists between the economic and political aspects of long-standing conflicts in the region, it is not clear how – in precise terms – to characterise the nature of the region's economy in comparative terms within the international system. More specifically, the connection between economic structure and protracted conflict in the region needs to be clarified in order to grasp both the nature of difficulties as well as opportunities in regional cooperation, and also the potential for settlement of conflicts.

In attempting to move towards this objective, we follow the 'two-level-game' approach discussed in Chapter 3. We identify first the characteristic economic structure of the region: We underline the implications of regional economic structure for domestic economic interests and political groupings. In light of recent world trends towards reforms of more market-oriented economic liberalisation, we try to trace the difficulties and opportunities offered by regional domestic forces. From a regional perspective, we evaluate the trade patterns among the Middle Eastern countries. On the international scene, we specifically focus on the impact of new institutional arrangements to regulate world trade.

The economic structure of the Middle East

The unique nature of the economic structure of the Middle East can be attributed to a peculiar combination of several factors. Among these an odd mix of the region's natural resources rises to the forefront. As Richards and Waterbury (1996: 45) rightly point out, '[t]he political economy of the Middle East is dominated by three simple facts: little rain, much oil, and increasingly many (and therefore young) people'. Its climate is the most serious obstacle to the region's economic development. It acts as a natural barrier impeding agricultural development. Combined with a rapidly expanding population, bottlenecks in agricultural production lead to dependency on other regions of the world for food supplies. Vast oil reserves give the region a dominant role in world markets and create huge revenues for some countries in the region. However, as we will illustrate in the following sections, a considerable portion of these revenues are absorbed by a dependency on imported food and the need to develop material and human infrastructure that are currently inadequate.

From a simplistic perspective, most countries in the region are not short of resources. The inefficient way the available resources of the region's economies have been used constitutes the most important characteristic of Middle Eastern economic policy-making. Economic policy-making in the Middle East is shaped by what we call the 'war-prone economy'. This is especially true for the countries that are directly involved in the Arab–Israeli conflict. However, due to particular circumstances all other countries in the region suffer from the same 'security-minded policy-making'. The terms 'war-prone economy' and 'security-minded policy-making', adapted here from Richards and Waterbury's (1990: 255) 'war capitalism' to describe *infitah* (an Arabic term used to refer to economic opening) in Iraq, are used to refer to the non-economic rationale behind public policies that is dominated by strategic, political and often militaristic concerns in the Middle Eastern policy-making environment.[1] Here, we are specifically refering to policy choices that result in inefficient economic dynamics but are made for the sole purpose of maintaining a strategically important constituency or militaristically important economic activity.

Climatic characteristics of the Middle East

Underlying many of the issues that shape the political economy of the Middle East is a lack of sufficient agricultural production in the region. The agricultural sector in the Middle East simply cannot produce enough food in response to the rapidly growing needs of its population. The primary factors responsible for this phenomenon is the unfavourable climatic and geographic characteristics of the region. Approximately 75 per cent of the land stretching from Morocco through Iraq is desert. Desert areas lack water resources to support urban or agrarian populations. The overall population density in the region is at the same level as that of the United States, that is, about 28 people per km^2, compared with 242 in the United Kingdom and 128 in China (WDI 1997). For Libya the figure is 3 and for Egypt it is 58 people per km^2. In Turkey the figure is higher at 79, in Israel it is 267, in Lebanon 391 and in Bahrain 836 people per km^2. However, in arable parts this figure goes up more than tenfold reflecting a denser population than many highly populated regions of the world. For example, in Egypt the population density in rural areas is 1,011 people per km^2 compared with 404 in India and 909 in China (WDI 1997). An overwhelming majority of Middle Easterners lives in relatively small stretches of arable land and settlement is highly concentrated along major rivers and coastal zones.

In much of the region, rainfall is not only scarce but also shows great regional variation making unirrigated agriculture highly risky. Much of Algeria, Libya, Egypt, Saudi Arabia, Oman, Qatar and the United Arab Emirates receive annually, on average, less than 100 mm of rain. Average annual precipitation is above

1,500 mm only in some parts of Morocco and Yemen, in the Central and Black-Sea regions of Turkey, on the Caspian shore of Iran, and in narrow stretches of land in Syria and Iraq.[2] Other regions of the Middle East not only get very little rain but the precipitation is also quite irregular. Accordingly, only irrigated lands are suitable for agricultural production in much of the region.

There is a long history of irrigation in the region. However, the geography of the region does not offer much opportunity for easy exploitation of the scarce water resources. Table 4.1 provides a list of perennial rivers of the region. In all cases except the Litani River in Lebanon, the river basins are shared by more than one country. The use of these rivers is problematic due to the fact that they cross many national boundaries. This attribute has contributed significantly to international tension in the region.[3] Of these significant rivers in the region, only the Tigris-Euphrates system has a substantial water surplus.

Table 4.1 Perennial rivers in the Middle East

River	*Catchment area (000 km²)*	*Length of main river (km)*	*Riparian and basin countries*
Nile	2,900	4,800	Uganda, Egypt, Ethiopia, Sudan and others
Tigris	258	1,718	Turkey, Iraq, Syria
Euphrates	444	2,330	Turkey, Iraq, Syria
Jordan	18	360	Jordan, Israel, Syria, Lebanon
Orontes	17	511	Lebanon, Syria, Turkey
Litani	2	145	Lebanon

Source: Government of Israel (1995: 4–7)

Table 4.2 provides details on the extent of the water problem from a comparative perspective as well as providing indicators of climatic problems and environmental degradation. A simple indicator of environmental degradation and a reflection of climatic characteristics of the region is the total forest area across the Middle East. Of the total 11,920,000 km^2 of area, only 632,000 km^2 are forested. Although the annual rate of deforestation has stopped, and in some cases reforestation is under way, forests are very rare in the region. Only Turkey has a significant portion of land forested. However, bushes rather than forests cover most of these areas. Per capita non-industrial domestic freshwater available in the region is about 89.7 m^3. Compared to other countries, this figure is higher than all 51 countries in the low-income country group, 38 in the lower middle-income country group and 16 in the upper middle-income country group. According to the World Bank (1996) classification[4] it only ranks as second to 16 in the high-income country group. Therefore, from a purely comparative statistical point of view there is no water shortage in the region for at least domestic usage. From the perspective of other industrial usage of water per capita across the region, the Middle East has a figure of 464.5 m^3, which is considerably higher than that of the low-income

Table 4.2 Basic environmental indicators for various years

	Population (millions of inhabitants)	Area (thousands of km^2)	Forest area: Total area (thousands of km^2)		Annual deforestation (% of total area)	Annual freshwater withdrawal (1970–94): Total (km^3)	As a % of total water resources	Per capita (km^3) (domestic)	Per capita (km^3) (other)
	1995		*1980*	*1990*	*1981–90*				
Algeria	28.6	2,382	18	41	0.8	3.0	20.3	35	125
Bahrain	0.6	1	0	0	–				
Egypt	59.2	1,001	0	0	–	56.4	97.1	67	889
Iran	63.8	1,648	38	180	0	45.4	38.6	54	1,307
Iraq	20.5	438	12	12	0				
Israel	5.5	21	1	1	-0.3	1.9	84.1	65	343
Jordan*	4.1	89	0	1	-1.0	0.4	32.1	50	123
Kuwait	1.6	18	0	0	–	0.5		336	189
Lebanon	4.0	10	0	0	–				
Libya	5.8	1,760	2	2	0				
Morocco	27.9	447	32	90	-1.3	10.9	36.2	23	404
Oman	2.2	212	0	41	0	0.5	24.0	17	547
Qatar	0.6	11	0	0	–				
Saudi Arabia	18.2	2,150	2	12	–	3.6	163.6	224	273
Syria	14.2	185	2	2	0				
Tunisia	8.9	164	3	7	-1.8	2.3	60.5	41	276
Turkey	61.6	779	202	202	0	33.5	17.3	140	445
UAE	1.8	84	0	0	–	0.9	300.0	97	787
Yemen	15.7	528	0	41	–	3.4	136.0	17	318
Total	344.8	11,928	312	632		162.7	84.2	89.7	463.5

Source: World Bank (1992, 1996)

Notes: *Forest areas* refer to natural stands of woody vegetation in which trees predominate. *Total water resources* include both internal renewable resources and river flows from other countries. Estimates are from 1992. *Total per capita water withdrawal* is calculated by dividing a country's total withdrawal by its population in the year for which withdrawal estimates are available (World Bank 1996: 230–231).

Table 4.3 Population figures in the Middle East, 1970–95

	Population (millions of inhabitants)						*Population share*						*Population growth (%)*					
	1970	*1975*	*1980*	*1985*	*1990*	*1995*	*1970*	*1975*	*1980*	*1985*	*1990*	*1995*	*1971*	*1975*	*1980*	*1985*	*1990*	*1995*
Algeria	13.8	16.0	18.7	21.9	25.0	28.6	8.1	8.2	8.3	8.4	8.3	8.3	3.1	3.2	3.1	3.2	2.6	3.6
Bahrain	0.2	0.3	0.3	0.4	0.5	0.6	0.1	0.1	0.1	0.2	0.2	0.2	4.8	4.0	3.1	4.9	2.0	5.4
Egypt	33.1	36.3	40.9	46.5	52.4	59.2	19.5	18.7	18.2	17.8	17.4	17.2	1.8	2.1	2.6	2.6	2.3	2.4
Iran	28.4	33.2	39.1	46.4	55.8	63.8	16.8	17.1	17.5	17.8	18.5	18.5	3.1	3.3	3.4	3.6	3.8	2.2
Iraq	9.4	11.0	13.0	15.3	18.1	20.5	5.5	5.7	5.8	5.9	6.0	5.9	3.3	3.4	3.3	3.4	3.3	2.7
Israel	3.0	3.5	3.9	4.2	4.7	5.5	1.8	1.8	1.7	1.6	1.5	1.6	3.4	2.4	2.4	1.7	3.1	2.6
Jordan	1.5	1.8	2.2	2.6	3.3	4.1	0.9	0.9	1.0	1.0	1.1	1.2	4.0	3.4	3.8	3.9	7.2	2.0
Kuwait	0.7	1.0	1.4	1.7	2.1	1.6	0.4	0.5	0.6	0.7	0.7	0.5	8.1	6.3	6.2	3.0	4.4	1.9
Lebanon	2.5	2.8	2.8	3.2	3.6	4.0	1.5	1.4	1.3	1.2	1.2	1.2	4.5	1.1	1.1	4.6	2.2	1.8
Libya	2.0	2.5	3.0	3.8	4.6	5.8	1.2	1.3	1.4	1.5	1.5	1.7	4.0	4.7	4.5	4.4	3.4	10.2
Morocco	15.3	17.3	19.4	22.1	25.1	27.9	9.0	8.9	8.6	8.5	8.3	8.1	2.6	2.4	2.4	2.7	2.3	1.9
Oman	0.7	0.8	1.0	1.3	1.5	2.2	0.4	0.4	0.4	0.5	0.5	0.6	3.1	4.1	5.3	4.1	3.4	2.9
Qatar	0.1	0.2	0.2	0.4	0.5	0.6	0.1	0.1	0.1	0.1	0.2	0.2	9.1	6.3	9.5	9.1	16.7	5.1
S.Arabia	5.8	7.3	9.4	12.4	14.9	18.2	3.4	3.7	4.2	4.7	4.9	5.3	4.3	4.9	5.6	5.4	3.0	2.4
Syria	6.3	7.4	8.7	10.4	12.1	14.2	3.7	3.8	3.9	4.0	4.0	4.1	3.7	3.3	3.3	3.6	3.4	2.2
Tunisia	5.1	5.6	6.4	7.3	8.1	8.9	3.0	2.9	2.8	2.8	2.7	2.6	1.6	2.2	2.6	2.4	2.0	1.0
Turkey	35.3	40.1	44.4	50.3	56.1	61.6	20.8	20.6	19.8	19.3	18.6	17.9	2.6	2.3	2.2	2.4	2.1	0.8
UAE	0.2	0.5	1.0	1.4	1.6	1.8	0.1	0.3	0.5	0.5	0.5	0.5	18.2	18.6	10.9	3.8	3.2	2.3
Yemen	6.3	7.0	8.2	9.7	11.3	15.7	3.7	3.6	3.7	3.7	3.7	4.6	1.7	2.5	3.4	3.0	3.5	6.4
Total	169.7	194.6	224.0	261.3	301.3	344.8	100.0	100.0	100.0	100.0	100.0	100.0	2.8	2.8	3.0	3.1	2.9	2.4

Source: Various issues of World Bank's World Tables and World Development Report (see under World Bank in bibliography)

country group. However, it is again striking to see that the Middle East has an average per capita industrial freshwater withdrawal rate that is quite close to that of the high-income economies with 473.4 m^3 per capita. Middle-income economies fare in comparison better than the Middle East in terms of per capita industrial freshwater withdrawal.

It is imperative here to point out that distribution and sharing of water supplies, rather than availability, surfaces as the main problem in the region. These figures are also quite undependable for arid regions and regions with serious seasonal variation. Clearly, all of these shortcomings are present in the region. Accordingly, the above figures should be used with caution.[5] Nevertheless, both the fact that all perennial rivers, except the Litani river in Lebanon, are shared by more than one country in the region, as well as the fact that seasonal variation is quite high requiring extensive irrigation efforts to render agriculture feasible in the region, point to a pressing need for cooperation among the countries of the region. Sharing of water resources cannot be considered separately from developing water resources for better use and for irrigation projects.

Population dynamics in the Middle East

Population growth underlies all major problems from agricultural self-sufficiency to water supply, from provision of health and educational basics to urban settlement problems in the region. As Table 4.3 shows, the population of the Middle East had increased from about 170 million in 1970 to about 345 million in 1995. This increase was especially strong during the 1970s and 1980s, but it seems to have slowed down considerably for the first half of the 1990s. As of 1995, Iran is the largest country of the region with about 64 million people, followed by Turkey (61.6 million) and Egypt (59.2 million). Iran's share quickly grew from 16.7 per cent of the region's population to 18.5 per cent, surpassing both Turkey and Egypt. Iran experienced population growth rates well in excess of 3 per cent throughout the 25-year period between 1970–95. Despite the fact that over the last decade or so the region's population growth has slowed down on average, countries of the Middle East still experience growth rates considerably higher than average growth rates in other parts of the world. The region's overall growth rate of 2.97 in 1994 is well above the weighted average of population growth in 'low-income' economies according to the World Bank (1996) classification of 2.1, 1.5 for 'middle-income' economies, 0.7 for 'high-income' economies over the 1990–94 period. The world average for the same period was 1.5 per cent. All Middle Eastern countries have population growth rates above the world average.[6]

Table 4.4 presents the developments in the labour force of the region. Of the total population of 344.8 million in 1995, only 119.8 million were in the 'economically active group'. Typically, the economically active group has a considerably higher growth rate than the population as a whole, aggravating the problem of job creation. Over the last 25 years many countries of the region have found their work force doubled. The Egyptian labour force rose to about 20 million in 1995 from only about 10 million in 1970. Similarly, Iran, Morocco, Saudi Arabia and

Table 4.4 Regional labour force, 1970–95

	Labour force (total in millions)			*Average annual growth (%)*			*Population aged 15–64 (total in millions)*			*Female (%)*			*Agriculture (%)*		
	1970	*1980*	*1995*	*1971–80*	*1981–90*	*1991–95*	*1970*	*1980*	*1995*	*1970*	*1980*	*1995*	*1970*	*1980*	*1990*
Algeria	2.99	4.85	8.63	4.95	3.80	4.14	6.53	9.25	16.19	5.95	21.50	24.25	47.37	35.97	26.05
Bahrain	0.06	0.13	0.25	7.98	5.49	2.30	0.11	0.21	0.35	4.92	11.42	18.45	7.06	4.18	1.96
Egypt	9.98	14.32	20.95	3.69	2.49	2.73	17.95	23.08	33.61	7.97	28.35	31.06	51.75	61.17	43.27
Iran	8.15	11.73	19.30	3.70	3.31	3.51	14.41	20.25	33.63	13.21	20.47	25.01	43.75	45.77	40.97
Iraq	2.39	3.53	5.39	3.97	2.72	3.13	4.77	6.67	11.06	6.52	17.28	18.16	47.03	28.46	16.10
Israel	1.10	1.45	2.19	2.87	2.34	3.59	1.79	2.26	3.46	29.95	33.78	39.87	9.66	6.10	4.14
Jordan	0.58	0.52	1.10	–0.80	4.97	5.46	0.77	1.03	2.32	6.36	19.69	27.94	27.90	23.93	20.51
Kuwait	0.25	0.50	0.82	7.23	5.97	–1.56	0.41	0.80	1.05	8.06	12.84	26.50	1.74	1.89	1.18
Lebanon		0.80	1.31		3.54	2.97	1.26	1.54	2.41		21.31			13.44	5.12
Libya	0.67	0.94	1.54	3.76	3.26	3.47	1.04	1.56	2.81	18.71	18.10	17.47	23.82	24.84	10.89
Morocco	4.05	6.97	10.28	5.58	2.63	2.63	7.39	10.22	16.10	13.93	33.53	35.12	57.62	56.02	44.67
Oman	0.20	0.30	0.55	4.37	3.47	5.19	0.38	0.58	1.11	6.06	7.24	14.62	56.95	50.08	47.90
Qatar	0.05	0.10	0.33	8.09	10.18	3.91	0.07	0.15	0.44	4.17	6.70	11.56	9.72	2.81	2.65
Saudi Arabia	1.59	2.76	6.26	5.70	6.76	3.30	3.01	4.96	9.97	5.03	7.78	12.34	64.15	44.57	19.52
Syria	1.57	2.48	3.99	4.66	3.07	3.57	2.92	4.20	7.14	11.58	23.49	26.87	50.23	38.68	33.85
Tunisia	1.35	2.19	3.34	4.97	2.74	3.10	2.56	3.48	5.43	12.77	28.93	30.06	41.77	38.88	27.79
Turkey	16.07	18.73	27.84	1.54	2.98	2.09	19.24	24.91	37.90	37.94	35.49	35.65	70.69	60.32	53.08
UAE	0.10	0.56	1.14	19.09	5.24	3.93	0.14	0.73	1.30	4.08	4.98	10.74	8.54	4.43	7.04
Yemen	1.75	2.49	4.61	3.62	3.76	5.07	3.38	4.03	7.60	7.85	31.31	27.22	70.40	69.84	58.04
Total (Middle East)	52.89	75.35	119.82	5.28	4.14	3.29	88.14	119.92	193.88	11.39	20.22	24.05	38.34	32.18	24.46
Low-income economies	889.04	1,155.62	1,574.82	2.66	2.27	1.72	1,048.46	1,351.46	1,934.40	35.82	39.97	40.51	75.88	73.20	69.36
Middle-income economies	402.95	512.91	688.43	2.44	2.08	1.79	569.57	717.24	981.27	33.76	36.40	38.09	45.11	38.39	31.86
High-income economies	316.66	368.21	432.15	1.52	1.18	0.86	461.95	521.67	605.50	34.73	38.57	42.40	12.48	8.68	5.72
World	1,608.66	2,036.74	2,695.40	2.39	2.03	1.60	2,079.98	2,590.37	3,521.17	35.00	38.40	40.14	57.39	53.49	49.12

Source: Various issues of World Bank publications (see under World Bank in bibliography)

Yemen have more than doubled their labour force. The slowest growing labour force over the last 25 years is in Turkey where a growth rate of only 73 per cent is observed. Female participation rates in the labour force are quite low in all countries of the region. None of the countries get even close to the world average in this respect, and the regional average was about 24 per cent in 1995 when the world average was about 40 per cent. Nevertheless, female participation has significantly increased over the last 25 years. The largest increase in share is observed in Egypt where the female labour force rose from 7.9 per cent in 1970 to 31 per cent in 1995. During the same period, female share in the labour force rose by about 21 per cent in Jordan and Morocco whereas it declined by about 1 per cent in Libya and 2 per cent in Turkey. The share of the agricultural sector is typically higher than all other sectors with an average for the region of about 24.5 per cent in 1990 (down from 32.1 per cent in 1980). In countries like Tunisia (33 per cent), Algeria (31 per cent), Israel (29 per cent) and Turkey (27 per cent), a considerable portion of the labour force is actively employed in the industrial sector. Service sector activities in these countries actually dominate all others. However, as of 1990 the Middle East has a higher portion of its labour force in industry than only the low-income economies of the world (24 per cent in the Middle East as opposed to 15 per cent in the low-income economies). In all other groups of economies, the industrial sector occupies a higher share of labour-force distribution across economic activities.

Due mainly to geographical and climatic reasons, but increasing as a result of a general trend of modernisation, the Middle Eastern economies are dominated by urban settlements. As Table 4.5 shows, about 50 per cent of the region's population was in urban areas in 1970. By 1995, this share had risen to about 67 per cent and the estimated figure for 2025 is 78 per cent. The Middle East is above the world average of 45 per cent urban population. The region's urban population ratio is above those of the low- and middle-income country groups and is also above the Asian average of 35 per cent. In this respect, it is closer to the average of North and Central America of 68 per cent (World Resources Institute 1997: 149–154).

For the 1990–95 period urban growth rates are typically well above those in the rural settlements. Over the 1990–95 period, the Middle East has a lower urban population growth rate (annual average of 3.6 per cent) than African countries (annual average of 4.4 per cent). It is the only area for which the rate is lower. In contrast, in countries like Kuwait, Lebanon, Libya, Qatar, Turkey and the UAE the rural population is actually shrinking in size. This is primarily due to migration to urban areas. However, it also points to an alarming tendency of decline of productive populations in the agricultural sector of the region.

Table 4.5 also presents urban dependency ratios in comparison to rural dependency ratios. Clearly, the modernising effects of urbanisation is evident in lower dependency ratios for the urban settlements. However, typically 40 to 45 per cent of the population is economically unproductive. In relation to this high level of economic dependency it is not surprising to observe that in those countries where data is available about 16 to 37 per cent of the population is below the poverty line. Typically, poverty is much more widespread in the agricultural sector. In countries

Table 4.5 Population and labour force

	Total urban population share (%)				*Growth rates (%)*			*Dependency ratio*		*People in absolute poverty (millions)*		
	1970	*1980*	*1996*	*2025*	*Urban 1990–95*	*Rural 1990–95*	*No. of cities**	*Urban 1992*	*Rural 1992*	*Total 1994*	*Urban 1994*	*Rural 1994*
Algeria	40	43	56	74	3.8	0.5	1	44	46	23	20	25
Bahrain	79	81	90									
Egypt	42	44	45	62	2.6	1.9	3	39	45	23	21	25
Iran	42	50	59	75	3.6	1.3	5	47	53			30
Iraq	56	66	78	85	3.2	0.4	1	45	52			30
Israel	84	89		94	3.9	3.1	1	38	40			
Jordan	51	60	72	84	5.9	2.6	1	45	50	16	14	17
Kuwait	78	90	97	99	–6.3	–1.3	1					
Lebanon	59	73	87	94	4.1	–1.4	0	39	44			15
Libya	45	70	86	93	4.3	–1.1	2	48	50			
Morocco	35	41	49	66	3.1	1.2	2	38	47	37	28	45
Oman	5	8	13	33	7.8	3.7	0					6
Qatar	80	86	92									
Saudi Arabia	49	67	79	88	2.9	–0.6	2					
Syria	43	47	53	70	4.3	2.6	2	48	54			54
Tunisia	45	51	57	74	2.8	0.9	1	37	44	17	20	15
Turkey	38	44	70	87	4.5	–2.5	5	36	43			14
UAE	57	72	84	91	3.4	–0.9	0	30	36			
Yemen	13	20	34	58	8.0	3.6	0					
Total (Middle East)	50	58	67	78	3.6	0.1	27	41.1	46.5	23.2	20.6	25.1
Low-income economies	18	21	29									
Middle-income economies	46	52	60									
High-income economies	72	75	75									
World	37	40	45		2.5	0.8	369					

Source: World Resources (1996–97: 149–154) and World Bank (1997).
* Number of cities with a population greater than 750,000

Table 4.6 Access to safe drinking water and sanitation (%), 1980–95

	Access to safe drinking water		*Access to safe sanitation services*	
	Urban	*Rural*	*Urban*	*Rural*
Egypt	82.0	50.0	23.0	6.0
Iran	89.0	77.0	82.9	36.5
Iraq	50.0	30.0	40.0	25.0
Israel	100.0	97.0	99.0	95.0
Jordan	91.8	82.8	41.1	1.7
Kuwait	100.0		100.0	
Lebanon	99.0	99.0	89.0	89.5
Libya	100.0	80.0	100.0	85.0
Morocco	98.0	14.0	66.5	17.9
Oman	97.0	50.0	97.0	68.0
Saudi Arabia	100.0	74.0	100.0	30.0
Syria	92.0	78.0	100.0	100.0
Tunisia	100.0	89.0	98.0	93.0
Turkey	100.0	70.0	95.0	90.0
UAE	100.0	100.0	100.0	77.0
Middle East (avg.)	93.3	70.8	82.1	58.2
Africa	67.2	46.6	64.8	30.5
Europe	99.7	97.8	99.1	98.6
North and Central America	85.9	66.1	72.4	61.8
South America	82.3	35.0	73.2	40.2
Asia	87.3	74.3	83.9	56.1
Oceania	93.2	271.4	92.4	60.2

Source: World Resources (1996–97: 149–154)
Note: data not available for Algeria, Bahrain, Kuwait (rural), Qatar and Yemen

like Morocco (45 per cent) and Syria (54 per cent) about half of the agricultural sector is below the absolute poverty line. Only in Tunisia is the portion of people below poverty line higher for the urban sector than the rural sector. In all others, the rural sector is typically much poorer.

Table 4.6 reveals that in terms of urban access to safe drinking water the Middle East ranks favourably as second on average; it is surpassed only by the European countries. However, when it comes to rural access to safe drinking water the Middle East average of about 70 per cent ranks only as fourth among the world regions listed. The same fourth ranking is obtained for rural and urban access to sanitation services. In particular, the rural access to sanitation services is clearly very poor in countries like Jordan (1.7 per cent), Egypt (6 per cent) and Morocco (17.9 per cent). Only Syria seems to have secured access to sanitation services to all rural settlements. The overall performance in urban settlements rises considerably for all the countries for which data is available. However, even in urban Egypt only 23 per cent have access to sanitation services. Morocco (14 per cent) and Iraq (30 per cent) have noticeable difficulty in maintaining basic requirements of public health as reflected in the low access rate to safe drinking water in rural areas.

With hardly any exceptions, the Middle Eastern countries have all experienced rapid population growth. However, there are only a few serious and successful attempts to control population growth and counteract the associated problems. There is evidence that rising urban populations in the region will become a distinct group in the politics of the region (Richards and Waterbury 1996: 251–276). Problems of health, education, poverty and infrastructure in urban settlements, and expectations and demands of urban populations all play a significant role in all countries of the region. Level II cooperation in the region will accordingly be created mainly in the urban segments of the Middle East. Any cooperation scheme in the region will have to take into account provisions to control rapid population growth as well as responses by urban settlers to their existing problems. Accordingly, a critical aspect of cooperation in the Middle East is to appeal and to control growing population segments especially those in the urban areas.

'Food security' in the Middle East

Besides rapid urbanisation and its consequent problems in Middle Eastern urban settlements, the immediate result of rapid population growth in the Middle East is a serious food shortage. It is not easy or simple for the Middle East to feed its young, fast growing and highly concentrated population. A growing population with more financial capabilities due to expanding revenues from oil exports has increased and diversified the demand for food. The domestic policy response, however, has largely been limited due not only to geographic and climatic constraints, but also to ineffective and inefficient policy initiatives. The rise of imported food in the region has led to a growing concern for food security on the part of the policy-makers. Reliance on foreign suppliers was seen as too risky. Consequently, agricultural policies were shaped with a vision of increasing self-sufficiency of the Arab world instead of relying on imported food. There came a costly confusion between the two concepts of food security and food self-sufficiency. Being food self-sufficient meaning 'minimising imported food supplies' is neither necessary nor sufficient for food security. 'Food security recognises that we all live in a risky world, and seeks to devise public policies to minimise the risk that consumption of food will fall below some minimally acceptable level' (Richards 1995a: 66). Domestic production is only one way of achieving food security which requires that food supply, domestic or imported, is dependable. If domestic supply is more risky in securing a steady flow of food supplies than importing these supplies from international markets then no clear preference for domestic production can be justified. The available evidence so far has not fared well in favour of domestic production because it has typically been more expensive and less reliable in the region.

Compared to other regions of the world, the Middle Eastern supply of food has not been responsive to the fast expanding domestic demand. Table 4.7 shows the development of yield, imports, and food aid in cereals over the last two decades. Three points stand out from the data. First is that the nineteen countries of the

Middle East import about 10 to 20 per cent of all world cereals imports and the region's share has been continuously increasing. Second, the Middle East used to get about 20 per cent again of world food aid during the 1970s and 1980s. However, as of 1994 the region only gets about 5 per cent of world food aid due largely to drops in cereal aid to Egypt, Morocco, Tunisia and Turkey. Third, cereal yield in the region is considerably lower than the world average. Only Turkey, Iran and Egypt produce cereals to a significant degree and among these only Egypt has a cereal yield that is above the world average. Both Turkey and Iran's yields are below the averages of even the low-income country group. Nevertheless, for most countries food production as of 1995 is higher than what it was in the 1989–91 period. Only Morocco, Oman, Saudi Arabia and Tunisia experienced a drop in food production in 1995 compared to the 1989–91. Among the significant food producers, only Egypt has a fertiliser use that is above world average, even being above that of the high-income country group. Both Iran and Turkey lag behind the world average whereas smaller agricultural producers in the region such as Lebanon, Saudi Arabia and the United Arab Emirates have considerably high fertiliser use which seems effective in raising their cereal yields.

For our purposes its is enough to underline the fact that, due to this high food dependency coupled with continuous 'war-minded' policy-making in the region, the Middle East is full of examples of failed policy initiatives and wasted resources.[7] The agricultural sector is a considerable drain on the scarce resources of the region. Fischer (1995: 432) notes for example that in response to the urgent need to diversify production in Saudi Arabia the development of 'the Saudi wheat industry, *is* both extremely expensive and inhibits the development of interregional trade based on comparative advantage (italics added).' Similarly, Clawson (1992: 86–87) notes that in order to maintain a politically powerful agricultural sector, while also keeping an eye on securing food and other agricultural self-sufficiency, inefficient use of valuable water resources is supported, wasting economic resources. Graham (1991: 152) also underlines that in a period of declining oil revenues Saudi Arabia's use of irreplaceable ground water for wheat production with subsidies it can no longer afford is becoming less and less justifiable. 'Food self-sufficiency is an expensive, wasteful, and ultimately doomed food security strategy' (Richards 1995b: 69).

Despite considerable potential for cooperation in agricultural production and trade in agricultural products amongst the countries of the region, not much is accomplished in this respect due to the security concerns of policy-makers. Once the 'war-minded' economic policy-making is left behind, considerable welfare gains are possible by cooperation amongst the Middle Eastern countries. Although food self-sufficiency is highly risky and wasteful for the increasingly resource-scarce countries of the region, development of their agricultural sector into a more efficient, technologically more sophisticated and demand-driven organisation remains a respectable objective. However, such development efforts, as will be emphasised in the following chapter, depend critically on available financing opportunities for expensive projects, development of market forces in the agricultural markets of the region for more efficient use of resources based on demand-driven incentives, as well as

Table 4.7 Agriculture and food in the Middle East

	Cereal yield (kg per hectare)			Cereal imports (thousand tons)		
	1970	1980	1995	1978	1980	1994
Algeria	638	760	877	3,137	3,414	7,760
Bahrain	–	–	–	68	84	122
Egypt	3,911	4,095	6,048	5,853	6,028	9,200
Iran	885	1,067	1,767	1,994	2,779	5,450
Iraq	1,012	826	907	1,707	2,942	1,099
Israel	1,183	2,313	2,200	1,735	1,601	2,311
Jordan	227	930	774	436	505	1,347
Kuwait	–	–	–	278	340	455
Lebanon	931	1,731	1,925	596	678	577
Libya	–	–	–	654	908	1,790
Morocco	942	1,019	453	1,689	1,821	1,678
Oman	1,333	667	1,667	65	120	460
Qatar	–	–	3,000	57	81	142
Saudi Arabia	1,277	587	4,196	1,352	3,061	6,182
Syria	353	1,437	1,665	413	726	952
Tunisia	553	916	626	793	817	1,592
Turkey	1,215	1,855	1,977	38	6	878
UAE	–	–	7,000	210	426	759
Yemen	780	1,016	1,091			
Middle East (total)				21,073	26,335	42,756
Middle East (avg.)	1,089	1,373	2,261			
Low-income economies	1,482	1,896	2,617	24,659	30,803	33,241
Middle-income economies	1,577	2,014	2,100	77,870	100,198	87,905
High-income economies	2,837	3,350	4,183	78,183	78,871	87,329
World	1,833	2,309	2,730	180,713	209,872	208,475
Middle Eastern share in world (%)				12	13	21

Source: World Bank (1988, 1989, 1990, 1992, 1994, 1997).

effectual voicing of demands in a more participatory environment; thus there is a dependence on democratisation in the region.

Two alternatives to self-sufficiency for achieving food security are food aid and trade. We have seen above that the Middle East has a significant share of world food aid. However, trade in foodstuff still leaves a lot of room for development. In the past, trade has been intentionally ignored in the region due to misconceptions in the understanding of issues to do with food security. As Richards (1995b: 70) argues, neither Singapore nor Korea can be considered as insecure in terms of providing food supplies for their citizens. Trade, and especially trade in foodstuff within the region, can provide the region with sufficient food supplies which are relatively cheaper and can be provided at a steady flow.

The above discussion of the Middle Eastern approach to resolving the existing cleavage between food demand and supply underlines an important dimension in what we call the 'war-minded' policy-making in the region. Leaving aside

Food aid in cereals (thousand tons)			Fertilizer consumption (100g/hectare of arable land)			Food production index (1989–91 = 100)		
1971	1980	1994	1970	1980	1994	1970	1980	1995
89,600	28,500	23,087	163	314	153	69	72	114
–	–	–	–	–	3,000	43	137	113
218,300	1,864,992	179,046	1,312	2,714	2,433	55	68	121
230,400	–	–	60	447	561	40	58	135
41,200	–	67,678	34	170	654	66	80	107
837,000	9,801	–	1,401	1,919	2,391	61	84	115
104,500	95,431	110,565	87	427	346	36	70	137
–	–	–	–	4,400	2,000	48	108	122
154,100	42,875	6,963	1,354	869	915	47	62	122
–	–	–	62	256	306	–	–	–
456,500	120,357	12,766	117	258	312	48	59	77
–	–	–	–	259	1,587	26	60	91
–	–	–	–	4,000	7,500	36	39	125
–	–	–	33	209	947	22	30	89
39,200	43,541	58,873	68	224	636	37	103	129
215,000	98,751	21,704	76	132	180	45	74	88
115,100	9,090	–	157	511	543	54	75	106
–	–	–	–	1,328	9,077	20	48	148
47,600	33,511	–	1	77	74	45	76	113
2,548,500	2,346,849	480,682						
			352	1,029	1,769	44	72	114
0	4,352,771	6,297,621	180	522	1,022	–	68	126
3,843,310	3,330,614	1,962,818	356	–	507	–	81	98
3,088,500	948,745	–	1,010	1,285	1,169	–	91	103
12,153,260	8,632,130	8,261,120	506	817	852	–	80	109
21	27	6						

considerations of economic efficiency, policy-makers have sought to protect those constituencies in the agricultural sector they have seen as politically important and strategically necessary.

In Israel, for example, farming interests have an established and powerful voice in the determination of water policy. This has frustrated the calls of Israeli water experts over the last two decades or more for a clear water policy emphasising the re-allocation of water away from agriculture into areas where returns to water are higher. The announcement of a policy of significant reductions in the supply of water to irrigation has only seemed possible in an atmosphere of crisis such as was generated by the drought of 1990–91. The fact that members of the Jordanian political elite have farming interests may increase resistance within government to cut-backs in the supply of water for agriculture. In Syria, Iraq, Sudan and Egypt, agricultural interests may not

> have the same access to those who make policy on water. However, farmers cannot be regarded as having no domestic political importance – if only because of the sheer weight of their numbers. For varying combinations of strategic, economic and domestic political considerations Middle Eastern leaders have avoided the public elaboration of a policy of re-allocating water away from agriculture.
>
> (Shapland 1995: 317)

Similarly, political pressure from the urban sector to secure relatively cheap and subsidised food supplies has contributed to the sensitivities of public policy-makers.

The Middle East in post-Uruguay round world trade

Our discussion in Chapters 2 and 3 is based on a simplified view that international and regional development in the Middle East is not only conducive towards economic cooperation in the region but also that it could strengthen political initiatives to resolve long-standing political animosities. Many different forms of cooperation in the literature range from cooperative sectoral development projects and joint ventures to various degrees of liberalisation in trade between the parties involved in the region. The above discussion on the population structure is the fundamental indicator of potential economies of scale in the regional market for traded commodities. However, obviously a cooperative new structuring of the region's economies in the form of increased trade, both intra- and extra-regionally, will neither depend solely on the international or regional forces conducive for more economic cooperation, nor potential enlargement and development of markets. Instead, existing patterns of trade, restructuring and new institutional regulation of world trade will play a critical role in these developments.

Developments in world trade

At end of 1995 it was clear that world trade is firmly growing at rates in excess of 7 per cent, due largely to economic recovery in the industrial countries. After the establishment of GATT in 1947 multilateral trade negotiations reached a new peak of success with the agreements achieved at the Uruguay Round (UR). As illustrated in Table 4.8, world trade in the aftermath of the UR is seen as 'the major engine of growth over the next decade. Assuming that liberalisation policies continue, world merchandise trade is projected to grow at more than 6 per cent a year, faster than any time since the 1960s' (World Bank 1995: 5). Notable in this table is that the forecasted GDP growth for the Middle Eastern economies is lower than any other region for the 1995–2004 period. A 4.9 per cent average growth of output for the developing countries is dependent on the provision that no significant turn from the liberalisation policies are undertaken over the next decade. If the liberalisation reforms are continued, then growth in output for the developing-country group is expected to be much faster than the rest of the world. This will result, as a consequence, in a 25 per cent developing-country share in world output

Table 4.8 World economic growth (annual percentage change in real GDP)

	Actual				*Estimated*	*Forecast*	
Region	*1966–73*	*1974–80*	*1981–91*	*1991–93*	*1994*	*1995–96*	*1995–2004*
World total	5.1	3.4	3.2	1.2	2.8	3.2	3.3
High-income economies	4.8	3.0	3.2	1.3	3.0	3.0	2.8
OECD countries	4.8	2.9	3.1	1.2	2.9	2.9	2.8
Non-OECD countries	8.4	7.0	5.0	6.2	5.8	6.0	5.6
Developing countries	6.9	5.0	3.2	0.8	2.0	4.0	4.9
East Asia	7.9	6.8	7.6	8.7	9.3	8.1	7.7
South Asia	3.7	4.0	5.7	3.2	4.7	5.0	5.4
Sub-Saharan Africa	4.7	3.4	1.7	0.6	2.2	4.0	3.8
Latin America and the Carribean	6.4	4.8	1.7	3.2	3.9	2.4	3.5
Europe and Central Asia	7.0	4.9	2.9	–9.4	–7.5	0.7	3.4
Middle East and North Africa	8.5	4.7	0.2	3.4	0.3	2.7	3.2
Eastern Europe and the Former Soviet Union	7.0	5.1	2.7	–12.5	–9.1	0.1	3.5
World trade		4.9	10.0	4.5	5.1	7.1	6.6

Source: World Bank (1995: 6–7)

over the next decade. Nevertheless, this overall evaluation hides wide differences among the developing countries. Only East and South Asia and Eastern Europe will actually experience real growth in per capita income in excess of the 2.3 per cent projected for the industrialised economies. At the end of this century other developing regions, among which the Middle East is present, will actually find themselves at about the same average real income level they were at in 1980.

It should also be noted at this juncture that trends in commodity prices are not expected to present any significant opportunities. As Table 4.9 shows, agricultural commodity prices, metals and minerals prices, as well as petroleum prices have exhibited a continual downward trend over the past two decades. Under normal conditions, no significant changes are expected from this trend over the next decade.

Further development, maturation and integration of the European market, and liberalised barriers to intra-regional trade among Canada, Mexico and the United States due to NAFTA agreement, underline expectations of a rapidly expanding world economy and rapidly expanding world trade. These developments will have major impact on international trading conditions that will create favourable as

Table 4.9 Commodity prices, 1965–94

Year	*Petroleum*	*Agriculture*	*Food*	*Non-food*	*Metals and minerals*
1965	6	46	47	44	41
1970	6	51	53	43	43
1971	8	48	49	43	39
1972	9	51	53	44	39
1973	13	81	84	70	53
1974	53	107	115	78	77
1975	51	86	91	68	68
1976	55	107	114	85	71
1977	60	144	159	87	79
1978	61	130	139	96	84
1979	88	143	150	116	103
1980	144	148	153	132	116
1981	161	129	133	113	103
1982	146	114	119	99	95
1983	132	123	126	112	97
1984	130	130	137	103	90
1985	126	113	120	87	86
1986	64	118	128	81	71
1987	81	103	104	99	80
1988	64	118	122	102	104
1989	77	109	111	100	110
1990	100	100	100	100	100
1991	82	98	98	99	92
1992	81	92	91	94	91
1993	72	91	92	89	77
1994	70	123	127	110	85

Source: World Bank (1995: 90–91)

well as risky conditions for the Middle East, since the integration of the European and North American markets create preferential access to member countries which could potentially displace non-member countries' exports.

Trends in the level, composition and direction of Middle Eastern trade

Depending mainly on the conditions of the oil market, exports of the region show an erratic development. Huge increases in exports in the early 1970s were partially lost during the 1980s when continual decline in Middle Eastern exports was experienced. Only towards the end of the 1980s did the region's export performance start to recuperate. With the exception of the mid-1980s, Middle Eastern imports continually increased in the 1970–91 period.

Table 4.10 summarises the growth in Middle Eastern trade. Taking 1987 as the base year we see that the value of Middle East exports for all countries except Libya has increased. Egypt nearly doubled its exports in 1991 compared to 1987, whereas Qatar and Saudi Arabia have increased their exports by about 230 per cent. The value of imports for all countries in the region except Jordan was higher in 1991 than it was in 1987. For Bahrain, Iran, Israel, Lebanon, Libya, Morocco, Turkey and the UAE import value increased more than the export value during the 1987–91 period.[8]

When we look at the composition of exports and imports we see that different components of trade show different rates of growth but the overall composition of

Table 4.10 Value of exports and imports in the Middle East (fob; based on US$; 1987 = 100), 1970–91

	Exports						*Imports*					
	1970	*1975*	*1980*	*1985*	*1990*	*1991*	*1970*	*1975*	*1980*	*1985*	*1990*	*1991*
Algeria	12	52	191	157	135	144	18	85	150	140	139	109
Bahrain	10	47	156	119	155	143	6	43	128	116	137	150
Egypt	37	69	150	90	127	191	10	52	64	72	121	103
Iran	22	182	120	121	139	144	18	121	128	122	164	227
Israel	9	23	65	74	142	140	12	36	68	70	129	143
Jordan	4	17	55	89	122	120	7	27	89	96	102	93
Kuwait	23	111	247	127	143	0	11	43	119	109	112	0
Lebanon	33	190	147	82	135	144	30	109	194	117	145	153
Libya	29	85	272	136	97	92	11	73	139	111	97	104
Morocco	17	55	86	77	151	152	16	60	99	91	164	163
Qatar	8	58	181	134	191	236	6	35	120	98	146	163
Saudi Arabia	10	128	470	118	191	236	3	21	150	118	121	128
Syria	5	24	54	42	109	145	15	68	167	161	97	122
Tunisia	8	40	104	76	163	172	10	47	116	86	181	171
Turkey	6	14	29	78	127	133	6	33	53	80	157	149
UAE	3	40	123	84	119	126	4	38	112	93	155	190

Source: Various issues of the World Bank's World Tables (see under World Bank in bibliography)
Note: data not available for Iraq, Oman and Yemen

Table 4.11 Export shares of various products in the Middle East (%), 1970–91

	Fuels						*Manufactures*						*Non-fuel primary products*					
	1970	*1975*	*1980*	*1985*	*1990*	*1991*	*1970*	*1975*	*1980*	*1985*	*1990*	*1991*	*1970*	*1975*	*1980*	*1985*	*1990*	*1991*
Algeria	70.2	92.4	98.4	98.0	96.5	96.9	6.7	2.2	0.3	1.2	2.6	2.2	23.0	5.4	1.2	0.8	0.9	0.9
Bahrain	77.9	81.5	93.6	88.1	88.1	88.1	16.7	9.8	3.0	6.9	6.9	6.9	5.4	8.8	3.4	5.0	5.0	5.0
Egypt	4.8	9.5	64.2	68.1	29.4	29.9	27.1	34.1	10.9	10.1	42.5	40.7	68.1	56.5	24.8	21.7	28.1	29.3
Iran	88.6	97.0	89.2	89.2	89.2	89.2	4.0	1.2	3.6	3.6	3.6	3.6	7.3	1.8	7.3	7.3	7.3	7.3
Israel	0.0	0.0	0.0	0.0	0.7	0.6	70.5	76.6	82.1	83.3	86.7	87.6	29.5	23.4	17.8	16.7	12.6	11.8
Jordan	0.0	0.7	0.2	0.0	0.1	0.0	16.2	20.0	33.8	43.3	46.1	45.7	83.8	79.3	65.9	56.7	53.9	54.3
Kuwait	94.0	91.5	88.9	77.4	77.4		4.8	8.0	10.4	21.0	21.0		1.2	0.5	0.8	1.6	1.6	
Lebanon	0.1	0.5	0.1	0.1	0.1	0.1	60.3	70.1	75.1	75.1	75.1	75.1	39.6	29.4	24.8	24.8	24.8	24.8
Libya	99.9	100.0	100.0	99.8	99.8	99.8	0.0	0.0	0.0	0.2	0.2	0.2	0.1	0.0	0.0	0.0	0.0	0.0
Morocco	0.4	0.9	4.8	3.9	3.6	2.9	9.7	12.5	23.5	40.5	52.3	51.2	89.9	86.6	71.6	55.6	44.2	46.0
Qatar	97.2	97.2	96.9	96.9	96.9	96.9	2.7	2.7	3.0	3.0	3.0	3.0	0.1	0.1	0.1	0.1	0.1	0.1
Saudi Arabia	99.7	99.3	99.2	98.8	98.8	98.8	0.1	0.6	0.6	1.0	1.0	1.0	0.2	0.1	0.2	0.2	0.2	0.2
Syria	60.6	70.3	79.0	74.1	59.7	59.7	9.4	7.8	8.5	12.2	23.8	23.8	30.0	21.9	12.5	13.8	16.5	16.5
Tunisia	27.2	43.6	52.5	42.2	17.3	18.5	19.2	19.6	35.8	44.8	69.1	67.9	53.6	36.8	11.7	13.0	13.6	13.5
Turkey	0.6	2.6	1.4	4.7	2.3	2.2	8.9	23.3	26.9	61.2	67.9	66.9	90.4	74.1	71.7	34.1	29.8	30.8
UAE	96.3	97.7	95.2	95.2	95.2	95.2	0.5	1.2	4.1	4.1	4.1	4.1	3.2	1.0	0.8	0.8	0.8	0.8
Middle East (avg	51.1	55.3	60.2	58.5	53.4	51.9	16.1	18.1	20.1	25.7	31.6	32.0	32.8	26.6	19.7	15.8	14.9	16.1

Source: Various issues of the World Bank's World Tables (see under World Bank in bibliography)
Note: data not available for Iraq, Oman and Yemen

trade in the region remains fairly constant. Exports of fuels typically occupy a dominant position for the Middle Eastern countries.[9] While for Algeria, Bahrain, Iran, Libya, Qatar, Saudi Arabia and the UAE fuel exports have typically been in excess of 80 per cent of total exports, for Israel, Jordan, Lebanon and Turkey fuel exports occupy a share less than 2.5 per cent of total exports. Syria, Egypt and Tunisia lie in between these two groups of countries. Syria has approximately 60 per cent of fuel exports in its total exports over the 1970–91 period with the exception of the 1979–82 period when fuel exports rose above the 70 per cent share in its exports. Egyptian fuel exports rose to a 25 per cent share in 1976 and reached eventually 66 per cent in 1982, dropping down to about 30 per cent in 1991. For Tunisia, fuel exports occupied a share of about 27 per cent in the early 1970s, eventually reaching a share of about 54 per cent in 1981. During the 1980s, the share of Tunisian fuel exports has steadily declined down to about 18 per cent of total exports by 1991 (see Table 4.11).

Share of manufactured products in total exports in the region have steadily increased over the 1970–91 period rising from an average of 16 per cent in 1970 to an average of 32 per cent in 1991. However, countries show great variation in the share of manufactured goods in their exports. Those countries with a dominant fuel-export sector typically have less than 7 per cent of their exports in manufactured goods. The following countries (percentage of exports in manufactured goods is given for each in brackets) stand in contrast to these oil-rich countries: Egypt (40.7), Israel (87.6), Lebanon (75.1), Morocco (52.1), Tunisia (67.9) and Turkey (66.9) (see Table 4.11). While Israeli exports in manufactured goods have always been in excess of 70 per cent of its total exports, Moroccan, Tunisian and Turkish manufactured exports have risen from a modest level of 9.7 per cent, 19.2 per cent and 8.9 per cent respectively to a share in excess of 50 per cent in each country. Egyptian manufactured exports had steadily declined in share over the 1970–85 period and rose again to about 40 per cent of total exports by the end of 1991.

The share of non-fuel, non-manufactured goods' exports has been typically highest in the region for Egypt, Jordan, Lebanon, Morocco and Turkey. This sector's share has steadily declined, but as of the end of 1991 it still occupied a share in excess of 20 per cent in all four countries. The largest drop in this sector took place in Turkey where 90.4 per cent of exports were in this sector in 1970, whereas in 1991 it occupied 30.8 per cent.

In short, Algeria, Bahrain, Iran, Kuwait, Libya, Qatar, Saudi Arabia and the UAE primarily export fuels and no other significant agricultural or manufactured goods. On the other hand, the export of manufactured goods in Egypt, Israel, Jordan, Morocco, Tunisia and Turkey is in excess of 40 per cent of their total exports. Non-fuel, non-manufactured exports (the significant portion of which are agricultural) occupy one third or more of total exports in Egypt, Jordan, Morocco and Turkey.

As Table 4.12, shows fuel imports occupy highest shares in the region for Jordan (14.5 per cent), Morocco (15.3 per cent), Syria (18.2 per cent) and Turkey (20.7 per cent). The share of manufactured goods' imports occupies on average 65 to 70 per cent of imports in the region over the 1970–91 period. With the exception of Bahrain, manufactured imports are more than 50 per cent of total imports in all

Table 4.12 Import shares of various products in the Middle East (%), 1970–91

	Fuels						Manufactures						Non-fuel primary					
	1970	*1975*	*1980*	*1985*	*1990*	*1991*	*1970*	*1975*	*1980*	*1985*	*1990*	*1991*	*1970*	*1975*	*1980*	*1985*	*1990*	*1991*
Algeria	2.1	1.7	2.5	1.9	1.1	3.2	79.4	72.9	71.7	67.0	68.4	65.3	18.5	25.4	25.8	31.1	30.5	31.5
Bahrain	1.1	50.8	58.3	40.6	40.6	40.6	76.5	41.7	32.7	48.4	48.4	48.4	22.4	7.4	9.0	11.0	11.0	11.0
Egypt	9.4	6.9	1.1	3.8	2.6	2.5	55.8	49.8	59.0	61.0	56.3	58.6	34.8	43.3	39.9	35.2	41.0	38.9
Iran	0.2	0.2	0.2	0.2	0.2	0.2	85.0	79.3	82.1	82.1	82.1	82.1	14.8	20.5	17.6	17.6	17.6	17.6
Israel	4.9	15.3	26.5	16.4	8.8	7.7	72.6	62.5	56.7	68.7	78.2	80.5	22.5	22.2	16.8	14.9	13.0	11.9
Jordan	5.7	10.6	17.1	21.9	18.6	14.5	59.3	64.3	61.9	55.3	61.3	54.8	35.1	25.1	21.0	22.8	20.1	30.7
Kuwait	0.7	0.6	0.8	0.6	0.6		77.6	80.9	82.0	82.6	80.1		21.7	18.6	17.2	16.9	19.4	
Lebanon	5.9	5.2	7.6	7.6	7.6	7.6	59.6	65.3	58.0	58.0	58.0	58.0	34.5	29.4	34.3	34.3	34.3	34.3
Libya	3.2	1.9	0.7	1.3	1.3	1.3	71.7	77.7	77.7	78.3	78.3	78.3	25.1	20.4	21.7	20.3	20.3	20.3
Morocco	5.5	10.9	23.6	27.9	16.9	15.4	63.7	53.2	46.5	42.1	61.0	60.2	30.9	35.9	29.9	30.0	22.1	24.4
Qatar	1.0	0.9	1.2	0.8	0.7	0.7	75.6	83.8	78.4	76.9	75.7	75.7	23.4	15.2	20.4	22.3	23.6	23.6
Saudi Arabia	1.4	0.7	0.6	0.5	0.3	0.3	68.1	81.4	82.8	82.6	81.4	81.4	30.6	17.9	16.6	16.9	18.3	18.3
Syria	9.8	6.5	13.3	29.3	18.3	18.3	68.9	67.6	63.3	47.4	57.8	57.8	21.3	25.9	23.4	23.3	23.9	23.9
Tunisia	4.8	10.4	20.7	14.2	9.0	9.2	58.6	65.2	57.7	62.9	71.6	65.7	36.6	24.4	21.6	22.9	19.4	25.1
Turkey	7.5	17.5	48.4	33.4	20.8	20.7	76.8	68.8	43.1	54.1	61.1	60.2	15.7	13.8	8.5	12.5	18.1	19.1
UAE	3.3	7.2	5.4	5.4	5.4	5.4	78.0	79.9	81.1	81.1	81.1	81.1	18.7	12.9	13.6	13.6	13.6	13.6
Middle East (avg.)	4.2	9.2	14.2	12.9	9.6	9.8	70.4	68.4	64.7	65.5	68.8	67.2	25.4	22.4	21.1	21.6	21.6	22.9

Source: Various issues of the World Bank's World Tables (see under World Bank in bibliography)
Note: data not available for Iraq, Oman and Yemen

Table 4.13 Export and import price indices in the Middle East (fob; based on US$; 1987 = 100), 1970–91

	Export						Import					
	1970	*1975*	*1980*	*1985*	*1990*	*1991*	*1970*	*1975*	*1980*	*1985*	*1990*	*1991*
Algeria	10	66	178	156	128	128	30	64	100	90	121	134
Bahrain	9	62	163	140	136	109	13	55	121	108	131	114
Egypt	29	87	158	119	114	128	21	64	101	91	137	138
Iran	18	122	375	272	124	105	58	127	198	169	71	120
Israel	40	71	106	91	131	119	25	54	96	87	120	114
Jordan	38	94	110	92	110	120	27	64	108	96	105	103
Kuwait	7	60	161	142	124		30	55	88	82	144	
Lebanon	37	63	102	83	167	170	25	64	113	100	165	157
Libya	7	58	160	139	125	104	24	51	85	81	135	122
Morocco	36	101	112	86	112	119	28	69	112	98	124	121
Qatar	7	58	160	139	125	104	24	51	85	81	135	122
Saudi Arabia	7	60	166	146	131	103	30	57	90	83	145	130
Syria	22	58	142	120	54	70	24	65	110	96	42	39
Tunisia	22	61	130	97	122	123	27	62	103	92	127	130
Turkey	37	63	102	83	167	170	25	64	113	100	165	157
UAE	7	58	160	139	125	104	24	51	85	81	135	122
Middle East (avg.)	21	71	155	128	125	118	27	64	107	96	125	122

Source: Various issues of the World Bank's World Tables (see under World Bank in bibliography)
Note: data not available for Iraq, Oman and Yemen

countries of the Middle East. There is no significant change in the share of manufactured goods' imports for any one of the countries in the region. Non-fuel, non-manufactured imports also show a steady share of about 20 per cent on average throughout the region. Algeria, Qatar and Lebanon, however, have about one third of their imports in this sector. In short, the countries of the region predominantly import manufactured goods while some non-oil-producing countries depend on fuel imports.

Table 4.13 shows that export prices for the Middle Eastern countries have typically been in decline whereas import prices remained stagnant for the 1979–88 period. This indicates a disadvantageous trend in the world markets for the Middle Eastern countries. While the Middle East continues to pay about the same price for its imports, exports become cheaper and cheaper thus making the relative price of imports with regard to exports higher and higher.

A summary measure of developments in both the import and export markets is given by the terms-of-trade-index in Table 4.14. We see that, due to oil-price hikes, the oil-rich countries experienced favourable developments in their terms of trade during the 1970s. The terms of trade steadily deteriorated throughout the region during the 1980s. As of 1994 only Israel, Jordan, Morocco and Turkey had an improvement in their terms of trade compared with 1987. The relatively more diversified structure of the export sector of these countries is partly responsible for such a favourable development. Nevertheless, these improvements are quite modest.

Fast growing population and sluggish employment creation in the Middle East have created significant flows of migrant workers.[10] Significant numbers of migrant

Table 4.14 Terms-of-trade index in the Middle East (based on US$; 1987 = 100), 1970–94

	1970	*1975*	*1980*	*1985*	*1990*	*1994*
Algeria	35	103	179	174	106	83
Bahrain	67	113	134	129	104	
Egypt	140	135	157	131	84	95
Iran	31	96	189	160	176	90
Israel	160	131	111	105	109	113
Jordan	141	146	102	95	105	118
Kuwait	24	110	184	175	86	88
Lebanon	145	100	91	82	101	
Libya	29	112	187	171	92	
Morocco	130	145	100	88	90	107
Qatar	29	112	187	171	92	
Saudi Arabia	24	104	184	176	90	92
Syria	92	89	129	125	128	
Tunisia	81	99	127	105	96	93
Turkey	145	100	91	82	101	109
UAE	29	112	187	171	92	93
Middle East (avg.)	81	113	146	134	103	96

Source: Various issues of the World Bank's World Tables (see under World Bank in bibliography)
Note: data not available for Iraq, Oman and Yemen

Table 4.15 Workers' remittances received in the Middle East (in US$ and %), 1970–1992

	Balance of payments (US$)							*As share of total exports (%)*					
	1970	*1975*	*1980*	*1985*	*1990*	*1991*	*1992*	*1970*	*1975*	*1980*	*1985*	*1990*	*1992*
Algeria	211	412	406	313	352	233	774	21	10	3	2	3	2
Egypt	29	366	2,696	3,496	3,743	3,755	5,430	4	26	89	190	145	97
Jordan	0	167	715	1,021	500	450	800	0	133	178	157	56	51
Morocco	63	533	1,054	967	2,006	1,990	0	13	35	44	45	47	47
Oman		0	35	43	39								
Syria	7	52	773	350	375	0	0	3	6	37	21	9	0
Tunisia	29	144	319	271	599	570	633	16	17	14	17	17	15
Turkey	273	1,312	2,071	1,714	3,246	2,819	3,008	46	94	71	22	25	21
Yemen	0	308	1,256	785	1,366	800	0						

Source: Various issues of the World Bank's World Tables (see under World Bank in bibliography)
Note: data not available for Bahrain, Iran, Iraq, Israel, Kuwait, Lebanon, Libya, Qatar, Saudi Arabia and the UAE

workers from the Middle Eastern countries have gone to work in countries both within and outside the region. Major labour-force exporting countries are Algeria, Morocco, Tunisia, Egypt, Jordan, Lebanon, Syria and Turkey. Typically, workers from the North African countries have gone for work predominantly in France. Turkish migrant workers are spread across the European continent but found work predominantly in Germany. Table 4.15 provides a measure of the extent of the flow of workers' remittances to their country of origin. While the regional receipt of remittances is about US$10 billion, for Egypt and Turkey workers' remittances amounted in total to about US$8.4 billion in 1992. Workers' remittances amount to a declining percentage of total exports in both Algeria and Turkey. However, in Turkey they still amounted to about one fifth of total export revenues in 1991. Jordan and Morocco receive remittances amounting to about 50 per cent of their export income whereas Egypt makes as much from remittance revenues as it does from exports.

As will be presented below, intra-regional trade within the Middle East is relatively small. However, labour flows are quite significant. As of the early 1980s, over half the labour force of the 8 labour importing countries of the region; (that is, Bahrain, Iraq, Kuwait, Libya, Oman, Qatar, Saudi Arabia and the UAE) came from other countries (Fischer 1995:437). A dominant portion of this imported labour force comes from countries within the region. The size of remittances from the Gulf countries to total volume of intra-regional trade is also quite significant, with Yemen having a remittance flow of about 43.8 per cent, Egypt 5.9 per cent, Jordan 4.6 per cent, Syria 1.9 per cent and Libya a negative 400 per cent (i.e., a net outflow from Libya to other Middle Eastern countries) of their intra-regional exports (Fischer 1995:438). It should be noted here that a migrant worker population of roughly 5 million people (Fischer 1995: 437) forms a significant constituency in their native countries for increasing intra-regional economic cooperation. In many host countries, these migrant workers have limited rights, suggesting the need and demand for renewed labour market regulations. As will be touched upon

Table 4.16a Direction of trade in the Middle East: Exports (millions of US$); figures also given for per cent distribution

	Algeria	*Bahrain*	*Egypt*	*Iran*	*Iraq*	*Israel*	*Jordan*	*Kuwait*
Total	10,230	6,439	4,686	14,890	12,284	14,770	1,232	10,536
Industrial countries	8,827	662	2,987	9,292	6,844	10,253	131	5,192
Developing countries	1,037	1,362	1,616	5,598	5,403	2,975	759	3,256
Africa	199	109	151	272	416	241	69	2
Asia	155	936	661	3,272	645	1,646	256	2,998
Europe	131	91	337	1,410	2,194	695	51	0
Western hemisphere	473	0	16	399	1,608	384	5	255
Algeria	0	0	30	0	0	0	2	0
Bahrain	0	0	4	8	0	0	14	0
Egypt	0	1	0	0	23	0	10	0
Iran	68	8	2	0	0	0	31	0
Iraq	0	0	0	0	0	0	0	0
Israel	0	0	15	0	0	0	0	0
Jordan	1	5	39	7	339	0	0	0
Kuwait	0	0	0	0	108	0	0	0
Lebanon	0	0	25	0	0	0	21	0
Libya	8	0	62	0	0	0	16	0
Morocco	92	0	7	173	350	0	2	0
Oman	0	27	3	1	0	0	3	0
Qatar	0	25	10	15	0	0	14	0
Saudi Arabia	0	137	217	8	27	0	118	0
Syria	1	0	35	18	0	0	13	2
Tunisia	54	8	22	7	65	0	5	0
Turkey	11	0	23	365	951	129	28	0
UAE	0	33	21	174	43	0	44	0
Yemen	0	0	20	14	1	0	21	0
Total for Middle East	235	244	535	790	1,907	129	342	2
Percent distribution								
Industrial countries	86.3	10.3	63.7	62.4	55.7	69.4	10.6	49.3
Developing countries	10.1	21.2	34.5	37.6	44.0	20.1	61.6	30.9
Africa	2.0	1.7	3.2	1.8	3.4	1.6	5.6	0.0
Asia	1.5	14.5	14.1	22.0	5.3	11.1	20.8	28.5
Europe	1.3	1.4	7.2	9.5	17.9	4.7	4.1	0.0
Western hemisphere	4.6	0.0	0.3	2.7	13.1	2.6	0.4	2.4
Middle East	2.3	3.8	11.4	5.3	15.5	0.9	27.8	0.0

Source: IMF (1997)
Notes: Figures are for 1993 apart from: Iraq (1989), Lebanon (1985), Qatar (1992), Turkey (1992) and Yemen (1990)

later in Chapter 5, these communities of migrant workers form an important interest group in Level II.

Perhaps the most striking feature of Middle Eastern trade is neither its volume, nor its composition (reflecting heavy dominance of oil exports and manufactured goods imports), but its low degree of intra-regional flow of goods and services. In 1983 intra-regional trade only accounted for 6.2 per cent of total trade. The picture does not change even when oil trade is excluded, since only 6 per cent of non-mineral fuel trade

Lebanon	*Libya*	*Morocco*	*Oman*	*Qatar*	*Saudi Arabia*	*Syria*	*Tunisia*	*Turkey*	*UAE*	*Yemen*
576	8,047	4,970	7,251	3,624	47,442	3,284	3,804	14,716	23,664	1,383
103	6,839	4,099	1,843	2,149	28,008	2,054	3,293	9,363	10,597	1,252
344	1,207	830	5,408	1,379	19,335	1,117	619	6,290	8,161	131
32	339	232	138	17	1,043	72	129	829	650	4
1	184	174	2,489	1,028	11,772	30	98	1,172	4,507	86
12	593	75	1	0	1,854	316	94	1,747	387	1
1	7	96	15	79	1,380	7	15	32	102	0
6	1	77	0	0	7	20	67	106	0	0
8	0	0	46	8	1,774	7	10	0	72	0
16	52	2	0	9	105	18	7	173	5	0
0	0	27	197	4	75	0	8	455	1,075	0
14	0	0	0	0	0	0	7	212	0	0
0	0	0	0	0	0	0	0	0	0	0
21	13	6	1	7	58	62	8	163	9	0
44	0	0	0	0	0	43	1	65	14	0
0	9	3	6	0	32	356	4	9	0	0
6	0	140	0	0	7	22	188	247	0	0
2	103	0	0	16	409	8	35	56	262	3
2	0	0	0	9	70	0	1	0	986	0
8	0	0	5	0	85	8	0	0	75	0
115	0	70	30	90	0	151	20	485	226	28
27	7	1	0	0	41	0	25	216	6	1
1	47	44	0	0	18	41	0	48	1	0
2	451	35	0	0	1,674	65	51		356	0
29	4	1	2,420	129	937	20	4	65	0	12
8	0	1	57	0	101	6	0	0	29	0
309	687	407	2,762	272	5,393	827	436	2,300	3,116	44
17.8	85.0	82.5	25.4	59.3	59.0	62.6	86.6	63.6	44.8	90.5
59.8	15.0	16.7	74.6	38.1	40.8	34.0	16.3	42.7	34.5	9.5
5.5	4.2	4.7	1.9	0.5	2.2	2.2	3.4	5.6	2.8	0.3
0.2	2.3	3.5	34.3	28.4	24.8	0.9	2.6	8.0	19.1	6.2
2.2	7.4	1.5	0.0	0.0	3.9	9.6	2.5	11.9	1.6	0.1
0.2	0.1	1.9	0.2	2.2	2.9	0.2	0.4	0.2	0.4	0.0
53.7	8.5	8.2	38.1	7.5	11.4	25.2	11.5	15.6	13.2	3.2

is intra-regional (Fischer 1995:435). Tables 4.16a and 4.16b show that 6 out of 19 countries in our definition of the Middle East export less than 6 per cent of their total exports within the region (these are: Algeria, Bahrain, Iran, Israel, Kuwait and Yemen). Nine countries in the region export between 6 to 17 per cent of their total exports to the region (these are: Egypt, Iraq, Libya, Morocco, Qatar, Saudi Arabia, Tunisia, Turkey and the UAE). Jordan has 27.7 per cent, Lebanon 53.6 per cent, Oman 38 per cent and Syria 25.1 per cent of their exports directed to the region.

Table 4.16b Direction of trade in the Middle East: Imports (millions of US$); figures also for per cent distribution

	Algeria	*Bahrain*	*Egypt*	*Iran*	*Iraq*	*Israel*	*Jordan*	*Kuwait*
Total	7,982	4,766	14,226	15,617	9,890	22,619	3,420	6,580
Industrial countries	7,116	1,926	10,373	10,608	6,586	16,877	1,981	5,194
Developing countries	768	2,596	3,462	4,947	3,258	2,035	1,428	928
Africa	261	28	134	152	109	325	83	1
Asia	212	275	2,123	1,646	420	1,083	539	779
Europe	162	91	657	1,007	1,189	378	399	34
Western hemisphere	73	0	304	721	415	233	113	68
Algeria	0	0	0	69	4	0	1	0
Bahrain	0	0	1	9	0	0	5	0
Egypt	33	4	0	3	69	0	66	0
Iran	0	9	0	0	0	0	7	0
Iraq	0	0	0	0	0	0	0	0
Israel	0	0	10	0	0	0	0	0
Jordan	3	16	10	34	233	0	0	0
Kuwait	0	0	0	0	426	0	0	0
Lebanon	0	12	20	3	0	0	53	0
Libya	0	0	59	0	0	0	15	0
Morocco	84	0	0	30	46	0	5	0
Oman	0	4	0	200	119	0	2	0
Qatar	0	8	12	5	0	0	9	0
Saudi Arabia	4	2,021	119	76	180	0	67	0
Syria	22	7	8	0	0	0	56	47
Tunisia	74	11	7	8	52	0	9	1
Turkey	124	0	150	531	490	92	171	0
UAE	0	67	5	1,091	97	0	10	0
Yemen	0	0	0	1	0	0	2	0
Total for Middle East	344	2,159	401	2,060	1,716	92	478	48
Percent distribution								
Industrial countries	89.2	40.4	72.9	67.9	66.6	74.6	57.9	78.9
Developing countries	9.6	54.5	24.3	31.7	32.9	9.0	41.8	14.1
Africa	3.3	0.6	0.9	1.0	1.1	1.4	2.4	0.0
Asia	2.7	5.8	14.9	10.5	4.3	4.8	15.8	11.8
Europe	2.0	1.9	4.6	6.5	12.0	1.7	11.7	0.5
Western hemisphere	0.9	0.0	2.1	4.6	4.2	1.0	3.3	1.0
Middle East	4.3	45.3	2.8	13.2	17.4	0.4	14.0	0.7

Source: IMF (1997)
Notes: Figures are for 1993 apart from: Iraq (1989), Lebanon (1985), Qatar (1992), Turkey (1992) and Yemen (1990)

On the import side Algeria, Egypt, Israel, Kuwait, Saudi Arabia and Tunisia import less than 6 per cent of their total imports from the region. Iran, Iraq, Jordan, Lebanon, Libya, Morocco, Qatar, Syria, Turkey, the UAE and Yemen's imports from the Middle East range between 6 to 18 per cent of their total imports. Only Oman with 26.8 per cent and Bahrain with 45.3 per cent obtain more than 25 per cent of their imports from the region.

Lebanon	*Libya*	*Morocco*	*Oman*	*Qatar*	*Saudi Arabia*	*Syria*	*Tunisia*	*Turkey*	*UAE*	*Yemen*
2,184	5,316	8,652	4,226	1,871	35,654	4,345	6,215	22,872	22,348	1,509
1,353	4,004	6,191	2,689	1,383	26,667	2,410	5,392	15,421	12,527	902
820	1,277	2,444	1,537	487	8,711	1,437	830	8,920	9,289	586
29	384	366	9	5	378	35	159	240	78	55
75	224	273	364	172	5,896	251	168	1,843	7,281	303
416	433	456	21	17	642	836	261	3,232	155	21
53	95	225	22	40	657	92	90	356	102	12
29	9	105	0	0	0	1	60	11	0	0
24	0	0	30	26	139	0	9	0	171	5
13	68	11	5	10	262	48	24	59	23	14
7	0	198	1	16	8	20	8	362	177	0
52	0	0	0	0	0	0	0	1	0	0
0	0	0	0	0	0	0	0	0	0	0
5	18	1	2	14	103	23	5	25	48	16
28	0	0	0	0	0	2	2	67	0	15
0	27	5	2	12	116	65	3	1	69	4
0	0	0	0	0	0	8	52	447	4	1
1	153	0	0	0	96	1	48	30	1	4
0	0	0	0	6	33	0	0	0	8	0
0	0	20	9	0	94	2	0	0	135	0
102	3	466	71	77	0	45	20	1,659	950	116
6	24	6	0	9	122	0	28	52	22	1
0	207	39	1	0	22	26	0	29	4	0
107	288	103	14	0	381	230	57		76	1
9	0	299	1,000	81	248	7	1	353	0	20
1	0	1	0	0	13	4	0	0	3	0
385	797	1,254	1,135	251	1,637	482	317	3,096	1,691	197
62.0	75.3	71.6	63.6	73.9	74.8	55.5	86.8	67.4	56.1	59.8
37.5	24.0	28.3	36.4	26.0	24.4	33.1	13.4	39.0	41.6	38.9
1.4	7.2	4.2	0.2	0.3	1.1	0.8	2.6	1.1	0.4	3.6
3.5	4.2	3.2	8.6	9.2	16.5	5.8	2.7	8.1	32.6	20.1
19.0	8.2	5.3	0.5	0.9	1.8	19.2	4.2	14.1	0.7	1.4
2.4	1.8	2.6	0.5	2.1	1.8	2.1	1.5	1.6	0.5	0.8
17.6	15.0	14.5	26.9	13.4	4.6	11.1	5.1	13.5	7.6	13.0

Industrial countries form the single largest group of trading partners of the Middle Eastern region. In both the export as well as import markets, their share is typically larger than any other group. For example, Algeria obtains 89.1 per cent of its imports from the industrial countries group and exports 86.2 per cent of its exports to the same group of countries. Industrial countries occupy more than 75 per cent of both the imports and exports of Libya and Tunisia and approximately two thirds of Egyptian, Israeli and Turkish foreign trade.

Developing countries of Africa typically occupy a very small percentage of Middle Eastern trade. Asian countries occupy significant shares in excess of 20 per cent for only Iran, Jordan, Kuwait, Oman, Qatar and Saudi Arabia. Countries of the American continent except the US and Canada occupy less than 5 per cent of the trade of Middle Eastern countries.

Seen from a different perspective, Tables 4.16a and 4.16b also show the extent of trade within the region as shares of each Middle Eastern country's trade with other countries of the region. Only Bahrain has about 42.2 per cent of its imports from Saudi Arabia, and Oman sends 33.3 per cent of its exports to, as well as receiving 23.6 per cent of its imports from, the UAE. Similarly, Lebanon also sends 19.8 per cent of its exports to Saudi Arabia. For the rest of the Middle Eastern countries, trade with another country of the region occupies a small portion of their total trade volume. It should also be noted here that due primarily to the Arab boycott, Israeli trade in the region is negligible. Even with Egypt, and despite recent increases in trade volume with Turkey, Israel has almost no trade.

Turkey's role in intra-regional trade should be emphasised here. Turkey is by far the largest importer from the region. Saudi Arabian oil exports to Turkey constitute the largest single bilateral trade flow in the Middle East. Accordingly, Saudi Arabia is the largest exporter of goods to within the region, followed by UAE, Oman and Turkey. Considering the fact that Turkey's trade with the region is seriously hampered by the post-Gulf War crisis in Iraq, one notices the importance of Turkey as a trade partner in the region.

Besides the macro-level composition of trade and its distribution across the countries of the region, the product composition of Middle Eastern exports shows interesting patterns. Yeats (1995) provides a list of thirty of the largest non-oil products in Middle Eastern exports. In this list textiles surfaces as not only the largest product group but also as the one that has grown considerably faster than most others. As textiles have experienced considerable growth, agricultural exports have declined, due primarily to rising protection in European markets (Laird and Yeats 1990). The expansion of textiles offers opportunities for the region, so long as they can remain price competitive in a more liberalised world-trade environment. Besides textiles, agricultural products such as barley and rice also appear on the list of fastest growing items. Agricultural products are more labour intensive and use mainly rural labour, which helps to alleviate rural poverty. Table 4.17 shows that Israel and Turkey are the major suppliers of most of the fastest growing products in Middle Eastern exports. In only 9 out of 30 products do other countries have some exports, usually with either Israel or Turkey featuring as exporters of the product in question. Accordingly, one is led to conclude that a few countries are exploiting these fastest growing or 'dynamic' products, and Israel and Turkey in particular are leaving the others behind.[11]

The above analysis relies on the latest available data on countries from the late 1980s and early 1990s. Consequently, the observations are valid for the most recent years. However, there is no indication in the literature that trade patterns, especially intra-regional ones, in the past have been significantly different from the picture revealed above. In short, the Middle Eastern do not trade with each other to any

Table 4.17 Exports to OECD markets of dynamic products from Middle Eastern countries, 1986–92

SITC Description	*Major 1992 Suppliers (% share)*	*OECD Imports (thousands of US$)* 1986	1988	1992	*Growth Rate* 1988–92	1986–92
Rice (042)	Egypt (88)	114	3,235	6,062	17	94
Cement and building products (661)	Turkey (89)	7,708	42,473	150,722	37	64
Lead (685)	Lebanon (48) Israel (27)	91	1,678	1,397	-4	58
Clay and refractory products (662)	Turkey (88)	4,740	13,258	62,029	47	54
Domestic electrical equipment (725)	Turkey (83)	5,906	82,489	73,263	-3	52
Leather (611)	Saudi Arabia (66)	2,558	11,502	29,133	26	50
Plumbing and heating equipment (812)	Turkey (85)	8,428	21,716	73,949	36	44
Wire products (693)	Turkey (86)	4,320	8,359	34,497	43	41
Woven textiles noncotton (653)	Turkey (74) Israel (21)	41,403	162,717	302,675	17	39
Electrical distributing machines (723)	Turkey (86)	32,508	20,657	234,996	84	39
Natural abrasives (275)	Israel (60) Turkey (39)	4,921	26,551	34,625	7	38
Silk (261)	Turkey (100)	105	1,464	719	-16	38
Special textile products (655)	Israel (61) Turkey (36)	11,143	28,994	75,062	27	37
Leather manufactures (612)	Turkey (75)	979	3,437	6,571	18	37
Wood in the rough (242)	Turkey (94)	1,057	581	6,721	84	36
Telecommunications equipment (724)	Israel (54) Turkey (26)	133,954	349,010	835,700	24	36
Iron and steel castings (679)	Turkey (84)	211	3,203	7,469	24	35
Zoo animals and pets (941)	Turkey (48) Egypt (33)	767	2,421	4,726	18	35
Radioactive materials (515)	Israel (92)	235	549	1,376	26	34
Wood shaped (243)	Turkey (93)	1,688	1,729	9,768	54	34
Iron and steel wire (677)	Turkey (87)	328	5,418	1,882	-23	34
Non-alcoholic beverages (111)	Turkey (32)	1,163	3,769	6,283	14	32
Wheat meal or flour (046)	Turkey (38) Lebanon (34)	143	499	678	8	30
Road motor vehicles and parts (732)	Turkey (70) Israel (13)	45,052	87,370	203,604	24	29
Base metal household equipment (697)	Turkey (83)	11,656	20,568	50,712	25	28
Wheat unmilled (041)	Saudi Arabia (96)	3,652	21,955	15,851	-29	28
Soaps and cleansing preparations (554)	Israel (58) Turkey (32)	2,789	2,888	12,012	43	28
Milk and cream (022)	Israel (50) Saudi Arabia (13)	341	399	1,454	38	27
Iron and steel forms (672)	Turkey (80) Egypt (9)	17,785	149,734	73,520	-16	27
Total of above products		345,743	1,078,624	2,317,456		

Source: Yeats (1995)
Note: In order to be included in the above tabulations, OECD imports of the product had to total at least US$500,000 in 1992

significant degree. The Middle East also trades very little with any specific geographical region other than industrial Europe and other developed economies of the world. These results, however, do not take into account the extent of Middle Eastern trade in the world, which is about 4 per cent of global trade. If a given country in the Middle East has part of its trade with the region's countries that is above the share of the Middle East in world trade then it can be considered to have a higher than average propensity to trade within the region. As Table 4.16 shows, some countries depend heavily on trade with other Middle Eastern countries: Bahrain (45 per cent imports from the Middle East), Jordan (27.7 per cent of exports), Lebanon (53.6 per cent of exports), Oman (26.6 per cent of imports and 38 per cent of exports), Syria (25.1 per cent of exports). Table 4.16 clearly indicates that – with the exception of Algeria, Egypt (for the case of its imports), Israel and Kuwait – all of the regional economies' intra-regional trade shares are considerably higher than the group average in world trade. This alone is an indication that trade within the Middle East is relatively higher than the world average propensity to trade with the Middle East. This is a promising sign of regional dynamics for trade that could be conducive to more regional economic cooperation through trade and more economic integration within the region. Next we turn to sectoral characteristics of intra-regional trade to diagnose any sectoral complementarities in the region.

Sectoral breakdown of intra-regional trade in the Middle East

The most limiting obstacle facing the analysis of sectoral breakdown of intra-regional trade in the Middle East is lack of data. Some countries do not report their import and export statistics to the United Nations on a regular basis. Consequently, instead of using these irregular reporters' own data, their partner countries' statistics must be used as estimates of intra-regional trade. We rely in this section on data analysis carried out by Yeats (1995).

The trade intensity index (TII) is a standard tool for the analysis of two countries' propensity to trade with each other. TII is based on the simple idea that if the value of trade between two countries is greater (smaller) than what would be expected on the basis of their share in world trade then these two countries have a higher (lower) than expected intensity of trade between them. As of 1992, Turkey sends approximately 12 per cent of its exports to Europe whereas it imports about 14 per cent of its total imports from Europe. Based on shares of Turkey and Europe in world trade, can we consider this trade as above or below the two partners' expected shares?

TII is given by the ratio of the share of one country's exports going to a partner to the share of world exports going to the same partner:

$$TII_{ij}=(x_{ij} / X_{it}) / (x_{wj} / X_{wt})$$

where x_{ij} and x_{wj} are respectively the value of i's and world's exports to j. X_{it} and X_{wt} are respectively i's and world's total exports. Accordingly, when TII exceeds (falls short of) unity it reflects that bilateral trade flow is larger (smaller) than expected given the partner country's share in world trade. Table 4.18 below shows the values of trade intensity indices for 1992 calculated by Yeats (1995).

Table 4.18 Trade intensity index for selected Middle Eastern countries' exports, 1990

	Partner country				
Exporter	*All OECD countries*	*European Union*	*North America*	*Japan*	*Middle Eastern region*
Egypt	0.71	0.92	0.49	0.51	4.19
Israel	1.07	0.85	1.66	1.38	0.31
Jordan	0.12	0.08	0.03	0.40	6.00
Libya	1.21	2.04			1.32
Oman	0.25	0.25	0.21	0.40	17.27
Saudi Arabia	0.36		1.40		
Syria	0.63	1.00	0.05	0.01	5.84
Turkey	0.93	1.29	0.44	0.35	4.07

Source: Yeats (1995: 24)

Trade with OECD countries as a group is only slightly above expectations for Libya and Israel. The rest of the countries have a considerably smaller than expected tendency to trade with OECD countries in general. Libya and Turkey have above the expected tendency to trade with the European Union. Similarly, only Israel and Saudi Arabia trade with North American countries with an above-expected intensity, and with Japan only Israel's trade is above expectations. In comparison, with the exception of Israel, all countries' trade within the Middle East is higher than expectations. For example, Turkey's share of exports to the region is about 4 times larger than expected while Oman's is 17 times larger. Accordingly, despite the fact that most Middle Eastern trade is with countries outside the region, the relative importance of the regional markets is above that expected on the basis of Middle Eastern share in world trade.

If trade is to be promoted and expanded within the region, it is imperative to diagnose those product groups that offer opportunities for intra-regional trade. For this purpose the revealed comparative advantage (RCA) index can be used. The RCA index offers a rough indication of where countries' advantages are. Accordingly, those countries that have a similar RCA index value will not be expected to engage in significant trade. Those who have disparate index values are more likely to engage in trade.

More specifically:

$$RCA_{ij} = (x_{ij} / X_{tj}) / (x_{iw} / X_{tw})$$

where x_{ij} is the value of country i's exports of j and X_{tj} is the country's total exports and the w subscripts refer to world totals. The interpretation of the RCA index is straightforward; if it exceeds unity then the country in question has a 'revealed comparative advantage' in the product. If the RCA index is less than unity then the country has a comparative disadvantage in the item. Yeats (1995: 28–29) calculates the RCA index values for 9 single digit Standard International Trade Classification (SITC) product groups over three decades (for the years 1970, 1980 and 1992) for 13 countries in the Middle East.

The SITC is the most commonly used classification of traded goods in the international market. Products are grouped under a series of 'digits' in increasing order of disaggregation. There are five different levels of disaggregation. At the one-digit level there are 10 'sections'. At the two-digit level, there are 63 'divisions'. At the three-digit level, there are 233 'groups'. At the four-digit level there are 786 'subgroups' and at the five-digit level there are 1,486 'items' of traded goods and services. Yeats (1995: 28–29) uses 9 of the 10 sections to produce RCA indices. For example, food and live animals at the one-digit level is disaggregated into 10 two-digit 'divisions' ranging from live animals (00 as its SITC digit), meat and meat preparations (01 as its SITC digit) to dairy products and eggs (02 as its SITC digit) and fruits and vegetables (05 as its digit). At the three-digit level of disaggregation these two-digit 'divisions' are further sub-grouped under 233 'groups'. For example, fruits and vegetables have fresh fruits and nuts excluding oil nuts, dried fruits including artificially dehydrated, and raw sugar beet and cane.

According to Yeats (1995: 28–29), under the food and live animals 'section', Egypt, Iran, Israel, Jordan (except for 1987), Lebanon, Syria and Turkey enjoy comparative revealed advantage. However, all of these countries except Iran have had declining comparative advantage over the years for this group of products. Under beverages and tobacco, Jordan had lost its comparative advantage over the last three decades. In contrast, the UAE and Lebanon had apparently developed a considerable comparative advantage, indicating, for example, that the share of beverages and tobacco in the UAE exports are approximately 3 times larger than the corresponding world-trade share.

For crude materials including materials such as coal, lignite and the like, none of the countries have had a comparative advantage for the last three decades. On the other hand, 9 of the 13 countries show a strong comparative advantage over the refined fuels category. Not surprisingly, only Israel, Jordan, Lebanon and Turkey have a comparative disadvantage in this 'section'. While Egypt, Libya, Oman, Qatar, Syria and the UAE increased their comparative advantage for this 'section', the comparative advantage for each of Bahrain, Iran and Saudi Arabia has declined considerably. This is also an indication of the inner competition between the countries of the region in the world oil markets.

The only country that has ever had a slight comparative advantage in animal and vegetable oil was Turkey and it has lost this advantage over the last two decades. In chemicals, while Israel has persistently had a comparative advantage over the last three decades, Jordan, Libya and Saudi Arabia have also developed an advantage in chemicals. Qatar's comparative advantage has declined slightly. In both refined fuels and chemicals the comparative advantage of the Middle Eastern countries is due to oil-related industries that intensely use petroleum inputs.

Under manufactured goods classified chiefly by material, Bahrain, Egypt, Iran, Israel, Lebanon and Turkey have slight comparative advantages. These manufactures include leather and leather products, rubber manufactures, wood and cork manufactures (excluding furniture, paper and paperboard and manufactures thereof) textile yarn and fabrics, non-metallic mineral manufactures such as glass, iron and steel, non-ferrous metals, and manufactures of metal. While Oman, Qatar and Syria once had a comparative advantage in this 'section', Egypt and the UAE's advantage has been declining and Turkey's advantage has been fluctuating.

Under the machinery and transport equipment 'section', none of the Middle Eastern countries have a comparative advantage. Only Libya (in 1970) and Oman (in 1980) had a comparative advantage in this section but they both lost their advantage. The miscellaneous manufactured articles 'section' includes items such as furniture, clothing, footwear, scientific control equipment and clocks, cameras and the like. Israel and Egypt have lost their advantage in this 'section' while Turkey and the UAE have both developed an advantage. Lebanon and Syria have maintained their advantages over the last three decades.

The above discussion is at the lowest degree of disaggregation only showing some general patterns in Middle Eastern trade and thus is not very helpful in diagnosing specific product groups with which each country enjoys a comparative advantage in world trade. For this purpose, Table 4.19, summarised from Yeats' (1995) detailed appendix on revealed comparative advantage (RCA) indices, shows only those products in which each country has a revealed comparative advantage in the 1990–92 period. The first pattern that attracts attention is the number of items in which each country has a comparative advantage. Without taking the volume of trade into account, this can be taken as a reflection of the degree of competitive diversification in these economies. For example, while Iran has 7 product groups in which it has a revealed comparative advantage, Bahrain has 4, Egypt 16, Israel has 28, Jordan 14, Lebanon 38, Libya 8, Oman 10, Qatar 9, Saudi Arabia 7, Syria 15, Turkey 34 and the UAE 28. While Lebanon's exports are considerably smaller than other countries in the region, it nevertheless exports the largest number of product groups to the world with a clear comparative advantage. Turkey and Israel follow Lebanon in the highest number of exported product groups that reveal a comparative advantage.

At the first SITC group of products for food and live animals (SITC 'section' 0) only a few countries have an advantageous position in world trade and this only occurs for a limited number of product groups. Only Egypt and the UAE have a comparative advantage for glazed or polished rice (SITC 0422). In tinned or prepared fish (SITC 032) only Iran and Turkey enjoy a comparative advantage. In dried fruit (SITC 052) most countries of the region have been performing well above the world trade patterns; Israel, Jordan, Lebanon, Oman, Syria, Turkey and the UAE have a comparative advantage. In preserved or prepared fruits (SITC 053) Iran, Israel, Lebanon, Syria and Turkey have a comparative advantage. Similarly, in preserved or prepared vegetables (SITC 055) Egypt, Israel, Iran, Lebanon,

Table 4.19 Revealed comparative advantage indices (selected for indicating a comparative advantage)

		Commodities	*1970–72*	*1980–82*	*1990–92*
Bahrain					
1	332	Petroleum products	28.29	11.09	21.22
2	512	Organic chemicals	0.00	0.00	1.59
3	513	Inorganic elements, oxides, etc.	0.00	0.02	1.54
4	684	Aluminium	3.97	5.77	16.96
5	897	Gold, silverware, jewellery	0.11	20.14	1.21
		Mean	6.47	7.40	8.50
Egypt					
1	0422	Rice, glazed or polished	58.84	6.37	3.58
2	055	Vegetables, preserved, prepared	12.39	7.30	4.05
3		Prepared sugar	9.45	1.71	2.15
4	521	Coal, petroleum, etc., chemicals	0.10	2.63	2.56
5	551	Essential oil, perfume, etc.	14.98	7.07	3.06
6	561	Fertilisers, manufactured	1.44	0.63	4.92
7	651	Textile yarn and thread	15.71	15.03	15.35
8	652	Cotton fabric, woven	21.23	7.35	8.78
9	656	Made-up articles, wholly or chiefly of textile material	0.73	2.95	5.00
10	657	Floor coverings, tapestries, etc.	1.14	5.25	2.62
11	671	Pig iron, etc.	1.68	0.00	2.41
12	673	Iron and steel bars, rods, angles, shapes, sections	0.00	0.00	4.04
13	684	Aluminium	0.00	13.29	9.09
14	696	Cutlery	0.01	0.04	1.08
15	734	Aircraft	0.32	0.22	5.52
16	841	Clothing not of fur	0.20	0.75	2.59
		Mean	8.64	4.41	4.80
Iran					
1	032	Fish, etc., tinned, prepared	4.04	3.23	12.67
2	053	Fruit, preserved, prepared	28.28	22.19	65.72
3	055	Vegetables, preserved, prepared	0.26	0.16	7.87
4	332	Petroleum products	12.78	7.68	11.76
5	657	Floor coverings, tapestries, etc.	107.19	95.51	154.04
6	671	Pig iron, etc.	0.00	0.00	1.86
7	682	Copper	0.00	0.00	3.28
		Mean	21.79	18.40	36.74
Israel					
1	052	Dried fruit	0.85	2.43	2.64
2	053	Fruit, preserved, prepared	34.37	18.93	14.21
3	055	Vegetables, preserved, prepared	3.83	4.95	1.51
4	099	Food preparations, nes	4.42	5.28	3.46
5		Worked wool	4.88	4.1	4.95
6	512	Organic chemicals	1.15	2.26	2.59
7	513	Inorganic elements, oxides, etc.	1.33	2.6	3.14
8	514	Other inorganic chemicals	3.3	5.22	7.53

Table 4.19 Continued

		Commodities	*1970–72*	*1980–82*	*1990–92*
Israel (cont'd)					
9	551	Essential oil, perfume, etc.	1.47	0.67	1.03
10	561	Fertilisers manufactured	15.17	8.84	10.82
11	571	Explosives and pyrotechnic products	0.6	3.17	3.79
12	581	Plastic materials, etc.	0.73	1.2	1.59
13	599	Chemicals nes	1.24	1.14	1.51
14	621	Materials of rubber	0.14	1.17	1.52
15	629	Rubber articles nes	5.28	2.7	1.48
16	651	Textile yarn and thread	3.91	2.19	1.47
17	655	Special textile, etc. products	0.15	0.44	1.73
18	656	Made-up articles, wholly or chiefly of textile material	0.73	4.27	2.95
19	695	Tools	1.18	2.35	4.2
20	696	Cutlery	0.99	1.01	1.56
21	724	Telecommunications equipment	0.41	0.77	1.77
22	726	Electromedical, X-ray equipment	3.5	9.62	4.7
23	729	Electrical machinery	0.41	0.53	1.12
24	734	Aircraft	0.58	3.57	1.88
25	841	Clothing not of fur	6.14	3.37	1.83
26	861	Instruments, apparatus	0.49	1.06	2.19
27	893	Articles of plastic, nes	2.19	2.35	1.87
28	897	Gold, silverware, jewellery	1.99	10.86	9.78
		Mean	3.62	3.82	3.53
Jordan					
1	052	Dried fruit	0.03	0.86	1.33
2		Synthetic rubber	0	0.07	1.22
3		Vegetable oils	0	0.65	2.91
4	513	Inorganic elements, oxides, etc.	1.58	0.49	4.5
5	514	Other inorganic chemicals	0.11	2.44	3.65
6	561	Fertilisers manufactured	6.44	9.1	83.84
7	661	Cement, etc., building products	0	8.74	65.81
8	684	Aluminium	0	0.04	1.54
9	697	Base metal household equipment	0.1	6.4	1.74
10	711	Power generating machinery, other than electric	5.3	2.49	1.89
11	734	Aircraft	0.9	3.42	3.16
12	841	Clothing not of fur	0.06	0.66	1.1
13	861	Instruments, apparatus	0.68	1.22	1.26
14	897	Gold, silverware, jewellery	0.61	6.97	2.43
		Mean	1.13	3.11	12.60
Lebanon					
1	046	Wheat, etc., meal or flour	18.41	0.08	1.35
2	052	Dried fruit	0.91	6.68	1.42
3	053	Fruit, preserved, prepared	0.48	2.87	2.59
4	055	Vegetables, preserved, prepared	3.02	1.69	7.55
5		Prepared sugar	0.59	0.6	2.04
6	099	Food preparations, nes	1.09	0.77	2.01

Table 4.19 Continued

		Commodities	*1970–72*	*1980–82*	*1990–92*
Lebanon (cont'd)					
7	111	Non-alcoholic beverages	0.98	32.63	2.03
8	112	Alcoholic beverages	0.06	0.17	1.84
9	2219	Oil seed flour and meal	8.08	6.63	115.94
10		Vegetable oils	0.19	0.53	2.12
11	514	Other inorganic chemicals	0.27	0.82	2.01
12	553	Perfume, cosmetics, etc.	0.31	4.47	1.87
13	561	Fertilisers manufactured	7.08	4.77	1.87
14	611	Leather	7.21	0.56	1.93
15	642	Articles of paper, etc.	3.56	4.99	5.07
16	656	Made-up articles, wholly or chiefly of textile material	3.78	2.34	5.26
17	657	Floor coverings, tapestries, etc.	4.24	3.2	1.43
18	661	Cement, etc., building products	18.87	13.76	14.79
19	662	Clay, refractory building products	0.22	2.41	3.1
20	665	Glassware	1.52	1.27	4.22
21	671	Pig iron, etc.	0.16	0.26	1.94
22	673	Iron and steel bars, rods, angles, shapes, sections	0.76	1.07	3.84
23	677	Iron and steel wire excluding wire rod	0.14	0.08	2.37
24	679	Iron and steel castings unworked	0.34	2.29	1.92
25	684	Aluminium	1.22	1.96	3.05
26	685	Lead	0.08	1.87	8.51
27	694	Steel, copper nails, nuts, etc.	0.08	0.31	1.4
28	696	Cutlery	0.07	0.21	1.26
29	698	Metal manufactures nes	0.4	0.1	1.12
30	722	Electric power machinery and switchgear	0.27	0.3	1
31	723	Equipment for distributing electricity	0.44	4.48	3.75
32	812	Plumbing, heating, lighting equipment	0.74	4.78	1.26
33	821	Furniture	1.01	1.58	1.36
34	831	Travel goods, handbags	55.49	5.36	1.42
35	841	Clothing not of fur	0.65	2.91	3.14
36	864	Watches and clocks	0.05	0.26	5.14
37	892	Printed matter	5.38	8.94	10.66
38	897	Gold, silverware, jewellery	2.33	42.33	43.63
		Mean	3.96	4.48	7.30
Libya					
1	332	Petroleum products	16.52	10.98	24.18
2	513	Inorganic elements, oxides, etc.	0	2.23	1.58
3	521	Coal, petroleum, etc., chemicals	0	0	38.09
4	561	Fertilisers manufactured	0	0.23	2.93
5	672	Iron and steel primary forms	0	0	1.2
6	673	Iron and steel bars, rods, angles, shapes, sections	16	0.01	1.25
7	675	Hoop and steel of iron or steel	0	0	6.05
8	712	Agricultural machinery	0.5	0	1.77
		Mean	4.13	1.68	9.63

Table 4.19 Continued

		Commodities	*1970–72*	*1980–82*	*1990–92*
Oman					
1	046	Wheat, etc., meal or flour	0	0	1.29
2	052	Dried fruit	0.01	3	2.14
3	332	Petroleum products	0.01	0.87	16.14
4	682	Copper	0	0	4.1
5	694	Steel, copper nails, nuts, etc.	0	0.03	1.77
6	711	Power generating machinery, other than electric	0.24	11.59	2.08
7	734	Aircraft	0.19	4.93	2.75
8	841	Clothing not of fur	0	0.11	2.52
9	864	Watches and clocks	0.17	2.27	4.69
10	897	Gold, silverware, jewellery	0.02	35.58	7.47
		Mean	0.064	5.838	4.495
Qatar					
1	332	Petroleum products	5.32	2.09	17.37
2	512	Organic chemicals	0.08	2.25	1.84
3	513	Inorganic elements, oxides, etc.	0	3.01	1.44
4	561	Fertilisers manufactured	0.17	18.11	23.54
5	581	Plastic materials, etc.	0.02	6.09	2.89
6	673	Iron and steel bars, rods, angles, shapes, sections	0.01	39.67	9.63
7	841	Clothing not of fur	0.35	0.02	2.03
8	864	Watches and clocks	0.1	0.44	1.04
9	897	Gold, silverware, jewellery	0.71	3.49	6.83
		Mean	0.75	8.35	7.40
Saudi Arabia					
1	332	Petroleum products	28.5	11.21	21.39
2	512	Organic chemicals	0.01	0	3.98
3	521	Coal, petroleum, etc., chemicals	30.02	1.41	7.36
4	561	Fertilisers manufactured	0.06	1.24	1.29
5	581	Plastic materials, etc.	0	0.06	3.4
6	661	Cement, etc., building products	0.04	0.01	1.64
7	897	Gold, silverware, jewellery	0.19	4.24	3.58
		Mean	8.40	2.60	6.09
Syria					
1	047	Meal and flour, non-wheat	0	0	1.94
2	052	Dried fruit	7.91	1.62	2.88
3	053	Fruit, preserved, prepared	2.58	1.65	2.12
4	055	Vegetables, preserved, prepared	2.07	2.04	1.17
5		Synthetic rubber	0.73	0.02	2.77
6	332	Petroleum products	1.08	10.73	23
7	651	Textile yarn and thread	1.08	0.13	2.16
8	652	Cotton fabric, woven	8.81	0.62	2.55
9	653	Woven textiles, non-cotton	2.73	0.72	1.69
10	654	Lace ribbons, tulle, etc.	2.86	1.31	1.05

Table 4.19 Continued

		Commodities	*1970–72*	*1980–82*	*1990–92*
Syria (cont'd)					
11	656	Made-up articles, wholly or chiefly of textile material	5.85	1.82	3.71
12	657	Floor coverings, tapestries, etc.	0.37	0.18	2.11
13	661	Cement, etc., building products	0.02	0.08	7.99
14	841	Clothing not of fur	3.18	1.44	2.72
15	842	Fur clothing and articles of artificial fur	0.49	1.57	3.84
		Mean	2.65	1.60	4.11
Turkey					
1	032	Fish, etc., tinned, prepared	0.14	0.25	1.18
2	048	Cereal, etc., preparations	1.12	3.15	1.14
3	052	Dried fruit	205.78	168.07	79.29
4	053	Fruit, preserved, prepared	1.07	3.68	5.74
5	055	Vegetables, preserved, prepared	5.54	6.96	5.6
6	091	Margarine, shortening	0.02	0	6.83
7	266	Synthetic and regenerated artificial fibres	0.36	5.18	2.85
8	332	Petroleum products	1.5	1.02	1.12
9	514	Other inorganic chemicals	1.51	1.25	3.13
10	521	Coal, petroleum, etc., chemicals	0	0.06	1.23
11	532	Dying and tanning artifacts, synthetic tanning materials	5.04	1.08	1.18
12	612	Leather, etc., manufactures	0.07	0.06	1.13
13	629	Rubber articles nes	0.39	0.29	1.28
14	651	Textile yarn and thread	8.79	19.67	6.39
15	652	Cotton fabric, woven	5.08	4.19	4.54
16	653	Woven textiles, non-cotton	0.29	0.64	2.4
17	656	Made-up articles, wholly or chiefly of textile material	0.53	6.04	7.46
18	657	Floor coverings, tapestries, etc.	5.39	20.48	9.43
19	661	Cement, etc., building products	15.26	7.87	9.71
20	662	Clay, refractory building products	0.05	0.74	2.13
21	664	Glass	0.99	2.49	2.52
22	665	Glassware	1.64	4.88	4.47
23	671	Pig iron, etc.	3.64	7.93	3.39
24	672	Iron and steel primary forms	0.15	0.14	3.99
25	673	Iron and steel bars, rods, angles, shapes, sections	0	0.59	7.44
26	675	Hoop and strip of iron or steel	0.03	0.03	7.17
27	678	Tubes, pipes and fittings of iron-steel	0.15	0.08	1.39
28	679	Iron-steel castings forgings unworked	0.35	0.89	1.44
29	682	Copper	0.74	0.05	1.42
30	693	Wire products non-electric	0	0.27	2.81
31	697	Base metal houshold equipment	1.36	1.96	1.78
32	812	Plumbing, heating, lighting equipment	0.25	0.67	1.34
33	841	Clothing not of fur	1.88	4.08	7.63
34	842	Fur clothing and articles of artificial fur	37.27	10.79	10.3
		Mean	9.01	8.40	6.20

Table 4.19 Continued

		Commodities	*1970–72*	*1980–82*	*1990–92*
UAE					
1	0422	Rice glazed or polished	0	0.07	4.36
2	046	Wheat, etc., meal or flour	0	3.15	1.73
3	052	Dried fruit	0	1.25	1.6
4	055	Vegetables, preserved, prepared	0	1.11	1.28
5	099	Food preparations, nes	0	1.77	1.06
6	111	Non-alcoholic beverages	0	14.27	9.18
7	122	Tobacco Manufactures	0	0.23	6.95
8	332	Petroleum products	0.2	5.6	12.21
9	521	Coal, petroleum, etc., chemicals	7.07	2.47	42.15
10	553	Perfume, cosmetics, etc.	0.03	1.33	1.41
11	561	Fertilisers manufactured	0	0.04	1.16
12	629	Rubber articles nes	0.03	0.13	1.21
13	631	Veneers, plywood, etc.	0	0.76	1.06
14	642	Articles of paper, etc.	0	0.64	1.26
15	653	Woven textiles, non-cotton	0.03	0.56	1.37
16	656	Textile yarn and thread	0.03	0.44	1.85
17	657	Floor coverings, tapestries, etc.	0.06	1.21	1.54
18	661	Cement, etc., building products	0	8.92	2.98
19	673	Iron and steel bars, rods, angles, shapes, sections	0	0.7	1.41
20	684	Aluminium	0.05	6	9.04
21	691	Finished structural parts and structures	0.45	1.25	1.24
22	692	Metal containers for storage and transport	0.15	1.08	3.32
23	693	Wire products non-electric	0.01	2.01	1.07
24	718	Machines for special industries	0.11	1.03	1.1
25	735	Ships and boats	0.15	0.49	2.22
26	841	Clothing not of fur	0	0.26	1.94
27	864	Watches and clocks	1.58	0.98	1.55
28	897	Gold, silverware, jewellery	0.44	8.75	5.09
		Mean	0.37	2.38	4.37

Note: 'nes' stands for 'not elsewhere specified'

Syria, Turkey and the UAE show a comparative advantage. Turkey is the only country in the region that has a comparative advantage in processed cereal preparations such as malt, malt-flour, macaroni and noodles, bakery products and the like. Turkey has exported approximately US$28 million worth of these products over the 1990–92 period, increasing its exports over the last two decades to a great extent from about US$475,000 in the 1970–72 period. Turkey is also the only country with a comparative advantage in margarines, shortening, poultry fat and lard in the region. Turkey's exports reached US$11.2 million in the 1990–92 period in this product group from an almost non-existent level in earlier periods (Yeats 1995: Appendix). Similarly, Israel, Lebanon and the UAE enjoy a comparative advantage in food preparations such as roasted coffee substitutes, mustard flour, mixed seasonings and sauces, soups and broths, natural yeast and prepared baking powders and the like.

In short, the region's food dependency, as underlined above, also resurfaces in a sectoral analysis. Most of the countries of the Middle East do not have significant export competitiveness in food products. Accordingly, they do not export these products above the world-trade shares, thus revealing a comparative disadvantage in them. Only Israel and Turkey, and to a lesser extent Lebanon, have significant export capacity in foodstuff. The other countries of the region either export quite small amounts of food products or are at a comparative disadvantage in these markets.

Most countries in the region are competitive in petroleum products (SITC 332) and related industries such as inorganic elements and oxides (SITC 513) and crude chemicals derived from coal, petroleum and gas (SITC 521). Bahrain, Egypt, Israel, Jordan, Lebanon and the UAE have quite high degrees of comparative advantage in this sector. With no significant oil reserves Turkey also exports about US$226 million worth of petroleum products. However, this can only be taken as an indication of the existence of processing facilities in Turkey, not as a competitive edge in regional trade based on resources. This clear separation of oil-rich countries and the rest is the largest area of complementarity in the region.

Besides oil, the following countries have a comparative advantage in aluminium (SITC 684) (approximate value of exports in the 1990–92 period given in millions of US$ in brackets): Egypt (135.2), Jordan (3.1), Lebanon (6.8) and the UAE (266.7) For copper (SITC 682) the countries are: Turkey (69.7), Iran (21.7) and Oman (15.3) For lead (SITC 685), Lebanon has a comparative advantage with approximately US$0.75 million worth of exports in the 1990–92 period (Yeats 1995: Appendix).

Most countries of the region also have a comparative advantage in manufactured fertilisers. Turkey, with one of the largest agricultural sectors in the region, does not have a comparative advantage in this item. Despite its comparative advantage, Egypt only exports a small amount of fertilisers (Yeats 1995: Appendix).

In the textile sector – textile yarn and thread (SITC 651), woven cotton fabric (SITC 652), made-up articles wholly or chiefly of textile material (SITC 656) – the following countries have comparative advantages (approximate value of exports in the 1990–92 period given in millions of US$ in brackets): Egypt (277), Israel (119), Syria (91) and Turkey (614) (Yeats 1995: Appendix). Clearly, Turkey has by far the largest capacity in this sector. Apart from these 4 countries, no other country has a significant and internationally competitive textiles sector. In floor coverings and tapestry (SITC 657) the following countries, with respective figures in brackets, have a comparative advantage: Egypt (10.9), Iran (378.4), Lebanon (0.89), Syria (1.69), Turkey (172.1) and the UAE (12.7) (Yeats 1995: Appendix). Iran and Turkey have a considerable lead in both the export capacity and the degree of comparative advantage they possess in floor coverings and tapestry.

Turkey (with approximately US$131 million worth of exports in the 1990–92 period) and Lebanon (with approximately US$2.4 million worth of exports in the 1990–92 period) are the only two countries in the region that have developed some comparative advantage in glass (SITC 664) and glassware (SITC 665) (Yeats 1995:

Appendix). Turkey's dominant position in this sector is apparent considering the relatively small capacity in Lebanese exports.

In iron and steel products – pig iron (SITC 671), iron and steel primary forms (SITC 672), iron and steel bars, rods, angles, shapes and sections (SITC 673), hoop and strip of iron (SITC 675), tubes, pipes and fittings of iron and steel (SITC 678) and unworked iron and steel castings, forgings (SITC 679) – Turkey (in all SITC groups listed above with approximately US$503 million worth of exports in the 1990–92 period), Libya (in only SITC 672, 673 and 675 with approximately US$23.8 million worth of exports in that period), Qatar (in only SITC 673; US$25.1 million), Iran (in only SITC 671; US$4.2 million) and Egypt (in only SITC 671 and 673; US$45 million) have a comparative advantage (Yeats 1995: Appendix). Once again Turkey's capacity and comparative advantage is well above the rest of the group of Middle Eastern countries indicating not only a dominant position but also an opportunity to export to other countries of the region with no comparative advantage in this sector.

Israel appears as the only country in the region with a comparative advantage in telecommunications equipment (SITC 724), electromedical X-ray equipment (SITC 726) and electrical machinery (SITC 729) with approximately US$682 million of exports in the 1990–92 period. Lebanon, with a comparative advantage in equipment for distributing electricity, exported about US$4.6 million worth in the 1990–92 period (Yeats 1995: Appendix). Clearly, Israel's technological capacity dominates the region in the cutting-edge telecommunications sector. Electricity distribution is a major hindrance in the region, and Lebanon's capacity there offers the only locally competitive industry.

In conclusion, on the basis of Yeats' (1995) analysis we should underline that opportunities for developing a more intensified intra-regional trade relationship between the countries of the Middle East exist chiefly between the countries of the region exporting oil and petroleum products, and those which hold relatively high comparative advantages in manufactured goods, unprocessed food and processed foodstuffs. Turkey, Israel, Lebanon and to some extent Syria are candidates for exploiting such markets within the region (Yeats 1995: 30). At a more disaggregated level we also see that Israel has the only capacity in the region for telecommunications. Turkey dominates the iron and steel, glass and glassware sectors. Turkey and Israel, and to a lesser degree Lebanon, are candidates for a competitive supply of processed and unprocessed food to the region. The textiles sector is quite competitive in the region and offers relatively few complementarities for increased regional cooperation.

Post-Uruguay Round trade in the Middle East

For a total of 8 times since 1947, trade barriers in world trade have been subject to multilateral tariff reductions. The last one – that is, the Uruguay Round (UR) in 1994 – accomplished a series of tariff as well as non-tariff measure (NTM) liberalisation in previously excluded sectors such as agriculture, textiles and clothing. In addition, UR extended,

> multilateral rules to trade in services, trade related intellectual property rights and trade related investment measures; *it reformed* some GATT rules such as those on subsidies, countervailing duties, anti-dumping actions and safeguards; as well as forming new institutions for dispute settlement and functioning of the GATT system.
>
> (Yeats 1995: 31, italics added)

Countries like Israel, Turkey, Iran, Jordan and Lebanon already had preferential access to OECD markets, European markets and some other regional markets. However, since these regional countries' preference margins are expected to be reduced due to new UR arrangements, Middle Eastern exports will be affected. According to Yeats:

> UR liberalization of … major OECD markets' trade barriers could increase all regional countries' exports by US$800 million – an annual change of less than one per cent … due to the erosion of their preferences Israel, Syria and Libya are projected to experience overall losses from the Round.
>
> (Yeats 1995: 41)

These changes are net effects of trade lost due to preferential treatment of some products as well as trade gains due to tariff reductions. These estimates do not include reactions of economies like Australia, Canada, New Zealand and EFTA. If these economies behave as others, regional gains for the Middle East could be approximately US$100 million higher. Similarly, these estimates do not incorporate trade effects of the removal of non-tariff measures, which could have considerable impact on some of the Middle Eastern economies. Low and Yeats (1994) estimate that about 18 per cent NTM in pre-UR will be reduced to about 3 per cent.

Although the elimination of NTMs at the UR is generally good for developing countries some negative impact may still be felt due to the gradual phasing out of export quotas. These quotas were kept under the Multi-Fibre Arrangement (MFA) and some countries today still use these quotas even though they may not be competitive in international markets. Some of these countries may be Middle Eastern countries and, as quotas are slowly reduced, they may find their exports severely curtailed. Accordingly, more liberalised world trade will make international textiles and clothing markets less promising. The UR agreement is also expected to raise food prices. If food prices rise, those countries that are net importers of food will find their food import bills rising while, as noted previously, their traditional export prices are stagnating, if not declining (Yeats 1995: 47).

Macro-economic structure and policy-making in the Middle East

The arguments presented so far are primarily based on an assumed relationship between peace and economic cooperation in the region. The starting point of our analysis is that with recent breakthroughs in resolving the long-standing Arab–Israeli conflict in the region, the economic as well as political isolation of the region may come to an end. At the starting point of our analysis, we assume a causal direction from peace to increasing economic and political cooperation. However, as noted previously, for a long-term solution to political animosities in the region the economic structure of the region may also become a significant obstacle. In a region where countries do not trade with each other and face serious structural macroeconomic problems, domestic constituencies as well as strategic concerns of the countries' elites may feel pressures that run against the deepening of the peace process. In short, we should also underline a causal flow from economic structure to peace. Establishing trade partnerships within the region and thus creating domestic constituencies that complement and develop each other is crucial for the deepening of peace in the Middle East.

Our theoretical treatment in Chapters 2 and 3 distinguishes itself from the prevailing literature in that it underlines the crucial role of domestic constituencies in inter-state negotiations. Very simply put, we argue that no settlement in the international arena is going to be long-lived unless domestic constituencies of each one of the negotiating countries ratify it. The isolation of the Middle East from the rest of the world and, more importantly, the alienation and isolation of the countries of the Middle East from each other is to be interpreted from this perspective. Given that peaceful agreement between parties of the Arab–Israeli conflict is reached, what are the necessary conditions for a peaceful ratification by the domestic constituencies of each one of the countries? The answer, we argue, necessarily lies in the structure of trade in the region as well as the character of domestic economic structures. We have seen that the trade sector is not developed to a significant degree. Now we turn our attention to the general character of the Middle Eastern economies.

The prolonged political conflict in the Middle East between Israel and the Arab countries has had impacts on all aspects of the social, political as well as economic structure in the region. From the economic perspective, armed hostilities have led to heavy reliance on military expenditures. As noted in our introductory chapter, the Middle Eastern countries have, on average, a much larger share of military outlays as a proportion of their GNP than the world average. As Table 4.20 reveals, the Middle East has a share of military expenditure in GDP about twice the size of the world average. A total of 3.2 million people are in the military and a considerable number are reservists and sizeable paramilitary forces exist.

Servicing these large armies depends primarily on more and more expensive imports of military hardware. Due to rapid technological change that accelerates the rate of product obsolescence in military hardware, pressures rise for modernising regional military forces. Despite a lack of considerable oil revenues in some, all countries in the region are using valuable economic resources to service and continue building up their military forces. As of 1991, the region absorbed more than 41 per cent of the world's total arms imports (up from 35.9 per cent in 1981). The Middle East is by far the largest importer of arms in the world, with Saudi Arabia leading the pack. With respect to percentage share of military expenditure

Table 4.20 Military expenditure in the Middle East, 1985–94

Totals for given region	*Amount (millions of US$)*			*Per capita (US$)*		
	1985	*1993*	*1994*	*1985*	*1993*	*1994*
Algeria	1,252	1,360	1,249	57	50	44
Bahrain	198	251	246	476	475	439
Egypt	3,394	2,477	2,641	70	45	47
Iran	18,689	1,977	2,237	419	34	37
Iraq	16,909	26,000	2,628	1,064	141	132
Israel	6,638	6,197	6,543	1,568	1,211	1,230
Jordan	791	439	422	226	97	96
Kuwait	2,360	3,110	3,009	1,380	2,032	2,019
Lebanon	263	275	301	99	71	75
Libya	1,774	967	1,062	471	190	210
Morocco	842	1,086	1,197	38	40	44
Oman	2,834	1,920	1,854	1,771	951	991
Qatar	394	330	294	1,251	685	559
Saudi Arabia	23,603	16,473	13,917	2,045	1,339	1,109
Syria	4,577	2,383	2,358	436	172	168
Tunisia	548	231	219	77	27	25
Turkey	3,016	7,073	5,242	60	119	86
UAE	2,685	2,110	2,055	1,954	1,241	1,149
Yemen	643	356	401	64	27	29
Total NATO	539,587	485,008	456,002	477	446	427
Total NATO Europe	190,074	177,442	168,031	415	401	388
Total other Europe	43,968	25,850	26,104	270	145	141
Russia	n/a	107,900	106,927	n/a	729	718
USSR	317,000	n/a	n/a	1,144	n/a	n/a
Central Asia	12,650	12,905	13,080	15	14	13
East Asia, Australasia	98,163	118,672	123,108	231	205	218
Caribbean, Central and Latin America	18,546	17,839	18,423	65	37	37
Subsaharan Africa	10,062	8,971	8,111	28	21	19
Global totals	1,128,437	821,622	794,425	232	148	141

Source: IISS (1995)

in the world, in 1991 the list of top 30 countries in the world included 13 countries from the Middle East. A similar ranking of military expenditure per capita reveals that 10 of the Middle Eastern countries are in the list of the top 30 countries with the largest share of military expenditure in the world. Fourteen Middle Eastern countries also have the largest number of armed forces (that is, soldiers) per 1,000 individuals (USACDA 1994: 36–44). In other words, in all respects the Middle East has one of the largest military arsenals in the world, with huge resources

			Numbers related to armed forces			
Percentage of GDP			*In armed forces (thousands)*		*Reservists (thousands)*	*No. of para-militaries*
1985	*1993*	*1994*	*1985*	*1994*	*1994*	*1994*
1.7	2.9	2.7	170.0	121.7	150.0	41.2
3.5	5.5	5.5	2.8	8.1	n/a	9.3
7.2	5.7	5.9	445.0	440.0	254.0	374.0
36.0	3.4	3.8	305.0	513.0	350.0	45.0
25.9	14.4	14.6	520.0	382.0	650.0	24.8
221.2	9.5	9.5	142.0	172.0	430.0	6.1
15.9	7.8	7.1	70.3	98.6	35.0	10.0
9.1	13.1	12.2	12.0	16.6	23.7	5.0
9.0	4.4	4.4	17.4	44.3	n/a	13.0
6.2	3.3	3.7	73.0	70.0	40.0	n/a
5.4	4.0	4.3	149.0	195.5	150.0	42.0
20.8	16.7	15.9	2.5	42.9	n/a	4.0
6.0	4.3	3.8	6.0	10.1	n/a	n/a
19.6	13.2	11.2	62.5	158.0	n/a	15.5
16.4	8.9	8.6	402.5	408.0	400.0	8.0
5.0	1.6	1.4	35.1	35.5	n/a	n/a
4.5	4.0	3.2	630.0	503.8	952.3	71.1
7.6	5.9	5.7	43.0	61.5	n/a	n/a
8.9	4.6	5.2	64.1	66.0	85.0	75.0
3.3	2.6	2.5	5,378.0	4,197.6	6,605.2	713.9
3.1	2.5	2.4	3,143.4	2,469.0	4,520.0	601.8
4.5	5.7	6.1	1,449.1	2,198.1	7,580.2	401.4
n/a	9.3	9.6	n/a	1,714.0	2,400.0	280.0
16.1	n/a	n/a	5,300.0	n/a	n/a	n/a
4.6	2.8	2.7	2,113.7	2,542.5	1,628.7	1,470.7
6.9	4.4	4.5	8,057.7	6,963.3	12,179.2	2,055.7
3.1	1.7	1.7	1,344.1	1,407.2	2,625.8	749.5
3.5	3.3	2.8	958.5	991.6	467.0	341.6
4.8	2.8	2.6	27,131.8	22,873.7	36,053.8	6,713.7

being spent on relatively large armed forces given the region's population and limited resources. These military expenditures consequently absorb scarce public-sector financial means.

Given a pre-commitment to maintain large military forces in order to continue credibly to be a player in Middle Eastern conflicts, the regions' economies have failed to undertake large-scale long-term investments in productive activities. As a result, despite huge oil revenues pouring into the region for the last three decades, regional infrastructure, human resources and diversity in economic activities do not develop at a worldwide competitive rate. Consequently, the economies all have a long way to go before they reach their full economic potential.

The fact that the Middle East falls behind its true economic potential is also due to the lack of significant flow of investment resources from the world to the Middle East. Especially when the world economy is living through its relatively large economic boom with expanding world trade, absorption of investment sources to the Middle East is extremely difficult since these international sources continue to face new and dynamic world markets such as the former Soviet Union and Eastern Europe where profit margins are larger and risks considerably low.

> In this context, the Middle East countries increasingly risk being the laggards in a process of greater global competition for development finance resources – all the more so if account is taken of the emergence and consolidation of regional trading arrangements in Latin America (including the NAFTA) and Europe.
>
> (El-Naggar and El-Erian 1993: 205)

Perhaps the most important impact of protracted armed conflict in the region has been the institution of 'war-minded' economic policy-making. It is true that not all countries in our definition of the region have been directly involved in the Arab–Israeli conflict. However, conflicts between the two Yemens, the Southeastern Anatolian conflict in Turkey, Libya's long-standing animosities with the West, and Algerian domestic armed conflict all are evidence to the fact that political and especially militaristic incentives have played a relatively more important role than purely economic ones in economic policy-making of the region.

Evidently, the cost of such a militaristic tendency in economic decisions by the governments of the region is most apparent in the opportunity costs of resources devoted to the military. Every year approximately 6.5 per cent of the regional GDP, or about US$450 per inhabitants of the region, is being spent on military outlays. Simply pulling the level of military expenditure down to the world average would free substantial economic resources that could be invested in human resources and economic infrastructural development, which would help the region to diversify its economic production and become competitive in the world markets. Fischer (1995:429) estimates that a realistical and gradual reduction of Middle Eastern military expenditure to world levels would free up 'about US$50 billion per annum, well in excess of any estimates of the amount of assistance the much called for and unlikely to happen Marshall Plan for the Middle East could hope to deliver'. The fact that much of this spending is on imports, a reduction in military outlays would greatly help restore balance of payments' deficits, provided of course that economic assistance is available on the same terms as military assistance. It should be noted here that some countries of the region like Saudi Arabia and Libya have been undertaking massive investments on human capital. However, other oil-rich countries of the region have been reluctant to make a concerted effort to increase social-sector investments. Any resources freed from the military sector should be especially effective in these countries' efforts to raise social capital.

A perception of high risk for investment in the region, coupled with high rates of taxation to finance militarisation efforts, lead to serious resource misallocation. Such misallocation of resources inevitably leads to difficulties in attracting voluntary external savings. Since resources are directed to military build up, taxes are raised to finance such a build-up. This reduces the return on investments, as well as raising financial return requirements for them, thereby reducing the private sector's incentives. At the regional level, protracted military conflict leading to misallocation of factors of production has contributed to 'slowing of important regional infrastructure projects such as management of scarce water resources, electricity, and energy grid networking and integrating financial relations' (El-Naggar and El-Erian 1993: 211).

Taking the case of the agricultural sectors, especially in Israel and Jordan, it has been suggested that, for the sake of maintaining agricultural constituencies as well as securing the food self-sufficiency that is deemed to be of strategic importance, heavily subsidised water supply in the region leads to high demands on scarce water resources (Clawson 1992: 87). Israeli officials have taken restrictive measures in water supply to farmers following the drought of 1990–91. Jordanian officials, due primarily to pressures from the World Bank, also used similar measures but they relied on administrative rather than price incentives. However, this example illustrates the impact of non-economic policy incentives on the allocation of scarce resources. Once the emphasis on policy objectives is on non-economic concerns such as agricultural independence, a domestic constituency is immediately created that acts to block any attempt to shift policy objectives to purely efficiency-based concerns. Such policy moves become politically costly and thus further aggravate the problem of inefficient allocation of resources.

Like any government programme with substantial financial resources, military resources have certainly created their own constituencies both within and outside the region. These constituencies may be used in developing the military expenditure programme. However, when any attempt is made to downsize this sector, it is a relatively simple matter to calculate who will lose what and thus anticipate their reaction and resistance. For our purposes it is enough to underline the fact that these constituencies are going to be inherently very cautious of, if not outright opposed to, political cooperation which will bring their very *raison d'être* into question. The same constituency may also not benefit from increased economic cooperation, which will inevitably replace military concerns with economic ones and thus redirect public resources for investments to build and create comparative advantages between economies.

World Bank (1996) classification of world economies places Israel, Kuwait, Qatar and the UAE into the high-income group of countries.[11] Bahrain, Oman, Saudi Arabia and Libya are classified as upper-middle income; Turkey, Iran, Iraq, Jordan, Lebanon, Syria, Algeria, Morocco and Tunisia are in the lower-middle income group. Only Yemen and Egypt among the 19 Middle Eastern countries are classified as in the low-income group.

Table 4.21 Macroeconomic indicators, 1980–94

	GNP per capita		*PPP estimates of GNP per capita*					*Distribution of GDP (%)*							
	Amount (US$)	*Avg. annual growth (%)*	*(US = 100)*			*GDP (millions of US$)*		*Agriculture*		*Industry*		*Manufacturing*		*Services*	
					Current int'l $										
	1994	*1985–94*	*1987*	*1994*	*1994*	*1980*	*1994*	*1980*	*1994*	*1980*	*1994*	*1980*	*1994*	*1980*	*1994*
Algeria	1,650	-2.5				42,347	41,941	10	12	54	44	9	11	36	44
Bahrain	7,460	-0.7	57.7	51.1	13,220										
Egypt	720	1.3	14.4	14.4	3,720	22,192	42,923	18	20	37	21	12	15	45	59
Iran						92,664	63,716	18	21	32	37	9	14	50	42
Israel	14,530	2.3	56.5	59.1	15,300	22,690	77,777								
Jordan	1,440	-5.6	25.4	15.8	4,100		6,105		8		27		14		65
Kuwait	19,420	1.1	84.3	95.6	24,730	28,639	24,289	0	0	75	53	6	11	25	47
Morocco	1,140	1.2	13.1	13.4	3,470	18,821	30,803	18	21	31	30	17	17	51	49
Oman	5,140	0.5	34.7	33.2	8,590	5,982	11,628	3	3	69	53	1	4	28	44
Qatar	12,820	-2.4	90.4	73.8	19,100										
Saudi Arabia	7,050	-1.7	45.7	36.6	9,480	156,487	117,236	1		81		5		18	
Syria		-2.1													
Tunisia	1,790	2.1	18.5	19.4	5,020	8,743	15,770	16	15	36	32	14	20	48	53
Turkey	2,500	1.4	20.9	18.2	4,710	56,919	131,014	23	16	30	31	21	20	47	52
UAE*		0.4				29,625	35,405	1	2	77	57	4	8	22	40
Yemen	280														
Middle East (avg.)	5,842	-0.3	42.0	39.1	10,131	44,101	49,884	11	12	52	39	10	13	37	50

Source: World Bank (1996)
Note: data not available for Iraq, Lebanon and Libya; limited data given for some countries
*UAE value for GNP per capita is for 1992

Data on income in the region are summarised in Table 4.21. Average annual growth over the last decade is predominantly negative in the region. Those countries with positive average growth rates over the past decade have grown at only moderate levels. The highest growth rates were observed in Israel. We also observe enormous regional disparities. On the one hand, Egypt and Yemen with a total population of about 75 million have US$720 and US$280 per capita GNP, respectively, which amounts to an average of US$628 dollars per capita GNP in these two countries combined. On the other hand, Israel (average GNP per capita US$14,530), Kuwait (average GNP per capita US$19,420), Qatar (average GNP per capita US$12,820) and the UAE (average GNP per capita US$22,020) with a total population of 10.56 million have an average of US$17,161 per capita GNP.

A more detailed description of per capita incomes in the region is presented in Table 4.22. These figures are obtained from the Penn World Table (Mark 5.6) which has the unique feature of representing expenditure entries denominated in a common set of prices in a common currency which enables one to make real international quantity comparisons between countries and over time.[12] The first observation is that over time the region's per capita GDP figures show great variation due primarily to changes in world oil-market prices. Regional average per capita GDP figures increased considerably up to 1980 but then continuously shrank during the 1980s. By 1989, the average per capita GDP was only slightly higher than its level in 1976. Equally important in this erratic development of per capita GDP in the region was rapid population growth. As previously discussed, rapid population growth puts heavy pressure on the economic performance of the region. Especially in Iraq, Iran, Kuwait, Qatar, Saudi Arabia and the UAE per capita growth rates were predominantly negative over the 1976–92 period.

Fischer notes that,

> the region's social and human accomplishments do not match its income. … Except for Israel and Lebanon, every country in the region [which excluded Turkey, Morocco, Algeria and Tunisia from his definition of the Middle East] is ranked higher by income than by Human Development Index, and some gaps are very large. These gaps help define the economic development tasks confronting the region in the coming decade.
>
> (Fischer 1995: 425–426)

The distribution of income within the countries of the Middle East also reflects income inequalities of varying degrees. Income distribution data are only available for 6 out of 19 countries of the region. Typically, for these 6 countries the lowest 20 per cent of the population receive between 6 and 8 per cent of total income. However, the highest 20 per cent of the people receive approximately 40 to 50 per cent of total income. Such cleavages can also be taken as reflections of the economic policies' failure to create a more equitable income distribution despite their general success in increasing economic welfare as reflected in overall

Table 4.22 Real GDP per capita and changes in real GDP per capita (1995 international prices; Laspeyres index), 1977–1992

	Real GDP per capita					*Changes in real GDP per capita (%)*				
	1977	*1980*	*1985*	*1990*	*1992*	*1977*	*1980*	*1985*	*1990*	*1992*
Algeria	2,518	2,758	2,988	2,777	2,723	2.6	–1.7	0.9	–2.3	–0.0
Bahrain	13,458	12,733	9,547			6.5	–1.0	–7.8		
Egypt	1,403	1,647	1,953	1,912	1,869	2.8	7.9	2.4	0.3	–2.3
Iran	6,018	3,341	4,043	3,393	3,641	–6.5	–26.7	1.2	5.1	3.6
Iraq	6,533	7,267	4,249			7.7	–15.5	–13.8		
Israel	7,122	7,887	8,310	9,289	9,801	–2.9	4.3	1.3	3.7	3.4
Jordan	2,727	3,387	3,561	2,922		8.6	5.1	0.5	–2.5	
Kuwait		20,040	13,114					–3.4		
Morocco	1,768	1,945	1,956	2,150	2,176	1.5	3.3	2.5	–0.5	–3.0
Oman	6,795	6,521	9,199			–12.0	10.8	12.7		
Qatar		33,946	16,986					–15.0		
Saudi Arabia	12,549	13,766	8,313			7.5	4.8	–9.6		
Syria	4,030	4,471	4,240	3,899		1.7	7.5	6.6	4.7	
Tunisia	2,225	2,530	2,758	2,909	3,073	4.1	6.8	1.1	5.1	4.8
Turkey	3,113	2,872	3,077	3,743	3,818	3.4	–2.9	1.8	9.6	3.9
UAE		32,014	19,648					–8.7		
Yemen	1,229	1,313	1,574			–0.6	5.5	16.4		
Middle East (avg.)	5,106	9,320	6,795	3,666	3,872	1.7	0.6	–0.6	2.6	1.5

Source: Pen World Table (Mark 5.6)
Note: data not available for Lebanon and Libya

increases in the income of Middle Eastern economies (Table 4.23). These deep income differentials both across and within countries not only create domestic and regional economic problems that can only be addressed by increased cooperation between the involved parties, but they also create constituencies that are inherently opposed to the resolution of conflicts that created and continue to feed them.

Table 4.23 Percentage share of income or consumption

	Survey year	*Gini Index*	*Lowest 10%*	*Lowest 20%*	*Highest 20%*	*Highest 10%*
Algeria	1988	38.7	2.8	6.9	46.1	31.5
Egypt	1991	32.0	3.9	8.7	41.1	26.7
Israel	1979			6.0	39.6	23.5
Jordan	1991	43.4	2.4	5.9	50.1	34.7
Morocco	1990–91	39.2	2.8	6.6	46.3	30.5
Tunisia	1990	40.2	2.3	5.9	46.3	30.7

Source: World Bank (1996)
Note: data given only for Algeria, Egypt, Israel, Jordan, Morocco and Tunisia

Relying again on the Penn World Table (Mark 5.6), Table 4.24 shows the developments in the real share of consumption, investment and government expenditure in regional economies. The first pattern that surfaces from the data is that the Middle Eastern economies only have a lower share of consumption than the low-income economies with a 65 per cent share of consumption in GDP. The regional average share of investment in GDP is lower than all country groupings according to the World Bank classification (World Bank 1990:194). In contrast, average share of government expenditure in GDP is higher than all country groupings. The trend in consumption over time has been positive (rising to 60 per cent of the Middle Eastern average in 1988 from 57 per cent in 1976), whereas the trend of the regional average investment share in GDP has been negative (decreasing to 17 per cent of the Middle Eastern average in 1988 from 21 per cent in 1976). The share of government expenditure, however, has been stable at around 23–24 per cent over the period 1976–88. In short, governments in the Middle East dominate their country's economy. Compared to world standards consumption is high and investment is low (statistics as shares of GDP). Considering the 'security-minded' economic policy in the region such development is not at all surprising.

The development of the annual inflation rate for the region for the 1970–95 period is given in Table 4.25. The region has a moderate rate of inflation compared to some other regions of the world. Only Israel and, to some degree Turkey, experienced inflation rates in excess of 60 per cent in the 1980s. Israeli inflation has been successfully controlled in recent years and Turkey's inflation has never shifted to a sustained hyper-inflationary phase. It has remained well above 50 per cent but has never exceeded a ceiling (prior to hyper-inflation) of around 80 per cent for a long period of time. Nevertheless, Algeria, Egypt, Iran, Iraq and Syria have had the moderate range of double-digit inflation rates of around 20 per cent since 1990 indicating considerable discomfort in the economy. Due to especially

Table 4.24 Real consumption, real investment and real government share of GDP (% at current international prices), 1977–88

	Real consumption				*Real investment*				*Real government*			
	1977	*1980*	*1985*	*1988*	*1977*	*1980*	*1985*	*1988*	*1977*	*1980*	*1985*	*1988*
Algeria	58	51	57	59	33	27	26	23	19	18	20	26
Bahrain	44	35	40	43	34	46	30	26	13	12	20	22
Egypt	63	70	67	69	6	6	7	5	36	30	32	31
Iran	55	50	68	73	26	33	19	16	16	21	13	12
Iraq	54	43	44		9	12	19		30	24	37	
Israel	51	49	52	57	25	22	18	18	36	40	35	31
Jordan	77	81	78	74	22	22	14	13	35	32	29	27
Kuwait		31	50	57		13	20	16		10	19	22
Morocco	72	74	68	67	17	12	10	9	23	22	25	24
Oman	28	28	39	35	29	22	24	26	28	24	26	32
Qatar		18	29	34		17	19	19		17	30	38
Saudi Arabia	22	30	53	52	14	13	19	16	19	19	35	35
Syria	72	71	67	80	20	18	19	10	17	19	19	12
Tunisia	72	71	71	73	16	15	12	9	20	18	19	19
Turkey	67	67	67	67	27	24	23	21	11	14	12	11
UAE		23	33	43		26	26	30		7	13	15
Yemen	79	79	77	74	25	23	10	7	23	33	28	26
Middle East (avg.)	58	51	56	60	22	21	18	17	23	21	24	24

Source: Penn World Table (Mark 5.6); see also Summers and Heston 1991
Note: data not available for Lebanon and Libya

Table 4.25 Inflation, 1970–95

	Inflation, GDP deflator (annual percentage)						*GDP deflator (1987 = 100)*					
	1970	*1975*	*1980*	*1985*	*1990*	*1995*	*1970*	*1975*	*1980*	*1985*	*1990*	*1995*
Algeria	5.42	5.45	25.59	4.34	34.61	28.25	17.25	34.25	66.88	92.65	174.23	609.71
Bahrain	–	–	–	–1.54	6.91	1.43	–	–	91.87	117.00	110.00	108.52
Egypt	1.81	9.22	17.18	9.04	17.49	8.34	21.52	28.58	53.77	77.05	158.66	300.38
Iran	–	6.47	25.22	4.06	19.60	39.74	–	16.00	39.25	70.57	170.02	683.17
Iraq	5.36	12.08	46.51	21.32	45.00	–	9.94	26.79	52.63	80.47	166.06	–
Israel	9.64	37.12	123.22	266.71	15.73	9.57	0.01	0.02	0.24	55.61	164.16	298.14
Jordan	–	–	–	–0.33	12.06	–	–	–	–	98.73	159.62	–
Kuwait	0.57	0.15	45.40	3.68	–	5.16	13.80	51.02	109.60	118.17	–	100.77
Libya	0.08	–9.42	33.31	17.35	–	–	14.32	50.16	88.81	104.89	–	–
Morocco	3.29	1.51	9.46	8.49	5.38	6.46	27.18	39.27	58.48	87.11	115.67	143.14
Oman	–6.23	2.37	54.39	–0.25	16.66	3.68	11.41	58.69	136.07	112.23	114.55	98.36
Saudi Arabia	14.71	10.06	26.11	–6.57	16.07	5.00	16.08	67.54	145.07	117.89	121.90	132.05
Syria	1.68	7.98	18.96	4.13	18.45	10.00	15.21	24.68	44.86	62.88	189.42	287.92
Tunisia	6.84	4.99	12.79	3.62	4.50	4.82	24.76	38.20	56.88	91.69	122.17	159.52
Turkey	8.77	20.54	84.18	52.48	59.10	82.45	0.60	1.53	10.38	55.12	472.26	7,739.03
UAE	–	19.00	8.82	4.40	3.99	–	–	72.50	95.98	98.11	108.26	–
Middle East (avg.)	4.33	9.11	37.94	24.43	19.68	17.07	14.34	36.37	70.05	90.01	167.64	888.39

Source: World Bank (1997)

Notes: Inflation as measured by the annual growth rate of the GDP implicit deflator. The GDP deflator is the price index that measures the change in the price level of GDP relative to real output. It is calculated using GDP in current and constant 1987 local currencies.

severe economic circumstances after the Gulf War, Iraq remains a unique case with severe economic difficulties especially on the inflation front.

Conclusion: The need for structural reform and reconstruction

Our review of economic data on the Middle Eastern economies points to several macroeconomic problems and structural characteristics that shape the economic policy-making environment commonly shared in the region. First, the Middle East is primarily constrained by severe geographical and climatic constraints. Given the large and fast-growing population, the Middle East region faces serious economic bottlenecks. Second, the Middle East comprises countries with many common economic problems and yet the region has the potential for considerable development within a framework of regional cooperation. Some countries are oil rich and thus enjoy huge revenues from basically a single export item; that is, crude oil. These economies, however, are constrained by a lack of diversification in economic activity. Others have considerable experience (and accumulation of experience) in diversifying their economies through long-lasting industrialisation programs with relatively few natural resources. However, the region typically has a shortage of social and human capital due to severe misallocation of resources in favour of military layouts, leaving infrastructure and social investment relatively neglected. Third, trade relationships within the region are almost non-existent. Due to the protracted militarised conflict between Israel and Arab countries of the region, Israel is almost completely isolated from trade relations within the region. However, despite some complementarity of factors of production, even the Arab nations do not trade or engage in cooperative projects with each other to a significant degree. The region heavily depends on manufactured goods imports, an important part of which is arms supplies from the industrialised countries of the world.

Nevertheless, considerable numbers of migrant workers are spread across the region, especially the Gulf countries. They come from non-oil exporting countries of the region. A considerable number of migrants, especially in the Gulf area, necessitates some Level I cooperation among the countries involved, in order to regulate the flow of labour. It also forms an important resource for countries with an excess labour supply, encouraging them to be more receptive to regional cooperation. These migrant worker communities, and their relatives in their home countries, stand out as potentially an important group of Level II cooperation in the region.

Income distribution between, as well as within, the countries of the region is severely skewed. Until 1980 intra-regional flow of capital from the oil-rich countries to those less endowed with natural resources have been significant. The post-1980 decline in oil prices as well as some important political disagreements in the area have reduced these flows considerably. Although inflation has not been a persistent problem, some countries of the region have experienced high double-digit inflation for a long period of time. However, despite similar and interdependent problems of the Middle Eastern countries, perhaps the most limiting constraint on policy responses to persisting economic problems has been the 'war-minded' policy stand prevalent across the region. Long-standing animosities in the region have pushed military incentives to the forefront of economic-policy objectives. Accordingly, scarce resources are misallocated creating constituencies that act as a barrier to economic cooperation in the region.

It has long been argued that unless a political solution to the Arab–Israeli conflict is created no cooperation in the region is feasible. Recent breakthroughs in this respect bring, however, the issue of deepening peace in the region by relying on building economic bridges between the countries of the region to the forefront. A crucial aspect of these efforts will be reforming the policy-making framework in the region. Now that political initiatives have been taken by the parties involved to resolve their differences in the political arena, consolidation of these steps towards building peace in the region will depend on cooperative economic-policy initiatives bringing the economic rather than military rationale to the forefront of policy priorities.

5 Potential for regional economic cooperation

As signals of a fast approaching end to the Arab–Israeli conflict have been surfacing in the past few years, public interest has shifted from the immediate consequences of long-standing animosities in the Middle East to the underlying social and economic structure of the region. Immediate observations on the regional socio-economic character were far from optimistic: the Middle East was obviously one of the most underdeveloped and isolated regions of the world economy. On the international scene the protracted Arab–Israeli conflict impeded the economic, social and, equally important, political development of the region's countries. The economic costs associated with a continuing militarised conflict gained new momentum in the aftermath of the Cold War due to rapid technological change. This increased the renewal costs of military hardware and thus imposed a serious drain on shrinking regional resources in an era of falling oil revenues.

The potential opening up of the Central Asian oil reserves to world markets shifted the attention of energy markets from the Middle East to the newly independent states of Central Asia. Coupled with new opportunities offered by market reforms in Eastern Europe and the former Soviet Union as well as similar developments in Latin America and Asia, international investors' attention has also shifted more and more away from the Middle East. Considering the expectations of a fast growing world economy due to new trade arrangements in the post-Uruguay Round era, the Middle East increasingly risks not gaining the attention of internationally competitive sources for development finance, as well as being left out of impending global economic development.

Underlying the region's economic problems were fast population growth, a limiting climate and, with the exception of oil, a lack of natural resources for agricultural and industrial development. Issues of rapid population growth could not be dealt with by creating jobs and ultimately led to growing income inequalities. Prolonged Arab–Israeli conflict was also responsible for a distorted set of economic priorities leading to tightly controlled and consequently largely inefficient economies in the region. As a reflection of the regional war economy, the Middle East accounted for a disproportionately large segment of world arms trade that was siphoning out scarce resources. The region's socio-economic policy-making was also dominated by a 'war-minded' approach consequently leading to an insufficient material and human infrastructure and inefficient investment projects.

The Middle Eastern economies suffered from a lack of agricultural self-sufficiency and a heavy reliance on imported food. Inefficient, 'war-minded' policy-making resulted in less and less competitive regional economic structure in a rapidly expanding world economy. On the domestic scene, distorted social and economic policies created popular forces that reflected the deep suffering of the region's masses. At the same time, due to their heavy dependence on the existing socio-economic system, they acted as a barrier to development efforts, impeding international political and economic cooperation in the region and isolating it from the rest of the world.

As a consequence, it became more and more evident that the regional disputes could not be stabilised without a considerable social and economic development effort. The extent and nature of the region's problems, however, impedes any solution by individual nations in isolation. Even bilateral or multilateral effort in this direction is likely to fail unless backed by a framework of regional cooperation on both political and economic dimensions. Comprehensive and non-exclusive regional cooperation is not only conducive to peace and security, but will also promote stable economic development, and national growth and prosperity at the level of the individual. 'The region's only chance to compete and to catch up – despite past mistakes – is through economic cooperation. Cooperation, and cooperation alone, will increase the productivity of extant resources and amenities: human capital, climate, location, and historical and cultural uniqueness' (Fishelson 1992: 107).

Previous attempts in this direction have largely failed. Following again the two-level-game framework described in previous chapters, we aim in this chapter to demonstrate that any future effort to integrate the region into the newly arising world order in a cooperative way is also bound to experience similar failure unless regional domestic forces are carefully taken into account and cooperative incentives on the international scene are balanced with the expectations and open demands of the domestic forces that shape the region.

Economic cooperation in the Middle East: A conceptual framework and assessment

As recent attempts to promote regional cooperation in the Middle East increased, a common underlying assumption became evident. All parties involved seemed to assume that economic cooperation could contribute to a peaceful settlement and normalisation of relations between Israel and the Arabs, as well as other animosities within the region at large. So far, we have also maintained this assumption. However, as noted earlier in Chapter 2, separation and clarification of the nature, scope and dynamics of these two different kinds of cooperation, i.e. economic and political, and their degree of dependency upon each other is of utmost importance for the understanding and design of successful cooperation schemes. Accordingly, before beginning to discuss the potential for economic cooperation in the Middle East, we need to clarify some aspects of the underlying logic of the assumption about regional economic and political cooperation.

Our discussion of regional cooperation mechanisms in Chapters 2 and 3 points to two distinct paths for creating regional cooperation which fit into our two-level-game framework quite well. The first path is created primarily at the negotiation table through a legal political process. Using our two-level-game terminology, this path is created at Level I and gradually permeates down to actors at Level II. The second occurs on its own among interacting domestic actors of the region who are fuelled by purely economic incentives. Firms, business associations and other economic interest groups, following their own strategies that are aimed to maximise their microeconomic gains, create in reality institutions for regional cooperation. This happens even if legal mechanisms are not present. Clearly, in cases of successful cooperation both paths are at work simultaneously, though one typically dominates the other. However, our diagnosis in Chapters 2 and 3 is that cooperation at Level I is likely to fail if it is not accompanied by cooperation at Level II. In other words, Level I arrangements are neither necessary nor sufficient for a successful regional cooperation mechanism whereas Level II cooperation is both necessary and sufficient in the long term.

In this chapter, and also later in Chapter 7, we assess the likelihood of regionalisation in the Middle East from the economic as well as political perspective. Both political and economic dimensions of cooperation in the region have Level I and Level II components. However, due to its nature, economic cooperation is more of a Level II phenomenon than a phenomenon played by Level I actors. Clearly, though, it needs crucial Level I arrangements to succeed. Accordingly, it should be stressed that economic cooperation in the short run is neither necessary nor sufficient for a peaceful settlement of long-standing animosities in the region (Tuma 1995: 288). As long as militarised political conflict continues, it is very unlikely that any significant willingness on all sides to engage in economic exchange will be observed.

While animosities continue between any two parties, not only will there be no significant opportunity to engage in economic exchange between groups in these countries, but significant impact by third parties on the economic relations of the parties involved will also be observed. The Arab boycott of Israel has not only limited the ability of Israel to trade with the region's economies but has also severely curtailed significant trade relations with other third parties like Japan. The Arab boycott, which began with the establishment of the state of Israel, has led to a strict refusal by the Arab countries to buy products that are produced in Israel or that have any discernible Israeli input. Indirectly, Arab countries also inhibit trade with any firms that do business with Israel or with identifiably Jewish owners. As such, the Arab boycott constitutes the most important barrier for direct foreign investment in Israel. 'The indirect boycott reduces the willingness of some foreign firms, most notably Japanese firms, to operate in Israel' (Clawson 1992: 92). This severely limits Israeli access to Japanese electronics technology.

The settlement of long-standing conflicts in the region is not solely motivated by potential economic benefits to be reaped due to cooperation among the countries of the Middle East. Peace has its own, relatively independent, dynamics that do not need to be supported by economic benefits. Peace in the region will end the suffering and loss of life that has been going on for generations. The economic benefits that are supposed to follow peaceful settlement of regional conflicts is necessary, but not sufficient, for full exploitation of the region's economic potential in a newly arising world economic order (El-Naggar and El-Erian 1993: 207).

Chatelus (1996: 95) notes that 'it is essential to put an end to the state of emergency which for the last 50 years has been used to justify the most irrational economic conduct and the distortions that have cost the area so much'. For any significant impact of peace on economic relations of the region it is critical that the resolution of the conflict is perceived by all parties involved as real, durable and comprehensive (El-Naggar and El-Erian 1993: 206). As noted in Chapter 4, economic decisions in the past have been shaped not on the basis of economic benefit and efficiency but instead largely on the basis of strategic military incentives. Cooperation in the economic arena depends on shifts in decision-making criteria of the relevant parties in each and every one of the countries in the region.

Like most decisions, economic cooperation decisions are also forward looking. Unless the parties involved perceive peaceful settlement of protracted conflicts in the region as acceptable, comprehensive and long-standing, non-economic strategic considerations will not be abandoned. The duration of a peace settlement critically depends on its being perceived by the relevant parties involved as real and comprehensive, thus addressing the pressing issues of concern in strategic as well as economic dimensions. If one of a group of parties in the region perceives a critical issue for itself is being left out of the peace settlement it will exert pressure to break the peace for a new settlement. Unless all parties see the settlement as their own best option for the long-term political as well as economic decisions, it will not be shaped on the basis of a cooperative approach, but instead will continue to be dominated by strategic military considerations. In other words, any successful peace settlement will have to be inclusionary and take into account the long run incentives of all relevant parties.

Solingen (1996a) underlines the pivotal role played by domestic coalitions in creating and strengthening regional cooperation. The determining impact of domestic coalitions on regional cooperation mechanisms depends critically on democratisation and economic liberalisation reforms: 'there is a distinct possibility that democracy might bear a generally positive relationship to cooperation, but it is equally possible that political freedom is neither necessary nor a sufficient condition for the emergence of regional cooperation'. Solingen (1996a: 86) argues that two basic types of coalition arise in the analysis of regional cooperation schemes: one favouring economic liberalisation and another opposing it. The very nature of liberalising coalitions leads such coalitions to support regional cooperation for three main reasons. First is that regional cooperation frees up resources to carry out reform and liberalisation in domestic markets. If regional conflicts persist, economic resources will have to be allocated for policies extending a given state's militaristic and other strategic ambitions, leaving the domestic markets insufficient financial power. Second, stances that follow a cooperative policy typically reduce the importance of the military, industrial collaborators that are economically dependent on military activities, and also advocates of nationalistic rhetoric and policy. (All of these three groups are inherently against economic liberalisation and would prefer extensive state intervention and the regulation of markets in order to create distinct advantages for themselves.) Third, cooperative regional arrangements reduce foreign investors' risks in a given economy and open up possibilities for more intense economic collaboration in international markets thus helping the general objective of liberalising a given economy.

Nationalist–populist coalitions, on the other hand, would oppose regional cooperation. These groups 'have affinity with import-substituting models of industrialisation and classical populist programs, involving a strong, active government controlling prices, protecting workers, wages and state enterprises, allocating credit at low interest rates and dispensing rents to private industry' (Solingen 1996a: 91). For reasons similar to those previously given for groups supportive of regional cooperation, these groups would oppose it. A cooperative regional arrangement makes it difficult, if not impossible to justify extensive military outlays and protection of some markets and industrial groups. When no close-by enemy exists, the myth of a protective state becomes less and less convincing which further restricts the ability to 'justify societal extraction and the allocation of state resources to a wide array of economic, military and confessional interests' Solingen (1996a: 91). These two analytical groups of coalitions will thus shape the outcome at Level II. For successful regional cooperative mechanisms, then, the emphasis should be placed on developing and supporting those coalitions that favour economic liberalisation.

When and if the peace settlement is perceived as the region's long-term and most fundamental institutional framework, then the challenge shifts from the international environment to the domestic decision-making apparatus, shaped by interactions amongst various interest groups, i.e. it shifts to Level II interactions. There is considerable potential for new markets and business opportunities in the region. Groups that stand to significantly profit from increased economic cooperation are all expected to contribute significantly to efforts for more cooperative economic or political relationships in the region. From a two-level-game perspective, those groups that see a beneficial future for the markets on both sides of the conflict are expected to push for more cooperative stands at the negotiation tables. Fischer (1995: 434–446) underlines the fact that 'most economies in the Middle East need large-scale reconstruction and reform, with or without regional integration. … However, the constituencies for change have not yet clearly emerged.' Clearly, the non-existence or non-saliency of these constituencies depend critically on 'the prior existence of mutual trust, which can only be based on politics and is not simply a matter of agreement between technical specialists' (Chatelus 1996: 95). When these latent beneficiary groups are ignored, those groups who stand to lose most will be most vocal in blocking cooperative action.[1]

As noted in Chapter 4, non-economic principles that shaped the decision-makers and policy priorities of the region in the past have created their corresponding supporting social groups. The Middle Eastern bureaucracy and military being at the core of this support group for the pre-settlement, intense conflict period form the legitimacy base for misallocation of resources in these countries. For peace to lead to full exploitation of economic potential of the region through cooperative arrangements there needs to be significant structural reform in the region's economies. As noted by El-Naggar and El-Erian:

> for the potential economic benefits of peace to be fully realised the resolution of the conflict would need to be supported by the sustained implementation of policies aimed at eliminating financial imbalances, improving the pricing structure of the economies, and enhancing their supply responsiveness through fundamental structural reforms in the areas of, inter alia, trade liberalisation, and deregulation of domestic economic activities.
>
> (El-Naggar and El-Erian 1993: 207)

These reforms will be opposed by many powerful social groups not only on the basis of economic rationale but also for ideological and strategic reasons. 'In certain cases there are military lobbies that profit from the present situation and will try to limit the demilitarisation of the economy as much as possible' (Chatelus 1996: 97).

The strategy to be followed for a successful implementation of structural reform is complex.[2] While some neo-liberal economists argue that elimination of the role of the state in the economy is the key to successful reform, others argue that an 'embedded autonomy' of the state is necessary for successful reforms (Evans 1992). For neo-liberals, state intervention creates market distortion and rent-seeking behaviour leading to costly and unproductive investment. In contrast to this approach, Evans argues that only those states that operate according to market logic and internalise the market signals – but are free from the penetration of various interest groups and can thus avoid falling prey to different demands and rent-seeking behaviour – can undertake successful reforms. The key to successful reform lies then, for Evans, not in eliminating the role of the state in the economy but in restructuring it.

How these reforms are put into effect is a source of yet another controversy. While some economists defend the view that a technocratic approach to reform is necessary and provides the best results, others argue that consolidation of economic reforms might in fact hinge on the governability of democracies (Haggard and Kaufman 1992). Indeed, discussion and negotiation of the reform program as well as transparency might go a long way towards filling the credibility gap in a reform strategy. As Przeworski *et al.* (1993: 209) argue,

> if the (reform) program is forged in negotiations with diverse political forces, it will emerge in a form that will be easier for these forces to support. Such a program may retard the pace of reforms and may eliminate the element of surprise necessary for stabilisation measures. ... Yet, such a program may be more, not less, credible, because it creates political conditions for continuation of reforms.
>
> (Przeworski, *et al.* 1993: 209)

In short, how the reform program is implemented might have crucial implications for the credibility and success of both the state and the reform program.

Despite all these difficulties, structural reforms are indispensable in the Middle East. In the absence of such reforms, peace will not lead to increased cooperation, which would then result in improved integration of the region into the world economy and the resolution of long-standing economic problems of the Middle East. It should also be noted that even in political contexts favourable to demilitarisation, the economics of converting resources invested in military installations would be costly, especially in the short run. Such difficulties are apparent from the experiences of western democracies in the aftermath of the Cold War. Large numbers of military personnel will have to be absorbed by the civilian economy and that certainly requires high rates of growth. Such a capacity for extra labour supply in these economies needs both extra financial assistance as well as expanding markets. Flow of financial resources as well as expanding markets are only two of the expected benefits of regional integration in the post-peace-settlement era of the Middle East that will facilitate such transitional problems.

Our discussion in Chapter 2 diagnosed a new trend in regionalisation in the world economy. Simple mutual liberalisation of trade have failed especially in the developing world successfully to create exploitable advantages to member countries eventually leading to de facto suspension of these regional integration schemes. Following the unprecedented rise of economic liberalisation coupled with equally forceful democratisation in the developing world, harmonisation of institutional structures and coordination of economic policies within regional boundaries is seen as the recipe for successful regional economic cooperation. As indicated previously, incompatibility of relevant interest groups' incentives within regional arrangements is the most compelling challenge facing successful regional cooperation. Instead of trade liberalisation, isolated from country-specific programmes for industrialisation and development of production systems, the newly emerging regional cooperation schemes aim to create regional production systems.

Theoretically, proponents of the so-called 'new' or 'strategic' trading policies argue that active state policies to create a favourable environment for the transfer of rent from international markets as well as to follow strategically aimed policies to create positive externalities, enhancing comparative advantages of countries, are necessary for improved trade gains in world markets.[3] Applying the same logic to the problems of economic regionalisation, we observe that mechanisms for regional cooperation aim to impose some common rules of conduct, institutional harmonisation and coordination, as well as eliminate barriers to investment following policies to create worldwide competitive sectors in a given region.

The need for economic reforms in the Middle East, as argued for in this section, should be evaluated as a necessary step towards harmonising regional economic structures and institutions. Coupled with political liberalisation, such reforms will necessarily undermine the power of traditional regional groups that block initiatives towards more regional economic cooperation. Incentives of relevant groups within each country will accordingly be harmonised and economic policymaking in various countries of the region would then be expected to complement and support each other on the sole basis of economic rationale for more efficiency. Only then will countries be able to cooperate with each other, not only for mutual economic gains but also for the enhancement of security in the region. Since only then will the domestic support base (Level II actors) in each country be able to voice demands for enhanced regional economic as well as political interaction. However, the support of the domestic base for a policy change in this direction will be forceful enough to bring about political will and change.

It should also be noted at this juncture that economic cooperation necessarily requires a certain degree of complementarity between countries. Many have seen the lack of economic complementarities in the Middle East as the main economic explanation for the weakness of intra-regional relations (Chatelus 1996; Clawson 1992; Fischer 1995). The scope of cooperation among countries with very similar factors of production will be limited. Complementarity of the goods and products produced as well as complementarity in the supply sectors are necessary conditions for successful economic cooperation. On the demand side, enlarged markets provide opportunities for increased returns on large-scale production which eventually lead to improved competitiveness in the international market. Complementarity on the supply side, coupled with opportunities for economies of scale due to enlarged markets for traded commodities, will then tend to create efficient productive capacity that can be targeted for a larger market due to regional cooperative arrangements.

The degree of complementarity among the nations of the region is at best limited. As discussed in Chapter 4, the region's economies resemble each other with respect to the composition of the respective GNPs. Most countries produce a limited set of goods that are (1) not in high demand in other countries of the region and that are (2) highly competitive in international markets. Accordingly, 'there is no general category of commodities for which intra-Middle Eastern trade is very important' (Fischer 1995: 436). This poor trade relationship among the Middle Eastern countries is surprising since trade regulation in the region is seemingly supportive of regional trade. The oil-rich Gulf Cooperation Council (GCC) countries have practically zero tariff rates for most goods, including food (Fischer 1995: 436). Just the opposite situation is observed, however, in non-oil producing countries, excluding Israel. Importance of trade barriers are also apparent in a UNCTAD (1986) study of tariffs:

> [A]verage tariffs in Syria, Turkey and Libya ranged between 27 to 34 per cent and actually reached 100 per cent in Iran. Over 70 per cent of Turkey's imports encountered some form of non-tariff measure while this ratio was 99 per cent in the case of Iran.
>
> (Yeats 1995: 25)

Given the balance of payment advantages of oil-rich countries, the lack of exports from non-oil producing countries to GCC countries can only be explained by the fact that the structure of demand in the GCC countries cannot be met by non-oil producing economies, that is, whatever they offer can be obtained cheaper and at a higher quality from other producers outside the region. From a realist perspective, partner countries in regional cooperative schemes need to become somewhat similar in their economic and strategic objectives before they surrender some of their national autonomy. Yeats (1995) also notes that 'transport links within the region can be an important constraint to increased trade as most established liner conference routes follow a North–South pattern'.[4] Unless cooperation increases for the development of transportation infrastructure, further development of regional trade will continue to be hampered.

As we emphasised in Chapter 4, the most important impediment facing regional economic cooperation and trade in the Middle East is the low degree of product diversification in the region. Not only is there a limited number of efficient industries in the region's economies, but whatever is being produced in one country is typically not complementary to another country's production. Some degree of complementarity exists between oil-rich countries and those countries of the region that have a considerable experience and quite a large number of efficient manufacturing industries. Similarly, some of the countries of the region do not have sufficient, nor efficient enough, agricultural production while others, such as Israel, Turkey, Lebanon and Syria, have developed relatively efficient industries in processed and unprocessed food. Some degree of complementarity in the region exists in the telecommunications, iron and steel, glass and glassware sectors. Israel has the only internationally competitive telecommunications sector in the region. None of the other countries can match that capacity. Similarly, Turkey has a dominant position in the iron and steel, glass and glassware sectors.

This diagnosis of the sectors, in which countries exhibit revealed comparative advantage, is not of much help if one is more interested in the sectors or products that have had the greatest opportunity to expand. Yeats (1995) identifies 'dynamic' or, simply, fastest-growing export items in the Middle East.[5] Clearly, these items represent competitive product groups in the region and, with continued growth in the export of these items, they may come to occupy an important share of the region's export earnings. Yeats (1995: 12) also notes that diagnosing these items is necessary for 'ensuring that foreign trade barriers are not imposed on these items, or that existing restrictions are removed'. Yeats' (1995) list of 'dynamic' products is dominated by manufactured goods that require locally available natural resources and that are produced by above-average labour intensive technologies.

> This raises the question of whether other similar types of exports could be developed on the basis of further processing of domestically available natural resources? Petroleum based chemical and plastic industries may be one such suitable sector for further export development given the availability of crude petroleum in many Middle East countries. The fact that these plants require sizeable capital investments could make multi-country regional investment in jointly owned plants to process and refine petroleum an attractive option.
>
> (Yeats 1995: 12)

Furthermore, it is also noticeable that OECD countries have imported significant quantities of fresh vegetables, fruits and nuts from the region. Further processing these agricultural products and increasing their value may not only increase the export opportunities in these products but also create a significant number of jobs. Similarly, Yeats (1995: 12) notes that unprocessed tobacco, cotton and oil seeds along with crude minerals (such as natural asphalt, clays, borates and mica) offer important market opportunities.

It is a commonly held assertion among economists that the free trade of goods and services as well as free flow of factors of production will improve regional welfare. However, if those who can afford to import have a set of preferences for goods and services that cannot be met by those who need to export, such an optimistic policy change will not help the region's economies. On the other hand, consider the situation if those countries, whose preferences and needs for goods and services can be easily met by regional economies, cannot afford to import these in significant amounts. In that situation, not much will change even if these poorer countries were to free their trade regulations. Given these difficulties, there is still at least one reason to be hopeful for increased trade among countries of the Middle East, provided that the necessary Level I initiative is taken. Another issue concerns considerations of increased Level II interaction and support for Level I cooperative efforts. However, in both instances, de facto cooperation among Level II players cannot arise without either significant help from the Level I negotiations or without first establishing political settlements at that level.

The first consideration concerns the fact that factor endowments in the region are highly complementary; that is, oil-rich countries of the Gulf Area have abundant capital with highly flexible financial services at their disposal whereas non-oil-producing countries of the region are typically labour abundant. Moreover, the capital-abundant countries are typically engaged in immense projects that require significant labour inputs that could be supplied by the region's labour-abundant economies. The capital-scarce countries need capital inflow to finance their development efforts that could be directly supplied by the oil-rich economies through not only loans or other types of arrangements, but also by remittances of workers they send to oil-rich economies. Clearly, to a limited extent, this type of exchange of factors of production is perhaps the only significant cooperation that exists in the Middle East. However, as noted in Chapter 4, 'the mobility of these factors is largely subject to political and nationalistic decisions rather than economic rationality, e.g. labor and capital mobility … is highly restricted regardless of market demand' (Tuma 1995: 292). It is unrealistic to expect that Level II actors could ignore the restrictions imposed on them by their governments and go ahead and respond to market forces. First steps here should be taken by Level I actors to settle their differences and free the mobility of factors of production within the region as much as possible.

An institutional framework within which especially international as well as regional financial resources can be channelled to a coherent set of regional development projects is lacking in the Middle East. Fischer (1995: 442) rightly argues that, given the existing political cleavages and rivalries in the region, the existing cooperative organisations such as the OPEC Fund and other Arab aid agencies will not be effective in providing such a framework. Moreover, participation of other external powers might bring valuable funds from the international markets as well as providing the necessary political balance to the process. Fischer supports the option of a development bank similar to the World Bank or simply the Middle Eastern Bank for Reconstruction and Development (MEBRD). Although many conceivable difficulties exist in such an institutional framework the need for an organisation still justifies the efforts to build it.[6]

The second issue concerns the existing perceptions of Level II actors concerning their counterparts in other countries of the region. It is clear from theoretical considerations as well as empirical assessments that open economies with reduced, or preferably abolished, barriers to trade and barriers to engage in cooperative productive economic activities in the region will increase incomes in the region. This, in turn, will enhance regional competitiveness in the world economy and help regional economies gain a new momentum in their development efforts. However, this fact in no way ensures that actors, especially at Level II, will choose this option. Peoples of the Middle East have long been opposed to each other. In addition, they have frequently been engaged in militarised conflicts which have resulted in considerable loss of life, damaged lives and consequent suffering attributed to each other's actions. Even if considerable hurdles at Level I negotiations are resolved to an extent and a certain degree of cooperative agreement is achieved, given the existing mutual hatred of peoples of the region it will be difficult to convince them to engage in cooperative economic linkages with each other. This is primarily a political preference of the masses. Shifts in these preferences will take time and careful fine-tuning on the part of the Level I players.

After long-standing conflict between the two, it is only normal to expect that in the short run Arabs will be reluctant if not openly opposed to buying Israeli goods, and Israeli businessmen will not be wholeheartedly forthcoming in cutting business deals with their Arab counterparts (Clawson 1992: 91). The results of a series of interviews with Israeli and Palestinian business and academic communities by Hisham Awartani and Samir Awad of the Center for Palestine Research and Studies in 1994 provide support for this line of thinking. Awartani and Awad underline that

> the case for joint ventures is strong, reaping complementarities and comparative advantages for both Palestinians and Israelis. Joint ventures have the potential to generate employment and create trade. They can increase capital flows, technology transfers and expertise exchange between the two partners, stimulating both economies. There are also political gains to joint ventures since they can serve as a catalyst for and guarantee of peace by raising the costs of dissociation.
>
> (Awartani and Awad 1994: 42)

The Israeli as well as the Palestinian perspectives are dominated by political concerns. The Israeli side sees normalisation of economic relations as a high priority with a potential to further develop political legitimacy and as the final blow to the Arab boycott. From an economic perspective,

> the Israelis appreciate joint ventures as an advanced form of normalisation of relations. Their perception of joint ventures as 'stabilisers of peace' is especially true in infrastructure projects, which have greater potential for interdependency. Similarly, Israelis attach high hopes on commercial joint ventures, since many leading Israeli economists believe that trade with Arab countries may not be very promising for Israel due to high labor costs in Israel and their effect on the price of her exports. Joint ventures may provide the answer to the problem of how competitively to interact economically in the region from an Israeli perspective.
>
> (Awartani and Awad 1994: 42)

The Palestinian perspective is equally politically motivated. They seem to emphasise timing of such joint ventures as the most important issue.

> Political legitimacy could work both ways through economic interdependency, as the Israelis are not the only party who could benefit from such a development. However, a premature normalisation of relations can have adverse effects on political leverage. If Palestinians promote normalisation at this stage, the Israelis have no incentive to further negotiate outstanding political issues, such as settlements and Jerusalem. … Notwithstanding this cautious attitude, however, most Palestinian businessmen and economists seem to agree that economic benefits of joint ventures can be very strong. These projects can be considerably competitive, a prospect with both positive and negative aspects for local business. Improvement in quality standards resulting from greater competition can be very good for business development and for consumers. However, increased competition may hurt those Palestinian firms which fail in raising their competitiveness at the same pace as that of joint venture projects. The failure to do so may cause detrimental effects on the economy, as some firms may suffer or even collapse.
>
> (Awartani and Awad 1994: 43)

Potentially, this divisive dynamic of joint ventures between Palestinians and Israelis may create a dual and hostile grouping of business groups against not only the joint ventures but also the peace process itself.

It is extremely important to note that especially Palestinians consider joint ventures as a 'prelude to Israeli economic domination of the Arab world'. The implications for further political settlements between the Israelis and Palestinians are far reaching since the perception in the Arab world that Palestinians are in a compromising position may lead them to abandon further settlement of issues regarding the Palestinians. Such a view of the end of the peace settlement accordingly leads to an uncompromising position of Palestinians until political settlement is finalised.

This worry of the Palestinians that there is a serious danger of losing supporters, if not being left alone in their long struggle for recognition first and political rights next, is not totally unwarranted. The peace process alone has greatly improved the Israeli position in the international community. Since the Madrid

Conference in 1991 Israel's diplomatic representation increased by approximately 60 per cent reaching a record number of diplomatic representations with a total of 160 states in 1997. Special note should be made of the establishment of links with the two Asian giants: China and India. Such critical links hold tremendous strategic and economic potential. In 1997, Israeli diplomatic missions are present in all but 5 Asian countries: North Korea, Pakistan, Afghanistan, Bangladesh and Bhutan. Similarly, Israelis have been very successful in initiating relations with non-Arab predominantly Moslem countries, such as Albania, Gambia, Nigeria, Azerbaijan, Kazakhstan, Kyrgyzstan, Turkmenistan, Tajikistan and Uzbekistan. Considering the recent amelioration in the late 1990s of its relations with Turkey, Israel's political and economic leverage in the Moslem world has considerably increased since the start of the peace process. In addition to all these successes – coupled with equally impressive developments in Israeli relations with the Vatican and African countries, and consequent amelioration of its position within international organisations notwithstanding – Israel's relations with the Arab world have also significantly improved. In addition to full diplomatic ties with Egypt, Jordan and Mauritania, an Israeli liaison office is functioning in Morocco, an interest office has been opened in Tunisia, and a trade office in Oman. Israel also has contacts with Qatar and Bahrain in the Persian Gulf. Although this certainly does not means that Israeli policies and positions are being fully accepted in its newly built links, the developing ties are clear indications that Israel is beginning to break its isolation from the world community and is communicating its interest directly to Level I actors. One of the first concrete expressions of the change which has occurred in the region as a result of the peace process was the public declaration by the Gulf States on 1 October 1994 to support a review of the Arab boycott of Israel, which would in effect abolish the secondary and tertiary boycott against Israel.

An equally important finding of Awartani and Awad's (1994: 38) research is the reaction obtained from the following question: 'What do you think is the extent to which Palestinian public opinion will accept joint ventures if the PLO clearly agrees to these projects?' While 23 per cent of the respondents stated no opinion, 36 per cent said that 'the majority of the people will accept the idea' whereas 41 per cent indicated that 'public opinion will refuse it even if the PLO accepts it'. Clearly, the political cost of a cooperative attitude by Level I actors – the PLO in this case – is considerable due to resistance by Level II actors. Given these costs, manoeuvring room for Level I players on the Palestinian side will be severely constrained until Level II reactions are smoothed.

The necessity for structural reforms in the regional economies will not only serve to create Level II players that are open to cooperation but also create dynamics that remedy the existing hostile predisposition of the peoples of the Middle East. 'The Middle East countries reflect almost totally irreconcilable variations of regimes, levels of participation in governance, ideology, sources of decision making, and political history, tradition and policy orientation' (Tuma 1995: 293). Despite Level I settlement of differences in the region, reconciliation of historically based ideological differences that manifest themselves best in the form of governance types can only be realised in the middle to long term. As noted previously, it is quite clear that the model of regional cooperation and integration in other parts of the world cannot be directly applied in the region. A transitional period of confidence-building is required to eliminate the roots of long-standing conflicts especially at Level II. Democratisation coupled with serious economic liberalisation reforms is necessary to achieve these objectives. Such an institutional change has important implications for the short-to-long-term peace process in the region. We leave this discussion for Chapter 7.

An equally important dimension of cooperative arrangements is technological equity among potential regional partners. Technologically stronger economies typically dominate weaker ones, and dependent relations with the stronger economy tend to surface after regional cooperation arrangements. The fact that the weaker as well as the stronger sides are mutually aware of this possibility will constitute a serious barrier to regional economic cooperation. Being in an advantageous position, stronger economies will be much more willing to cooperate whereas the weaker sides will be reluctant to engage in a potentially dependent relationship with the stronger side. As has been underlined by Awartani and Awad's (1994) research, the stronger economy will also have a disadvantageous position, since its labour market will typically be more developed and thus more expensive compared to that of the weaker economy. Accordingly, labour costs will be an impediment to trade with the weaker economy.

Although trade and other forms of cooperation will benefit both sides, relative gains will not be shared equally. Given the fact that political animosities exist in the period prior to economic cooperation, potential regional partners, especially the technologically weaker ones, will be reluctant to accept economic cooperation due to inequity of sharing future economic benefits. Accordingly, political concerns of potential economic dependency on the stronger sides will dominate the negotiation phase and be a serious barrier to enhanced regional economic cooperation. Given such potential inequity in sharing economic benefits of cooperation, countries will be reluctant to surrender a certain amount of their economic sovereignty within an economic cooperation arrangement since any such arrangement will have important political implications within the underlying dependency relationship. Accordingly, mutual compromise on the economic front will be hard to reach (Tuma 1995).

Such difficulties for economic as well as political cooperation in the region have been recognised. From an optimistic point of view the potentially dominant position of the Israeli economy should not be overemphasised. Other countries of the region also stand to gain from increased cooperative links within the region. Considering the fact that most of these economies have long been engaged in liberating and restructuring their economies, such a move towards more cooperative economic relations within the Middle East is only a natural development.[7]

The opposing view, however, emphasises the economies of scale gained by the Israeli economy due to their new access to the huge Middle Eastern market. The addition of the relatively small Israeli economy constitutes not much of a gain in this respect for the other partners in the peace process. Adding to this, the relative inefficiency and non-competitiveness of the Arab economies underlines the disadvantageous position of the Arab world. Moreover, the relatively more modern Israeli economy will be much more attractive to foreign investors, which will also have open access to the Middle Eastern market by simply locating themselves in Israel.

The optimistic response to these challenges is simply that overall long-term gains from cooperation will be so great that potential inequities in sharing the benefits in the short-term will be overshadowed. The cooperative arrangements should be all-inclusive leaving no crucial partner outside. They should involve capital from the Gulf, cheap manpower from Egypt and other Arab countries, water from Turkey and Israeli technical know-how and management (Chatelus 1996: 96). Only then can peace and cooperation be institutionalised and only then will the resulting benefits satisfy all parties involved.

As we emphasised in Chapter 4, the climate and endowments of natural resources, with the exception of oil, are quite similar across the region. However, the same is not true for the endowment of physical and human capital in the countries of the Middle East. Tables 5.1a to 5.1c report capital stock per worker at 1985 international prices for five Middle Eastern countries: Iran, Israel, Morocco, Syria and Turkey for the 1965–92 period. Israeli non-residential capital stock per worker is approximately 30 per cent higher than both Iran and Syria whereas Turkey and Morocco only have, respectively, approximately 30 and 10 per cent of the Israeli capital stock per worker (Table 5.1a). Israel's advantageous position remains unchanged when capital stock in producer durables (Table 5.1b) as a percentage of total non-residential capital stock is taken into consideration. Israel is by far ahead of the rest of the group in allocating capital stock to producer durables that is directly relevant for productive capacity. Although Turkish capital stock per worker is below that of Iran and Syria, it allocates a higher percentage to producer durables than both these countries. Transportation equipment as a percentage of total non-residential capital stock per worker (Table 5.1c; Morocco not included) is highest in Syria among the countries reported. However, for all countries transportation equipment is only a small portion of total capital stock. Despite the fact that Israel has considerably higher capital stock per worker, the level of transportation equipment still remains above those of the other countries in the region.

Measurement of capital stock is quite difficult and is typically prone to measurement error. However, the general tendency in the above data is clearly in favour of Israel, and as such creates an obstacle for regional cooperation arrangements:

> Dualities or major gaps in technology levels between Israel and the other countries and in economic wealth between the oil-rich countries and the others allow domination of certain countries by others. This is contrary to cooperation. These Middle East countries range so widely in their endowments, levels of development, and growth prospects that the better endowed countries may find it too taxing to cooperate with the poverty stricken less endowed countries.
>
> (Tuma 1995: 293)

Table 5.1 (a) Non-residential capital stock per worker, 1965–92

						% of Israel's capital stock				
Year	*Iran*	*Israel*	*Morocco*	*Syria*	*Turkey*	*Iran*	*Israel*	*Morocco*	*Syria*	*Turkey*
1965	2,718	12,179	1,482	9,705	2,365	22.3	100	12.2	79.7	19.4
1970	4,522	14,824	1,686	9,671	3,354	30.5	100	11.4	65.2	22.6
1975	6,696	19,967	1,911	9,512	4,717	33.5	100	9.6	47.6	23.6
1980	10,442	21,578	2,669	13,442	6,513	48.4	100	12.4	62.3	30.2
1985	10,686	22,307	2,803	15,681	6,989	47.9	100	12.6	70.3	31.3
1990	15,548	21,453	1,991	14,994	7,589	72.5	100	9.3	69.9	35.4
1991	N|A	20,809	1,911	14,941	7,686	N|A	100	9.2	71.8	36.9
1992	N|A	21,618	1,832	14,463	7,626	N|A	100	8.5	66.9	35.3

Source: Penn World Table (Mark 5.6); see also Summers and Heston 1991
Note: 1985 international prices

(b) Capital stock per worker in producer durables, 1965–92

						% of Israel's capital stock				
Year	*Iran*	*Israel*	*Morocco*	*Syria*	*Turkey*	*Iran*	*Israel*	*Morocco*	*Syria*	*Turkey*
1965	19.6	35.5	11.6	9.5	26.3	55.2	100	32.7	26.8	74.1
1970	19.1	32.8	11.7	13.3	23.3	58.2	100	35.7	40.5	71.0
1975	19.5	38.7	12.1	17.1	27.2	50.4	100	31.3	44.2	70.3
1980	17.8	38.6	14.3	26.2	29.8	46.1	100	37.0	67.9	77.2
1985	15.2	42.5	13.3	23.2	28.5	35.8	100	31.3	54.6	67.1
1990	5.7	45.9	12.5	20.0	29.5	12.4	100	27.2	43.6	64.3
1991	N|A	47.6	12.5	20.3	29.9	N|A	100	26.3	42.6	62.8
1992	N|A	50.6	12.4	20.3	29.6	N|A	100	24.5	40.1	58.5

(c) Capital stock per worker in transportation equipment, 1965–92

						% of Israel's capital stock				
Year	*Iran*	*Israel*	*Morocco*	*Syria*	*Turkey*	*Iran*	*Israel*	*Morocco*	*Syria*	*Turkey*
1965	4	2	N|A	3	3	200	100	N|A	150	150
1970	4	2	N|A	4	2	200	100	N|A	200	100
1975	4	2	N|A	6	3	200	100	N|A	300	150
1980	3	2	N|A	10	3	150	100	N|A	500	150
1985	2	2	N|A	8	3	100	100	N|A	400	150
1990	N|A	2	N|A	6	3	N|A	100	N|A	300	150
1991	N|A	2	N|A	7	3	N|A	100	N|A	350	150
1992	N|A	3	N|A	6	3	N|A	100	N|A	200	100

Source: Penn World Table (version 5.6); see also Summers and Heston 1991

Similar views surface from the interviews conducted with business and academic circles in Israel and Palestine by Awartani and Awad (1994: 38) who find that 83 per cent of respondents agree with the statement that joint ventures between Israelis and Palestinians 'is a prelude to Israeli economic domination over the world'.

One possible way that Level I actors could alleviate the strains imposed by these fears, held by both the laymen as well as the academics, of domination by the stronger economies in the region, especially Israel, is to ensure that trade in the region is not dominated by a stronger partner. Chatelus (1996: 94) notes that 'there must be built-in safeguards to protect the interests of weaker parties and, if need be, the possibility of calling upon help from outside to guarantee this protection'. Once such safeguards are incorporated into the Level I negotiations and communicated to Level II actors their support could be much more easily obtained.

In conclusion, our discussion above indicates first of all that complementarity of traded goods and services in the region is limited. However, some sectors – such as processed and unprocessed food, iron and steel, telecommunications and glass and glassware – still offer opportunities for further development of regional trade. In addition, obvious complementarity in factor endowments, such as capital and labour, has not been adequately exploited due primarily to long-standing animosities in the region and its reflection on the political arena with a lack of political will to abolish non-economic barriers. One further complication in the region has been the prospect of economic domination by Israel due to its advantageous position in technological capabilities. An added complexity to the peace process is introduced by opposing perceptions of the two hostile sides for each other. While the Level II actors perceive each other as either intending to dominate the region or as not having the economic potential to benefit the other side, the capacity of Level I actors to broker a settlement becomes extremely tricky and renders the Level II side of the game an equally, if not more, important part of the whole process of peace-making efforts.

All in all, it seems quite unreasonable to expect a natural tendency among the region's countries to cooperate and trade with one another.

> Rather, attempt to improve and develop economic relations among the countries of the region should start from collaboration in functional areas, encouraging officials and private citizens of the different countries of the region to work together on subjects of mutual interest, leading gradually to more general economic relations.
>
> (Fischer 1995: 441)

A gradual development of relations 'predicated on the search for an effective pragmatic compromise between what the economy requires and what the state of political relations allow' seems a more realistic alternative (Chatelus 1996: 94).

As we tried to underline above, initiatives of cooperation will, in all likelihood, not be forthcoming from the domestic constituencies of the region in a decisive way. Such lack of incentives to cooperate intra-regionally can and should be promoted by a proper regulatory environment (as depicted above) following the necessary economic reforms towards more market oriented and relatively freer economies. Only then can a base of popular support for the impending cooperation mechanisms be created. From this perspective functional projects offer opportunities that can not only overcome possible popular resistances due to ideological reasons but also allow a cooperative spirit to permeate down to the masses.

Areas of potential economic cooperation in the Middle East

The literature on the Middle East peace process is full of expositions of numerous projects in varying degrees of complexity and detail. Our objective here is not to add a new list of projects to the literature. Clearly there are wide-ranging areas in which the Middle Eastern countries can cooperate, including water, energy-sharing arrangements, public health, tourism, telecommunications and canals. What we aim, instead, to demonstrate is how some of the fundamental projects that are on the table in the region can help establish what we call a 'functional approach to peace.' In other words, by exploring the dynamics of cooperation of the two major issues in the region, namely water and energy, we focus on the degree to which the Level II actors can play a constructive role. Our target is to utilise the cooperative projects on these two issues as examples to emphasise the importance of Level I but most importantly Level II actors. As elaborated throughout this book, only when the two-level dynamics – the intergovernmental ties and transnational pathways as well as the cross-level processes – are explored can we best analyse economic routes to peace. That is why, instead of giving a detailed account of the proposals on these issues, we will provide a discussion of the general principles upon which these functional projects need to be built and can indeed succeed.

Water issues

The scarcest natural resource in the Middle East that is of critical importance for the livelihood of masses is water. By all estimates Israel, Syria, Jordan, the West Bank and the Palestinian Authority in the region are currently using virtually all replenishable water sources which regularly fall short of the required necessities in dry years. 'Projections for water requirements for the coming fifty years forecast significant water deficits for many countries in the region as early as the year 2000. This deficit will increase significantly later' (Government of Israel 1995: ch. 4: 1).[8]

> Only Turkey and Lebanon amongst Middle Eastern countries have the water resources to meet current and all future water needs including those of agriculture. All other countries, including some of the major economies such as Egypt and Israel, need more than twice as much water as currently available to them in surface flows and renewable groundwater.
>
> (Allan and Mallat 1995: 1)

The basis of the problem is geographic and climatic; that is, precipitation in the region is typically deficient and average temperatures lead to rapid and massive evaporation. However, human sources of the water problem are not to be underestimated: one would expect that the management of the scarcest resource would be the most efficient and carefully planned. To the contrary, however, water resource management in the region leads to wasteful utilisation and deterioration of water sources and quality. Two aspects of the water problem need to be underlined for the future of the peace process in the region.

The first is that, due to the vital nature of water, disputes over it have largely been politicised very often leaving economic and technical aspects of the dispute obscure. The technical aspects of the water questions have always been at best ambiguous. Much contradictory information exchange can be identified that leaves the impression of deliberate misinformation on the subject (Chatelus 1996: 105). Shapland notes that

> the importance of agriculture in the minds of Middle Eastern decision-makers ... reflects their perception of its strategic and economic value. Their unwillingness to espouse policies aimed at cutting back the share of water given to agriculture may often be based on internal political considerations.
> (Shapland 1995: 317)

National ideology in Israel critically depends on creating and sustaining fertile agricultural land not only as a means for 'building up the land' but also as a way to populate remote areas for defensive purposes. Besides, due to food security considerations discussed above policy-makers in the region seem also to have an eye on maintaining people in the agricultural sector as a means to control already problematic urbanisation. Subsidies in the agricultural sector not only provide cheap inputs for the export sectors and save increasingly scarce foreign exchange, but also provide incentives not to migrate to the cities.

The second is the fact that the international legal basis of water sharing from a river source has largely been a source of conflict in the region rather than a means of easing the existing tensions. A disputed legal basis on the topic has led nations to resolve their differences largely on an ad hoc basis through bilateral negotiations. However, such an approach in the Middle East has proved to be detrimental to the process since the rivers typically cover more than just two countries and involvement of many parties is necessary to resolve the long-standing issues.

In addition, comprehensive measures to be taken to improve both the demand and the supply sides of the water shortage in the region require huge amounts of financial investment.

> In order to even contain current trends of deterioration, required investment ranges between [US]$200–300 million dollars a year for the coming two decades. In order to gain substantial improvement in the current and expected situation, approximately US$9–10 billion will be needed within the coming decade. Long-term solutions involving the creation of additional water sources

> involve time and money-intensive projects and heftier and highly concentrated investment schedules. All projects involve investment in physical infrastructure as well as managerial programs and administration. Some require allocations in research and development as well, in order to develop new and improve the cost effectiveness of existing technologies.
>
> (Government of Israel 1995: ch. 4: 1).

Clearly, such sums of money cannot be obtained from those countries directly benefiting from the projects since none of them possess significant natural resources such as oil. Since no long-term settlement of hostilities in the region is possible without a credible solution to the water conflict in the region, both technical as well as financial aspects of the proposed projects have to be resolved. Existing hostilities in the region have led to a block of effective use of international financing of expensive water projects. The most important international lender, the World Bank, has developed a policy to turn down an application for funding if another riparian objects to the project. This policy has been initiated as a result of

> Turkish protests against Syrian proposals for the Asi river between 1949 and 1956. ... The blocking of Bank funding has also been used by Israel against Jordan and Syria (Unity Dam), by Syria against Turkey (Atatürk Dam) and by Iran against Turkey (Aras river). Other international lending institutions work with similar if less formal guidelines. In the face of Egyptian objections, the African Development Bank declined to lend Ethiopia funds for the development of sugar-cane plantations with water drawn from the Fincha barrage. The policy of [the] European Investment Bank is to finance projects on international rivers only when all states affected can reach agreement.
>
> (Shapland 1995: 310)

These restrictions on international resources are by no means enough to keep countries from undertaking these projects on their own. Turkey has financed its water projects in the South-Eastern Anatolia Development Project (GAP) largely dependent on domestic sources. However, this certainly added to its financial bottlenecks leading to delays in the project and efficiency losses.

In providing solutions to sensitive water problems, symbolic and political aspects should not be underestimated. For these very reasons, 'the region's external partners have a vital role to play in keeping negotiations calm by producing impartial technical studies of the problem dealing with needs, resources and the consequences of the policies pursued by the various parties involved' (Chatelus 1996: 106).

Both of the above mentioned aspects of water conflict restrict the solutions for efficient and peaceful use of water resources. The political nature of water-resource management coupled with highly controversial technical discussions lead to the dominant position of engineers in the process which ultimately results in emphasising the supply-side solutions of the problem to the exclusion of demand-management issues. Richards stresses that engineers

> tend to treat 'use' (demand) and 'availability' (supply) as if they were fixed quantities, varying only with population for use or rainfall for supply. Such an 'engineering view' is the basis for the conventional wisdom, now echoed by many political analysts, that Israel/Palestine suffers from a 'water shortage'.
> (Richards 1995b: 332)

We also stressed in Chapter 4 that from a comparative perspective the Middle East does not suffer from a shortage of available water but instead from the irregularity of the natural supply, the lack of distribution channels and inefficient resource management due to what we call 'war minded policy making'.

Pushing aside concerns about economic efficiency due to strategic considerations in a 'war minded' policy-approach leads to total neglect of price mechanisms in the management of water-resource allocations. Especially when inefficient use of resources is present, however, a pricing mechanism will be very effective in curbing demand. Since we have already underlined the inefficient use of water resources, simply resorting to shortage-driven pricing mechanisms should greatly reduce water demand as well as increase the efficiency of its use to a great extent.[9] Although water price elasticity is not a thoroughly studied subject in the region, similar studies in the US suggest that there is considerable scope for water saving by using pure economic rationale in water-pricing policies.[10]

It should also be stressed here that adjustments in water prices to curb demand alone will not work unless they are coupled with efficiency seeking regulations in agriculture and related credit policies. As long as agricultural products are subsidised, the marginal value product of water will be inflated and water demand will remain high. Similarly, since water-saving technology requires considerable capital investment, making credit available to farmers should induce them to adopt water-saving investments. Water and capital should be seen as substitutes. If one uses water less efficiently then savings on the capital requirements for efficient use of water can be created. Accordingly, subsidies in the credit markets will make the water-saving investments more likely, thus reducing the water demand and increasing efficiency of water use. At this juncture we should emphasise that successful policy choice and implementation on water issues critically depends on cooperation by Level II actors including players in financial and agricultural sectors. Unless mutually beneficial arrangements for all critical parties are adopted, their incentives will not be mutually compatible leading to the eventual collapse of the policies adopted.

The use of demand-side management of water resources, as presented above, critically depends on property rights upon the water sources, and this brings us back to the legal aspect of the dispute. We agree with Richards (1995b: 332) that heavier reliance on efficient pricing and market mechanisms would be politically very difficult to achieve since both sides of the existing disputes in the region see the water issue as not only a zero-sum game of allocation but also as an integral part of their national sovereignty. Accordingly, the resolution of the water conflict will critically depend on a Level I settlement of these sovereignty issues. 'Regional water planning must ultimately allocate water on political grounds. There is no scientific or economic basis for determining a *just sharing* of water resources' (Clawson 1992: 90, emphasis added). However, our argument here is that by exemplifying how market and pricing mechanisms can resolve local problems in the short run, it could create its own Level II constituencies that would be more willing and ready to cooperate than they are under present circumstances. Such constituencies would form the foundation of a larger constituency on both sides that would have to ratify the settlements at Level II. Moreover, since the demand-side aspects of water scarcity require an effective and efficient management, involvement of local constituencies in these projects would also create and mobilise local human resources that would maintain the economic use of these water resources. In short, once the Level I barriers – such as war minded policies, or politicisation of the water sharing – are removed, the Level II actors can easily be mobilised to demand a rational and effective management of scarce water resources.

Energy-sharing arrangements

The energy sector also offers immense opportunities for regional cooperation in the Middle East. As noted previously, vast oil reserves in the region not only present opportunities for trade between the region's countries on the basis of complementarity but also options for developing efficiency-increasing projects. Energy projects in the region can be grouped under two main headings. The first one concerns the power supply and interconnection of electricity grids and the other concerns the oil and natural-gas conveyance systems.

The basis of the idea of interconnecting the electricity grids is complementarity of electricity supply in countries of the region. Linking up the transmission grids can result in significant economic benefits for all involved parties due to two main reasons. 'At times of peak demand in a given country, the country would be able to buy electricity from the existing generating capacity of the other country, thus obviating the need to actuate the more expensive production reserves of its own. The overall amount of installed electrical power reserves which either country would have to maintain over time would be lower, enabling all countries to reduce their investments in the production infrastructure in the long run' (Government of Israel 1996: ch. 10: 2).

Such an interconnected grid system was in the making due to an agreement signed between Turkey, Syria, Iraq, Jordan and Egypt prior to the Gulf Crisis in 1991. During the peace process the building of a similar grid system was also proposed between Egypt, Israel, Jordan and the Palestinian Authority. Technical surveys for these projects have been completed since 1993 (Government of Israel 1996: 10–2). In the long run, the possibility is also open for a connection between all countries around the Mediterranean. Seasonal differences in electricity demand create possibilities to exploit energy-supply complementarities between the countries. Typically the northern side of the Mediterranean experiences high electricity demand due to electricity demand for heating during the winter; during this time the climate is milder on the southern side. In contrast there is high electricity demand in the southern countries in the summer due to air conditioning (Chatelus 1996: 109). If an interconnected grid system is present, all countries around the Mediterranean could use each other's excess electricity supply and energy investments in electricity generation.

Although an extensive system of pipelines exists in the Middle East to transport oil to ports in the Mediterranean, political conflicts have precluded export via pipelines from Saudi Arabia, Kuwait and other Gulf states. The price of transporting oil to western Europe around Africa in tankers is US$20 per ton whereas transporting oil by tankers from the eastern Mediterranean costs only around US$6 per ton (Government of Israel 1996: ch. 10: 11). These cost advantages are smaller for transportation to North America. Clearly, the cost advantage of using the Mediterranean ports is substantial. Countries involved in pipeline projects can easily offer competitive but still profitable prices by sharing the difference in transportation costs. These revenue estimates critically depend on developments in the oil markets in general and developments particularly in the economies of eastern Europe. Considering the fact that only half of a pipeline capacity of approximately 390 million tons per year is currently being used, new projects will inevitably be set up only when existing pipelines are being fully used. Some potentially beneficial projects exist linking the Saudi Arabian oil reserves to the port of Aqaba – which is already linked to the Mediterranean port of Ashkelon – or linking the Qatar oil fields first to the Iraqi pipeline system which in turn is linked through Turkey to the Turkish eastern Mediterranean port of Dörtyol. However, given the political problems concerning the use of the Iraqi pipeline system through Turkey in the post-Gulf War period, any new projects will have to rely on a peaceful settlement and efficient use of the existing link.

Natural gas is also abundant in the region. Turkey has relatively recently started extensive use of natural gas. Israel, due to its geographical isolation and political animosities, has not yet started to exploit this resource. Use of natural gas requires substantial investments by both the user and the supplier. In natural-gas deals the buyers commit themselves to a specific minimum amount on a regular basis in order to keep the system running. Natural gas can be imported either in gas or in liquefied form. Among the proposed projects are two pipelines: one would run from Egyptian reserves discovered relatively recently and the other from Qatar to Israel with potential extensions to Lebanon and Turkey. Projects for liquefied gas use the same sources but involve liquefaction plants at the source and gasification plants plus a pipeline at the destination. These projects are answers to serious energy needs in a potentially expanding Middle Eastern market. Like any economic expansion, dependable energy supply is a must. Another important player in natural-gas projects in the region is of course Iran which also holds control of huge reserves. A recent natural-gas deal between Turkey and Iran also brings another factor to the region's natural-gas distribution network. Turkey also signed an important deal with Egypt to import liquefied natural gas. In short, all major economies in the region will have some part in the natural-gas deals of the future, which could be much more easily developed if economic cooperation is sought.

A comparison of solutions to water and energy issues in the Middle East from a two-level-game framework

Our argument in support of functional policies in the region as a driving force of regional cooperation both from the political as well as the economic perspective was based on our observation that a cooperative environment, especially at Level II, is practically non-existent in 1998. Although some niches of hope exist, peoples of the Middle East are by and large still hostile to each other. An intrinsic aspect of such an environment is basically the non-existence of mutually beneficial relationships between the Level II actors. We have diagnosed some hopeful complementarities between the economies of the region. However, full exploitation of these opportunities also critically depends on Level I settlements of disputes that are amenable to supportive Level II cooperation. Functional projects can be used to promote a regional cooperative environment within a proper regulatory environment, as depicted above, following the necessary economic reforms towards more market-oriented and relatively freer economies. Such an economic milieu will necessarily involve a more participatory political environment which forms the political framework during the obviously long adjustment period of the peace process in the Middle East.

The political framework of increased economic cooperation is certainly not easy to create. We agree with Richards (1995a: 76) that 'the habits of the past will die hard: entrenched interest groups, engendered over nearly a half-century of state centralisation, will not be easily persuaded to abandon their privileges'.[11] However, as underlined above, the economic and social problems of the region can no longer be kept under close control. As structural reforms in the Middle Eastern economies are undertaken with an explicit objective of creating well-functioning market economies in the region, the political implications of these reforms should also be underlined. It seems quite unlikely, if not outright impossible, to have a well functioning market economy under repressive political regimes.[12] Although many uncertainties exist as to the nature of proper political system design as 'democratic' in the current western sense, the nature of the economic and political problems faced in the region and successful political settlement of the regional disputes as a result of the continuing peace process implies a greater role played by intensifying participation.[13]

The argument for increased and institutionalised participation in the countries of the Middle East is primarily based on the necessity of reforming the region's economic structure. Without repeating the arguments as to the reasons for reform in the Middle Eastern economies, we should here underline that structural adjustments in the economic sphere will necessarily involve reduction of the size of and demilitarisation of the government's role in regional economies. As the policy-making environment is reshaped by establishing the economic rather than strategic and military rationale as its foundation, many social groups will be hurt and thus a considerable resistance is to be expected. Successful transformation of these economies will depend on considerable reductions in subsidies so far taken for granted. Unless the participation of those groups that stand to lose as well as those that stand to benefit from these structural reform policies are integrated to the policy process, chances for success are significantly reduced.[14]

Related arguments for increased participation are based on the observation that efficient functioning of markets critically depends on the free flow of information as well as a secure legal foundation for property rights. Without a stable legal environment securing property rights in markets, successful functioning of the market-oriented structural adjustment programs cannot be expected. Stabilisation and re-adjustment of the legal system to fit the market system aspired to, as well as the free flow of information, both have serious political implications.[15] Liberalisation of information flow within the region's economies will be coupled with wider access to politically sensitive information and greater opportunity for free expression of political exchanges. This would, by implication, increase the level of participation in the region. Success in structural adjustments depends on the integration of these political aspects into the reform package. Participatory schemes also support political and economic opening-up and liberalisation of the region.

We should stress here that our argument is not only a policy recommendation for increased participation. We argue that not only economic but also political reforms are necessary in order to achieve regional integration through more cooperative relations in both economic as well as political spheres, thus creating the long-awaited peace in the Middle East. These two aspects will go hand in hand, complementing and providing support for each other. Our argument is not of a predictive nature. We do not claim that this is the inevitable path the region will have to take. As Richardson (1990: 77) argues, some countries will rise to this challenge of economic and political restructuring via liberalisation while some others will likely fail. In all likelihood, those who fail will not only incur heavy costs to themselves but will also create damaging repercussions for the region as well as the international community. Our arguments shaped around economic necessities do not mean that political choices will be shaped accordingly. We simply hope to underline the overall implications of distinct paths facing policy-makers both for the economic as well as the political sphere.

Staying with the above framework on the relationship between the economic and political aspects of regional cooperation, we can identify several principles upon which the functional projects can be shaped. We should underline once again that functional projects are seen as instruments with which Level I actors try to enlarge Level II constituencies that support economic as well as political cooperation in the region. Accordingly, the projects should be chosen so as to maximise constituency involvement from all sides of Level II actors within a cooperative environment. Resolving problems that affect these constituencies' lives in cooperation with their counterparts from the other side, it is hoped that a cooperative spirit and willingness to communicate with each other to resolve community problems will be brought about. By implication, projects should be encouraged to include community involvement from conflicting sides. Parties from Level II should be encouraged to create their own solutions. They should be involved in creating their own projects. They should be involved in the implementation and management of the projects as much as possible.

Clearly, not all functional projects are suitable for this kind of Level II participation from different sides of the conflict. Some, like the interconnection of electricity grids, are technically too complex. Nevertheless, opportunities should be sought to include local expertise, human resources and private businesses in these large-scale projects to provide an opportunity for all parties to work for a common objective of creating a service to each others' communities. Policies should accordingly be designed to promote business-to-business relationships across communities.

As underlined, the above policies' capacity to promote Level II participation will differ to a great extent no matter how hard Level I actors try to promote such interaction. Diagnosing those projects which offer more opportunities for Level II interaction is critical. Priority should accordingly be given to those projects that have involvement and if possible active participation of Level II actors in the design and implementation of the projects. In comparison with the interconnection of power systems, projects geared towards the resolution of water conflicts in the region could offer more community links. Besides designing grand water-supply projects, projects for the efficient use of common resources between conflicting communities, projects for managing demand and the like should be promoted. Governments should, of course, balance economic benefits with the creation and mobilisation of Level II support for regional cooperation.

Similarly, projects on tourism, agriculture and the environment will offer great possibilities for the creation of a support base across countries that interact with each other. Equally importantly, these Level II actors' self-justification of their function both within their own counries as well as across regional boundaries during the slow-paced peace process will eventually depend on their cooperation with each other. Certainly, creation of such micro-level networks of Level II actors is a slow process. Functional projects, however, will not only provide a fertile environment for such relations to be formed but will also resolve common problems in a more efficient way.

Conclusion

How likely is economic cooperation in the Middle East? This chapter has argued that economic cooperation in the Middle East is indeed possible provided that the Level II actors are mobilised and encouraged to interact. Still, there are a number of barriers to economic cooperation in the region such as a low degree of complementarity of the economies, a low degree of diversification and deepening of industrialisation. Perhaps the most important barrier to cooperation, however, is the degree of state involvement in the Middle Eastern economies. Political considerations of a non-democratic nature have impeded these nations from adopting economic rationale in the decision-making processes. Most decisions on allocation of scarce resources have been made either on the basis of security concerns or have been spent for rent-seeking purposes. The inefficiencies embedded in these economies coupled with political distortions have made the institutional reforms in these countries very difficult.

These barriers, however, can be overcome through market-oriented reforms coupled with democratisation in the political arena. Such reforms can also be enhanced through various functional cooperation schemes. As indicated above, those schemes which support grass-roots activities and encourage civil-society mobilisation are most likely to play a crucial role in the democratisation processes in the Middle East. These projects are most likely to last if the Level II actors, namely the domestic constituencies, are mobilised. The projects can thus be an instrument not only for economic cooperation but also for peace and democratisation. It is to those political implications and requirements that we now turn in Chapters 6 and 7.

6 Dynamics of political change in the Middle East

In Chapter 2, it was argued that the growth of regionalism is a function of globalisation, the end of the Cold War and a growing trend favouring economic liberalism. The aim of this chapter is to examine how these trends affected the Middle East. Why is the Middle East lagging behind other regions in regional economic and political cooperation? Are there any political changes occurring in the Middle East that might raise the prospects of regional economic and political cooperation? The argument in this chapter will be based on the premises that developments at three levels of analysis – international, regional and domestic – seem to be creating an environment that is increasingly more conducive for cooperation.

International Level

One of the major regional consequences of the Cold War was that the rivalry between the two superpowers was reflected in regional divisions. As early as 1946, the former British Prime Minister Winston Churchill, speaking in Fulton, Missouri, remarked that an iron curtain was separating Europe into two blocs (McWilliams and Piotrowski 1993: 42). Similar observations could be made about other regions of the world as colonies gained their independence. The African continent experienced divisions from the very first days of independence as conservative pro-Western countries joined the Brazzaville group of countries against the Soviet-leaning Casablanca group. This division not only complicated the Pan-African dream of a united Africa but also delayed the foundation of the Organisation of African Unity. Africa experienced the consequences of Cold War divisions in numerous civil wars from the Congo to the Horn of Africa as well as in southern Africa. Similar divisions surfaced in Asia too. The first Third-World summit in Bandung in 1955 failed to achieve much success when participating countries split into two camps over Chinese and Soviet participation. Practically every country in South-East Asia in one way or the other suffered the consequences of Cold War divisions. Today, the division of Korea into two countries remains as a relic of the Cold War in Asia. Latin America was not spared either from divisions driven by the Cold War. By the late 1950s, there were guerrilla movements in Latin America challenging the supremacy of the United States. The arrival of Castro to power in Cuba in 1959 followed by the Sandinistas in Nicaragua in 1979 and the civil war in

El Salvador and Guatemala were clear manifestations of the Cold War rivalries in Latin America.

The Middle East experienced its share of the effects of the Cold War. In the mid-1950s efforts to set up the Baghdad Pact reflected the emergence of Cold War fault lines in the Middle East. The situation became aggravated by the Suez Canal crisis in 1956 and by the rise of Pan-Arabism in the Arab World. The conservative, relatively pro-Western, regimes in Syria and Iraq were overthrown and the ones in Jordan and Lebanon were seriously challenged. The conflict between the pro-Soviet Pan-Arab regimes in Egypt, Iraq and Syria on the one hand and the conservative regimes in Jordan, Saudi Arabia and emerging Gulf states on the other developed, in the words of Kerr (1975), into an Arab Cold War. This was a cold war within the larger Cold War characterised by intense political confrontation which at times spilled into violence.

This confrontation attracted the active involvement of the superpowers. The development of close relations between Pan-Arab regimes and the Soviet Union were perceived in the West as Soviet expansionism. The adoption of the Eisenhower Doctrine in 1958 reminiscent of the 1947 Truman Doctrine signalled a growing active involvement of the US in the Middle East at a time when the former colonial powers – Britain and France – were withdrawing from the area. Clearly, both for the Soviet Union and the United States, the Middle East had tremendous strategic importance in the context of the Cold War. The Middle East was not only strategically located between Asia, Africa and Europe but it was also the part of the world with the largest oil reserves. The West became very much dependent on Middle Eastern oil, engendering the need to control the supply of oil as much as possible. The Soviet Union was much less in need of this oil. Yet, as Golan suggests, the Soviet Union may well have had a 'an interest in gaining control over this resource, at least to the extent of being able to threaten the regular flow of vital oil supplies to the West and Japan' (Golan 1990: 16). Furthermore, close military relations between the Soviet Union, Egypt and Syria enabled the Soviet navy to use the port facilities of Alexandria and Lattakia on the Mediterranean Sea. This was the product of an ever-expanding, multi-dimensional relationship between the Soviet Union and radical Arab states. Lewis puts the consequence of this as follows: 'at one time or another, Egypt, the Sudan, Syria, Iraq, South Yemen, Libya, and Algeria seemed to be moving into the Soviet orbit, acquiring Soviet weapons, accepting Soviet instructors, adopting a pro-Soviet alignment at the UN and other international fora, and – most portentous of all – adopting a form of socialist, though not Communist, planning in their economies' (Lewis 1994: 5–57).

There were a number of occasions during the Cold War when the effect of the confrontation of the superpowers in the Middle East manifested itself in violent clashes between pro-Western and pro-Soviet groups. The first significant confrontation occurred in 1958 when pro-Nasserites in Lebanon, encouraged by the political union formed between Egypt and Syria, tried to overthrow the government. The crisis very quickly escalated into a Cold War confrontation when the US government dispatched marines to the beaches of Beirut under the Eisenhower

Doctrine. This Doctrine had promised to defend the Middle East against the aggression of 'states controlled by international Communism' (Kerr 1975: 4–5). A similar crisis in Jordan was averted as a result of British support for the royalist regime. In the eyes of the West, and in particular the Americans, Pan-Arabism was very much seen as a sign of Soviet and communist influence. In the 1960s, the civil war in Yemen to some degree might also be seen as a reflection of the confrontation between pro-Western and pro-Soviet forces. Saudi Arabia, with the blessing of the United States, supported the conservative regime in North Yemen while Egypt, with the military assistance of the Soviet Union, supported the rebels (Golan 1990: 236).

The civil war in Jordan in 1971 erupted as a function of the increasing threat mounted by Palestinian groups to the regime of King Hussein. However, it might also be possible to argue that the civil war did also have a Cold War dimension. It pitted radical forces such as the pro-Soviet Marxist-Leninist Palestinian groups against the pro-Western regime of King Hussein. The Jordanian regime was able to reinstate order after forcing the Palestine Liberation Organisation (PLO) to leave Jordan for Lebanon. Lastly, the long and destructive Lebanese civil war attracted the involvement of both superpowers. The US lent support to the Christian dominated government. In 1983, the US even provided military assistance for the Lebanese government by committing US troops in a manner reminiscent of the 1958 military intervention. Similarly, though in a more limited manner, the Soviet Union too extended political support to Syrian presence in Lebanon, especially after the first Israeli invasion in 1978.

One last example of the Cold War intruding into Middle Eastern politics was as a result of the Soviet invasion of Afghanistan in 1979. The invasion very much reinforced the Cold War-related ideological divisions in the Middle East. Radical Arab regimes in Iraq, Libya and Syria remained reluctant to condemn the Soviet invasion while conservative Arab regimes, in particular Saudi Arabia, not only condemned the Soviet Union but also extended financial assistance to opposition forces in Afghanistan. When coupled with the revolution in Iran, Saudi Arabia and the Gulf States decided to support the Carter Doctrine announced in January 1980. Accordingly, the security of the Gulf region was considered to be of vital interest to US security. This led to the deployment of US military forces in the area and the authorisation of the use of tactical nuclear weapons in the event of Soviet advances into the Gulf area (Halliday 1989: 227).

The Cold War divisions in the Middle East were further complicated by the Arab–Israeli dispute. Although during the 1956 Suez Canal War both superpowers cooperated in forcing Britain, France and Israel to withdraw from the Canal area and the Sinai, this cooperation turned out to be of a very transient nature. Instead, by the 1960s, the United States threw its weight behind Israel while the Soviet Union lent its support to the Arab side, in particular to Egypt, Iraq, Libya and Syria. This support took a political, economic as well as a military form. The 1967 War became a confrontation between American and Soviet military equipment. Both sides during the course of the war and its aftermath poured military assistance on their respective allies. In October 1973 the situation became even more aggravated when the Soviet Union threatened a military intervention, forcing both superpowers to go on a nuclear alert.

With the rise of the PLO in the 1960s as a new player in the Arab–Israeli conflict, the PLO was able to attract the support of the Soviet Union. It provided considerable diplomatic, military and political support to the PLO. The presence of Marxist-Leninist groups within the PLO offered an additional ideological incentive for relations between the PLO and the Soviet Union to grow extensively throughout the 1970s. The United States, on the other hand, refused to deal with the PLO or recognise it as the representative of the Palestinian people. Instead, the US administration considered the PLO a terrorist organisation until towards the very end of the Cold War when the latter recognised Israel.

The Cold War dimension of the Arab–Israeli conflict complicated the search and attainment of a solution. The United States supported the Israeli preference for bilateral negotiations with neighbouring Arab states and her refusal to have any dealings with the PLO. Under this approach the United States and Israel were successful when Egypt was persuaded to sign the Camp David peace treaty in March 1979. The Soviet Union opposed this agreement and took a position extremely critical of Egypt's President Anwar Sadat who had, after the death of Nasser in 1971, taken Egypt out of the Soviet sphere of influence in the Middle East. The Soviet Union instead supported the idea of multilateral negotiations and a comprehensive settlement which meant the withdrawal of Israel to the 1948 borders and the right of the Palestinians to establish a state of their own. The Camp David agreement remained the sole breakthrough in the Arab–Israeli conflict while the deadlock over confrontation persisted throughout the 1980s.

Arab countries and the PLO too have used the Cold War at the international level to further their interests. Radical Arab countries were able to play the Soviet card against both Israel and the conservative Arab regimes. In turn, conservative Arab countries were able to mobilise Western support without compromising on the Arab–Israeli conflict. The US often found itself having to maintain good relations with Saudi Arabia and the Gulf States to be able to keep Soviet influence out of these countries. On the other hand for radical Arab regimes, the Soviet Union became a convenient weapons' supplier at a time when the United States refused to supply them. The refusal of the United States and Western countries to supply weapons to Egypt in the mid-1950s played an important role in Nasser's decision to acquire Soviet weapons. During the 1960s Egypt, Libya and Syria were able to trade naval- and military-base facilities for Soviet military and economic support. By the late 1970s, after Sadat terminated the close relationship with the Soviet Union, Syria's status as the last major Soviet ally gave it considerable leverage over the Soviet Union (Ismael 1986: 190). Also, just as the Soviet Union benefited from close relations with the PLO to further its influence in the region, the PLO too was able to make use of the Soviet Union especially with regard to bringing the Palestinian issue to world attention and receiving material assistance (Reppert 1989: 110–111). These examples are indicative of the extent to which regional actors could use the Cold War to further their interests. Furthermore, it should also be added that it was often pragmatic considerations rather than ideological ones that determined the basis of close relations. This frequently led the Soviets to have to overlook the repression of Communist groups by their allies.

It is possible to argue that Cold War divisions in the Middle East, exacerbated by the Arab–Israeli conflict, prevented the possibility of a conducive environment for region-wide cooperation across the Middle East to emerge. Instead, whatever cooperation did emerge in the Middle East was the kind of cooperation achieved within each camp. However, the cooperation that did occur between the Arabs against Israel was a very ineffective one. Ideological divisions between radical pro-Soviet regimes and conservative pro-Western regimes prevented these countries from achieving a level of cooperation that went beyond the bare minimum of an agreement to oppose Israel and not to negotiate. The deadlock in finding a solution to the Arab–Israeli conflict began to weaken with the end of the Cold War.

Effect of the end of the Cold War

Traditionally, Churchill's observation during his speech at Fulton in March 1946 that an iron curtain was descending separating Europe into two blocs is taken as the beginning of the Cold War. However, it is difficult to determine a specific date for the end of the Cold War. Many consider the opening-up of the Berlin Wall in 1989 as a convenient date signifying the end of the Cold War, while others prefer the more definitive event marked by the disintegration of the Soviet Union in December 1991. The significance of the latter event was that it unequivocally marked the victory (to use 'war' terminology) of the West over the Soviet Union, particularly in ideological terms. This naturally had important repercussions on the Middle East. However, for the purposes of this book, the period in the second half of the 1980s when Gorbachev began to introduce his policies of perestroika and glasnost is chosen as the period characterised by at least the thawing of the Cold War if not its actual end. More specifically, the Soviet decision to sign the agreement paving the way to its withdrawal from Afghanistan in April 1988 can be taken as an historical marker. The thaw in the Cold War had an immediate and visible consequence in the Middle East which helped to pave the way to a conducive environment for regional cooperation.

The first significant sign of constructive engagement on the part of the Soviet Union in respect to efforts to bring about peace in the Middle East came in 1988. Gorbachev, in his speech to the United Nation's General Assembly, made it very clear that the Soviet Union's approach to international relations was changing. He was promising that the Soviet Union would be abandoning its confrontationist policies in favour of efforts to resolve conflicts peacefully. In June 1988, he announced that the Soviet Union would not only be prepared to revise its position on the form of negotiations to resolve the Arab–Israeli conflict but also that it was ready to re-establish diplomatic relations with Israel (Lukacs 1992: 32–33). Gorbachev also made an important contribution towards creating the background for peace negotiations when he played a critical role in helping the reunification of the PLO in 1987 and assisting Arafat in moderating his views on the settlement of the Palestinian–Israeli conflict (Golan 1990: 274–277). After its forced evacuation from

Beirut in 1982 the PLO had suffered deep internal divisions as a result of challenges mounted to Arafat's leadership by radical pro-Syrian factions. In turn, this situation was preventing Yasser Arafat from making much headway in translating his moderate views into policy.

Gorbachev played a critical role in the reunification process by persuading the Syrians and the radical pro-Soviet groups within the PLO to realign themselves behind Arafat's moderate leadership. It is quite possible that without this Soviet assistance Arafat would have failed to mobilise the political strength and influence that led to the Palestine National Council (PNC) decision in November 1988. In this decision, the PNC declared that an independent state alongside Israel should be achieved by negotiation rather than armed struggle. This decision eventually led to the lifting of the US Congressional ban on any interactions or relations between the US and the PLO. More significantly, it robbed the right-wing Israeli government of its popular argument that Israel could not deal with an entity that advocated the destruction of Israel. In turn, this facilitated the hand of the liberals in Israel to push their policy of 'land for peace' more effectively, opening the way to an eventual electoral victory for the liberals in 1992.

Gorbachev, by permitting Soviet Jews to emigrate to Israel and by unequivocally committing the Soviet Union to Israel's right to existence, helped to improve Soviet–Israeli relations. This also contributed to the emergence of a positive political atmosphere which facilitated Israel lifting its previous objections to any Soviet role in the quest for peace in the Middle East. This was a critical breakthrough in paving the way for the Madrid talks in October 1991. The thawing of the Cold War also manifested itself in improved relations between the Soviet Union and conservative Arab states. There had been early signs already when the Soviet Union leased three ships to Kuwait in 1987 to help avoid Iranian attacks on Kuwaiti shipping. Furthermore, Soviet withdrawal from Afghanistan in 1988 followed by the growing Soviet efforts to moderate the policies of radical regimes in the Middle East diffused the fears of conservative Arab regimes. The diminishing role of ideology in Soviet foreign policy was also reflected in the Soviet decision not to prevent the unification of the pro-Soviet People's Democratic Republic of Yemen with the conservative Yemen Arab Republic in 1990.

Another very important development occurred when the Soviet Union did not hesitate to cooperate with Western allies in the adoption of a series of United Nations Security Council Resolutions. These resolutions imposed embargoes on Iraq and prepared the ground for the US-led military intervention to force Iraq out of Kuwait. Clearly, without the Soviet Union's cooperation none of these Resolutions could have been adopted. The Soviet decision not to support one of its most reliable and traditional allies in the Middle East is considered as an important symbol of how far the Cold War had thawed and also how far Saddam Hussein had failed to draw the appropriate lessons from this. The successful concerted effort to force Iraq out of Kuwait generated international pressures to also address the situation resulting from the Israeli occupation of Arab territories.

In the context of President Bush's discourse about an emerging 'new world order' that would replace the old order characterised by the Cold War, addressing the Arab–Israeli conflict became urgent for the credibility of the United States in the Middle East. Hence, in the light of the Soviet Union's cooperative foreign policy, the pressure on the United States to convince Israel to come to the negotiating table increased. This pressure could be recognised in the speech given by the US President to the American Congress in March 1991 when he argued that 'We must do all that we can to close the gap between Israel and the Arab states and between Israelis and Palestinians. … The time has come to put an end to Arab–Israeli conflict' (quoted from Appendix L in Quandt 1993: 496).

There were a number of other developments that were precipitated by the thawing and then the end of the Cold War that in one way or another helped to generate a more positive climate for cooperation. One such development resulted from a growing reluctance and inability of the Soviet Union to provide economic and military assistance to its allies. As the Cold War thawed not only the need and the logic for such assistance diminished but, more significantly, under Gorbachev's efforts to make the Soviet economy more transparent and efficient, it became difficult to find resources for assistance. An important consequence for the decrease in assistance manifested itself in growing pressures to make local economies more efficient and productive. This became yet another important factor fuelling pressures in radical Arab countries for economic liberalism and greater interactions with the external world.

Efforts by Gorbachev to reform the Soviet regime, and then the eventual disintegration of the Soviet Union, had two important consequences for the Arab world. First, it diffused the significance of ideological divisions in the Arab world. As the Soviet Union's emphasis on the ideological aspects of world politics diminished the conflicts between radical and conservative regimes decreased too. Egypt, as early as 1971, had toned down the role of radicalism in its foreign policy and ruptured its close relations with the Soviet Union. Similar developments also occurred within the PLO as well as Algeria and, to a lesser extent, in Syria. Secondly, the collapse of Communist regimes first in Eastern Europe and then in the Soviet Union precipitated what Huntington (1991) called the third wave of democratisation. These developments had a 'demonstration effect', generating increased pressures for democratisation and more representative government in the Arab world. The consequences of growing pressures for both economic and political liberalism in the Arab world, and its relationship to increased prospects of cooperation, will be examined in greater detail in the section focusing on the domestic level.

The United States also demonstrated its commitment to push forward the Arab–Israeli peace process when the US administration declared it would not extend guarantees for a US$10-billion loan that the Israeli government sought. The loan would be used to provide housing for growing numbers of Soviet-Jewish immigrants. The Likud government in power in Israel had hoped to use this loan to gain the support of these immigrants during the 1992 national elections. The US government feared that these loans would be used to build settlements in the occupied territories. The reluctance of the US to support the Israeli government on the loan issue, according to Hadar, was a sign that 'Washington was not going to continue to treat with benign neglect Likud's annexationist policies. It was about to force

Israel to choose between continued support from Washington and the implementation of the Greater Israel agenda' (Hadar 1992: 608).

One last factor that should be considered when examining the gradual emergence of an environment increasingly conducive to cooperation is the place of the Middle East in Western security. The importance of the Middle East for the West during the Cold War was a function of oil supplies, its geo-strategic location and Israel's security, particularly in the case of the United States. Comprehensive cooperation between the West and a divided Arab world was very limited. The oil crisis of 1973 forced the European Community to try to develop what became known as the Euro-Arab Dialogue. Divisions in the Arab world and the Arab–Israeli conflict prevented this dialogue from achieving much (D'Alançon 1994: 42–43). Instead, Western interests were basically secured through the mechanics of the Cold War and the balance of power between pro-Western conservative Arab countries and the pro-Soviet Arab regimes. In the late 1970s and early 1980s, European countries advocated, in contrast to the US position, the idea of the need to include the Soviet Union in efforts to achieve peace in the Middle East (Parson 1985: 27). They energetically pursued this idea in the period preceding the Madrid conference. With the end of the Cold War and the start of the Arab–Israeli peace process, prospects for Western European involvement in cooperative efforts in the Middle East has increased. Yet, more importantly, there has been a growing recognition that the security of Europe has become more intertwined with Middle Eastern security and stability.

In this matrix for new European security, massive population growth in the Middle East has become an important factor. This factor led many in Europe to fear massive illegal immigration across the Mediterranean Sea if the Middle East fails to achieve a significant degree of stability and economic growth. Fast demographic growth accompanied by a very young population often with little prospects of employment can be seen to form a large pool of potential recruits for anti-Western Islamic fundamentalist groups. This has raised the fear of situations similar to Algeria emerging in other Middle Eastern countries. This fear has also been closely associated with the danger of fundamentalist terrorism spreading across Europe where there are large and often alienated Middle Eastern immigrant communities. The wave of terrorism that engulfed France during the summer of 1995 was considered to be a case in point. Furthermore, the proliferation of weapons of mass destruction and ballistic missiles is another growing source of concern for European security, especially for countries along the Mediterranean (Lesser and Tellis 1996).

The more diffused nature of threats at the end of the Cold War led to the adoption of NATO's new strategic concept in November 1991. The concern of NATO was no longer of a massive military assault from the Soviet Union. Instead, the new strategic concept focused on a wide range of security issues which ranged from the economic and social dangers associated with large-scale immigration into Western Europe to threats emanating from the proliferation of weapons of mass destruction and ballistic missiles. Though NATO's new strategic concept was adopted at a time when Eastern Europe was going through tremendous change, if not turmoil, clearly it also reflected concerns about threats and risks from the

Middle East. Many still had in their minds the Libyan missile attack on the southern Italian island of Lampuseda in April 1986. Furthermore, the rise of political Islam and the manner in which this seemed to be associated with Islamic fundamentalist terrorism was also reflected in this new strategic thinking. This concern was somewhat reflected in the widely misunderstood but controversial remark that the then Secretary General of NATO, Willy Claes, made in February 1995 about the need to contain violent Islamic fundamentalism.

The words of Willy Claes led to misunderstandings and not surprisingly alienated many countries of the Middle East, drawing criticisms from them (Faria and Vasconcelos 1996: 23). One positive development is that since then NATO has embarked upon a policy to develop better relations with countries of the Mediterranean. This effort is far from aiming to introduce a Partnership-for-Peace programme of the kind that was developed with Eastern Europe. However, it nevertheless reflects a new and more constructive approach to the search for greater stability and security. The Western European Union (WEU), too, is in the process of developing a dialogue with the Mediterranean countries. As the Cold War came to an end, another initiative that aimed to improve security and stability of the Middle East and the Mediterranean was based on the idea of emulating the European experience with the Conference on Security and Cooperation in Europe (CSCE). At a CSCE meeting in September 1990 the idea of a 'Conference on Security and Cooperation in the Mediterranean' was launched under an Italian–Spanish initiative. However, the deep divisions and mistrusts among Middle Eastern countries prevented this idea from gaining practical life.

A more ambitious and promising initiative came from the European Union in the form of the Euro-Med initiative. As a part of this initiative in November 1995, a summit of EU members and Mediterranean countries was held in Barcelona. The Barcelona Declaration that was adopted reflects a comprehensive approach to security and stability in the Mediterranean and the Middle East. The Declaration clearly recognised the interdependence between the security and stability of the two shores of the Mediterranean. It also put the emphasis on the development of internal as well as regional political and economic institutions to achieve greater stability. Most importantly, it also reflected a commitment on the part of the EU to transfer financial resources to assist economic and political development in the Mediterranean basin.

The common denominator of these new policies adopted by the EU, NATO and WEU is a growing recognition that security cannot any more be conceived as narrow national-military security. Instead security is conceived in a comprehensive manner, taking into account its military, economic, social, cultural and internal as well as regional political dimensions. Furthermore, recognition of the interdependence between security in the Middle East and security in Europe has played an important role in developing these policies. These policies still have a long way to go but the rationale behind them is not very different from that behind the policies the EU has adopted towards Eastern Europe during the transition from one-party political systems and centrally-planned economies to pluralist democracy and market economies.

This evolving EU policy might have, in itself, contributed to the emergence of a conducive environment for greater cooperation by creating international pressures on governments and providing funds for civilian projects aiming at greater economic and political liberalism. Governments have to learn to cooperate on common regional projects and the same applies to groups in civil society. Most of the projects that the Barcelona Declaration supports are those which aim at developing transnational relations and interactions. They are policies reflective of the EU's commitment to participate actively in the search for and development of a stable and secure Middle East. Combined with the more positive international climate that has resulted from the end of the Cold War, it is possible to say that the Middle East is presently facing an environment much more conducive to regional cooperation compared with that during the Cold War period. The next section will examine the regional dimension of prospects for cooperation.

Having looked at how the global environment has changed in the aftermath of the Cold War, and how a new cooperative framework has emerged in the Middle East, we also have to explore how the regional dynamics influence the Middle Eastern states. Using Putnam's terminology, the game at Level I is played both globally and regionally in the Middle East. Although the region is significantly shaped by the global power balance as outlined above, interstate relations cannot be fully understood without looking at regional problems and issues peculiar to the Middle East.

Regional level

Three sets of violent intra-state conflicts have stood in the way of effective region-wide cooperation for security and stability. The first one is the result of the confrontation between Israel and Arab countries since the establishment of the former over a part of the British mandate of Palestine in 1948. This confrontation escalated to the levels of inter-state wars on four occasions between 1948 and 1973. Furthermore, it also led to the Israeli invasions of Lebanon in 1978 and 1982 in addition to the numerous military incursions into neighbouring Arab countries. These incursions were often preceded by Arab or Palestinian, armed, terrorist attacks on Israeli targets. The second set of confrontations was a product of conflicts between Arab states turning violent. Ideological and territorial ambitions have played an important role in these confrontations. What Kerr has termed as the 'Arab Cold War' has led to inter-state as well as intra-state violence on a number of occasions (Kerr 1975). Syria has invaded Lebanon and Jordan (although it withdrew from Jordan within a short period of time). Egypt was deeply involved in the civil war in Yemen from 1963–1970. The ideological confrontation between Egypt and Libya over unification turned violent in July 1977 when a series of armed clashes occurred on the border between the two countries. There was also the invasion of Kuwait by Iraq in 1990. The third set of violent inter-state conflicts was the one between Iraq and Iran. In the early 1970s the Shah supported Kurdish groups in northern Iraq in an uprising against the government in Baghdad. It was not until Iraq accepted the Algiers Treaty in 1975, which expanded Iran's sovereignty over the Shattul-Arab, that Iran ceased to support the violent Kurdish rebellion. In many ways it was the Iraqi discomfort with the Algiers Treaty and the arrival of a radical regime in Tehran that paved the way to the almost-decade-long war between Iraq and Iran. It is no wonder that in this conflict-ridden region, often characterised by violent and coercive actions, there has not been much room for cooperation aimed at achieving greater region-wide security and stability.

The creation of Israel in 1948 against the will of local Arab inhabitants and Arab states immediately led to an effort on the part of neighbouring Arab states to destroy this nascent state. The defeat of the Arab armies and the enlargement of Israel beyond the territories allotted to the Jewish state by the United Nations Partition Plan led to the displacement of more than half a million people as well as the deep resentment of the Arab world (Smith 1992: 135–147). This resentment determined the nature of Arab–Israeli as well as intra-Arab relations. The first Arab–Israeli war not only paved the way to other wars but also played a critical role in fuelling the rise of Pan-Arabism in the Arab world. Pan-Arabism first came to power in Egypt in 1952 and gathered influence in the Arab world after the political success that Egypt's President Gamal Abdel Nasser achieved during the 1956 Suez Canal crisis. This led to the formation of a temporary union between Egypt and Syria followed by the establishment of Pan-Arab regimes in Syria, Iraq, Libya, South Yemen and Algeria.

Pan-Arab regimes came to power very much as a result of a popular resentment against conservative regimes which were blamed for the loss of Palestine (Smith 1992: 159–161). The Pan-Arab regimes, and in particular Nasser's, enjoyed widespread popularity in the Arab world. Pan-Arab discourse was revisionist in its demands calling for the replacement of royalist regimes with Arab socialist ones. The ultimate aim would be the unification of the Arab world into one state and this, in turn, would help to mobilise the necessary strength to liberate Palestine (Nasser 1959). The emphasis put on radicalism, Arab territorial unification and the violent manner in which Pan-Arab regimes came to power became a major source of insecurity for conservative regimes. This generated deep distrust between radical Pan-Arab regimes and Arab conservatives. One consequence of this situation was that relations between the two groups remained very poor and prevented the development of much cooperative behaviour among Arab countries. Whatever economic and political cooperation did emerge was directed towards the destruction of Israel rather than the development of region-wide cooperation aiming at enhancing security, stability and economic prosperity for all the countries of the region.

George Lenczowski (1980:750) identifies the Arab–Israeli conflict as one of the most important issues that has engendered political cooperation between Arab countries. One multilateral forum where this cooperation has been most visible is the Arab League. The Arab League was founded in 1945 and, from the establishment of Israel until the late 1980s, it served as a forum where Arab governments expressed their opposition to Israel even if they often remained divided on what policies to follow with regard to Israel. In 1948 the Arab League considered Israel an illegal entity and played an important role in mobilising the necessary support for launching a war on the country. The defeat of the Arab armies and the additional loss of Arab land increased the resentment against Israel. The Arab League became even more radical in its rhetoric especially with the arrival of Pan-Arab regimes to power. After the defeat of the Arab armies against Israel, members of the Arab League at their fourth summit in Khartoum in September 1967 agreed that there would be 'no peace with Israel, no recognition of Israel, no negotiations with it' (Lukacs 1992: 454). These principles remained in force as far as direct negotiations with Israel were concerned. This was the case until the visit of Anwar Sadat to Israel in 1977.

Political cooperation among Arab countries also took the form of efforts at creating unions. The most significant one was the union between Egypt and Syria. However, this union – known as the United Arab Republic – lasted for only 3 years between 1958 and 1961. The 1960s and 1970s witnessed a number of attempts at forming other unions. Some of the more ambitious ones included the attempt to form a federation between Egypt, Libya, Sudan and Syria soon after Colonel Muammar Gaddafi overthrew the royal regime in Libya in September 1969. However, after the death of Nasser in 1971, the idea lost momentum and in 1973 it was completely abandoned. There was also a failed attempt to form a union between Libya and Tunisia in 1974. The failures were mostly due to the fact that once Pan-Arab revolutionaries attained power in their respective countries, their taste for exercising that power nationally often exceeded their zeal for unions or even federations (Lenczowski 1980: 758).

Sadat's visit to Israel and than the eventual signing of the Egyptian-Israeli peace treaty in March 1979 led to tremendous resentment against the Egyptian government both among Arab governments as well as with the Arab public at large. In December 1977, immediately after Sadat's visit to Israel, the PLO and radical Pan-Arab regimes in Algeria, Iraq, Libya, South Yemen and Syria formed a rejectionist front refusing the idea of unilateral solutions or negotiations with Israel. Although, this rejectionist front failed to gain the support of conservative regimes at the time, the situation changed after the signing of the peace treaty. In March 1979 the Arab League decided to suspend Egypt's membership and to transfer the league headquarters from Cairo to Tunis. Israel's decision in July 1980 to declare Jerusalem to be its undivided and eternal capital, its decision in August 1981 to incorporate the Golan Heights into Israel and the Israeli invasion of Lebanon in 1982 exacerbated the situation in the Middle East. Most of the 1980s continued to be characterised by an environment of confrontation between Israel and the Arab world including the PLO. This was also, however, a period when early signs of differences began to occur among the Palestinians and Arabs in respect to political cooperation against Israel. These developments will be examined separately with respect to the impact they had on opening the way towards a more conducive environment for a peace process between Arabs and Israelis.

Arab governments have also tried to use economic cooperation amongst themselves as a means of strengthening their capability to confront Israel. The first manifestation of this occurred in December 1945 when the Arab League introduced a boycott of Jewish goods in Palestine and set up an office based in Syria to monitor compliance with this boycott. The creation of the state of Israel led to an expansion of the boycott to include foreign companies dealing with Israel. The boycott was seen as a weapon to prevent Israel enhancing its economic power and to block its integration into the region. Arab governments also tried to achieve a certain degree of cooperation in respect to using oil as a political weapon against Israel. In 1968 the Arab Organisation of Petroleum Exporting Countries (AOPEC) was formed. The nationalisation of oil production in a number of radical Arab countries, such as Iraq and Libya, opened the possibility for Arab governments to regulate the supply of oil for political purposes. The most striking example of this occurred in 1973 when AOPEC succeeded in imposing an oil embargo on a range of countries they considered to have been supportive of Israel. They also forced the price of oil to increase from US$2.90 a barrel in June 1973 to US$11 by the end of 1973 (Bill and Springborg 1994: 400).

The establishment of the Arab League in 1945 engendered an interest in achieving greater economic cooperation between the member states. Furthermore, the formation of the European Economic Community (EEC) in 1957 led to a desire among Arab governments to emulate the experience of economic integration in Europe (Owen 1988). However, their efforts to emulate the European Economic Community did not bear fruit until 1965 when the actual agreement establishing an Arab Common Market (ACM) was signed. The ACM had little economic logic because of a conspicuous lack of complementarity between Arab economies. More than ten years after its formation, intra-ACM trade in 1978 between the major four members – Egypt, Iraq, Jordan and Syria – was just over 2 per cent of their foreign trade (Bill and Springborg 1994: 420). The preference of individual governments to protect their own markets for domestic political reasons was another major obstacle to the further development of this economic integration (Owen 1992: 101). More importantly, as Musrey notes, Arab countries lacked a community of interests and aspirations to achieve economic integration (Musrey 1969: 144–145). An effort to strengthen overall Arab ability to confront Israel through economic integration was clearly not adequate to put the ACM into effect.

In contrast to the ACM, Saudi Arabia and the Gulf States were able to set up the Gulf Cooperation Council (GCC) in 1981 which succeeded in creating a free trade area among its six member countries. However, it should be noted that the GCC was established in the context of the Iranian revolution and the Iran–Iraq war to further the common security and defence interests of a group of oil-producing conservative Gulf states. It would be difficult to say that the GCC had much of a connection with the Arab–Israeli conflict. Lastly (although not much intra-Arab economic integration was achieved this way) wealthy oil-exporting Arab countries extended generous economic and financial assistance to other Arab countries. At the 1967 Khartoum summit of the Arab League, oil-rich countries agreed to extend financial assistance 'to strengthen the economy of the Arab States directly affected by the aggression, so that these states will be able to stand firm in the battle' (Lukacs 1992: 454). Accordingly, over the years, a large amount of financial assistance was channelled into Egypt, Jordan, the PLO and Syria. This assistance played a critical role in sustaining these countries', and especially Syria's and the PLO's, ability to confront Israel.

The Arab–Israeli conflict and the desire to confront Israel were the most significant motivation behind efforts to enhance inter-Arab political and economic cooperation. The ambitious schemes of achieving an Arab Union advocated especially by the Pan-Arab movements, as well as the desire to establish an Arab Common Market, was very much a product of a belief that it was Arab disunity which had caused the loss of Palestine and the defeats suffered against Israel. However, these schemes achieved very little in concrete terms other than serving as ideological rallying points. Conservative governments, often for domestic political reasons, felt the need to go along with at least the rhetoric surrounding these schemes. Oil-rich conservative countries successfully used programmes of financial assistance to other Arab countries and the PLO to reinforce their commitment to the Arab cause and the confrontation with Israel. The Arab League remained the only forum which has succeeded in functioning continually since it was founded. However, the Arab League has not gone beyond being a forum where decisions are taken on the basis of strict recognition of each member's sovereign rights. A common characteristic of all these efforts for political and economic cooperation has been that they are exclusively Arab and the Arab–Israeli conflict and the Palestinian problem have often remained as part of the hidden agenda.

Regional pressures for change

At the regional level the origins of change go back to the early 1980s and to a gradual 'evolution of Arab politics toward concluding that war was futile and compromise was inevitable. Israel was not going to be destroyed, and that continuing the conflict damaged both Arab state and Palestinian interests' (Laqueur and Rubin 1995: 478). The causes and manifestations of this change at the regional level can be grouped into three. First, the 1980s were characterised by a period during which radical Pan-Arab regimes lost their influence in Arab politics, and Egypt became reintegrated into Arab League ranks without having to renegade on the peace treaty with Israel.

The Iran–Iraq war played a critical role in this process, especially after Iran recaptured the territories it had lost to Iraq in the early stages of the war and began to occupy Iraqi land and threaten the security of the Gulf states. Iraq's retreat in the light of Iranian military success not only undermined the influence of Pan-Arab rhetoric that had played an important role in Saddam Hussein's decision to invade Iran, but also enhanced the need to bring Egypt back to mainstream Arab politics. There was a clear recognition that Egypt remained the largest and most powerful Arab country and that without Egypt's support for the Arab cause, Iraq risked being defeated. Syria's decision to maintain support for Iran against Iraq increased Egypt's importance. At the November 1987 Arab League meeting, the way was opened to the reintegration of Egypt into Arab ranks. Such a decision was a major departure from the position advocated by the rejectionist front and adopted by the Arab League in 1979. Indirectly, this departure also meant a recognition of

Egypt's peace agreement with Israel, and the need to face up to the reality of Israel's existence, a development that had already been set in motion to some extent with King Fahd's peace plan of August 1981 and the Arab League Fez summit statement of September 1982. Both statements had indirectly recognised Israel's right to exist (Aras 1996: 32).

The rise of political Islam as a formidable opposition to existing regimes in Arab countries engendered yet another development which contributed to the emergence of an environment conducive to the peace process. Arab governments found themselves compelled to align themselves more closely with the West, particularly the US. In the 1980s, from Syria through Lebanon and the occupied territories in Palestine to Egypt, radical Islam was on the rise in a very conspicuous manner. The Iranian revolution and the determination of the Khomeini regime to support radical Islamic groups exacerbated fears about Iranian influence across the Arab world as well as among the Palestinians. Radical Islamic groups challenged the legitimacy of both Pan-Arab as well as conservative regimes including the PLO. Syria violently repressed such radical Islamic groups while Lebanon experienced a further deterioration of the civil war as a result of the growing influence of radical Islamic groups in the country. Conservative regimes ranging from Jordan to Saudi Arabia and Egypt felt the need to seek security by approaching the United States. They hoped that the US would be able to assist them to counter the influence of Iran.

These were concerns clearly reflected in the content of both the Fahd and Fez peace plans. These two documents continued to put emphasis on a multilateral and comprehensive peace settlement, a position with which Israel disagreed. In December 1982, in line with the Fez Plan, the PLO and Jordan agreed to start negotiations to explore the possibility of reaching a confederal arrangement between Jordan and a liberated Palestine composed of occupied territories. The general expectation among moderate circles was that such an arrangement would gain the support of the US, which, in turn, would be able to pressurise Israel to agree to withdraw from the occupied territories. However, the PLO leadership remained trapped between moderate and radical forces and failed to bring about a major breakthrough. The talks were discontinued in 1986. Nevertheless, these talks suggested that moderate voices in Arab politics, prepared to recognise Israel's existence and negotiate an agreement with Israel, could now be increasingly heard. It is no wonder that this was also a period when Egypt, that had broken ranks by signing a peace treaty with Israel in 1979, was gradually being allowed to return to the Arab fold.

The new approach reflected in these developments was starkly different from the one represented in the 1967 Khartoum decisions characterised by their famous 'three "no"s'. An important cause behind this transformation can be attributed to what Ismael calls the fragmentation of the Arab political system in which, once, the Pan-Arab regimes could maintain an important degree of unity at least towards opposing Israel. This, he argues, increased the influence of external powers, particularly the United States (Ismael 1986: 56–65). Hence, the diminished influence of Pan-Arab regimes, accompanied with their inability to balance the rising influence of Iran and radical Islam, induced the conservative Arab regime to seek US support. Efforts in seeking this support played an important role in bringing about a critical transformation in Arab governmental stance on Israel. Ajami had aptly detected the beginnings of this process and the end of Pan-Arabism's influence in Middle Eastern politics as early as 1978 (Ajami 1979).

The third critical development at the regional level was the Gulf crisis which resulted from the Iraqi invasion of Kuwait in 1990. An overwhelming majority of Arab governments reconciled themselves to accepting the dominant role of the United States in ending Kuwait's occupation by Iraq. The Arab political system had failed to prevent the Iraqi invasion and Arab governments simply did not have the power to ensure an Iraqi withdrawal. The threat to the existing Arab political order was of such a magnitude that, in spite of Saddam Hussein's effort to mobilise Arab public opinion by raising the Palestinian problem, Arab governments maintained their unity and continued to support the decisions of the United Nations Security Council.

This constituted an important psychological turning point. For the first time a position supported by conservative pro-Western Arab governments prevailed and could not be undermined by radical Arab rhetoric. Furthermore, among Arab governments there was a clear recognition that with the end of the Cold War their security had become much more dependent on the United States. An important consequence of this dependency in the 1990s meant that most Arab governments had to reconcile their regional interests as much as possible with those of the United States. This dealt the final blow to any ability to resist accepting the right of Israel to exist in the Middle East. Unlike previously, the Palestinian problem could no longer be used to bolster regime legitimacy domestically or regionally by calling for the destruction of Israel.

Another consequence of the Gulf crisis was that it demonstrated that non-Arab countries, such as Israel and Turkey, could have a constructive role to play with respect to regional security and stability. Since the mid-1950s, Turkey had remained outside Middle Eastern politics especially with respect to intra-Arab politics. Turkish cooperation during the crisis facilitated the imposition of UN economic sanctions against Iraq. Furthermore, the Turkish decision to permit the use of NATO military bases for mounting allied aerial operations provided an important strategic advantage against Iraq. Similarly, Israeli behaviour during the Gulf crisis showed that Israel, too, could have a regional role to play. In spite of Iraqi scud attacks aiming to draw Israel into the war, Israel succeeded in refraining from becoming actively involved in the crisis. An Israeli retaliation against Iraq could have complicated the internal dynamics, especially of the Arab wing of the coalition against Saddam Hussein, which would have put the whole military operation against Iraq at risk. This demonstrated that non-Arab countries in the region could also have a role to play in the resolution of regional conflicts.

There were also developments outside the context of the Arab–Israeli conflict that helped to contribute to the emergence of a more positive cooperative environment. One such development arose from the drastic fall in oil revenues. Arab states, which earned a total of US$213.6 billion from oil exports in 1980, received only US$147.4 billion two years later (Bill and Springborg 1994: 423). This fall continued throughout the 1980s. In 1994, oil producers were putting out even less than they did in 1982 (Roberts 1995: 23). Arab states, including oil-producing ones like Saudi Arabia, started to accumulate large foreign debts. The per capita income of Saudi Arabia fell from just over US$16,000 in 1981 to US$7,410 by 1991 (World Bank 1995: 4–5). This was happening at a time when the population of Arab countries had doubled compared with twenty years previously. Furthermore, the cost of the Iran–Iraq war was measured in hundreds of billions of US dollars. As Roberts notes, by the late 1980s the value of oil as a military and political weapon had diminished too (Roberts 1995: 16). Under these circumstances, it had become increasingly difficult to continue with the financial assistance that confrontation states and the PLO had enjoyed previously. The pressure of less financial support was most acutely felt by the PLO and Jordan.

The unification of Yemen was yet another indication of how the influence of Arab radicalism was decreasing. At independence in 1967, South Yemen saw the arrival of a Pan-Arab regime that developed very close relations with the Soviet Union. In 1977, it was one of the regimes that took the lead in the formation of the rejectionist front and supported armed struggle against Israel. However, by the late 1980s economic pressures inside the country, as well as diminishing Soviet economic support, were the most important factors that pushed the regime in South Yemen towards unification with conservative North Yemen (Dunbar 1992: 463–467). Hence, in May 1990 one of the last bastions of Pan-Arabism and radical Arab socialism had fallen. The remaining Pan-Arab regimes were in difficulty as well. Iraq shortly after the war with Iran had ended, drifted into yet another adventure with the invasion of Kuwait. When Iraq had been forced out of Kuwait Iraq was no longer a serious player in regional politics. Syrian President Hafiz Assad, on the other hand, toned down his Pan-Arab rhetoric and even supported the Allied coalition against Iraq. Pan-Arabism's influence that once had played a critical role in regional politics was falling (Ajami 1991; Tibi 1993). Clearly, by the early 1990s Pan-Arabism could no longer withstand the growing preference towards moderation and pragmatism among Arab governments and the PLO leadership. This has also been accompanied by 'an erosion of the credibility of pan-Arabism' in the eyes of the public (Karawan 1994: 454).

As we suggested in earlier chapters, domestic dynamics, or what happens at Level II, are a crucial part of understanding inter-state ties. What are indeed the domestic dynamics of interest groups, state structures and policy networks in the Middle Eastern states? What are the changes occurring at that front? It is to those questions that we now turn.

Domestic level

The last level of analysis focuses on domestic political factors that impeded the possibility of any region-wide cooperation and demonstrates how domestic economic and political developments since the late 1980s helped to change this situation. An important factor that exacerbated the Arab–Israeli conflict was the nature of regimes in Arab countries. Owen identifies two types of political regimes in the Arab world (Owen 1992). The first type is characterised by single-party regimes, often Pan-Arab in ideology. The second type is based on the rule of monarchs and royal families. The common denominator, until the late 1980s and early 1990s, to both types of regimes was that they were more often than not repressive and non-democratic with hardly any room for freedom of expression. The only exception was Lebanon where a relatively free and competitive political system operated until civil war broke out in the mid-1970s. Kuwait, too, permitted some degree of freedom of the press until the early 1980s and the rise of radical Islam.

The creation of Israel and the subsequent Arab–Israeli conflict played an important role in sustaining these repressive regimes although the political culture of the area did, to a certain extent, also play a role in this. The political elite in both types of regimes exploited the Arab-Israel conflict to perpetuate their rule (Norton and Wright 1995: 8). In many ways, the two reinforced each other. The conflict helped to justify the repressive nature of these regimes and deflect attention away from domestic grievances (Tessler and Grobschmidt 1995: 144), while this situation in turn prevented the possibility of any alternative approach to the resolution of the Arab–Israeli conflict to emerge. Both types of regime were locked in dynamics that only permitted the expression of views that advocated the destruction of Israel. This was particularly the case for the radical regimes led by the military or a Pan-Arab elite. These regimes developed a complex bureaucratic and military apparatus characterised by their emphasis on security and authoritarianism (Hinnebusch 1993: 183; Owen 1992: 38).

There were a number of distinct economic, military and political characteristics of these regimes. First, they based their legitimacy on Pan-Arabism. Pan-Arabism became an ideology that explained why the Arab world had become divided and attributed the occupation of Palestine and the creation of Israel to this division. The cause of this 'calamity' was attributed partly to western imperialism and partly to conservative Arab regimes considered to be pro-Western. Second, these regimes advocated a solution of the problem of Palestine which called for the destruction of Israel. Third, Arab 'socialism', a mixture of policies which emphasised the redistribution of wealth and the nationalisation of the economy, was introduced to achieve social and economic development. Fourth, considerable importance was attributed to expanding military capabilities. The implementation of these policies demanded the silencing of any opposition. Emphasis was put on the need to achieve unity and mobilise the public against Israel. Values associated with democratic and pluralist regimes were suppressed or considered as either inappropriate for the Arab world or a luxury until the achievement of Arab unity and the destruction of Israel.

Before the creation of Israel, conservative regimes in Egypt, Jordan, Iraq and Syria had developed a certain degree of parliamentarianism, however, this did not last for long. Conservative regimes in Egypt, Iraq and Syria were replaced by radical Pan-Arab ones in the 1950s. The remaining conservative regime in Jordan became repressive in an effort to protect itself from the rise of Pan-Arabism. Furthermore, with the emergence of Palestinian nationalism in the 1960s, the Jordanian regime also felt threatened by the PLO and this led, in 1971, to a major violent confrontation between the two. Saudi Arabia, throughout the period and until after the Gulf crisis, remained a closed society with little room for dissent of any kind. Although conservative regimes lacked the kind of ideological fervour in confronting Israel, the leadership often felt the need to keep up with the anti-Israeli rhetoric of radical regimes. This became an indispensable requirement for maintaining a minimum degree of legitimacy among the Arab public. This was, to a certain extent, in contrast to the early 1950s when King Abdullah of Jordan did not hesitate to maintain contact with the Israelis. However, his assassination by a Palestinian quickly demonstrated the dangers of cooperating with Israel. A similar fate awaited President Anwar Sadat of Egypt almost thirty years later for having negotiated a peace agreement with the Israelis.

The repressive nature of Arab regimes also helped to cover for the zeal with which the leadership in each country tried to protect their domain of power. In spite of the Pan-Arab call for unification, radical Arab regimes shied away from unification and instead argued over who would lead Arab unity. Some of the fiercest conflicts took place between Pan-Arab regimes (Kerr 1975). Yet, the existence of Israel provided the basis for a minimum degree of cooperation. However, Pan-Arab political parties in each radical Arab country, that were tightly organised and led, prevented the possibility of a leadership favourable to an authentic Arab-unification process from emerging. The only success in Arab unification took place between Egypt and Syria in 1958 and did not last beyond 1961. Other Pan-Arab unification or cooperation projects failed to materialise as the leadership in each radical Arab country used Pan-Arabism to bolster their rule. More often than not this reinforced the repressive nature of these regimes.

The rise of Palestinian nationalism can be partly attributed to the frustration experienced by the failure of Pan-Arabism to liberate Palestine (Kirişci 1986: 41). The leadership of Palestinian nationalism in its early years in the mid-1960s met fierce criticisms from the Pan-Arab regimes in Egypt and Syria. Yasser Arafat was imprisoned on a number of occasions in both countries and was considered a traitor to the cause of Arab unification (Frangi 1983: 102–103; Quandt *et al.* 1973: 166–167). There was no room permitted for dissent by Pan-Arab regimes. However, the defeat of Arab armies against Israel in 1967 strengthened the hand of the Palestinian nationalist leadership and made it possible for Arafat to become the leader of the PLO in 1969. A tense relationship continued between the PLO and other Arab regimes until the PLO was recognised as the representative of Palestinians in 1974. Compared to Arab countries, the PLO was able to achieve a greater degree of pluralism when it permitted the possibility for groups advocating Palestinian nationalism, Pan-Arabism and socialism to coexist at the Palestine National Council (PNC). However, the idea of negotiations with Israel, and the recognition of Israel, remained taboo and met fierce opposition from radical left-wing groups within the PLO until the late 1980s. It can be argued that the rise of the PLO made surrounding radical Arab and conservative regimes more repressive as the individual leaderships in these countries felt threatened by Palestinian nationalism.

Another development that reinforced the repressive nature of Arab regimes was the rise of radical Islam in the 1980s (Owen 1992: 178–188). The revolution in Iran, combined with the growing frustration felt as a result of both Pan-Arabism and Palestinian nationalism's inability to liberate Palestine or solve the Palestinian problem, were critical factors that helped the rise of radical Islam. Radical Islamic groups, such as the Muslim Brotherhood, Hizbullah and Hamas, accused Arab regimes of being corrupt and of having betrayed Islam. Secular regimes, such as the ones in Syria, Iraq and the PLO, felt particularly threatened. Syria repressed radical Islamic groups violently while Iraq, due to the Iran–Iraq, war did not permit such groups to surface in the country at all. Even the PLO, which traditionally did permit a degree of pluralism, did not give any representation to such groups in the PNC or other bodies of the PLO (Abu-Amr 1994).

The Muslim Brotherhood Society, which had originally been set up in Egypt in 1928, existed among the Palestinians since it participated in the 1948 war. Islamic Jihad and Hamas on the other hand emerged in 1980 and 1987, respectively. The *intifada* increased their influence among Palestinians in a very significant manner. This led to arguments that Israeli authorities encouraged the growth of radical Islamic groups purposefully to undermine the PLO's influence and Arafat's leadership (Abu-Amr 1994, xvi and 35; Saliyeh 1988: 142). Conservative regimes in Saudi Arabia and the Gulf States felt threatened as well because of these groups' close links with Iran and their fear that Iran aimed to destabilise their regimes. The radicalism with which these groups attacked Israel and called for its liquidation was yet another source of threat. No radical Arab government, let alone a conservative one, seemed keen to enter a war with Israel especially in the absence of Egypt that had made its peace with Israel. Yet, at the same time they were also reluctant to moderate their policies towards Israel too, openly fearing a backlash from Islamic radical groups.

Domestic politics within Israel did not help the emergence of a conducive environment for negotiations and peace either. It was Labour coalitions that had ruled Israel since its establishment and up until 1977. The policy of the Labour governments since 1967 was based on a readiness to exchange some of the occupied territories for peace on the basis of United Nations Security Council Resolution 242, as long as bilateral agreements could be reached with neighbouring Arab countries. The Arab intransigence against such an approach and the Israeli refusal to deal directly with the PLO blocked the way to any significant progress. The situation was exacerbated by the arrival of the right-wing Likud coalitions in 1977. Menachem Begin and his leadership considered the West Bank as liberated territories and referred to them as Judea and Samaria (Peretz 1986: 17). They opened these territories to Jewish settlement and declared Jerusalem as the undivided and eternal capital of Israel. Furthermore, a ban on any dealings with the PLO was imposed. The influence of Likud governments also played a critical role in the adoption of the US Congressional decision that closed down PLO offices in the US and introduced a ban on US relations with the PLO until the latter recognised Israel. This stance prevented any possibility of achieving a common basis for negotiations between Israelis and Palestinians.

Changes at the domestic level

Just as developments at both the international and regional levels contributed to the emergence of a conducive environment for cooperation, there were also similar developments at the domestic level. The most critical were probably the ones that took place among the Palestinians. In December 1987 a simple traffic accident in the Gaza Strip evolved into a fully fledged rebellion against the occupying Israeli forces in the Gaza Strip and the West Bank (Abu-Amr 1994: 53; Schiff and Ya'ari 1989: 17). The *intifada*, as the rebellion became known, had erupted relatively spontaneously with radical Islamic groups playing a critical organisational role in its early stages. It was with great difficulty that the PLO, and particularly Yasser Arafat's Fatah group, was able to reinstate some semblance of political control over the *intifada*. The PLO had suffered considerable loss of influence in the occupied territories after it was forced out of Beirut to Tunis by Israel in 1982. This had also weakened the PLO internally and had led to major splits within the organisations in the early 1980s (Gresh 1985: 226–238). The splits were also exacerbated by Arafat's efforts to negotiate a confederation with Jordan.

The *intifada* had a lot to do with the frustration experienced by the inhabitants of the occupied territories at a time when the Arab governments seemed preoccupied with the Iran–Iraq war (Khalidi 1991: 21). At the same time, the Likud governments were energetically expanding Jewish settlements and increased their repression of the Palestinians. This situation was benefiting radical Islamic groups to the detriment of secular Palestinian political organisations, and constituted a potent alternative voice and threat to Arafat's leadership (Abu-Amr 1994; Cobban 1990: 231). However, there was also a growing number of local moderate leaders especially in the West Bank which successfully articulated the frustrations felt by Palestinians with the lack of any improvement in their day-to-day lives in the occupied territories (Saliyeh 1988: 163–188). Pan-Arabism as well as Palestinian nationalism represented by the PLO had failed to liberate them from Israeli occupation.

Radical Islamic groups, however, seemed only to promise more of the same with their calls for the destruction of Israel and creation of an Islamic Palestinian state, calls that were increasingly being recognised as unrealistic. Arafat's concern about the potential challenge that Islamic radical groups could pose to his leadership was reflected in his remarks in February 1989 identifying such groups as a greater threat to his leadership than hostile Syrian-supported secular left-wing groups (Cobban 1990: 231). Arafat with the support of moderates in the PLO recognised the danger of losing ground to radical Islamic groups in the occupied territories and allied himself with the increasingly assertive moderate leadership in the occupied territories. The 'insiders', as Rubin calls them, played an important role in acting as an interest group which pressed the PLO towards diplomacy and pragmatism (Rubin 1993: 156). Traditionally, the elite of the occupied territories particularly in the West Bank has been more moderate in their approach than Palestinians based outside.

The period also coincided with one when the Cold War had started to thaw and the Soviet Union under Gorbachev was increasingly moderating its policies in the

Middle East. Previously, in an effort to increase its influence in the Middle East the Soviet Union used to provide significant levels of economic, military and diplomatic support for the PLO (Golan 1990: 110–123; Reppert 1989: 111). However, Gorbachev's policies preferred moderation and pragmatism in place of radicalism. One manifestation of this preference for pragmatism was reflected in the role that the Soviet Union played in persuading radical left-wing groups within the PLO to transcend their differences with moderate groups and reunite behind Arafat's leadership in 1987 (Duncan and Ekedahl 1990: 124). This development facilitated the ability of Arafat to reinstate his control within the PLO and the occupied territories.

This paved the way for the declaration of an independent Palestine alongside Israel at the nineteenth PNC held in Algiers in November 1988. According to the decisions taken at this meeting, the PLO laid down a clear strategy to attain this independence, based on international negotiations and accompanied by an implicit recognition of Israel. Under US and international pressure Arafat, in a speech he gave to the United Nations General Assembly in Geneva in December 1988, renounced the use of terrorism and unequivocally recognized the right of Israel to exist. (For the text of the speech see Lukacs 1992: 420–434.) In May 1989 the Arab League summit held in Casablanca approved the PNC decisions and Arafat's policies. In this manner, a major threshold in the Arab–Israeli conflict was crossed.

However, this major breakthrough in the PLO's stance towards Israel did not bring about any significant change in Israeli policies towards the occupied territories. Instead, the *intifada* continued with mounting frustration. It was not surprising, that when Saddam invaded Kuwait and linked his withdrawal from Kuwait to Israel relinquishing the land of Palestinians, he received great support among Palestinians. Palestinians were frustrated with the lack of progress since the PNC decision of 1988 and saw a certain double standard in the swift US reaction to the Iraqi occupation to Kuwait compared to the US inaction towards Israel. Arafat found himself expressing support and solidarity with Saddam (Mattar 1994: 32–36). This cost the PLO and Arafat very dearly.

Once Iraq was forced out of Kuwait almost 300,000 Palestinians were compelled to leave for Jordan and the occupied territories. The consequence of this mass influx of Palestinians to Jordan and the occupied territories together with the loss of commerce, financial assistance and remittances led standards of living to fall by almost a third compared to the late 1980s (Abed 1991: 37–38). There were also serious political costs attached to the PLO's support for Saddam. The PLO offended conservative Arab governments in particular. More importantly, it lost considerable prestige in its international standing (Khalidi 1991: 23). Furthermore, the PLO's credibility as a reliable partner for peace negotiation was seriously undermined. As Mattar notes 'it took the PLO more than a quarter of a century to achieve Arab and, except for Israel and the United States, international consensus on the need for Palestinian self-determination, and only one week to damage it' (Mattar 1994: 45).

After the Gulf crisis was over, the PLO was in such a weakened position that it found itself excluded from the Madrid Peace Conference. Instead, it was

Palestinians acceptable to the US and to Israel who were allowed to take part in the talks, but only as part of the Jordanian delegation. Hence, the PLO was absent from the most important meeting after the Gulf crisis concerning the establishment of a new order in the Middle East. Arafat had been trapped between radical Islamic and left-wing groups in the PLO – which opposed Palestinian participation in the Madrid conference – and a moderate local leadership – which seemed to be determined not to miss the opportunity to be represented at the conference (Köksaloğlu 1995: 95–96). In the end, fearing that he might lose his position in the occupied territories, he decided to support the position held by the moderates, and succeeded in persuading the twentieth PNC meeting in Algiers in September to accept participation at the conference. (For the text of the PNC decision see Laqueur and Rubin 1995: 567–573.) This decision turned out to be a very significant one as it locked for the very first time the Israelis and the Palestinians into a long and arduous series of bilateral negotiations. The negotiations developed a momentum of their own which reinforced the commitment to achieve a successful outcome. In September 1993 the international community discovered that in secret meetings held in Norway the PLO and Israel had succeeded in reaching an historic agreement expressed in the Declaration of Principles. (For the text see Laqueur and Rubin 1995: 599–612.)

Changes within Israel also played a critical role in paving the way for greater Arab–Israeli political cooperation. In the early 1980s Peace Now had emerged as a powerful movement against the Israeli occupation of Lebanon. This movement, which was closely associated with the Labour party, pushed for the idea of 'land for peace'. They opposed the views of the Likud governments throughout the 1980s and instead argued that Israel was more likely to achieve peace in return for withdrawing from the occupied territories. In spite of the ban on contacts with the PLO, Peace Now developed a dialogue with the PLO as well as moderate Palestinians in the West Bank (Schindler 1991: 205–211). They were also successful in mobilising a large number of Israelis in support of this position and played an important role in assisting the victory of the Labour Party over the Likud at the 1992 Israeli national elections. Furthermore, there were also a growing number of Israelis who were uncomfortable with the long reign of Likud that had put so much emphasis on expenditure for settlements rather than more pressing economic needs (Flamhaft 1996: 148). Another factor that played an important role in the weakening of the Likud was the refusal of the US administration to provide any financial assistance to help the Israeli government with the integration of Jewish immigrants from the Soviet Union who were streaming into the country in their thousands. This cost the Likud dearly when an overwhelming majority of these Jewish immigrants voted in favour of the Labour Party and other moderate political parties (Flamhaft 1996: 176–183; Reich *et al.* 1993: 474–475).

After the 1992 elections the coalition government led by the Labour Party opened the way to direct negotiations with the PLO. The task of the Labour-led government had in some ways been made easier because the previous right-wing government had already agreed to sit at the negotiating table in Madrid. The Gulf crisis and the Iraqi scud-missile attacks in many ways helped to strengthen the arguments of those who supported the need to reach an accommodation with the Arab world. The scud attacks and Saddam's threat to burn half of Israel in April 1990 demonstrated in a clear manner how military technology had reached such a level that simply maintaining a powerful Israeli military apparatus was not adequate. Military measures in themselves could no longer be considered as adequate to ensure Israel's security. 'Already in 1991, close to two-thirds of the public favoured trading land for peace, a formula backed by both Labour and the US administration' (Hadar 1992: 610). This led to growing demands to seek security through negotiations and political compromise.

Internal developments together with US pressure on the Likud government, accompanied by a visible improvement in Israeli–Soviet relations, helped to change the Israeli position on an international peace conference. Previously, Israel opposed the idea of multilateral negotiations, preferring direct bilateral talks. The US and the Soviet Union persuaded both the Israeli and Arab governments to accept a formula which allowed the Madrid talks to start in October 1991 with both multilateral as well as bilateral negotiations. This constituted a major psychological breakthrough that subsequently facilitated the task of Labour in dealing with the PLO. As noted earlier on, not much progress was achieved in the bilateral talks between Israelis and Palestinians until after the election of a Labour government led by Yitzhak Rabin who, in December 1992, lifted the ban on contacts with the PLO. This played a critical role in paving the way to the September 1993 agreement between Israel and the PLO.

Domestic political developments in Arab countries played a critical role in creating a conducive environment for cooperation, too. Anwar Sadat had become the first leader to take Egypt out of the confrontationist path against Israel. Economic factors had played a critical role in this respect. Sadat had come to realise that the Nasserite policies had led the country to a deadend. Egypt needed foreign investment and assistance to create a viable economy that could generate employment for a fast-growing population. Scarce resources needed to be diverted away from the acquisition of military armaments and the military-industrial complex. This could only be achieved if peace could be made with Israel. In addition, there was also recognition that the deteriorating economic situation could well lead Egypt into instability and turmoil. This became even more important as radical Islam began to grow in strength and mobilised support particularly among the economically disadvantaged. These economic considerations also played a critical role in Hosni Mubarak's decision not to go back on the peace agreement with Israel after the assassination of Sadat in October 1981 by Muslim extremists. However, it should also be noted that the concerns about radical Islam and political opposition to peace with Israel were also critical in slowing the deepening of the peace with Israel.

Although other Arab regimes resisted following Egypt and making peace with Israel, the Iran–Iraq war and Iraq's invasion of Kuwait enhanced the importance of Egypt for the Arab world. At least in terms of conservative Arab governments the political and economic strategy adopted by Egypt seemed much less threatening than Pan-Arabism and Nasserite policies. Hence, it could be argued that for all its problems Egypt, by the end of the 1980s and early 1990s, seemed a much better model to live with than the radical Pan-Arab regime that had fought two wars at considerable cost. The loss of legitimacy that Pan-Arabism suffered and the rise of radical Islam made conservative countries much more receptive to following Egypt's leadership. Furthermore, in Jordan, Saudi Arabia and the Gulf states there was also a recognition that with the Cold War ending the role of the Soviet Union was changing in the Middle East. Pan-Arab regimes like the ones in Iraq and Syria were much less likely to enjoy Soviet support and hence be much less of an ideological threat to conservative Arab countries. Instead, the Pan-Arab threat was being replaced by radical Islam. This was a radical Islam that was finding fertile ground among an Arab public demanding greater participation and accountability from half-a-century-old corrupt and repressive regimes.

Domestically, conservative Arab governments chose to confront this threat by a cautious political liberalisation process. The Jordanian government in 1989 allowed the first national elections to be held since 1967, legalised political parties and relaxed censorship on the press (Peretz 1994: 357–358). Kuwait permitted the reopening of the national assembly after elections were held in 1992. The government under the threat of Iranian support for radical Islamic groups in the country had suspended the national assembly in 1986 and censored the press (Peretz 1994: 495). King Fahd too was affected by the winds of liberalism in the Middle East. In 1992, in an effort to diffuse the disaffection among the middle class Islamic fundamentalist groups, he authorised the establishment of a 61-member consultative council, the first of its kind in the kingdom where power had been monopolised by the ruling Suud family very jealously (Peretz 1994: 477).

It is possible to argue that these developments made the conservative Arab governments much more receptive to sitting around the negotiating table with Israel. However, an important additional factor was clearly the US commitment to the protection of conservative regimes and the convincing role played by the US in dislodging Iraq from Kuwait. This lent greater credibility to the US at least among the elite of conservative countries, hence making them more amenable to US calls for liberalism and moderation in their relations with Israel. Syria remained the odd country out. However, the loss of Soviet support accompanied by a clear demise of Pan-Arabism left Hafiz Assad with little choice but reluctantly to sit at the Madrid talks. Furthermore, Hafiz Assad too was not immune to growing pressures to liberalise at least the Syrian economy (Hinnebusch 1993: 188–89; Lawson 1994: 47). Under these circumstances Pan-Arab rhetoric based on a confrontation with Israel became somewhat dysfunctional.

Conclusion

Developments at the international, regional and domestic levels played an important role in bringing about a transformation in the Middle East that made it possible to imagine region-wide economic and political cooperation. The critical turning point was clearly the decision to attend the Madrid talks. This was the first time in the history of the Middle East that a majority of Arab governments agreed to sit at the same negotiating table with Israel. The Madrid talks served as a threshold, and once this threshold was passed the Middle East entered a new kind of politics. The previous politics was based on a denial of Israel's right to exist and to become part of the Middle East. At the same time the Madrid talks symbolised a major turning point in Israel. It paved the way to accepting that the only way Israel could become integrated in the Middle East would be by agreeing to meet the aspirations of Palestinians and a 'land for peace' formula. These significant changes first opened the way to the signing of the PLO–Israeli peace agreement of September 1993. This was followed by the Jordanian–Israeli peace treaty. In 1998 Syrian and Lebanese peace treaties have not yet been made, but it would not be wrong to say that it is only a matter of time before both sign an agreement with Israel. Although the Gulf states have not yet formally recognised Israel they have nevertheless increased their contacts with Israel.

It would be wrong to say that all developments since the early 1990s have been positive in terms of consolidating and expanding region-wide cooperation. Little progress has been achieved in negotiations on achieving greater security and stability in the region. Yet, in spite of the major setbacks, it should also be noted that no Arab government has advocated views calling for a return to the situation prevailing before the Madrid talks. In Israel, the right-wing government came to power with a very slim majority but a commitment among Israelis to consolidate the peace process remains strong. Furthermore, the international community and particularly the US remains committed to the peace agreement.

How can the peace process be reinforced in the Middle East? What are the factors that might contribute to such a process? These are some of the questions that the next chapter will address.

7 Potential for regional political cooperation

In Chapter 6, it was pointed out that developments at the international, regional and domestic levels paved the way to the possibility of region-wide political cooperation in the Middle East. The structure of this cooperation is often referred to as the Madrid process and will briefly be evaluated with a view to preparing the basis for the model of cooperation to be developed in this chapter. The Madrid process consists of three elements. The first one was the opening conference which was convened under the auspices of the United States and the Soviet Union on 30 October 1991 and lasted for three days. This was the first time ever that a number of Arab states and Israel had come together to sit around the same negotiating table with the purpose of achieving peace. The second element was the ongoing direct bilateral negotiations between Israel and Syria, Lebanon, Jordan and the Palestinians. The direct talks between Israel and Arab states aim to achieve peace treaties while the negotiations between Israel and the Palestinians are based on a two-stage formula. The formula aims to achieve a five-year interim self-government arrangement for the Palestinians in the occupied territories followed by negotiations on the permanent status of these territories. The third element of the Madrid process, known as the multilateral track, started at a conference in Moscow in January 1992 and is meant to build the basis for a secure and stable Middle East for the future. The multilateral track includes five separate fora attended by representatives of Middle Eastern countries as well as the international community. The talks focus on five key issues of concern to the Middle East: water, environment, arms control, refugees and economic development. A working group focuses on each issue.[1]

Political cooperation: An assessment

The Madrid process has had both successes as well as some serious setbacks, particularly since 1996. A number of significant achievements under the Israeli–Palestinian and Israeli–Jordanian bilateral tracks of the Madrid process were made. The first track included the signing of the Israeli–PLO Declaration of Principles (DOP) in September 1993,[2] the subsequent Gaza–Jericho agreement in May 1994, the agreement on the transfer of power and responsibilities in August 1994 and the Interim Agreement on the West Bank and the Gaza Strip of September 1995.

Accordingly, the Palestinians were able to hold elections in January 1996 and form institutions to govern areas in the occupied territories transferred from Israel to the Palestinians. The Israeli–Palestinian track, as was envisaged in the DOP, entered a stage where the two parties hold negotiations to determine final and permanent status arrangements. Some of the issues over which agreements have to be reached (at the time of writing) include the final status of the city of Jerusalem, the question of Palestinian refugees and Jewish settlements, security arrangements, borders, relations and cooperation with other neighbours as well as additional issues deemed of common interests to both sides. Technically, agreements reached on these issues are supposed to come into force in May 1999 bringing about full peace and reconciliation between Israelis and Palestinians.

By Middle Eastern standards, what has been achieved by 1998 can be considered as a major success. Israelis and Palestinians have remained at the negotiating table since the Madrid process started. Israel has accepted the PLO as its partner in the search for peace between the two peoples and has actually transferred sovereignty to the Palestinians in most of the Gaza Strip and certain areas of the West Bank. The Palestinians were able to obtain what they had failed to achieve through armed struggle and warfare in the past. In return Israel gained greater legitimacy in the community of states and the PLO, in April 1996, amended its Covenant which made references to the destruction of Israel, sealing the commitment to exist in peace alongside Israel. Arab governments, and in particular the Egyptian and Jordanian governments, have also stood behind this process. This positive atmosphere led the governments of Mauritania, Morocco, Oman and Tunisia to permit the opening of Israeli diplomatic and trade offices. Furthermore, a gradual erosion of the Arab boycott occurred as secondary and tertiary boycotts were ended by these governments and other Gulf states.

However, in 1998 the peace process between the Palestinians and the Israelis remains fragile and faces many problems. Terrorism perpetrated by extremist groups has led to the repeated imposition of closures on the West Bank and the Gaza Strip, preventing Palestinians from entering Israel. This has aggravated the already depressed nature of the Palestinian economy and undermined the expectation that peace with Israel would bring economic prosperity. The Israeli government has continued with its controversial policies of permitting the construction of new Jewish settlements in the occupied territories. This has generated intense conflict and violence as well as considerable frustration about the future fate of the peace process. With the formation of a right-wing government in Israel following the May 1996 elections the situation became even worse. The growing political influence of right-wing Jewish groups and Jewish settlers exacerbated the situation and raised the tension between Israel and the Palestinians. In September 1996 the reopening of a tunnel in the Old City of Jerusalem led to rioting by Palestinians and pitted for the first time Israeli and Palestinian security forces against each other, causing the death of more than eighty people. Violence erupted again as a consequence of the Israeli government's decision to build a housing complex in East Jerusalem. In Hebron, too, life was marred with violence since an agreement was reached for a partial Israeli withdrawal from the town in January 1997. This situation deeply undermined confidence between the two sides and negotiations came to stalemate in March 1997. The Palestinians refuse to restart talks unless construction work for Jewish settlements is halted. From the other side, the Israeli government refuses to compromise on the grounds that the Palestinian Authority continues to support or condone terrorism and violence.

Yet, in spite of this negative climate, there is also a clear commitment at the time of writing to ensure that the peace process does not completely collapse and there are intense efforts to restart it. In October 1996, US President Bill Clinton became actively involved in diffusing the tunnel crisis, and in January 1997 he played an effective role in ensuring the transfer of a good part of Hebron to the Palestinian Authority against powerful opposition within the Israeli cabinet. President Mubarak of Egypt has repeatedly reiterated the need to keep the peace process alive. In November 1996 after the Middle East North Africa Economic Summit (MENA) in Cairo, he emphasised the importance of pursuing peace and noted that the alternative would be a drift back into deep instability, terrorism and generalised violence (*Al-Ahram Weekly* 21–27 November 1996). Again, in a similar manner, both the Israeli Prime Minister Binjamin Netanyahu and Husni Mubarak reaffirmed their respective governments' commitment to peace during their meeting in Egypt (*Al-Ahram Weekly* 6–12 January 1997).

Following the crisis over the Jewish housing project, which erupted in March 1997, there was intense diplomatic activity involving Egypt, Jordan, Israel, the Palestinian Authority, the European Union and the US to resolve the stalemate in the Israeli–Palestinian talks. During his visit to the US, Yasser Arafat, PLO chairman, seemed to demonstrate a willingness to control any temptation to revert to old ways of violent confrontation to resolve the crisis, when he reiterated to the US President his commitment to achieve lasting peace with Israel (*Turkish Daily News* 5 March 1997). In May 1997 there were news reports that Yasser Arafat might be returning to the negotiating table short of an end to the construction project in East Jerusalem provided that Israel permitted the building of a Palestinian harbour and an airport in Gazza (*Al-Ahram Weekly* 8–14 May 1997). In June and July there were also growing reports of secret talks being held between Palestinians and Israelis in an effort to break the deadlock (*Al-Ahram Weekly* 12–18 June; 3–9 July 1997). A breakthrough was achieved to restart the peace process after a meeting between Arafat and the Israeli Foreign Minister in July. Unfortunately, these efforts experienced a setback when deadly terrorist bombings by radical Islamic groups took place in Israel in July and September 1997. However, during the course of October and November intense US diplomacy led by US Secretary of State Madeleine Albright appeared to have brought the two parties closer to a possible agreement over Israeli troop redeployment in return for increased Palestinian efforts to meet Israeli security needs before the start of final status negotiations (*New York Times* 1 December 1997). In early December 1997 after Albright held meetings with both Binjamin Netanyahu and Yasser Arafat, an American official was optimistic enough to note that 'Now, we are into the nuts and bolts of a further deployment' (*New York Times* 7 December 1997). These were clearly developments suggesting that parties remain committed to the peace process, but at the same time there is also a tough bargaining process taking place involving many domestic, regional and international constituencies.

Possibly the most promising sign in terms of the future of the peace process is that, in spite of the many setbacks, frustrations and economic hardship the Palestinians have had to suffer, by and large they have remained supportive of the peace process. This can be seen from the results of the public opinion polls taken on a regular basis by the *Centre for Palestine Research and Studies* in Nablus (www.cprs-palestine.org). In their first poll taken in September 1993, 64.9 per cent agreed with the process laid down by the Israeli–PLO Declaration of Principles (*Poll number 1* 10–11 September 1993). In a poll taken in November 1997, 68 per cent of those polled indicated their support for the peace process (*Poll number 30* 27–29 November 1997). What is more promising is that 54 per cent of the supporters of Hamas, whose leadership has often violently opposed both the peace process and Israel, also expressed support for the peace process. In Israel, in spite of the influence of the hard-liners in government, the opposition, including President Ezer Weizman, has openly argued for the Israeli government to be more supportive of the peace process. In a poll taken in February and March 1997 it was revealed that for the first time in the history of Israel there was now a majority of 51 per cent of Israelis who were prepared to accept the establishment of a Palestinian state (Arian 1997). Furthermore, 89 per cent of those polled – compared to 53 per cent in 1994 – were supportive of the idea of negotiations with the Palestinians over military action. These results seem to be indicative of the way the peace process receives broad support from the public, both among Israelis and Palestinians and in spite of the positions taken by hard-liners on both sides that play such a critical role in stalling and undermining negotiations.

One area where the Madrid process has been particularly successful is with respect to Israeli–Jordanian bilateral negotiations. The negotiations after the Madrid conference led to the adoption of the Washington Declaration in July 1994 by King Hussein of Jordan and Prime Minister Rabin of Israel which ended the state of war between the two countries. Subsequently, the Prime Ministers of both countries signed a peace treaty in October 1994. This treaty became the second peace treaty ever signed between Israel and an Arab country. The two countries established full diplomatic relations and particular emphasis was put on expanding economic, military and political cooperation. The peace between Israel and Jordan has generally been viewed as one that has the potential of going well beyond the one between Israel and Egypt. However, the crisis in Israeli–Palestinian relations has dampened these expectations. Jordanians have been much less enthusiastic than their government, to deepen relations with Israel especially since the formation of a right-wing government in Israel. In March 1997, the killing of Israeli schoolgirls by a Jordanian soldier led to the resignation of the Jordanian Prime Minister who was known for his strong support for the peace process. Furthermore, a large number of professional associations and politicians called for an immediate halt to the normalisation of relations with Israel, leading to speculation that popular anger against Israel could pave the way to a showdown between the Jordanian palace and the people (*Al-Ahram Weekly* 20–26 March 1997). This naturally left King Hussein of Jordan in a very difficult position. The King has been an enthusiastic and energetic supporter of peace with Israel. However, he too expressed his growing despair over the breakdown in Arab–Israeli talks (*CNN* 12 July 1997). The situation became even more exacerbated in late September 1997 when a failed Israeli attempt to assassinate a member of Hamas in Amman left the King in a very difficult situation only weeks before the Jordanian elections. However, the King seemed to successfully overcome the crisis without undermining his commitment to the peace process when, at the opening session of the newly elected parliament at the end of November 1997, he announced the need to distinguish between the position of the government and the position of the people of Israel. He also made it very clear his intentions of becoming a part of the final status negotiations between the Palestinians and Israel (Satloff 1997).

Turning to the Israeli–Syrian bilateral talks, not much has been achieved in this area. The stumbling block was the stalemate over the Israeli withdrawal from the Golan Heights in 1997. Syria demands a total Israeli withdrawal, while Israel insists that it needs to negotiate the terms of its withdrawal and the final status of the Golan Heights. The matter is also complicated by the Syrian presence in Lebanon and the support that it extends to radical Muslim groups such as the Hizbullah. The Hizbullah has periodically launched rocket attacks on northern Israel. This has led to frequent Israeli accusations that Syria supports terrorism. In turn, Israel retaliated against the Hizbullah and supported the occupation of a security zone in southern Lebanon controlled by a Christian militia group. Syrian presence in Lebanon and the volatile situation in the south of the country have so far also prevented any progress being achieved in respect of the Lebanese–Israeli bilateral talks. However, during the previous Labour-dominated government the then Prime Minister Yitzhak Rabin had expressed readiness to negotiate the terms for turning over the Golan Heights to the Syrians. At the time, President Hafez Assad of Syria had declined the opportunity to cooperate; however, with the formation of the Netanyahu government in Israel he expressed an interest in negotiating the return of the Golan Heights. However, at this point the Israeli government was less willing.

Among those who participated at the Madrid conference the Syrian government was the least supportive of the peace process. It boycotted all meetings involving the Israelis and played a critical role in pushing the Arab League summit in June 1996 and the Arab League Foreign Ministerial meeting in March 1997 to adopt decisions calling for the halting of the normalisation process with Israel. Throughout 1997, Syria actively lobbied against the holding of the Fourth MENA summit in Doha, Qatar in November. In December, at the Islamic Conference Organisation's summit held in Tehran, Syria took a very critical position against Israel and those countries that maintained relations with Israel. Yet Assad does not seem to be against an eventual peace with Israel. He is, however, clearly keen to drive a hard bargain. He made this quite clear during talks with President Mubarak in Sharm El-Sheikh in Sinai, Egypt when he said 'We want this peace, but I can tell you now that the road is long' (*Al-Ahram Weekly* 8–14 May 1997: 2).

In their very essence, the multilateral track negotiations constitute an effort to transform the Middle East from a region characterised by conflict and confrontation to one where a structured and concerted effort is made to address and to solve the problems of the region. However, the purpose is not only to solve problems but also to use the negotiation process itself to serve as a confidence-building measure to promote cooperation and normalised relations among the countries of the region (Peters 1996: 2). The multilateral track is composed of a Steering Committee whose task is to oversee the meetings and decisions of five Working Groups. These are the Water Resources Working Group, the Environmental Working Group, the Arms Control and Regional Security (ACRS) Working Group, the Refugee Working Group and the Regional Economic Development Working Group. Each working group operates on the basis of projects aiming at addressing specific problems and is attended by representatives of participant countries from within as well as outside the Middle East.

Some of the key projects have included the development of a desalination research and technology centre in Muscat, training courses for refugees, the Gulf of Aqaba/Eilat oil-spill emergency centres, the linking of regional electricity grids and the establishment of a Regional Bank for Development. Some of the projects are slowly but surely reaching the point of realisation. This is mostly the case with projects addressing less controversial issues concerning technical and environmental matters, such as the establishment of the desalination research centre in Oman and the adoption of the Bahrain Environmental Code of Conduct for the Middle East. However, in spite of the initial enthusiasm, progress in the establishment of a Regional Bank had been very slow. There has also been much less concrete progress made in the ACRS Working Group dealing with military issues, which are invariably much more sensitive, involving arms control and verification issues. The highly heralded attempt to take the first steps towards emulating the early days of the Conference on Security and Cooperation in Europe (CSCE) by adopting a Declaration of Principles on Arms Control and Regional Security and establishing a Regional Security Centre in Amman have not materialised (Jentleson 1996).

The lack of progress on issues related to the ACRS Working Group stemmed partly from the thorny nature of security-related issues and partly from a confrontation between Egypt and Israel over nuclear weapons. However, more importantly, the whole of the multilateral talks was adversely affected by the change in government in Israel. Syria and Lebanon had, right from the start, boycotted the talks. Subsequent to the Arab summit in June 1996, all the other Arab governments withdrew their support and no meetings were held after that. Although this clearly constitutes a major setback, the fact that a certain degree of institutionalisation of multilateral cooperation and an overall agenda have been achieved in a region that has seen so many inter-state wars and ideological confrontation should be considered a major achievement. The Working Groups provided for the first time in history fora where former warring parties – Israelis and Arabs – were able to work together on a regular basis and develop a new set of norms for cooperative behaviour. It is highly likely that the multilateral talks will resume once the impasse between the Palestinians and Israelis is surmounted.

The three MENA summits held in Casablanca, Morocco (October 1994), Amman, Jordan (October 1995) and Cairo, Egypt (November 1996) are considered as significant developments in support of the Arab–Israeli peace process. Although these summits are not directly part of the Madrid process there is a close relationship and overlap with what the Regional Economic Development Working Group aims to achieve. The summits have seen a much larger number of participants from countries and business institutions from inside as well as outside of the immediate region. The first summit in Casablanca saw the attendance of representatives of 61 countries, international financial institutions such as the World Bank and 1,114 business people. A similar level of participation was also achieved at the meeting in Amman, while at Cairo the numbers increased to 87 countries and approximately 2,600 business people. This high level of attendance can be seen as a sign of the importance that the international community attributes to the relationship between economics and the success of the peace process in the Middle East. However, this performance was somewhat undermined at the fourth summit held in Doha, Qatar when a large number of Arab countries did not participate in protest of the setbacks in the peace process. Nevertheless, representatives from 65 countries together with 900 business people participated at the summit. There were important business and economic deals that were agreed involving Qatar, Jordan, Israel and other countries. The summit reiterated commitment to the Madrid process as well as to the key United Nations Security Council resolutions 242 and 338 (Plotkin 1997).

The summits so far have played a critical role in the gradual development of the institutional structure for greater economic activity in the region. At the first summit support was lent to the decision of the Gulf Cooperation Council to ignore the secondary and tertiary aspects of the Arab boycott. The Arab economic boycott of Israel had long been a major impediment to international business activity in the region. At the same summit decisions were also taken to establish a Middle East and North Africa Development Bank (MEDB), a regional Chamber of Commerce and Business Council, and a Tourism Board. Further progress was achieved in these areas in Amman in October 1995. However, since 1996 some setbacks in the realisation of these projects occurred with the slowing down of the peace process. Nevertheless, in Cairo delegates were hopeful that the MEDB and the Middle East Mediterranean Travel and Tourism Association (MEMTTA) would soon become a reality (*Al-Ahram Weekly* 21–17 November 1996). In Doha the summit welcomed the establishment of MEMTTA in Tunis and called on participants to speed up the process of ratification of the agreement for the MEDB. Business participants urged governments to resume their efforts to establish the Regional Business Council (Plotkin 1997).

The summits were also important in terms of the emphasis placed on the role of the private sector in the economic development of the region. Recognition of the growing importance attributed to economic liberalisation as a process that can assist the peace process and can help normalisation of relations between states of the region. Furthermore, these summits also demonstrated the international commitment for the idea of using economics as a vehicle for achieving and consolidating peace, particularly on the part of the US and the European Union. This position was reflected in the words of an EU official who underlined that 'there will be no peace without economic prosperity' (*Al-Ahram Weekly* 21–27 November 1996: 5). Yet, the Cairo summit also demonstrated that politics still matters. The fact that the summit was preceded by events that led to setbacks in the peace process showed how politics still influences economics. This was recognised when President Mubarak, during his opening speech, observed that '(o)ur economies have grown closer ... Yet, this is not close enough, for as long as comprehensive peace on all tracks is not firmly and irreversibly established among us, we will not reap the full benefits of our economic integration' (*Al-Ahram Weekly* 26 December 1996 -1 January 1997: 6). In Doha in spite of the discouraging political background, business people, including some from countries whose governments boycotted the conference, were present and keen to develop business contacts with their Israeli counterparts (Plotkin 1997).

Overall, the Madrid process and the economic summits transformed the Middle East in a manner that could not have been imagined ten years before. At the time of writing, in spite of the frustration with the recent lack of progress with the peace progress, and setbacks in the normalisation process, there still remains a strong commitment to peace in the Middle East both internationally and regionally. Clearly, this commitment seems to fluctuate with the ups and downs of the process but so far there have not been any significant signs of support for a return to the old days of the Middle East characterised by violence, radicalism and intransigence. It would not be too wrong to say that the old ways of conducting international politics in the Middle East have been replaced with diplomacy and negotiations. Still, there are nevertheless a number of fundamental challenges associated with the peace process that need to be urgently addressed.

Some of the most critical challenges have to do with the implementation of the Oslo Accords signed between Israel and the PLO in September 1993. One such challenge involves the future status of Jerusalem. In 1998, the Israeli government considers Jerusalem as its unified capital while the Palestinians argue that the future status of the city has yet to be determined. As the crisis over the construction of the Jewish housing complex near East Jerusalem has indicated, the Palestinians attribute great importance to keeping this part of the city as Arab as possible in the hope that they can eventually establish some form of control at least over East Jerusalem. Another important issue contested between the Palestinians and the Israeli government is the proportion of the remaining territories on the West Bank that will be transferred to the Palestinian Authority. Currently, the Israeli government, under the influence of right-wing groups, is reluctant to turn over more than 30 per cent of the West Bank to the Palestinians. The Palestinians on the other hand argue that at least 90 per cent of the West Bank should be transferred to the Authority. Another very tough and important source of contention is the future status of the occupied territories. The Israeli government seems reluctant to accept a fully-fledged Palestinian state, while the Palestinians clearly expect to achieve statehood by the time the final status negotiations are completed in May 1999. In December 1997, Arafat threatened unilaterally to declare a state if no agreement is reached by May 1999 while Netanyahu immediately retorted by threatening to annex the West Bank.

Another source of concern associated with the peace process is that, in spite of the normalisation occurring at the governmental level, the notion of peace between Israel and the Arabs has failed to involve ordinary people. The level of interaction between ordinary people is still considered to be at a level much lower than desired, especially lower than Israel desires. There are large numbers of Israeli tourists visiting Egypt and Jordan while the flow of tourism in the other direction remains low. This is particularly the case for Egypt, even though Egypt has been technically at peace with Israel since 1979. Although some of the imbalance may be attributed to the economic disparities between Israel and its Arab neighbours, an important factor has to do with the fact that, in the minds and hearts of many people, peace with Israel has not yet received wide popular support. Arab masses still remain under the influence of long years of anti-Israeli rhetoric and fear of Israeli domination. The setbacks in the peace process during the course of 1996 and first half of 1997 exacerbated the situation. Radical Islamic groups among Palestinians and in Egypt and Jordan have opposed the peace with Israel as well as the development of relations with Israel at the level of ordinary people.

The development of 'people-to-people' contacts is critical because, as we have pointed out, no agreement for cooperation can be long lived unless approved and ratified domestically. An important step in encouraging people-to-people relations in the Middle East was taken when a group of Arab and Israeli intellectuals met in Denmark in January 1997 and adopted the Copenhagen Declaration (*Al-Ahram Weekly* 6–12 February 1997). In this Declaration the need to encourage contacts between ordinary people and achieve 'a grassroots alliance' for lasting peace was stressed. However, this Declaration has triggered considerable controversy and criticisms in the Arab world (*Al-Ahram Weekly* 6–12 March 1997) suggesting that there are still important obstacles. However, the fact that such a declaration has been adopted should in itself be considered as a positive development, although injecting life into such a declaration will remain a major challenge which will call for special attention and effort.

Radical regimes such as the ones in Libya and Iraq have not yet joined, or lent their support to, the peace process. Both regimes remain isolated from the international community but continue to constitute a threat to regional stability and security. The Iraqi regime has not yet totally complied with United Nations Security Council Resolutions calling for the dismantlement of its offensive military capabilities. Libya remains branded as a state that supports terrorism. Both regimes refuse to recognise Israel's right to exist in the region and they maintain radical ideological positions reminiscent of the days of the rejectionist front. Iran is another important country in the region that has so far refused to support the peace process. This provides justification for radical Islamic groups in the Middle East to oppose and sabotage the peace process. At the time of writing it is not clear whether the election of the relatively moderate Ayatollah Mohammed Khatami as the new President of Iran will change Iranian foreign policy in favour of Israel and the peace process in any significant way. Although the Final Declaration at the Islamic Conference Organisation's summit in Tehran in December 1997 called for 'interaction, dialogue and understanding among cultures and religions', there was a conspicuous absence of any reference to the peace process, possibly reflecting the host country's influence over the wording of the declaration (*CNN* 11 December 1997).

Furthermore, Iran's supreme leader Ayatollah Khamenei, during the opening session of the summit delivered a speech critical and uncompromising towards the US and Israel (*New York Times* 10 December 1997). Although the President of Iran, Mohammed Khatami, was very much conciliatory towards the United States at a news conference after the summit, he reiterated the traditional Iranian line when he singled out Israel and its 'Zionist regime as the only country which we do not recognize these days' (*New York Times* 15 December 1997). At the same time he also emphasised that 'we have opposed the peace process and we still do. [Israel] is a racist, terrorist, and expansionist regime. … We hope that the roots of problems in the region and the world will be destroyed' (quoted in Clawson 1997). These remarks are clearly not very promising in terms of Iran's role in the Middle East, and make it difficult to judge whether it is possible to expect, in the near future, a major departure from the position held by hard-liners in Iran who had threatened participants in the Madrid peace conference with assassination (Ramazani 1992: 412). However, the fact that the Tehran summit also served as a venue for reconciling Iran with some of the moderate Arab states that have been supportive of the peace process might be seen as a positive development.

The growing acquisition of weapons of mass destruction and ballistic missiles by Iraq, Iran, Libya and Syria continues to constitute a major threat to the stability of the region. These are weapons systems that are capable of striking not only Israeli targets but also Arab and Turkish targets not to mention southern European ones (Lesser and Tellis 1996). What makes them particularly worrisome is that they are weapons systems that were actively employed in the past during the Iran–Iraq war as well as the Gulf crisis. Furthermore, the situation is complicated by the fact that these weapons are in the control of regimes for whom there are ideological as well as territorial disputes both amongst themselves and with some of their neighbours. Israel's nuclear capabilities and its reluctance to sign the non-proliferation treaty in the face of the threats constituted by these weapons systems and regimes has also adversely affected the possibilities of making progress in respect to arms-control and confidence-building exercises.

Lastly, it should also be added that there are serious problems in the region separate from the Arab–Israeli conflict. Syria remains in occupation of an important proportion of Lebanon and enjoys considerable political influence in the country. The Syrian presence in Lebanon was lent some degree of legitimacy in the 1989 Taif agreements which had helped to end the Lebanese civil war. However, when seen in the light of the Syrian dream of creating a Greater Syria in an area that corresponds to Syria, Lebanon, Jordan and parts of Turkey, Syrian presence in Lebanon reinforces her neighbours' concerns about Syrian territorial expansionism (Pipes 1990). Syrian support for organisations associated with terrorism in the region is yet another source of tension. The Syrian government has been condemned internationally for assisting the Workers' Party of Kurdistan (PKK) against

Turkey and for assisting extremist Islamic groups against Israel. This clearly leads to considerable distrust towards Syria while complicating the search for a stable and secure Middle East.

There are also serious problems between Syria and Iraq. Although the regimes in both countries have traditionally advocated support for Pan-Arabism they have bitterly clashed with each other in respect to the leadership of Arab unity (Kienle 1990). This rivalry led Syria to support Iran during the Iran–Iraqi war. In a similar manner during the Gulf crisis in 1990 Syria did not hesitate to join the military coalition against Iraq. The sharing of the waters of the Euphrates has also been another source of conflict between the two countries. The construction of the South-Eastern Anatolian Development Project from the early 1980s has led to fears in Syria that Turkey can restrict the flow of water to Syria for political reasons. The dispute over the waters of the Euphrates, along with Turkish objections to Syrian support for the PKK, results in frequently heightened tension between the two countries. Conflict over water is not limited to Iraq, Syria and Turkey. The scarcity of water and an ever-growing demand for water in the Middle East has been recognised as a potential source of war. However, the Madrid framework appears to have helped Jordan, Israel and Palestine to reach some degree of agreement on sharing common water supplies.

One other problem that needs to be mentioned stems from the uncertain situation prevailing in Iraq. The Iraqi invasion of Kuwait led to a United Nations trade embargo as well as to a massive defeat of the Iraqi military and the loss of Iraqi sovereignty for Iraq north of the 36 parallel and south of the 32nd parallel. However, in spite of these major setbacks Saddam Hussein's regime remains in power and at the time of writing, after six years, is still not fully cooperating with the international community in the application of the United Nations Security Council Resolutions. The situation in northern Iraq remains particularly unstable as rival Kurdish groups struggle among themselves for greater control over the region. The conflict complicated the task of Northern Watch (formerly Operation Provide Comfort) to protect the civilian population against the Iraqi military when the latter entered the area in alliance with one of the Kurdish groups in September 1996. Subsequently, the US showed its determination to keep the Iraqi military out of southern Iraq by launching missile attacks and enlarging the exclusion zone from the 32nd to 33rd parallels. In November, in accordance with United Nations Security Council Resolution 986 adopted in April 1996, the embargo on Iraq was partially lifted. Accordingly, Iraq was permitted to export oil for six months and allowed to purchase food and humanitarian goods with the revenue. In June and December 1997, the deal was renewed. Although, this may be a first step towards the rehabilitation of Iraq into the international community, these are not clear signs that Saddam Hussein, after fighting two wars and spending hundreds of billions of dollars, has actually been reformed. The crisis that Saddam Hussein provoked by expelling American members of the United Nations Special Commission (UNSCOM) inspectors from Iraq in October 1997 and his continued reluctance to cooperate with the United Nations over the destruction of weapons of mass destruction are clear signs that reform in Iraq's behaviour is not imminent.

According to Rolf Ekeus, the former chairman of UNSCOM, Iraq is still believed to possess an operational missile force equipped with chemical and biological warheads (Ekeus 1997).

How can these problems be resolved? How can the advancements that have been achieved by the Arab–Israeli peace process be consolidated and then expanded to address other problems of the Middle East that stand in the way of a more stable and secure Middle East? Can effective political cooperation be achieved in the Middle East? These are surely not easy questions to answer. However, the following section, by borrowing ideas from the literature on 'democratic peace', will argue that the best approach to follow might be to encourage greater political cooperation among a group of 'like-minded' countries: a group of Middle Eastern countries which respect each other's territorial integrity, are committed to resolving conflicts among themselves peacefully and have regimes that support political and economic liberalisation. Effective cooperation among such a core group of countries might help to create a pocket of stability and security in the Middle East. This process in itself and the advantages associated with stability and security could trigger a demonstration effect and have spill-over effects encouraging further economic and political liberalisation in the region as a whole.

Democratic peace

The proponents of 'democratic peace' argue that those countries that have democratic regimes are much less likely to wage wars against each other.[3] Doyle traces the origins of this notion to the works of Immanuel Kant (Doyle 1983). Kant's premise was based on the idea that democratic consent served as a restraint on governmental decision to go to war because of citizens' awareness that they would have to pay for all the costs associated with war. However, there is more to democratic peace than just that. The reasons why democracies do not fight against each other are complex and multifaceted. Furthermore, it is difficult to say that there is a complete consensus in the academic literature as to why exactly 'democratic peace' occurs. Russett (1993) has examined the behaviour of all pairs of independent states for the period 1946–86 and identifies two sets of factors that make it less likely for democracies to initiate wars against each other.

First, the norms and practices that liberal democracies have developed as a part of their political culture when dealing with domestic conflict help them to manage and resolve conflicts among themselves without resorting to force. Russett notes that 'when two democracies come into a conflict of interest, they are able to apply democratic norms in their interaction, and these norms prevent most conflicts from mounting to the threat or use of military force' (Russett 1993: 33). Dixon in this respect underlines the significance of the influence of domestic political norms, such as 'accommodation' and 'compromise', on the external behaviour of democratic countries and adds that '... if political leaders are accustomed to non-violent procedures of conflict resolution in domestic affairs, then it is likely that such methods will also prove useful in settling international disputes' (Dixon 1993: 45).

Second, structural and institutional factors play an important role in restraining democratic leaders from moving their countries towards war. These leaders have to mobilise broad popular support, including that of government bureaucracies, the legislature and many interest groups. In other words, the division of power provides checks and balances on democratic leaders. Furthermore, navigating through these checks and balances is very time consuming. What then actually keeps two democratic states from resorting to violence is that structural and institutional delays in the process of mobilisation for war provide enough time for negotiations and other means of peaceful conflict resolution to take place (Russett 1993: 39). At the same time, what is probably as important, is the expectation of democratic leaders that the same constraints work on their counterparts in other democratic countries. Therefore, Russett concludes, two democratic states – each constrained from going to war and anticipating the other to be so inhibited – are more likely to settle their conflicts short of war (Russett 1993: 39).

An important point that needs to be clarified about the notion of 'democratic peace' is that it does not suggest that democracies never go to war. On the contrary, democratic countries are as likely to go to war as are non-democratic ones. Quincy Wright's *Study of War* (1942) is considered to be one of the first to have noted this trend. Since then there has been a growing body of empirically tested literature that has confirmed this trend. As Rothstein underlines, the 'one argument all the analysts agree on is that democracies do not fight other democracies' (Rothstein 1993: 20). Hence, democracies do go to war but the significant point is that they go to war with non-democracies. How does one then differentiate a democracy from a non-democracy (autocracy)? This has been a major source of disagreement in the literature on 'democratic peace'. The problem arises to a large extent, from the fact that it is difficult to think of both terms in terms of simple opposites.

It is not the aim of this chapter to enter a discussion of what constitutes democracy on the one hand and autocracy on the other. Dahl associates a democracy with elected officials, free and fair elections, inclusive suffrage, the right to run for office, freedom of expression, access to alternative information protected by law, and associational freedom (Dahl 1989: 221). It is difficult to identify many countries in the Middle East which meet Dahl's definition of democracy. Israel and Turkey are frequently referred to as two-model democracies in the Middle East (Roberts 1995: 121). However, there are also many who point out the limitations of the democracy in these two countries. Solingen argues that by Dahl's standards Israel is a democratic country only within its 1967 borders (Solingen 1996b: 140). In spite of a long record of free and competitive elections, a growing democratic discourse and little fear of an authoritarian regression Özbudun argues that 'few analysts would call Turkey a stable or consolidated democracy' (Özbudun 1996: 123). The case seems even worse for most of the other countries of the Middle East. *Freedom in the World* (Kaplan 1997) provides a comparative freedom index of countries in the world based on a number of indicators which encompass the basic elements of democracy. In this index, apart from Israel and Turkey, only Jordan, Kuwait and Morocco appear as 'free or partly free' countries. Clearly, the present record is one that supports Norton and Wright's argument that one cannot expect a general and sustained 'outburst of democracy' in the Middle East (Norton and Wright 1995: 11).

This pessimistic state of affairs led Salame to observe that a region stretching 'from Tehran to Marrakesh' had been witnessing uninterrupted rule of authoritarian leaders at a time when other regions of the world were adopting growing forms of democratic government (Salame 1994a: 1). Kalaycıoğlu takes a similar view and concludes that it would be optimistic to expect the Arab countries and Iran to achieve any significant degree of democratisation in the near future, 'at least not before a fourth or fifth wave of democratisation is unleashed' (Kalaycıoğlu 1996: 87). However, as Rothstein notes, until recently 'in the Third World itself, liberal democracy has been denounced as a Western intrusion and its procedures (competition, participation, a free press, etc.) interpreted as luxuries for poor and divided countries' (Rothstein 1993: 24). Breakdowns in authoritarian government and transitions to democracy in the Third World are a relatively recent phenomenon (Huntington 1991). If democracy is viewed more as a process rather than just as a state of affairs, then a relatively less pessimistic view of the Middle East might be drawn. In that case it is possible to observe a slow and an unevenly distributed process of democratisation taking place in many Arab countries. Solingen calls this process 'incipient democratisation' and argues that this 'enables us to differentiate among regimes with varying degrees of democratic attributes, over time and across countries' (Solingen 1996b: 140).

Owen notes that all Arab states that, with the exception of Palestine, succeeded the Ottoman Empire had constitutions calling for elections (Owen 1992: 224). However, he adds that in the 1940s and 1950s the democratic and parliamentary system had many critics and few defenders in the Arab world and hence these systems were swept away by the military very easily. He quotes Nasser's unapproving remark of democracy as representing a generally shared attitude towards democracy and pluralism (Owen 1992: 230). It is no wonder that Kedourie is categorical in concluding that constitutional and representative government in the Middle East has, by and large, been a major failure (Kedourie 1994). Lebanon and Morocco were two Arab countries where a multi-party system persisted after independence while Kuwait did hold elections sporadically though without allowing for the operation of political parties. Jordan held what Rath calls its freest election in 1956, however the government was forced to resign in 1957 and political parties were subsequently banned. There was a short period of liberalisation in Jordan in 1967 which was brought to an abrupt end with the civil war in 1970 (Rath 1994: 532–534). Otherwise, the conspicuous absence of parliamentary democracy persisted in the Arab world until the 1980s when the very first signs of 'incipient democratisation' began to occur.

Although Egypt does not qualify as a free and democratic country in the *Freedom in the World* report (Kaplan 1997) it is in Egypt that the first early signs of 'incipient democratisation' emerged in the mid-1970s. Anwar Sadat, who had become the president of Egypt after the death of Nasser, was under growing pressure to liberalise the economy. The need to neutralise the opposition against economic restructuring forced Sadat to revive multi-party politics and introduce some political liberalisation. Nasser's Arab Socialist Union was broken into three platforms, encouraged to run against each other in a carefully managed election in

November 1976 (Owen 1994: 183–185). Since then, and especially during the presidentship of Husni Mubarak, the Egyptian political system has been liberalised to allow for carefully controlled political parties to emerge.

Periodic national elections for the People's Assembly have been held although these elections have tended to be run in a manner that has always favoured the ruling National Democratic Party. This situation has led Springborg to conclude that the Egyptian elections and parliament are sites of unequal contest (Springborg 1989: 197). Nevertheless, it can be argued, for reasons ranging from the need to bolster regime legitimacy to maintaining support for economic restructuring, that Mubarak continues to be supportive of democratisation, even if it remains an experience within the bounds of a limited democracy or what Owen calls a 'controlled multi-party system' (Owen 1994: 189–190).

In April 1989, major disturbances and riots erupted in Jordan as a result of a major economic crisis. In the face of these riots, King Hussein chose 'to seek popular support for the necessary economic reforms through a political opening and promises of democratisation and political freedom' (Rath 1994: 542). This took the form of parliamentary elections in November 1989 (the first ones to be held since 1967) followed by the adoption of a National Charter. The Charter opened the way for a multi-party system, and allowed for considerable freedom of the press, reflecting a clear commitment to democratisation (Nakhleh 1994: 113). Competitive elections, greater freedom and a clear commitment on the part of King Hussein's commitment to political liberalisation has led Perthes to conclude that in the Middle East 'the most far reaching democratisation has been taking place in Jordan' (Perthes 1994: 243). An additional important achievement for Jordan was its ability to incorporate Islamists into the system as well. This was reflected in the mainstream Islamic movement Muslim Brotherhood's acceptance to work within the framework of the parliamentary system (Rath 1994: 552). Yet a shadow was thrown on some of this progress when opposition parties, including the Islamic bloc, boycotted the November 1997 elections in Jordan and the participation rate fell from 68 and 63 per cent respectively in the 1989 and 1993 elections to 54.5 per cent (*CNN* 5 November 1997).

The Palestinians have also achieved considerable success in their democratisation process. This is occurring on top of a relatively long tradition of pluralism that evolved as a function of the experience of the Palestinian national movement (Abu-Amr 1996: 89). In accordance with the agreements reached between Israel and the PLO, elections were held in January 1996 for the presidentship of the Palestine Authority and the Council. The elections were declared free and fair by international observers. Another important step towards further democracy was taken when the Palestinian Legislative Council adopted a new law for holding municipal elections (*Palestine Reports* 28 February 1997, 2, 38). The Palestinians also enjoy an active civil society. However, it should also be noted that there have been reports critical of Arafat's repressive policies towards the media as well as of his human rights record (US Department of State 1996). Chan has argued that greater freedom in a previously authoritarian society is likely to be associated with more violence (Chan 1984: 632). However, so far it might, at least tentatively, be possible to argue that, in the case of the Palestinians, Chan's argument does not seem to hold. For example, the calls by radical Islamic groups for demonstrations after the Friday prayers following the 'tunnel' crisis in September 1996 went by and large unheeded by the majority of Palestinians. Instead, they seem to have preferred to follow the advice for calm and patience of Arafat. Similarly, relative calm was also ensured during the final negotiations over the transfer of authority in Hebron and the Jerusalem settlement crisis. The growing preference for non-violent means for resolving conflicts was also reflected in a public opinion poll taken in September 1993 when 83 per cent of those polled preferred dialogue to violence (*Poll number 1* 10–11 September 1993). A poll taken in April 1997 showed that 50 per cent of Palestinians in the West Bank and the Gaza Strip thought that the status of democracy had improved compared to 44 per cent in December 1996 (*Poll number 27* 10–12 April 1997). These are clearly promising developments in terms of democratisation. Furthermore, as Kaufman and Abed note, the mostly-Western educated Palestinian elite that is destined to play a central role in the building of a democratic Palestinian state, also seems to have a clear preference for democratic political culture (Kaufman and Abed 1993: 47).

Iraq and Syria are two countries that are critical to peace and stability in the Middle East. However, neither country has achieved much progress in respect of democratisation. Iraq is devoid of any semblance of democracy. Saddam Hussein, since he consolidated his leadership in Iraq in 1979, has completely personalised government power with virtually no role remaining even for the Ba'th party (Owen 1992: 262–264). As Perthes has noted, there is no civil society to speak of in Iraq and it seems that the Iraqi parliament's function is to do no more than rubber-stamp Saddam Hussein's decisions (Perthes 1994: 253, 265). The repression is so complete that no one has been allowed to challenge Saddam Hussein about the US$1 trillion that Roberts estimates he spent on the Iran–Iraqi war and the invasion of Kuwait (Roberts 1995: 158). It would be difficult to say that the situation is much better in Syria. Hafez Assad, President of Syria, like his counterpart in Iraq, has very much brought the Syrian Ba'th party under his personal control. As both Owen and Perthes note, there were minimal concessions made to single-party rule and no support for the emergence of a civil society independent of the party (Owen 1992: 280; Perthes 1994: 265). However, Hafez Assad, unlike Saddam Hussein, has been participating in the Arab–Israeli peace process although, at the time of writing, no agreement has been reached. He has also allowed some degree of economic liberalisation to take place. Yet, as Roberts notes 'democratisation in Syria will have to await Assad's demise and the end of his regime' (Roberts 1995: 118).

Iran is yet another country critical of any effort to achieve peace and stability in the region. Iran's regime is based on a Shi'a interpretation of Islam. Although Iranian leaders have claimed that their regime is democratic and constitutes a model for countries of Asia, very few people seem to agree. Ultimate power still remains in the hands of appointed religious leaders led by the Supreme Leader, Ayatollah Khamenei, the successor of the late Ayatollah Khomeini. Presidential and parliamentary elections are closely controlled by the Supreme Leader and the

Council of Guardians by determining who can run in the elections as candidates. In May 1997, Iranians elected Muhammed Khatami as the next President of Iran. Khatemi entered the elections on a platform of greater political and economic liberalism against the preferred candidate of the religious establishment, Ali Akbar Nateq-Nouri. Surprisingly, Khatemi won the elections with a large margin. However, it is very difficult to tell whether he will be able to alter the course of Iranian domestic and international politics in a significant manner, as he still needs to work with a parliament dominated by hard-liners and remains subordinate to Ayatollah Khamenei (*The Economist* 2 August 1997). Ayatollah Khamenei's threats to try moderate and dissident clerics who call for greater freedom and liberty for treason (which carries the death penalty) may suggest that the hard-liners are still far from allowing a pluralist form of democracy to operate in Iran (*New York Times* 16 December 1997).

As the above survey suggests, apart from Israel and Turkey there are at least 3 Arab countries in the Middle East that can be considered to be in a process of democratisation. They are mostly at different stages of democratisation but what is significant is that these are also the very countries who have been most supportive of the Middle East peace process. All these 5 countries together have diplomatic relations with each other, recognise each other's territorial existence, and are committed to resolving their differences through negotiations. Is this an adequate situation for peace and stability to consolidate itself in the Middle East? At first glance 'no' might probably appear as a more likely answer. This is primarily because the literature on 'democratic peace' argues that 'young democracies' – that is, countries in transition from authoritarianism to democracy – are at greater risk of becoming engaged in war than stable democracies.

Russett attributes this to two factors. First, 'democratic governments in which democratic norms are not yet fully developed are likely to be unstable … so they may be unable to practice norms of democratic conflict resolution internationally'. Second, 'democratic states with whom they develop conflicts of interest may not perceive them as dependable in their practices. Newness and instability cloud others' perceptions' (Russett 1993: 34). Similar observations are also made by Mansfield and Synder (1995). What then are the factors that make democratisation in the Middle East precarious and unstable which could throw the peace process and efforts to achieve stability into danger? Islam, religious fundamentalism, the lack of a strong civil society and economic difficulties are often cited as potential sources of instability and obstacles to democratisation in the Middle East. Furthermore, Norton and Wright predict that with the Middle East peace process in place 'instead of countries fighting against each other, conflict will mainly occur within countries, often pitting societies against their government' (Norton and Wright 1995: 7). The struggle for greater empowerment may generate instability and play into the hands of radicalism if governments remain unresponsive.

The question whether Islam and democracy can coexist has generated a very rich but inconclusive debate. There are many Muslim countries, which have failed to achieve any democracy and remain under authoritarian rule. How much of this can be attributed to the Islamic religion is difficult to determine. There are radical

Islamic groups who consider the *Shari'a* as perfect law and consider 'popular sovereignty as rebellion against God, the sole legislator' (Kramer 1996: 272). Such groups, Kramer observes, advocate Islam as an ideology whose 'effect has been to give new life to old rationales for oppression, authoritarianism, and sectarian division'. Yet, as Esposito and Piscatori, and many others note, there is a great degree of diversity in the actual practice of Islam and it would be wrong to automatically equate Islam with radicalism and write off Islam and democracy as incompatible (Esposito and Piscatori 1991: 440; Abed 1995; Kramer 1996). Salame argues that too much attention has been focused on the idea of the Islamic world's exceptionalism in explaining why there is little democracy. However, he notes that historically authoritarian regimes of various persuasions have been the norm and that democracy has been the exception. Therefore he adds that 'the basic intellectual effort should be to explain why democracy has flowered in certain countries at certain times rather than, as is usually the case, to try and discover the reason for its absence from most countries most of the time' (Salame 1994a: 4).

Such an approach may also facilitate a better understanding of the democratisation that is actually taking place in the Middle East at present. Turkey is often cited as the only Muslim country where democracy has taken some root and this is often attributed to the strength of secularism in Turkey and hence to Turkey's exceptionalism in the Muslim world. Therefore, there has been a growing concern that Turkish democracy may be at risk if the role of Islam in Turkish politics increases (Sayari 1996). However, Bayart observes that the revival of Islam in Turkish politics need not be seen as a danger to democracy but, on the contrary, as a force that could help to support democracy and strengthen the parliamentary regime (Bayart 1994: 292). Turkey is not the exception. Some Islamic groups and parties have also chosen to operate within the political system in Jordan, Palestine and to a lesser extent in Egypt. Nakhleh is right when he concludes that the idea that democracy and Islam cannot work together runs against evidence in the Middle East (Nakhleh 1994: 114).

In the case of this book, the issue is not so much whether Islam and democracy can coexist but whether fundamentalism and intolerance are a threat to democratisation and stability in the Middle East. Religious fundamentalism, both Islamic and Jewish, has tried to hamper the Middle East peace process. Particularly, Hamas has stood against the peace process and its Charter has advocated the destruction of Israel and the establishment of an Islamic state in Palestine (for details of the Charter of Hamas, see Laqueur and Rubin 1995: 529–536). Hamas declared its opposition to the Arab–Israeli Interim Agreement of September 1995 and called it a 'sell-out' (*The Economist* 30 September 1995: 54). Hamas also did not take part in the Palestinian elections and mounted together with the Islamic Jihad numerous terrorist attacks mostly in the form of bus-bombings in Israel in 1997 to sabotage the bilateral negotiations between the PLO and Israel.

Extremist Jewish groups have also opposed the peace process. As Solingen notes, although the Israeli electorate is overwhelmingly secular, political support for radical religious parties and movements has risen. Most importantly, 'within these parties lurks a hard core of religious nationalists who ... have shown a disturbing penchant for violent dissent and pose a genuine threat to both democratic procedures and the peace process' (Solingen 1996b: 148). Two violent manifestations of opposition against the peace process remain vivid in the minds of many. The first one was the killing of 29 Palestinians at a mosque in Hebron in February 1994 by a fanatic Jewish settler. The second one was the dramatic assassination of the Israeli Prime Minister Yitzhak Rabin on 4 November 1995 by an Orthodox Jew who could not accept the idea of relinquishing any land to the Palestinians. Since the new government came to power in Israel the say of the Jewish fundamentalist groups seems to have increased. This adversely affected and delayed the transfer of Hebron to the Palestinians as Jewish settlers in the area violently opposed the transfer. Some of the settlers in Hebron have also been involved in religiously provocative acts against Palestinians, sparking off street violence in June and July 1997.

With the peace process fundamentalism, however, does not seem to receive as broad public support as it had enjoyed previously. Hamas, under pressure from its leadership outside the occupied West Bank and the Gaza Strip, boycotted the Palestinian election. Nevertheless some of its members from the occupied territories ran as candidates and there was a high turnout in some of the Hamas dominated areas of the Gaza Strip (*Al-Ahram Weekly* 1–7 February 1996). Islamic groups achieved very little success during the elections as only six representatives of Islamic groups were elected to the 88-member Palestinian Council. The poor performance of Islamic candidates during the election led Solingen to tentatively argue that 'the appeal of radical Islam is at its lowest ebb where democratisation is at its highest'. She adds that the Palestine Authority is in a position to consolidate its popular support and weaken its extremist opponents because there is a recognition that with the peace process the Palestine Authority has succeeded in regaining Palestinian land where Arab standing armies failed for decades (Solingen 1996b: 147). Solingen's argument is very much supported by a public opinion poll taken in November 1997 in which respondents were asked who they would vote for if an election was held. Sixty-two per cent of those polled said they would vote for Yasser Arafat while only 3 per cent said they would vote for Sheikh Ahmad Yassin, the spiritual leader of Hamas (*Poll number 30* 27–29 November 1997). Even more telling is that 44 per cent of those who identified themselves with Hamas preferred Arafat, a name that has now become associated with moderation and support for the peace process, while only 11 per cent said they would vote for Sheikh Yassin. What is even more interesting is that the poll came only weeks after the Sheikh had made a triumphant return to the Gaza Strip after having being released from an Israeli prison.

Hamas seems to be drawing some critical lessons from their loss of support. In 1996, a Hamas leader Ghezi Ahmed recognised during an interview that some of their activities were mistakes and had contributed to the recent tension and level of confrontation (*Palestine Reports* 25 October 1996, 2, 20). This might also explain, to some extent, why, after his release from prison in October 1997, Sheikh Yassin repeatedly underlined that he was not in conflict with Arafat or the Palestinian Authority and why he even came up with the notion of a temporary truce with

Israel if Israel stopped building settlements and withdrew from the occupied territories. However, at this stage it would clearly be wrong to conclude that Hamas has reformed itself and abandoned its goal of destroying Israel. There is still plenty of evidence to the contrary. However, what it might be possible to conclude is that support for radical Islamic groups is variable and that growing political openness may either erode this process or moderate the behaviour of such groups (Tessler and Grobschmidt 1995: 160–162). In a similar manner, but at the other extreme of the political spectrum, the radical left-wing Palestinian groups too seem to be reconsidering their objections to the peace process. In February 1997, the deputy secretary of the Democratic Front for the Liberation of Palestine announced that the group was ready to drop the armed struggle and take a more active role in final status negotiations (*Al-Ahram Weekly* 20–26 February 1997).

Furthermore, transnational ties can play an important role in developing cooperation between countries. Exploring how cooperation can be developed among business groups, organisations in civil society, and across boundaries indeed constitutes a major part of the 'democratic peace' project. An important aspect of 'democratic peace' is the significant role that civil society and transnational relations between civil societies can play in dampening the likelihood of war between countries by acting as a check to governmental decision-making. Putnam has demonstrated in *Making Democracy Work* (1993) how non-governmental organisations have become important players in developing and consolidating pluralist democracy. The Middle East has long been associated with weak civil society. However, hand in hand with growing democratisation it is possible to observe a revitalisation of the civil society in the Middle East. As evidence Ibrahim notes that 'the number of Arab non-governmental organisations (NGOs) is estimated to have grown from less than 20,000 in the mid-1960s to about 70,000 in the late 1980s'. Ibrahim sees the expansion of the civil society as a product of a host of factors that include internal and external factors. He expects the process to continue with the 'demonstration' effect playing a very important role (Ibrahim 1995: 39, 51). Non-governmental organisations supportive of the peace process can play a critical role in acting as pressure groups. Putnam has argued that governments in their relations with each other are often involved in two-level games (Putnam 1988). Government officials, in the course of negotiations and bargaining, have to take into consideration the positions of their counterparts as well as the interests and positions of various domestic constituencies. In this context, a civil society committed to peace could play a critical role in mobilising support for transnational and inter-governmental peace-building and cooperation.

Economic problems and inequalities in income distribution remain an impediment to stability in the Middle East. However, there is growing recognition among governments in the Middle East of the need to combine economic restructuring policies with greater political liberalism. Richards, however, notes that the relationship is not an automatic one, but adds that at a time when old-style 'Arab socialist' options are no longer viable, those countries which do not have dependable sources of income will have to make a choice between repression, violence, and chaos versus broader participation and the rule of law (Richards 1995a:

56–57). One factor that complicates economic and political liberalisation stems from the fact that the private sector is often divided between those who have a vested interest in seeing the continuation of the role of the state in the economy, and those who are less dependent on the state and would wish to see a much smaller state (Richards and Waterbury 1990: 419). On the other hand, where economic liberalisation can take place it can plant the seeds of further change as governments loosen control of the economy and business groups become increasingly empowered (Norton and Wright 1995: 15–16).

What might work in favour of liberalisation is that there are clearly growing demands for democratisation in the Middle East coming from civil society accompanied with a recognition on the part of governments of the need to democratise. Although governments may hesitate about the speed with which to encourage greater popular participation in government they have become increasingly aware, at least in those countries experiencing 'incipient democratisation,' that this is in their own interest. This is the case because 'forms of political opening are increasingly viewed by leaders themselves … as a precious instrument through which a rapid deterioration of law and order, if not of the collapse of the whole state apparatus, might be avoided or at least delayed' (Salame 1994a: 2). This is accompanied by growing calls from the political and economic elite of many Arab countries for democratisation (Nakhleh 1994: 115). One last development that can be cited in support of growing prospects of democratisation in the Arab world is the way in which Arab intellectual discourse has changed. While in the past, democracy was defined mostly as 'popular democracy', today 'democracy is more and more operationalised according to the concept of liberal democracy, i.e. as a form of government whose attributes are human rights, free political organisation, government accountability and the change of government through periodic elections' (Perthes 1994: 256).

There is a close and dynamic relationship between economic liberalisation, democratisation and peace in the Middle East. The relationship is a multi-dimensional and interactive one. As Solingen points out 'economic restructuring is central to the connection between peace in the Middle East and democratisation' (Solingen 1996a: 150). An important factor here would be the emergence of domestic players with a stake in economic liberalisation capable of influencing governmental policy. This is more likely to happen in a more democratic and open domestic political environment. Such an environment would also facilitate transnational relations and coalition formation among national interest groups that would perceive a benefit from regional cooperation. Solingen also stresses that 'coalitions strongly committed to economic liberalisation are expected to be more likely to undertake regional cooperative postures, particularly when facing similarly committed regional partners' (Solingen 1996a: 79). Furthermore, with less inter-state conflict the common governmental justification for repression and control diminishes, enhancing prospects of democratisation (Richards and Waterbury 1990: 352). A less authoritarian environment would also diminish the influence of those very groups who have traditionally benefited from regional instability and insecurity. An increasing number of leaders in the Middle East are becoming aware that economic structures and policies dating from the 1950s and 1960s are not viable any more to manage economic growth, and recognise that economic liberalisation will bring increasing pressures for political liberalisation. The urgency of economic restructuring increases as demands for cashing in the economic dividends of peace from the public mounts. Yet, how can this complex relationship between 'incipient' democratisation, economic liberalisation and peace be sustained and encouraged to consolidate itself in the Middle East?

Political cooperation towards democratic peace in the Middle East

It is clearly too early to be able to talk about 'democratic peace' in the Middle East. Yet, it seems there is enough evidence of democratisation in a number of countries accompanied with considerable governmental commitment to Middle Eastern peace. The challenge is twofold. First, the inter-state peace that has been achieved between Egypt, Jordan and Israel on the one hand and the peace process between Israel and the Palestinian Authority on the other need to be strengthened. This can best be achieved if a normalisation of relations occurs between the societies as well. It is very important that not just governments but that also people switch from a confrontationist approach to a peace 'mode' in their approaches to relations with 'the other side'. Second, and probably most difficult, is to bring other Arab governments to normalise their relations with Israel and at the same time help to meet the challenge of assisting democratisation in those countries as well.

This section will primarily advocate the idea that the above goals can best be achieved if what Boulding calls a process of 'community building' can be started in the Middle East (Boulding 1994a: 39). A community of countries is a group of countries that share a common set of norms and values to guide their peaceful relations with each other. However, the emphasis would not be limited to inter-state or inter-governmental relations but would also involve an effort to develop and encourage non-governmental relations. This is very important because non-governmental relations would help the formation of transnational alliances that are not only supportive of the peace process but that would also strengthen democratisation and the expansion of civil society. This would assist the emergence and consolidation of what Doyle calls a 'liberal zone of peace' (Doyle 1983: 213). As Huntington (1991) has pointed out one factor that has affected the third wave of democratisation is the spillover or demonstration effect. It is expected that a similar spillover process could increase the pressures for other Middle Eastern countries to democratise and join in the 'liberal zone of peace'.

Mutual trust and confidence are going to be two key ingredients to encourage political cooperation in efforts to achieve a 'liberal zone of peace' in the Middle East. The task is made particularly difficult because the two ingredients will have to be developed at governmental as well as societal levels. Governments must come to trust each other and then encourage inter-societal relations to develop between the countries of the Middle East. The dilemma here is how to break the vicious circle of distrust and generate enough confidence in the Middle East so that political cooperation can start. The expectation is that once the process starts it should be able to sustain itself through feedback. It seems that two confidence-building processes are needed here – one between governments and the other between the societies.

Governments must manifest an unequivocal willingness to reconcile their differences and work together. This would take the form of a mutual recognition of each other's existence within recognised boundaries. No irredentist claims, at least at the governmental level, would be acceptable. Furthermore, these governments would have to show clear indications that they are committed to actively supporting cooperation among themselves. Internally, these governments must also be committed to political and economic policies that favour a more democratic and liberal environment for the individual. Politically, this would mean the introduction of democratic reforms, the encouragement of pluralism and the upholding of the rule of law. Economically, these governments would be expected to follow policies that encourage trade and financial liberalisation and the privatisation of their national economies. This would add an important dynamic in favour of stability in the Middle East because as Solingen argues 'coalitions advancing economic liberalisation have more often than not embraced the peace process for both economic and domestic political reasons' (Solingen 1996a: 151).

Countries that are closest to meeting these criteria are Egypt, Jordan, Israel, Palestine[4] and Turkey. These five countries have diplomatic relations with each other and their governments have demonstrated a willingness to cooperate on a wide range of issues. Israel and the three Arab governments have repeatedly manifested their commitment to the peace process regardless of the many treacherous political difficulties that have surfaced since the process started in 1991. Turkey, on the other hand, has been active in the multilateral track of the Madrid framework and has expanded its relations with all the four countries, and in February 1997 contributed to the International Supervision Force in Hebron. Israel and Turkey are two countries with a long tradition of democracy, even if the one in Turkey leaves a lot to be desired for. Jordan and Palestine have an elite that appears to be committed to democratisation in spite of the severe political difficulties they are facing. The pressures for democratisation in Egypt are on the rise and some important steps in that direction have been taken. These countries have relatively diversified economies which make the possibility of economic cooperation a little less difficult compared to some of the other countries of the region. Their economies are also considered by the *Index of Economic Freedom* (Johnson, Holmes and Kirkpatrick 1998) as 'mostly free' with the exception of Egypt. Furthermore, they happen to be those countries in the region where there is a growing private sector but also a blossoming civil society, a civil society increasingly in demand of greater freedom and democracy by Middle Eastern standards.

These countries can be termed 'like-minded' countries and it seems they could constitute the best nucleus for greater and deeper cooperation in the Middle East. Grandiose and ambitious schemes of economic or, for that matter political, integration should be avoided. Instead a loose form of cooperation at the governmental level should occur. The aim should be to create as conducive an environment as possible and for members of the business community and civil society in each country to take an interest in developing relations with each other. Of course, there are enormous political as well as economic difficulties especially in respect to the three Arab countries. However, the approach to surmount these difficulties should be an incremental one. As the difficulties are overcome and the interdependence between the economies of these countries increase the level of political cooperation can be deepened.

An important advantage of basing the nucleus of cooperation in the Middle East on the idea of 'like-minded' countries is that any other country that meets the above criteria could join in. This is the quality that would distinguish it from former Middle Eastern schemes of cooperation. In the past schemes of economic and political integration in the Middle East were very much exclusionist. For example, the Arab Common Market as well as the idea of an Arab Union was open to only Arab countries and generated considerable insecurity for other countries of the region. If ever the point can be reached where cooperation can be pushed to the ambitious level of regional economic and political integration, then for it to be able to serve the cause of peace in a manner similar to the European integration process, the whole process must be open to all countries in the region, including Israel. Otherwise, it would not be possible to transcend decade-old enmities. The failure to do so would perpetuate insecurities. In an environment characterised by tension and instability, it would be impossible to expect successful economic or political cooperation of any kind to take place.

Lebanon is a country with a past record of democracy and pluralism as well as a liberal economy which is being gradually rebuilt since the end of the Lebanese civil war. Furthermore, Lebanon has a relatively diversified and free economy. Hence, Lebanon would be a natural member of this group as soon as it can take up direct relations with Israel. Syria and Iraq have relatively well developed and diversified economies; however, the present regimes, at least at the moment, are far from manifesting any signs of 'like-mindedness' with the above group of countries. Hence, it is difficult to see how they could fit into this group in the near future. The same observation could be made about Iran too. Iran is a country with a large population and an important economy. Although in the near future there might be greater political and economic liberalisation taking place in Iran, there are no signs at the time of writing that the present governing elite will agree to cooperate in any regional scheme that involves Israel. The member countries of the Gulf Cooperation Council have already achieved an important level of intra-regional trade among themselves; however, they have so far not formally recognised Israel. Furthermore, many of them, with the exception of Kuwait, are far from being committed to democratisation and political liberalisation in their own countries. Morocco and Tunisia are two other countries that could be included in the 'like-minded' group as soon as they reach a formal agreement of peace with Israel. However, the proximity of these two countries to the European Union will probably continue to dominate their economic and political priorities.

It has already been pointed out that the focus of the governments of these 'like-minded' countries should not be restricted to political cooperation just at the governmental level. There should be a conscious effort to encourage expansion of relations at the societal level. Governments should make channels of communication and interaction available at the business as well as social level. The MENA summits have emphasised the need to establish a regional business council and a tourism board. Such institutions would surely provide at least formal channels that business people can use. Direct contacts between different professional groups should also be expanded. Some progress in respect to promoting relations between Mediterranean universities has been made through the European Union's Med-Campus project. 'Like-minded' countries should consider similar but more narrowly focused projects for their universities and research centres.

The *Istituto Affari Internazionali* in Rome prepared in 1994 a draft proposal for 'An Agenda for Partnership' in the Mediterranean (1994). In this proposal considerable emphasis has been put on 'cultural cooperation' so that 'the people in the countries concerned recognise their common historical and cultural background'. The focus of this proposal is on the development of direct contacts and exchanges between people from different Mediterranean countries to help people to discover common interests and shared values. The same approach could also be adopted for 'like-minded' countries. In this respect, NGOs (Non-Governmental Organisations) would have an important role to play. Encouraging greater contacts between NGOs would not only aid communication across frontiers but would also have the added advantage of strengthening civil society. 'An Agenda for Partnership' offers a rich array of activities in which NGOs could be engaged.

One important outcome of both democratisation and globalisation is a growing recognition of the role of NGOs in domestic as well as international politics. NGOs play an important role in raising issues to national, regional as well as international agendas and influence decision-making processes around these issues (Clark 1995). They have also become important players in pluralist democracy and effective vehicles in transmitting values of democratic participation. Such organisations would have a very central role to play in developing pluralist and democratic politics in the Middle East. Furthermore, these organisations can also contribute effectively to consolidating peace in the Middle East. It is specifically this particular role of NGOs that Boulding (1994b) stresses is an effective tool for strengthening and consolidating peace in the region.

Mitrany (1975) during the inter-war period had argued that security and stability in Europe could best be achieved by developing transnational functional schemes in which NGOs would play an important role. He had argued that such functional schemes would be critical in weakening the destructive hold of nationalism on individuals and would instead help individuals to recognise a vested interest in transnational cooperation. His ideas have been very influential in the many integration schemes that world politics has experienced. Clearly, it is this line of functionalist thinking that stood behind the multilateral Arab–Israeli talks. As Peters rightly points out 'continuous interaction between specialists from the different countries can, over time foster a convergence of expectations and the institutionalisation of norms of behaviour …' (Peters 1996: 67). This has been particularly evident in the work of the Working Groups on the Environment and Regional Economic Development. Cooperation in these two areas would benefit people in a clearly direct manner. As Peters rightly points out 'continuous interaction between specialists from the different countries can, over time, foster a convergence of expectations and the institutionalisation of norms of behaviour ...' (Peters 1996: 67). However, it is also important that this kind of cooperation does not remain limited to government experts but involves the civil society in a direct and effective manner.

'Like-minded' countries also happen to be located in the Middle East where the largest number of non-governmental organisations are found. Governments could help to create the circumstances that could assist these organisations to interact with each other with greater ease. In this ways, NGOs would help to weave a web of networks of contacts helping to deepen peace in the Middle East but at the same time also helping to expand civil society and a pluralist democracy. Also, an important role would fall on the international community. The European Union has developed a European-Mediterranean policy (a Euro-Med policy) that aims to promote security and stability around the Mediterranean. One of the methods adopted to achieve this in the Barcelona Declaration of October 1995 was a commitment to promoting civil society and pluralism. Similarly, the United States can play an important role. Surely, 'democratic peace' in the Middle East would benefit US interests too. Allison and Beschel (1992) argue that the US can help to promote democracy in the world and that it can benefit the US, too. Similarly, but with a greater focus on Palestinians, Quandt advocates that the US government should show greater commitment to Palestinian democracy because, this '... could be part of an initiative to encourage a zone of "peace, development and democracy" that could encompass Israel, Lebanon, Jordan, Palestine, Egypt, Turkey and perhaps eventually Syria' (Quandt 1994: 7). Rothstein also underlines the importance of external support for democratisation in the Middle East and notes that 'external powers cannot impose democracy on the region, but internal forces alone may be too weak to establish democracy. Only by working together will the prospects for success improve' (Rothstein 1995: 80).

The significance of economic liberalisation in promoting regional cooperation has already been stressed. In this respect, too, the international community could play an important role by extending greater support to those very countries that are involved in efforts to liberalise their economies. Barkey (1995: 125) points out that such support could help to create a regional momentum in support of economic liberalism. The need for active involvement and support from the international community to ensure the consolidation of peace in the Middle East is probably best recognised in the very nature of the multilateral talks (Peters 1996: 6). Lastly, Miller and Kagan, in a study of the involvement of great powers in regional conflicts, have demonstrated that great powers play a critical role as 'they can either intensify local conflicts or mitigate them' (Miller and Kagan 1997: 51). Therefore, it seems whether an environment conducive to regional cooperation can be achieved in the Middle East will also depend on the commitment of major powers to peace and stability in the region.

Conclusion

The conflict between Arabs and Jews, which has lasted since the adoption of the November 1917 Balfour Declaration, may finally be destined to become a historical relic. The Peace Treaty of 1979 between Egypt and Israel was an important political development but the watershed event came in October 1991 with the start of the Arab–Israeli peace process. The signing of the Jordanian–Israeli peace treaty in October 1994 and the Israeli–Palestinian Interim Agreement of September 1995 were very promising achievements in terms of the future of region-wide political cooperation in the Middle East. However, events since then show that consolidating peace is not an easy task at all. Nevertheless, maybe for the very first time in the modern history of the Middle East there is a window of opportunity to introduce the notion of 'democratic peace' to achieve lasting stability and security in the Middle East.

Recent waves of democratisation and liberalisation in some countries of the Middle East seem to be offering the prospects of 'democratic peace' in the region. These countries are still in a stage of transition and their gains in democratisation are fragile. Such countries are often considered too unstable to support 'democratic peace'. However, the particular circumstances of the Middle East, accompanied by general governmental commitment to the peace process and cautious democratisation, may help this transition process to succeed. International and domestic politics have become very much intertwined. Therefore, it is possible to argue that there is a strong dynamic relationship in the Middle East between regional peace and democratisation. It would be difficult to have one without the other as each feeds on the other. One way to sustain and strengthen this process would be to encourage greater political cooperation amongst members of a group of 'like-minded' countries. The significance of the formation of transnational coalitions among groups supportive of cooperation in promoting and consolidating peace has been mentioned. It seems it is among the 'like-minded' countries that the formation of such coalitions will be most likely. In accordance with the model of the two-level diplomatic game presented in Chapter 3, these coalitions would contribute significantly to the dynamics of achieving cooperation among this sub-set of Middle Eastern countries.

In Europe, it was six countries that started the nucleus of European integration. In the late 1990s, this project is evolving towards a fully-fledged political union encompassing fifteen countries with many others keen to join. The five 'like-minded' countries could play a similar role to the six European countries even if the integration process in the Middle East were to take a different path. The key factor for the integration process to start and develop successfully is to inject a sense of security and confidence into the hearts and minds of the people of the region. It is at this juncture that an important task falls on governments. Governments should cooperate to bring about a conducive environment to help the private sector take over the integration process, based on greater economic interactions. Governments should facilitate the process rather than impose grandiose schemes on people. In other words, the integration process should be a combination of top to bottom and vice versa.

8 Regional cooperation and the 'like-minded' states

The case of Turkey from a two-level-game perspective

Regional political and economic cooperation in the Middle East is at a historical turning point. Among the various factors that account for this claim, three in particular stand out. The first factor is the international environment within which the Middle Eastern countries find themselves operating. The effects of the end of the Cold War, the Gulf War and developments in its aftermath, and relatively recent accomplishments in the Arab–Israeli peace process are the apparent dominant factors that shape this new international environment. Perhaps equally important effects are to come from the new institutional arrangements stemming from developments in the Uruguay Round, NAFTA and the European Union reshaping the organisation and regulation of the world trade. These developments are expected to have significant impact on the economies of the Middle Eastern countries and their prospects for regional cooperation.

The second factor is the economic structure of Middle Eastern countries which have long been the basis of numerous conflicts in the region. The Middle Eastern economy is typically dominated by non-market forces driven by either domestically or internationally initiated military concerns. The heavy focus on non-market forces in the economy is the underlying force behind inefficient structure and performance of the economy. The region ranks at the top of the world's military as well as oil trade. With the exception of intense trade in these two sectors, the region's economies seem largely isolated from the rest of the world. The countries of the Middle East are often net importers in most other sectors and are unable to sell any other significant types of goods to the world. Population growth and internal migration underlie many of the social problems faced by the governments of the region. The government apparatus, however, seems to be bogged down with security issues creating not only an inefficient set of policy responses but also a rigid bureaucracy and interest group interaction that remains non-responsive and unaccountable to the people at large.

The third main factor is the complex of domestic political issues that affect the extent and nature of cooperation in the region. The composition and articulation of interests by different groups in the Middle Eastern countries are affected not only by the developments in the international environment but are also moulded by changes in their economies. Any move by the decision-makers of Middle Eastern countries to change the existing set of economic and political relationships towards greater cooperation will have to be approved by the relevant domestic political forces. We argue below that the actions and interactions of domestic and international players must be understood in order to explain the character and prospects of political and economic cooperation in the region. We base our analysis on the concept of the two-level-game framework of international politics developed by Putnam (1988), and discussed extensively in Chapter 3 of this book. Framing the policy analysis of the Middle East within a wider literature concerning the region's socio-economic structure, various armed conflicts and impinging developments in the world markets, we demonstrate that such an analysis can explain the hurdles as well as latent sources that might affect regional cooperation in general.

Putnam (1988) underlines that international negotiations in which governments represent constituencies must seek ratification of the negotiated agreement before it can be implemented. We argue throughout our analysis that the slowly moving experiment of creating a regional cooperative environment in the Middle East is essentially undergoing a similar negotiation and ratification process. Each government that is involved has concerns shaped not only by the international political and economic environment (Level I actors) but also by the domestic environment composed of different interest groups (Level II actors) with various conflicting motives and political leverage upon the government. See Chapter 3 for details on these levels and how they apply to the two-level-game framework.

In Chapter 5, we explored some of the functional projects that might lead towards establishing and deepening economic cooperation. In Chapter 7, we also discussed political options suggesting that a cooperation among 'like-minded' states such as Egypt, Israel, Turkey and Jordan together with Palestine might well form a nucleus of region-wide cooperation. In what follows, we focus on the case of Turkey, one of the 'like-minded' states, and apply the framework developed above to the specific bilateral and multilateral issues that Turkey faces regarding its ties with the region. In doing so, we aim to demonstrate the utility of the two-level-game framework in understanding the complex political forces opposing or supporting cooperation at the domestic front. Looking at the interaction of domestic and international factors also reveals that even though the 'like-minded' states with relatively open and competitive regimes might initially experience significant domestic opposition to regional cooperation, moderate, and pragmatic voices can also eventually gain influence in relatively democratic and open environments. Such regimes then constitute a significant basis for a 'new' Middle East.

However, the vision of the 'new' Middle East based on cooperation on the nexus of economic liberalisation, global integration and democratisation is clearly not the only vision in the region. There are powerful constituencies that are intrinsically opposed to a cooperative arrangement in the region. Unfortunately, but not surprisingly, many of these groups are presently in power in critical countries of the region such as Iraq, Syria, Iran and Libya. Similar coalitions are also greatly effective in Saudi Arabia, Algeria and Egypt and to a lesser degree in all other countries of the region.

For Turkey, there are considerable challenges both at the international and domestic levels for establishing and enhancing interaction between Levels I and II among the Middle Eastern countries. At the international level the challenge is one of dealing with the new geopolitical and geo-strategic role that Turkey came to play in the aftermath of the Cold War. In the light of a new post-Cold War era, with intensified attempts to reach a peaceful settlement of the protracted Arab–Israeli conflict and new challenges towards Turkish political and economic security, Turkish foreign policy offers a compelling case study for exploring prospects and problems of cooperation in the region.

Turkey and the Middle East in an international context

In an evaluation of Turkey and its ties with the Middle East, an initial overview is necessary of its position in the region along with the major issues and challenges the country faces. In what follows we will first discuss how the changing international dynamics from Cold War to post-Cold War have induced significant shifts in Turkey's status with regard to the Middle East. First, Turkey has come to assume new roles and responsibilities in the aftermath of the momentous changes in the strategic balance of Eurasia. Second, we will specifically focus on the fundamental issues that Turkey faces with regards to its ties within the Middle East. In doing so, we hope to demonstrate how the two-level-game framework can be used to explore some of the options open to foreign policy-makers in the region.

Geo-strategically Turkey is a unique country as it borders a number of regions that are very different from each other. During the course of the Cold War, Turkish foreign and security policy was, largely, a function of developments in the West and relations between the two different ideological and military blocs in Europe. One of the important consequences of the end of the Cold War, however, has been the way in which Turkish national interests have become intimately related to security and stability in all the regions surrounding Turkey. Its European territories make Turkey a Balkan country. The largest Turkish city, Istanbul, and a significant proportion of its population and industry are located in this area. Furthermore, Turkey, for historical, religious and ethnic reasons, has strong ties with the Balkans. Turkey is also a Black Sea country. Since the end of the Cold War, its trade and economic cooperation with countries around the Black Sea have been expanding. Turkey also has close ties to a large number of Muslim and Turkic communities in the Caucasus and Central Asia. Over the last few years Turkey's relations with these countries have acquired growing importance. At the same time, Turkey is also a Middle Eastern country and its security as well as stability and prosperity have become closely tied with developments in the Middle East. Furthermore, with the end of the Cold War Turkey is considered by many to have become an important player in Middle Eastern politics. This was particularly evident from Turkey's role in the events precipitated by the Iraqi invasion of Kuwait. It was also evident with efforts to create a new Middle East and the beginning of the Arab–Israeli peace process.

For Turkey, an important consequence of both the Gulf War and the Arab–Israeli peace process has been strategic. During the Cold War the Middle East was a region characterised by conflict and confrontation between radical and moderate Arab regimes. The radicals sought a revision of the status quo in the Middle East and were able to mobilise more often than not the support of the Soviet Union. Though in the main radical Arabs never succeeded in changing the status quo, the moderates were left on the defensive. The situation became more complicated when an Islamic radical regime came to power in Iran. Although its foreign policy actively sought a revision of the status quo as well, that revision was very different from the one sought by Arab radicals. All these revisionist attempts ran counter to the established interests of Turkey in the region.

However, during this period Turkish foreign policy remained passive with efforts to maintain balanced and pragmatic relations with all sides. In terms of the overall order in the Middle East, Turkey relied on the leadership of the United States. In other words, Turkey did not wish to see a change in the status quo favouring Iran or radical Arab regimes, but also did not in any way actively do much to pre-empt a revision of the status quo. The United States, on the other hand, basically used Iran and Iraq against each other to prevent any of the two from prevailing and altering the status quo throughout the Cold War and the 1980s. This was critical both in terms of protecting the existing order, safeguarding the supply and flow of oil to the West and maintaining Israel's security (Hudson 1996). Hence, at the strategic level, Turkey acted like a free-rider in the sense that it did not contribute in any effective way to the costs of maintaining the status quo in the Middle East, but nevertheless benefited from it.

The Gulf crisis and the Arab–Israeli peace process have changed these dynamics. In the 1990s Turkey has been drawn into involvement in the Middle East. The Turkish government's decision to assist efforts to force Iraq out of Kuwait changed Turkey's status from being a free-rider to an active cost bearer to bring about a return to the status quo ante. This was a major departure from Turkey's classic non-involvement policy in intra-Arab affairs. Turkey took a clear position against seeing the emergence of a Middle East dominated by a revisionist radical Arab power. By doing so, Turkey acknowledged that its security and national interests were being seriously challenged.

Another aspect of these changes in the Middle East is that it has enhanced Turkey's importance in the eyes of key actors in international politics. Turkey during the Cold War derived its strategic importance from its geographical location as a neighbour of the Soviet Union. Strategically, for the West to have Turkey on its side during the Cold War gave it an important advantage in its global confrontation with the Soviet Union. In return, Turkey was able to use this advantage as a source of bargaining power on many issues. However, as the Cold War began to unravel during the second half of the 1980s, Turkey's strategic value began to erode, very quickly precipitating considerable concern for areas of both foreign and military policy (Sezer 1992). Yet, the Gulf crisis, followed by efforts to achieve peace in the Middle East, helped to reinstate Turkey's strategic significance. This time, the emphasis was not so much on Turkey's geo-strategic value for the West per se, but rather on Turkey's value as the only major Muslim country in the world with a relatively democratic political system and a market economy. Thus, Turkey came to be seen as a source of stability in the region and was also considered as a possible model for other Muslim countries in the Middle East and Central Asia (Öniş 1995). Furthermore, in terms of Western and particularly US interests in the Middle East, a democratic and pro-Western Turkey is seen as more of an asset than a Turkey that would have closer relations with neighbouring radical regimes (*Wall Street Journal* 19 December 1997).

The US policy of dual-containment launched in 1993 and aiming to isolate and even precipitate regime changes in Iran and Iraq, for instance, could not be envisaged without Turkey's cooperation. The implementation of this policy required Turkey's cooperation in a number of areas. Turkey's support in maintaining effective UN economic sanctions against Iraq still remains critical. Furthermore, without Turkish agreement to the continuation of Operation Provide Comfort (renamed as Northern Watch in December 1996) it would have been very difficult to protect northern Iraq above the thirty-sixth parallel from Iraqi military activity. At the same time this also enabled the US, at least until August 1996, to organise opponents of the Saddam regime to form the Iraqi National Congress (INC) based in northern Iraq. It seems that the US had hoped to use the INC to overthrow Saddam Hussein. Furthermore, the major Kurdish groups in northern Iraq were able to remain beyond the control of Baghdad constituting a major force against Saddam's regime. In the case of Iran the US policy has been based on unilaterally declared sanctions requiring the goodwill and cooperation of its allies. Turkish restraint until recently in developing close economic relations with Iran has been critical to the US ability to ensure support for these sanctions. Furthermore, Turkish displeasure with Iranian support for the Workers' Party of Kurdistan (PKK) and Islamic fundamentalist groups in Turkey has also facilitated US efforts to contain Iran.

This strategic significance of Turkey appears to have been further reinforced as critics of the dual-containment policy attributed greater importance to Turkey (Brzezinski, Scowcroft and Murphy 1997; Sicherman 1997). Furthermore, US decision-makers have increasingly been advocating closer relations between Turkey and moderate regimes in the Middle East to counter the influence of radical states and assist the transition towards a more democratic, stable and secure Middle East. This new strategic importance of Turkey brings with it important advantages. One of Turkey's grand goals remains joining the European Union. It is difficult to see how the US government could have become a strong advocate of Turkey's membership to the European Union if it was not for a clear recognition by the US of the strategic value of a pro-Western, stable and democratic Turkey in the region. It is generally accepted that US lobbying played a critical role in ensuring the eventual signing and ratification of the Customs Union Treaty between Turkey and the EU in 1995. Most recently, however, the failure of the European Union to include Turkey among the list of 11 prospective members at the Luxembourg conference in December 1997 has dealt a significant blow to Turkey's aspirations to become a full member. Turkish foreign-policy-makers have expressed their frustration with the EU by seeking closer economic and political ties with the United States and Russia. This was demonstrated by the visit of the Russian Foreign Minister Yevgeny Primakov to Ankara followed by the Turkish Prime Minister Mesut Yilmaz's visit to the United States after the Luxembourg meeting. The Prime Minister received a warm welcome from the US. However, to what extent the current Turkish government's apparent tactics of using the further rapprochement with the United States and Russia – not only as an alternative to the EU but also as a mechanism to pressure the EU governments to recognise Turkey's strategic and economic value – will be successful remains to be seen.

Apart from international challenges Turkey also faces significant challenges on the domestic front in formulating its foreign policy towards the region. A recent rise of the pro-Islamist movement in Turkey, for instance, has been coupled with an increased focus among a certain constituency towards issues of the Middle East. It is to be expected that increased democratisation will go hand in hand with efforts on the part of these constituencies to influence Turkish foreign policy towards the region. A part of this constituency, for instance, has systematically opposed the peace process and Israel. What is critical at this stage is not to cave in to what might at times be non-cooperative demands coming from these constituencies. Such prospects have become realities in the recent past, especially with Turkish pro-Islamist groups taking sides with militant radical groups (like Hamas), amongst other public demonstrations.

The main reason for such a development is that the dominant position of these Turkish constituencies towards Middle East issues has often been linked to radical rather than moderate Islamic groups in the region. This seems to have caused a misperception not only on the part of the political party elite but also on the part of the general public. Any signs of tolerance on the part of Turkish authorities towards these groups run the risk of being interpreted as covert support for regional radical groups in the Middle East. Moreover, such a policy stand will immobilise any existing or latent Level II actors that might prefer to engage with more moderate groups in cooperative schemes in the region. There is certainly a need to balance such radical groups with a policy that encourages business-to-business interactions while setting up contacts with moderate and pragmatic Islamic actors in the region.

Turkey's specific regional concerns in the Middle East

Having elaborated on how Turkey constitutes a good case study in exploring international and domestic factors in the foreign-policy-making process in the Middle East, specific regional issues that the country faces will be discussed below. In so doing we attempt to clarify the difficulties and prospects of regional cooperation in the region from the perspective of a pivotal player among the 'like-minded' states. We also aim to demonstrate how a two-level-game framework might help us assess the circumstances under which cooperation might take place.

The Kurdish question and difficulties of cooperation

Since the end of the Cold War, developments in the Middle East have accentuated a number of political and security challenges facing Turkey. These challenges include the Kurdish question, the increased violent activities of the Workers' Party of Kurdistan (PKK), and broader military concerns about security. The Iraqi military operation against the Kurdish uprising in northern Iraq in late March 1991 precipitated one of the largest refugee crises in recent history. More than 1.5 million refugees, who were mostly Kurdish, fled towards Iran and Turkey. The crisis had two important effects on Turkey. First, the attention of the world was drawn to the Kurds and attention to Turkey's own Kurdish problem was accentuated. Second, in northern Iraq the creation of a safe haven above the thirty-sixth parallel increased the ability of the PKK to launch operations into Turkey. The lands traditionally inhabited by Kurds straddle four Middle Eastern countries. All of these countries face problems of varying intensity with their Kurdish populations. Turkey traditionally had long denied the existence of a separate Kurdish identity and had systematically tried to assimilate the Kurds into the larger Turkish identity. As a consequence of these policies in the 1980s the Kurdish problem became increasingly visible. However, it was at the time of the Gulf crisis that the problem came to the fore to such an extent that it led the government – at the time of the massive refugee crisis – to recognise a 'Kurdish reality' in Turkey.

It is not the purpose of this study to examine the Kurdish problem in Turkey as it has been dealt with extensively elsewhere (Kirişci and Winrow 1997). However, it should be noted that the Kurdish problem remains one of the most urgent and complicated problems facing the Turkish political system. More importantly from the perspective of this study, the Kurdish question is a transnational one whose resolution will require considerable inter-governmental as well as inter-societal cooperation. In other words, it is very difficult to see how the problem can ever be resolved in a satisfactory manner in one country without progress also being achieved in another. The old Middle East clearly has not achieved much in this regard. However, a Middle East in which at least some degree of democracy, pluralism and region-wide cooperation exists will be more likely to address the Kurdish question more effectively and constructively than it has up to now. Instead, at the time of writing the Kurdish problem is a source of violence in northern Iraq, Iran and Turkey while it is generally accepted that Turkey's neighbours actively exploit the Kurdish problem against Turkey.

Typically, the Kurdish problem remains a tool of power politics in the region. For example, the Turkish government regularly accuses Iran and Syria of supporting and encouraging the PKK to carry out attacks on Turkey. It has even been rumoured that the government considered planning a military attack on PKK bases in Iran in May 1995.[1] Turkish accusations against Iran have on a number of occasions led to diplomatic crises where tension between the two countries increased. In May and June 1996 Turkey and Syria came close to the point of military confrontation as both sides amassed troops along the border. Turkey has also mounted numerous operations into Kurdish controlled parts of northern Iraq from where the PKK was conducting most of its operations into Turkey (Kirişci 1986).

In the meantime, Turkish policy to counter Syria and Iran and their involvement with the PKK issue has contributed to the development of close military and strategic relations between Turkey and Israel. However, increased bilateral ties with Israel have had both benefits as well as a certain cost. In turn, Syria has tried to improve its relations with Iraq by opening its land borders, that were closed from 1980, and has also tried to mobilise the Arab world against Turkey (Danin 1997). The early departure of Turkish President Süleyman Demirel from the Teheran Conference in December 1997, largely due to increased criticism of Turkish ties with Israel, also demonstrates ongoing issues on the balance of power. These considerations regarding power politics help fuel a vicious circle of confrontation, weakening prospects of cooperation and dialogue.

Another aspect of this vicious circle of insecurity and power struggle is the increasing proliferation of sophisticated military capabilities in the region. The fact that Iran and Syria are equipped with ballistic missiles capable of delivering weapons of mass destruction, and that there are reports about Iranian efforts to acquire a nuclear capability, are sources of serious concern (Lesser and Tellis 1996; Egeli 1993). Many population centres, dams, power stations, air bases and military headquarters are within range of these missile systems. Furthermore, in 1998 there are still issues around Iraq's compliance with UN Resolutions demanding the dismantlement of all its weapons of mass destruction.

The security concerns that Turkey has with its neighbours have significant repercussions on the domestic front. The Kurdish question and the domestic responses, for instance, provide a good example. Throughout the 1990s there has been an increasingly intense public debate on how to resolve this problem: a problem that has engendered considerable violence and displacement of large numbers of people. However, a number of factors have stalled efforts to find a solution. The transnational nature of the Kurdish problem and the ability of the PKK to operate in and out of neighbouring Middle Eastern countries have led many in Turkey to define the problem as an issue of national security. Hence, the military and the security establishments have basically been the most important layers. They have seen the problem as a function of a regional power struggle and defined it as a serious threat to Turkey's territorial unity. They have very much determined the boundaries of permissible public debate on the Kurdish question and, so far, they have also come to dominate policy making on the problem, leaving very little room for alternative approaches to emerge.

Another factor that complicates the domestic aspect of finding a solution to the Kurdish question in Turkey stems from a disproportionate allocation of parliamentary seats with respect to their population share in the provinces of South-East and East Anatolia where the Kurdish problem is most concentrated. As a consequence a relatively low degree of electoral competition, particularly when contrasted with the Western provinces, has meant that, whichever party carries these regions gains a disproportionate advantage in the parliament. This has led governing political parties and coalitions systematically to allocate more resources to the region. In doing this they have made extensive use of patronage relationships in order to ensure parliamentary gains in these two regions of Turkey. Such an approach has led to considerable complacency on the part of those engaged in patronage relationships and a resultant failure to feel any need to address the Kurdish question or, for that matter, challenge the view and policies of the military and the security establishment. On the other hand, a 10 per cent national threshold requirement in nationwide elections and outright party closures (People's Labour Party – HEP – and Democracy Party – DEP) have been used as an effective tool in blocking ethnically-based political parties that seek cultural and minority rights for Kurds from gaining any representation in the parliament.

This situation not only stifles debate on the Kurdish question but also leads to a wasting of votes cast to such political parties (since they gain no representation in parliament) in many provinces of South-East and East Anatolia. In turn, this plays into the hands of the ability of other political parties to exploit patronage relationships, ensuring in many ways the perpetuation of a status quo.

The Turkish political system has so far failed to produce a viable solution to the Kurdish problem. However, what happens with respect to the Kurdish problem in Turkey is also intimately associated with what happens in neighbouring countries. These are countries that suppress their own Kurdish population, and have regimes characterised by authoritarianism. Under these circumstances it is difficult to achieve decisive progress in Turkey through democratic means when neighbouring countries will continue to exploit the Kurdish problem in Turkey in an effort to weaken the regime. For the regimes of these countries the fact that Turkey has a relatively democratic and open regime is a serious threat. Therefore, the more Turkey could contribute to the emergence of an environment in the Middle East that can sustain and eventually consolidate democracy and liberalisation, the more it will become easier to address the Kurdish problem meaningfully and effectively.

Turkey's urgent economic needs and the Middle East

The negative consequence of the Gulf War was not only limited to the strategic and national-security concerns described above. Another devastating consequence of the war for Turkey and particularly the South-Eastern provinces, has been the loss of commerce and trade with the Middle East. The sanctions against Iraq leading up to and continuing after the Gulf War not only closed the lucrative Iraqi market to Turkish business but also undermined Turkey's comparative advantage in supplying the Gulf States and Saudi Arabia with fresh and processed agricultural products. This significant loss of trade diverted many companies in Turkey to the newly emerging markets in former socialist countries, leading to the loss of a major constituency pushing for closer economic relations with the Middle East.

Turkish exports to the Middle East dropped from 23 per cent of its overall exports to 16 per cent (see Table 8.1). According to the calculations of the State Planning Organisation and the Undersecretariat of Foreign Trade, the projected exports to Iraq were estimated to be around US$5 billion between 1990–95. The amount of exports realised, however, reached only US$922 million (*Undersecretariat of Foreign Trade* 1996b: 22). A fleet of more than 40,000 trucks built up over previous years fell idle.[2] Most of these trucks were based in South-eastern Turkey and provided considerable employment possibilities for people in the region. Turkey also lost the revenues from the Kerkük–Yumurtalık oil pipeline. The government puts this revenue and the larger trade loss at approximately US$30 billion.

Table 8.1 Turkey's foreign trade with the Middle East (US$ millions), 1989–94

	1989		*1992*		*1994*	
	Exports	*Imports*	*Exports*	*Imports*	*Exports*	*Imports*
Egypt	140	21	174	59	195	124
Jordan	63	35	164	25	112	15
Israel	67	28	90	97	178	126
Bahrain	0	4	11	13	14	0.6
Kuwait	167	81	66	68	128	77
Oman	0	8	7	0.09	10	0.06
Qatar	1	8	6	1	9	0.7
Saudi Arabia	364	212	487	1,665	609	1,229
UAE	30	2	97	354	185	339
Iran	561	233	455	365	250	692
Iraq	445	1,650	212	1	141	0
Lebanon	77	3	99	5	161	7
Syria	177	18	216	54	254	44
Yemen	0	0	62	0.5	58	0.3
Algeria	237	154	108	10	238	95
Morocco	21	11	61	30	39	39
Libya	227	286	247	445	179	320
Tunisia	45	14	49	31	74	51
Sudan	43	14	9	7	23	11
Total	2,665	2,782	2,620	3,230.4	2,857	3,170.7
Overall total	11,625	15,792	14,719	22,870	18,105	23,170
Middle East %	22.92	17.61	17.80	14.34	15.79	13.62

Source: For 1989: International Monetary Fund (1991); for 1992 and 1994: from the Undersecretaries of Treasury and Foreign Trade, Ankara
Note: Overall total is Turkey's total foreign trade with all countries of the world

In depressing the economy of the region the embargo played an important role in aggravating the Kurdish problem and the violence surrounding it. In one rare example of active diplomacy, Turkey played a critical role preparing the background to the eventual adoption of Resolution 986 in April 1995 by the United Nations Security Council. The Resolution opened the way for a partial lifting of the embargo on Iraq. However, it was not until December 1996 that the Kerkük–Yumurtalık oil pipeline, after more than six years, was reopened. As a result Iraq was able to export, for the duration of six months, US$2 billion worth of oil. Although this is considered as an important step towards an eventual lifting of the embargo on Iraq, this will depend to a considerable degree on the policies of the Iraqi government. The United Nations Resolutions clearly demand that Iraq fulfil requirements concerning the destruction of offensive weapons before sanctions can be totally lifted. At this time of writing, Iraq's cooperation remains considerably below the level expected for lifting the sanctions.

There is a similarly difficult economic tension between Turkey and Syria. The tension between the two countries has not only adversely affected border trade that was formerly buoyant but has also closed the way to a possible expansion of cross-border trade. Furthermore, poor relations with Syria are also blocking the possibility of greater trade between Turkey and countries to the south of Syria, that is, Jordan, Israel and Palestine. At a time (the late 1990s) when the South-East Anatolia Development Project is beginning to bear economic fruits, the need to develop better relations with Syria and contribute to a more cooperative climate in the Middle East is acquiring growing urgency. However, in the case of Syria it is very difficult to foresee an immediate improvement. The present regime continues to control an important part of the national economy as well as Syria's external trade. In spite of an initial effort in 1990 to liberalise the economy, not much has been achieved since then. Under existing circumstances it is difficult to see how the present regime in Syria might change its policies.

Against the pessimistic background generated by the difficulties of surmounting the obstacles created by Iraq and Syria, some of the progress achieved in the Arab–Israeli peace process has enhanced the prospects for better relations between Turkey and some of the Middle Eastern countries. The peace process and the agreements signed between Israel and the PLO as well as between Israel and Jordan facilitated considerably the possibility for Turkey to broaden its relations with Israel (Aras 1997). Furthermore, the establishment of at least informal relations between Israel and some other Arab countries helped to erode the Arab economic boycott which used to make it difficult even for non-Arab countries to trade with Israel. Since these developments Turkish–Israeli trade has increased significantly and the prospects for even greater trade have emerged with the signing of a free trade agreement between the two countries. Turkish tourism has also largely benefited from an increased flow of Israeli tourists. The new climate created by the peace process has also enabled Turkey to develop better and broader relations with other countries, especially Jordan and Egypt. In contrast with the Cold War years, there have been frequent top-level visits between these countries. A close relationship has also evolved with the Palestinians. These developments have led many to speculate about an emerging political alliance between Egypt, Jordan, Israel, Palestine and Turkey supported by the United States. However, the change in government in Israel in May 1996 and the crisis that has surrounded the peace process since then has demonstrated that these speculations may have been somewhat premature. Nevertheless, when compared with the Cold War years, the Middle East offers better opportunities for Turkey in the post-Cold War years.

The future realisation of these opportunities will depend very much on progress achieved in the peace process and the regional cooperation that can be developed. Although absent from the Madrid summit in October 1991, further to the follow-up meeting in Moscow in January 1992, Turkey became active in the work of the Multilateral Working Group on Arms Control and Regional Security. In May 1993 Turkey was given the task of guiding the workshop on 'Military Exchanges of Information and Pre-notification of Certain Military Activities'. In respect of the Israeli–Palestinian peace process, Turkey extended US$2 million of aid and pledged US$50 million credit to the Palestinians. Turkey also participated in the Casablanca economic summit in October 1994 and put forward concrete proposals including the idea of establishing a regional bank to facilitate the growth of economic activity. However, since this initial engagement Turkish involvement has weakened. Turkey did transfer the $2 million assistance to the Palestinians, but no portion of the promised credits was released. Turkey's participation at the MENA summits in Amman, Cairo and most recently in Doha left a lot to be desired especially in terms of the level of governmental participation. This may, to some extent, be a product of problems with the peace process. However, it also seems to be a result of an inadequate appreciation of the benefits that would accrue to Turkey from an economically prosperous, stable and secure Middle East and the role that Turkey could play in bringing about such a Middle East.

Meanwhile, as the Turkish economy expands, Turkey's dependence on external energy sources is increasing. Turkey presently purchases most of its crude oil from Middle Eastern countries (see Table 8.2). Turkish energy consumption has grown exponentially over the last 11 years. While the consumption was 39.6 million tons of oil equivalents (toe) in 1986, it rose to 60.6 million toe in 1995. The dependence that Turkey has on Middle Eastern oil often creates an imbalanced trade structure. For instance, while Turkey imported US$1.382 billion worth of goods from Saudi Arabia, which was mostly oil in 1995, it could sell only US$470 million worth of goods in return. Oil trade accounts for more than 30 per cent of all trade Turkey has with the region (Undersecretariat of Foreign Trade 1996b: 20). The same is true for most of the Gulf states. While Turkey's major export products to the region include live cattle, cotton and textile products, wheat, potatoes, copper wires, some iron-steel products and fresh non-durable food products, Turkey's fundamental item of imports from the countries in the region has been oil and oil-related products. Turkey's dependence on Middle Eastern oil is likely to continue for the foreseeable future until Caspian and Central Asian oil can reach Turkey.

Furthermore, Turkey's natural-gas consumption is increasing. Turkey purchases most of its natural gas from Russia and a smaller quantity of natural gas in liquefied

Table 8.2 Imports of Turkish crude oil and natural gas for specified years (metric tons)

Country	*Natural Gas (1995)*	*Oil (1994)*
Saudi Arabia	–	9,868,786
Iran	–	5,499,011
Libya	–	2,465,661
UAE	–	2,616,402
Syria	–	383,280
Algeria	1,058,377	110,786
Egypt	–	14,927
Russia	5,560,443	236,021
Australia	240,120	
Kazakhistan	–	3,258
Total imports	6,858,940	21,198,132
Turkish production	–	3,686,668

Source: T.C. Petrol Isleri Genel Müdürlügü Dergisi (1997), BOTAS (1997)

Table 8.3 Turkey's primary energy consumption (millions of tons of equivalent oil), 1986–95

Type of consumption	*1986*	*1990*	*1991*	*1992*	*1993*	*1994*	*1995*
Oil	18.3	22.1	22.1	23.5	27	24.8	27.2
Gas	0.4	3	4	4.1	4.5	6.1	7.8
Coal	19.6	22.3	22	24.9	24.3	21.9	22.4
Hydro	1.3	2	2	2.3	2.9	3	3.2
Total	39.6	49.4	50.1	54.8	58.7	55.8	60.6

Source: Arab Press Service Organisation (1996)

form (LNG) is imported from Middle Eastern countries such as Algeria. In 1995, a total of 6.858 million cubic metres of natural gas was imported. Turkey also imported LNG from Saudi Arabia and has finalised deals with Egypt and Yemen to import LNG in the future (see Tables 8.2 and 8.3). The government appears to be determined to diversify and increase its supplies of natural gas. Indeed, with demand rising, Turkey desperately needs to increase its access to natural gas. Turkey's projected demand for natural gas for 2010 and 2025 is expected to reach 40–50 million and 63 million cubic metres respectively (BOTAS 1997). The existing agreements with Algeria and the Russian Federation can meet only one fifth of this projected demand. A number of Middle Eastern neighbours such as Iran and Iraq are the best-positioned potential suppliers. There are a number of projects under consideration which will, in fact, increase the dependence of Turkey on the region. One of these projects is carrying Turkmenistan's natural gas through a pipeline that may either pass through the Caspian Sea or Iran. Another project is the carrying of Russia's natural gas to Turkey and Israel through a pipeline. This 1,600 km pipeline is envisaged to pass through Tiblisi, Georgia, and through Ardahan, Kars, Erzincan, Sivas (in Turkey) and to reach Israel underneath the sea. Finally, also projected is a natural gas pipeline running from Iran through Turkey to Europe which will initially carry 3 billion cubic metres of Iranian natural gas starting in 1999, to be raised to 10 billion cubic metres from 2005 (BOTAS 1997). Two thirds of this natural gas is meant to be sold to Europe. All these projects indicate an increasing dependence of Turkey on the Middle East in terms of its energy resources. In the absence of alternative sources of energy and supplies, Turkey will continue to be dependent on Middle Eastern suppliers of crude oil and natural gas. This, too, constitutes another important reason to take greater interest in the stability and security of the Middle East. An unstable and insecure Middle East would not only cause the price of oil to rise but also make it more difficult to access.

Finally, Turkey is also in need of electricity. Turkey buys electricity from Iran and has also finalised negotiations to build an electricity grid between 5 countries in the region: Turkey, Syria, Jordan, Egypt and Iraq. The project aims to interconnect these five countries with each other by 2000. Such an electricity grid in the region might help increase interdependence (Undersecretariat of Foreign Trade 1996a).

How these economic needs of Turkey are addressed and how Turkey deals with its growing economic dependence on the Middle East will have important implications on domestic political configurations. In the course of the period of office of the coalition of the Welfare Party (RP) and the True Path Party (DYP) in Turkey, for instance, a natural-gas agreement was signed in August 1996 in the midst of international criticisms, particularly from the US. Similarly, the coalition government led by Mesut Yılmaz and the Motherland Party (ANAP) also signed a preliminary natural-gas agreement with Turkmenistan in December 1997, from where the natural gas will flow to Turkey through Iran. Because of the emergency of Turkey's energy needs, domestic variation of political strategies regarding this issue appears limited. However, the willingness of the RP government to sign a natural-gas agreement with Iran, where the Turkish government guarantees to pay for natural gas even though the pipelines have not yet been completed, has drawn extensive criticism. As will be discussed below, the earlier RP government had extensively used the rapprochement with Iran for domestic political purposes.

The water problem and the hydropolitics of the Euphrates–Tigris

The need for electricity and energy in Turkey is also linked to another major issue that Turkey faces in terms of its ties to the Middle East, namely water, and the sharing of water of the Euphrates–Tigris river system. Turkey has long defined the dams that it built over the Euphrates river as a 'hydro-imperative' which refers to its need to use these dams for its energy production (Kolars 1986). Indeed, it is calculated that in order to meet the demands of an annual GDP growth of 5 per cent, Turkey's electricity production will have to double every 10–15 years (Beschorner 1992a). These dam projects, however, have also been a source of strain and conflict among the other two riparian states, Iraq and Syria. As we discussed earlier, the water problem is not unique to Syria, Turkey and Iraq, which all have conflicting claims over the Euphrates–Tigris river basin, but is common in the entire Middle East. The dispute between Egypt and Sudan over the use of the Nile river system, the struggle over the Jordan basin and freshwater sources in the Israeli–Palestinian conflict, along with the discord over the use of water in the Euphrates–Tigris river system are just three examples of internationalised water conflicts in the region. Such conflicts over the water resources reflect a series of multi-faceted problems. First is the underlying geopolitical struggle among the states involved at the international negotiating table in order to secure access to a crucial resource. Second are the legal issues concerning the rights of states to use water resources. Third is the larger economic concern of the involved states with respect to development projects that depend on a steady supply of water. Fourth is intrinsically dependent on economic development projects and is concerned with the political implications of such development targets, ideological reasons and justifications used by politicians of the states involved.

Given the significance of water in the region, it is no wonder that water has emerged as potentially the next cause of war in the region (Gruen 1992; Naff and Matson 1984). Indeed, the relations between Turkey, Syria and Iraq have been particularly strained since the opening in July 1992 of the Atatürk Dam, the largest on the Euphrates River. Why is it so difficult to reach a compromise? One reason is that water conflict is a part of the ongoing power game between Syria, Turkey and Iraq (Starr 1991). The overall structural balance of power in the region explains the nature of the conflicting claims over these rivers. Indeed, the strict and inflexible positions that all three states have adopted suggest that the problem is one of a zero-sum game over the sharing of waters of both rivers. While Turkey claims sovereign rights over the Euphrates and the Tigris on the basis of being the upstream country, both Syria and Iraq argue that all riparian states should have *equal* rights over transboundary waters. The countries actually differ on the very definition of the river system. While Turkey defines the Euphrates–Tigris river system as a transboundary water system, Syria and Iraq call it 'international water' thus claiming their share. Turkey argues that both rivers should be seen as a single water system since both join before the Persian Gulf and since Iraq has developed the Tharthal Canal project, transferring waters of the Euphrates to the Tigris. Iraq and Syria, however, object to this interpretation arguing instead that each river (particularly the Euphrates) should be discussed separately and that the rights of the downstream states cannot be limited by the sovereignty claims of the upstream countries.

Turkey has also proposed, as part of what came to be called the three stage plan, allocation of water resources based on the systematic assessment of the water needs for irrigation of all parties. This assessment was to depend on land resources, economically viable irrigation of the riparians and optimal irrigation methods (Ministry of Foreign Affairs 1995; Mutlu 1996). This proposal, however, has largely been perceived both by Iraq and Syria as an infringement of internal affairs. Furthermore, both countries regard Turkey's building of the Atatürk Dam, the major scheme of the South-Eastern Anatolian Development Project (GAP), as a clear example of 'water imperialism' where Turkey's water consumption patterns will pose significant threats to future agricultural plans of both Syria and Iraq. The Atatürk Dam in particular and GAP in general are largely seen as projects to assert Turkey's territorial claims over both rivers and flow of water to downstream states as a tool in establishing dominance over Iraq and Syria. Meanwhile, Iraq has also insisted on 'acquired rights' based on 'ancestral irrigations'. Accordingly, since both the Euphrates and the Tigris have given life to the inhabitants of Mesopotamia and since Iraq developed their installations and dams earlier, both countries claim that they have acquired an historical right over the river basin. Given such irreconcilable interpretations, it is no wonder that water has emerged as a major thorny issue among these three states.

Another reason for the absence of compromise on this issue is the insufficiently articulated international law. Although a significant body of laws exists regarding the status of transboundary navigational waters thanks to early use of water in transportation, the sharing of non-navigational waters has become an international issue of conflict only in the course of the last hundred years or so (Picard 1994; Inan 1994). Documents such as the 1911 Madrid Declaration and Salzburg decision by the International Law Institute, 1956, 1958, 1960 and 1966 Declarations by the International Law Association and finally 1978, 1989, 1991 and 1994 reports by the United Nations International Law Commission constitute the point of reference for international law on water rights. Although most of these decisions are non-binding, the most recent 1994 draft report by the International Law Commission aims to establish some norms and principles upon which the signatories would agree and would be bound. When the 1994 United Nations draft resolution was finally voted in on 21 May 1997 as a Convention on the Law of the Non-Navigational Uses of International Watercourses, however, Turkey refused to sign along with two other countries (China and Burundi) while 27 other states chose to abstain on the issue. The attempts to resolve the issue through legal means have so far proved, in essence, ineffective.

Indeed, the existing international agreements, precedence, and general principles of law, which constitute the body of international law, are peculiarly ambiguous and vague in the case of transboundary waters. Part of the reason is the uniqueness of each water dispute, which makes it harder to reach general principles. The existing watercourse agreement that was reached between Mexico and the US, for instance, over Rio Grande, which established the Harmon Doctrine of absolute sovereignty, cannot easily be applied to the Euphrates and the Tigris. Nevertheless, some principles on sharing of international waters such as 'equitable and reasonable utilisation and participation' as well as obligation not to cause 'appreciable harm' to the downstream states have been proposed as general parameters by the International Law Commission. Regardless of how specifically the body of law might identify what really constitutes 'equitable and reasonable' distribution or 'appreciable' harm, the parties will interpret the law according to their own benefits. The initial 1994 draft resolution, for instance, was interpreted very differently by Turkey, on the one hand, and Iraq and Syria on the other. While Turkey has seen this resolution as a verification of the rights and claims of the upstream states, Syria and Iraq mainly consider the draft as an endorsement of equal rights over the transboundary waters. Turkey has rejected the final 1997 UN General Assembly framework convention mainly because the document requires prior approval of the water projects by the riparian states, which is seen as incompatible with the Turkish thesis on the issue.

The Turkish side insists on the 'Turkishness' of the rivers and argues that it does not have to justify its dams and development projects. The other two parties, however, see such projects as clear infringements on their riparian rights and a systematic attempt on the part of Turkey to economically and strategically dominate the region. Although Turkey has systematically denied any such claims and has offered a three-stage plan in order to resolve the issue on a trilateral basis, the negotiations among the three parties have largely failed. A Protocol that was signed in 1987 between Syria, Iraq and Turkey, in which Turkey promised to guarantee a flow of 500 cubic metres per second was later challenged by Iraq. Syria, also growing suspicious of Turkey's ambitious development plans in the framework of the Southeastern Anatolian Development Project (GAP), failed to attend a meeting in Ankara in late June 1993 which aimed to finalise the arrangements between the three parties. In short, the question over the issue has not really been whether, Iraq, Syria and Turkey can effectively manage the water for the future, which under normal circumstances is technically possible, but rather how the ideological and political barriers to cooperation can be eliminated in resolving the conflict.

Nevertheless, one of the fundamental reasons behind the water dispute is still an economic one. Clearly water is crucial not only for agriculture through irrigation but also for industry through hydroelectrics. Turkey has initially put particular emphasis on GAP in terms of its ability to meet the electricity demands of the country. Indeed, with its 22 dams and 19 hydropower plants, GAP is one of the world's most ambitious water-resources-development and energy-producing programmes. Another important dimension of the project is agricultural production. With the irrigation of 1.7 million hectares of land that is planned in GAP, Turkey aims to transform the economic and social landscape of the South-Eastern region of Turkey. That is why the scope and scale of GAP have increasingly broadened over the last decade, shifting from a largely hydroelectric development programme to a regional integrated development scheme. Increased flow of resources to the region, and overall economic development of Southeastern Anatolia, increasingly became a crucial part of the overall strategy of integrating the alienated Kurdish population in the region. This alienated and economically deprived Kurdish population was largely seen as fuelling PKK activity.

Indeed, even though most of the agricultural production of Turkey will still take place outside the GAP region, agricultural as well as industrial development in the region is particularly important for Turkey for political and strategic reasons. Not only is Southeastern Anatolia the nation's poorest region but also, as described above, it has the bulk of Turkey's Kurdish population. Gross domestic product in the GAP region is low and has deteriorated consistently over the last three decades (State Institute of Statistics 1996). The region is a backward one by all economic indicators, its economy is largely agricultural, it has no industry to speak of with the exception of the city of Gaziantep. Unequal distribution of land is also a major economic problem in the region. 'Some 61 per cent of the farmers (about 150,000 families) own less than five hectares, and 10 per cent of the population own 75 per cent of the land. The social structure has remained virtually unchanged since feudal times, with wealthy Kurdish landowners owning dozens of villages' (Bruan 1994: 26). The reasons behind such skewed land distribution along with large discrepancies in the region in terms of education, employment and other socio-economic indices are beyond the scope of this study. What is clear, however, is that this regional problem coupled with increased PKK activities in the region since 1984 have given new impetus to the GAP project as an integrated regional development programme.

The political and economic interests of Turkey in the South-Eastern region, coupled with the agricultural and industrial demands of both Iraq and Syria, help explain the dispute between the three parties. The difficulty of finding reliable data on the specific agricultural and industrial needs of all the parties also exacerbates the problem. For instance, the amount and degree of irrigable land has been a particularly thorny issue among the disputing parties. The land classification systems of both Iraq and Syria differ widely from that used in Turkey which makes reaching a consensus especially difficult. The amount of Syria's arable land varies, for instance, from 0.4 million hectares to 0.7 million hectares (depending on calculations used) but Syria has declared that it wants to use an annual average 11.5 billion cubic metres of water from the Euphrates (which has a total water potential of 35.5 billion cubic metres), well above the water needed for irrigation of this amount of land (Kolars 1994; Kolars and Mitchell 1991). A pure economic analysis would expect this problem to be solved through a technical analysis of what the long-term agricultural and industrial needs of each country is and would explore ways for more efficient agriculture and use of water (Bakour 1992; Biswas 1993). Once again, however, economic claims are made and needs are defined through political processes. Currently all three countries insist on food self-sufficiency regardless of its efficiency and its economic return. The lack of trust among the region's countries and the risk of a politically motivated embargo both explain the insistence on food security and water demands that go well beyond the capacity of the Euphrates.

Finally, there are also significant domestic barriers to the resolution of the problems. As Kut and Turan (1997: 140) suggest, 'water disputes may be handy to politicians in personifying real or perceived outside threats in the domestic context, and in this way serve to unite the society against "foreign enemies" and mobilise support for the government'. Indeed, the water issue has been effectively used in projecting the developmental needs in each country as a strategic priority and describing water as an indispensable part of independent, autonomous development. The maximalist positions that all parties adopt regarding this issue might indeed be explained through such ideological imperatives (Kut and Turan 1997). Changing the ideological make-up of the disputing states will thus be necessary for the long-term resolution of this conflict. Indeed, replacing the emphasis – or, as some might say, overemphasis – on food security and food self-sufficiency with mutual trust and interdependence will not be easy. Without installing some confidence-building measures that may help remove the ideological aspects of the dispute, carrying the issue from the rhetoric of national unity and national security to one of cooperation and effective use of water will not be possible.

Clearly, installing such confidence-building measures will involve significant transformations of regimes and domestic political structures particularly in Syria and Iraq. Such changes can be brought about through emphasising Level II actors and developing functional cooperation among the users of water in the region, namely the farmers, farmer organisations, water administration units as well as the industries that rely on hydroelectrics. Only through the involvement of such Level II actors can the issue be removed from the ideological biases that have long prevailed in the discussion of the issue and be carried to the issues of sustainability, best use of water, drainage issues, improving technologies for water use, as well as improving agricultural productivity. At a time when the terms of trade in agriculture are steadily declining, for instance, there is no reason why food self-sufficiency policies, which essentially lead to ineffective allocation of resources, cannot be replaced by policies of food interdependence and food trade. For Turkey, the returns of such a cooperative environment might well exceed the expected benefits of the expensive and giant GAP.

Based on the two-level-game framework, it is important to note, however, that the transformation of the GAP from one of hydro-energy production to an integrated regional development programme, had important repercussions both on the domestic and international fronts. On the international front, the transformation of the GAP has coincided with rising criticisms on the part of Syria and Iraq regarding the partitioning of water in the Euphrates–Tigris. The prospects of creating an agricultural power house in the region through the building of irrigation systems have not only increased concerns that not enough water will be flowing from Turkey to the bordering states but have also raised fears that Turkey can indeed become a dominant economic player in the region. Meanwhile, both the EU and the US have raised concerns that the project might exacerbate the international water dispute. It is not surprising that the issue on the use of non-navigational waters, which has been on the agenda of the UN for a long time, has resurfaced in the 1990s.

Domestically, GAP has offered a giant development vision for Turkey. Since the 1960s, GAP has long been associated, for instance, with a vision of a 'grand' Turkey by the then Prime Minister (and current President) Süleyman, Demirel who had spent many years at the Department of Water Management as an engineer. In the 1980s, Prime Minister Turgut Özal put his own stamp on this vision by transforming this power image of the GAP to one of a giant regional development programme. The rising Kurdish problem in the region also coincided with this transformation as the government tried to address the economic sources of this issue. Furthermore, given increasing budget constraints, the government thought that it would be easier to find international sources of project financing for regional development purposes than for building dams. Despite the rising costs of the GAP, however, which have been almost entirely financed domestically, the project has been consistently supported by the governing parties. The Turkish political parties have not only found it difficult to question this vision of a 'grand' Turkey but have also found it politically irrational and non-feasible to cut or limit funding for the overall project. This should not mean, however, that there have been no variations in the funding of the project over the years due to macroeconomic limitations or political considerations. Electoral concerns over votes in the South-East and the Kurdish issue were closely associated with the patterns of allocation, sequencing and timing of financing the GAP. All of these domestic political concerns not only underline the utility of the two-level-game framework but also point out the importance of the domestic political economy of the water dispute. (For further discussion of these issues, see Çarkoğlu and Eder 1997.)

Entry into the Customs Union and its influence on ties with the Middle East

Turkey's improved ties with Israel and some Arab countries were also propelled by its entry into the Customs Union with the EU. Most policy-makers have assumed that Turkey's completion of the 22-year-long transition period in its entry to the Customs Union in January 1996 would lead to significant reductions in economic and political ties with other regions, particularly the Middle East (Undersecretariat of Foreign Trade 1996a). Largely seen as a step towards full EU membership, the Customs Union agreement was hailed as Turkey's entry into the European bloc and a turning away from its neighbours to the East. However, such an argument lacks evidence. As Table 8.1 (see page 201) indicates, Turkey's trade fluctuations in terms of the trade volume with Middle Eastern countries were quite independent of Turkey's ties with the EU. Furthermore, as indicated above, Turkey's trade volume with the Middle East has neither increased nor decreased dramatically since 1994 and has stayed around the usual US$2 billion level (TUSIAD 1996: 66).

Nevertheless, the Customs Union Agreement that Turkey signed with the EU does mean that Turkey will have to accept a common customs tariff against the non-EU members including the countries of the Middle East. The harmonisation of commercial law with the EU is indicated in Articles 12–14 of the agreement. These articles require Turkey to adopt the same level of tariffs applied by the EU members to third parties. Furthermore, Article 16 of the Joint Council agreement also stipulates that Turkey will adopt the same preferential trade agreements that the EU has adopted with third parties within the five years starting from the date Council Agreements go into effect. These preferential trade agreements include a Generalised System of Preferences (GSP) which the EU adopted in 1971 with a number of developing countries. Not all countries, however, use GSP in their trade with the EU. North and Central African states, for instance, utilise the Lome Convention, which offers an even more preferential treatment for those states. Nevertheless, the GSP system offers non-discriminative and most importantly non-reciprocal tariff reductions for goods coming from the developing countries. This system, which was accepted as a waiver from the most-favoured-nation clause of the GATT regime in 1968, essentially aims to integrate the economies of the developing countries into the world economy.

Among the many Middle East countries that enjoy GSP status with the EU are Iran, Iraq, and Saudi Arabia. Jordan, Syria and Lebanon, on the other hand, benefit from the Lome Convention. Furthermore, the EU has concluded a series of bilateral partnership agreements with 8 of the 12 Mediterranean countries. The concepts of 'Euro-Mediterranean Partnership' was proposed and accepted in Barcelona in November 1995 by 12 EU members and 12 Mediterranean countries, which included Turkey. The Barcelona Declaration stated that these 27 countries

> agreed to establish a comprehensive partnership among the participants through strengthened political dialogue on a regular basis, the development of economic and financial cooperation and greater emphasis on the social, cultural and human dimension, these being the three aspects of the Euro-Mediterranean partnership.
>
> (Barcelona Declaration 1995: 1)

Among the most important goals stated in the Barcelona Declaration was the creation of a free trade area through new Euro-Mediterranean agreements and free trade agreements between partners of the European Union by 2010.

Another striking aspect of the Barcelona declaration was the emphasis put on democratisation and human rights which confirms the thesis presented throughout this work, namely, that economic cooperation in and with the region is highly unlikely unless accompanied by significant political aperture and democratisation. Another similarity is the focus on improving understanding between the people and civil societies in the region through programmes that support cultural exchange and community development, improving exchanges among local and regional authorities and education. Such level II contacts have also been recognised as crucial in building long-lasting partnerships between the EU and the Mediterranean countries.

These attempts to rejuvenate political and economic reforms in the region, however, still suffer from security concerns. One of the major conclusions from the May 1996 meeting of the Regional Economic Development Working Group, for instance, was that 'Israel's over-zealous security checks on its borders were a major impediment to regional economic cooperation' (*Reuter News* 6 November 1996). The EU indeed faces a major dilemma with the region of the Middle East and North Africa (MENA). As Hoekman summarises:

> The major policy issue facing the MENA region as a whole is to implement much more far reaching liberalisation, privatisation and deregulation than has been done up to the present. A basic tenet of the economic reform efforts in many of the countries in the region has been that this must not lead to social disruption. The consequence has been an insistence that reform be *gradual*. This has sometimes been complemented by a strategy of *non-transparency*, little effort being devoted to publicising reform efforts and mobilising political support. The result has been uncertainty on the part of firms, households and a lack of credibility. There is a trade-off between political feasibility of rapid efforts and the opportunity costs of gradualism. The slower the pace of reform and the less comprehensive its scope, the larger the gap between MENA's performance and that of the rest of the world is likely to become. The absence of a significant private sector supply response and inward foreign direct investment will in turn limit political support for reform. A vicious cycle may result. … Euro-Mediterranean Economic Area might provide the needed institutional framework that enhances the credibility of a gradual reform strategy.
>
> (Hoekman 1995: 1)

How fast should the EU countries then push for political and economic reforms in the MENA countries through cooperation without becoming a source of social disruption? Can the push for rapid economic liberalisation, for instance, create political backlash? Another fundamental concern on the part of some Middle East countries, for instance, has been the economic and political disparity between the two regions which has led to the questioning of the EU's motives in seeking cooperation with MENA countries. Such concerns surfaced at the Euro-Mediterranean meeting in Malta in April 1997. Nevertheless, increasing business and trade ties between the two regions can help overcome these suspicions and help institutionalise gradual reforms.

As a secular, relatively democratic state and open economy, Turkey can play a crucial bridging role in fostering ties between the EU and the Middle East. Turkish civil society can also help enhance social, cultural and business ties between the two regions. However, to be a part of the EU's Mediterranean policy, or part of its policies towards the MENA region, raises several dilemmas for Turkish foreign policy as well. There is also a fear shared by many policy-makers that it also runs the risk of losing the 'special status' it enjoys with the EU (Undersecretariat of Foreign Trade 1996a). In other words, agreeing to become a part of the EU's programme with respect to the Mediterranean and the Middle East, Turkey, in the words of a Turkish businessman, might end up helping the EU countries 'draw the line between the East and the West on the Aegean Sea', while pushing for a special and separate partnership 'might extend this line towards the Turkish–Iranian border' (Interview with Serif Egeli, 13 December 1996). In short, Turkey faces a tough balancing act, on the one hand setting an example for the region as a relatively democratic and secular state and acting as a liaison between the EU and the Middle East, while on the other hand securing its special status with the EU. This balancing act has become even more difficult with the refusal of the EU to include Turkey on the list of prospective member countries which included 11 other states, most of which where formerly Communist Eastern European countries.

On the economic side, however, there are more clear benefits to these agreements. What is most interesting in the Europe–Mediterranean Partnership agreements, is that they are reciprocal rather than one-sided concessions on the part of the EU. That is why it is much easier for Turkey to actually negotiate trade agreements with these countries, than if Turkey were to negotiate GSP concessions, namely, unilaterally open up its markets to the third parties. This is particularly the case since Turkey itself enjoys GSP status against a number of countries such as the US and Russia. What is also most advantageous for Turkey is that the EU has already developed formal economic ties with a number of Middle East and Mediterranean countries which will both encourage and make it easier for Turkey to develop similar economic agreements with these countries. In the 1/95 (Customs Union) decision of the EC–Turkey Association Council (which is a joint council between the two countries), Turkey has prioritised the countries with which it is willing to sign a preferential agreement. Some of the countries in the Middle East, such as Israel, Egypt, Morocco and Tunisia, are also included in this priority list (Customs Union Agreement 1995). Article 16 of the agreement also has an exemption clause indicating that Turkey will continue to carry out the obligations that stem from its membership of the Economic Cooperation Organisation which aims to foster links between Turkey, Iran, Pakistan, Afghanistan and most of the former Soviet republics. This means that Turkey will continue to implement the Preferential Tariff Protocol (PTP) that it signed with Pakistan and Iran, stipulating that Turkey will continue to apply 10 per cent lower tariffs on a series of products listed in the PTP.

The first fruit of agreements such as those discussed above has been the Free Trade Agreement that Turkey signed with Israel. This agreement, first signed in March 1996 and ratified in December 1996, has the aim of creating a free trade area between the two countries by 2000. This agreement – which is based on the global symmetry principle, meaning that all concessions given to the EU will also be given to Turkey – aims to liberalise trade on all industrial goods and some agricultural products. Plans to start negotiations to include services flowing into this free trade area are also under way. This agreement will benefit Turkey in a number of ways. It will be a step towards the harmonisation of Turkey's commercial policy with that of the EU. The agreement is likely to create an important boom between the two countries (Undersecretariat of Foreign Trade 1996a). It is also likely to create opportunities for Turkish and Israeli businessmen to invest jointly in the US, EU, Central Asia and the Middle East (Aras 1998). Such a partnership will also benefit Israel, helping it to dilute the deep-rooted hostilities towards Israeli investments in the Arab world. It could also ease some of the concerns of Israeli domination over the Arab economies. Furthermore, Turkey will also gain greater access to US, EU and EFTA markets through Israel. The Israeli government has already signed agreements with these countries which ensure zero tariffs on all industrial products. Subject to zero tariffs, Turkish products will have a better chance of competing in these markets while gaining cheaper access to some imported products, thus lowering import costs. In short, by creating a framework within which Turkey can undertake trade negotiations, Turkey's entry into the Customs Union has actually improved formal links between Turkey and the Middle East.

The argument that the increased ties with the EU can also help regulate, formalise and enhance ties with the Middle East runs counter to the usual dichotomy portrayed by Turkish political parties on the domestic front. The Turkish political parties have usually used the East–West dichotomy not only to identify their foreign-policy priorities but have also often associated increased ties with the West and the EU with modernisation and even civilisation. That is why, for instance, discussions over the Customs Union have rarely centred around the discussion of the possible economic repercussions of such an agreement but have instead focused on being 'European' and assuming a European identity. Such an emphasis has also assumed an exclusionary tone, implying that Turkey should only focus on the West and can afford to ignore its ties with the Middle East. As the above discussion indicates, such a dichotomy is indeed false but has been effectively used by the governing parties. During negotiations on the Customs Union, for instance, the then Prime Minister Tansu Çiller, was able to present the Customs Union agreement as a passage to 'Western civilisation' (Eder forthcoming). Similarly, the Welfare Party government has identified economic cooperation among the eight Islamic countries during a summit in Istanbul as an alternative to the G7 countries. Once again, such dichotomies defined along ideological and cultural lines rather than economic and political interests underline how foreign-policy realities might diverge from domestic political concerns. It is to this domestic dimension that we now turn.

Changing domestic dynamics of Middle Eastern foreign policy in Turkey

In spite of the developments that increase the importance of the Middle East for Turkey, the sensitivities, deep insecurities and divisions that continue to characterise the region's politics have imposed limits on Turkish involvement in the area. The military cooperation agreement signed between Israel and Turkey in February 1996, followed in less than a month by Israel's Operation Grapes of Wrath, caused a major uproar amongst Arab public opinion and drew strong criticisms from the governments of particularly Egypt and Iran. These criticisms became even more intense after the elections in Israel in May 1996, which brought to office a right-wing government much less willing to support the peace process. The already difficult relations with Syria were also affected when the Syrian government accused the Turkish government of inciting disturbances within Syria in May 1996 and saw a major strategic threat for itself from the Israeli–Turkish military cooperation. The tension between the two countries led to a troop build-up along the frontier during June 1996. The situation was further aggravated when Iran offered Syria a military pact that was similar to the one made between Turkey and Israel (*Turkish Daily News* 21 June 1996). The situation somewhat improved after the formation in Turkey of the coalition government between the pro-Islamist RP and conservative DYP in June 1996 (remaining in power until July 1997). The success of RP in the December 1995 elections and in the turbulent aftermath that led to its coming to power as the major partner in a coalition government signalled a turning point in the traditional centre-right politics in Turkey. Equally significantly, it also brought, for the first time in Turkish democracy, a party that openly challenges the secular basis of the Republic to executive office. From the perspective of Turkey's relationships with other Middle Eastern countries, the coming to power of the RP was also significant. This was because improved, solidified and deepened cooperation with the Muslim countries of the region had always been one of the critical issues advocated by the leadership of the RP, and this had been used extensively in its electoral campaigns.

The general policy preferences, and especially the ones concerning Turkish foreign policy of the new Prime Minister and leader of the RP, Necmettin Erbakan, were in marked contrast to previous governments. At the start of the RP/DYP coalition many were expecting that the RP would be shut out of foreign-policy circles that are traditionally under the strong influence of the military and the Ministry of Foreign Affairs. These two institutions are two of the strongest bureaucratic traditions in Turkey with powerful pro-secular stands in not only the policies created and implemented but also in the recruitment and promotion policies that they currently follow. When in opposition Erbakan and leading figures in the RP repeatedly challenged the secularist principles of the Turkish Republic and took a clear anti-western position in all critical foreign policy issues. Erbakan, for example, had promised to scrap the military agreement with Israel and replace traditional Turkish foreign policy with one that emphasised relations with Islamic countries with a view to establishing an Islamic common market and what he termed an Islamic NATO (Erbakan 1995: 58–61).

In a few short weeks after the new coalition government was formed, the claim of a foreign policy environment excluding RP was clearly being tested.

> In an early challenge, RP has reversed its long term policy stand against the Operation Provide Comfort (OPC), a multi-national air operation based in Turkey that aims to deter Iraq from attacking civilians and enforces a no-fly

> zone in northern Iraq. The coalition government extended the OPC for another five-month period.
>
> (Çarkoğlu 1997: 94)

Clear pressure from the military forced the RP not only to keep the military agreement with Israel but also extend it by authorising an additional agreement concerning the upgrading of Turkish F-4 fighter planes by Israel. However, it was only in December 1996, and with considerable reluctance, that Erbakan started the ratification process of the Free Trade Treaty with Israel. Although the ratification process was completed the Prime Minister's office held up its implementation on a technicality which delayed the effective date of the treaty until the formation of the new government in July 1997.

Against his reluctance to maintain good relations with Israel, Erbakan tried to put into effect his ideas about increasing economic cooperation among Islamic countries by launching the idea of the establishment of the group to be called the D-8, composed of Bangladesh, Egypt, Indonesia, Iran, Malaysia, Nigeria, Pakistan and Turkey. The foreign ministers of these 8 countries met in January in Istanbul to formalise its establishment. Another summit also took place in June 1997. Erbakan's emphasis on developing relations with Islamic countries was evident in two widely publicised foreign tours he held within months of coming to office. In August 1996, he set out on a visit of Islamic countries in Asia followed by a similar tour in Africa in October. The fact that these tours included radical Islamic countries such as Iran and Libya (Sudan was left out of the African tour at the last moment) generated considerable controversy in Turkey, as well as in the West and the Middle East. Although pragmatic considerations welcomed the signing of a US$23 billion dollar natural-gas deal, Erbakan's readiness to ignore Iran's support for the PKK generated strong criticism inside Turkey. In December 1996, Erbakan's enthusiasm to reach an Iranian–Turkish defence cooperation agreement during the Iranian President Hashemi Rafsanjani's visit was blocked by the military and his coalition partners. His meeting with the Libyan leader Muammar Gaddafi in October triggered a major governmental crisis. Gaddafi's remarks that Turkey should not impede the independence of Kurds led to a motion of censure in the parliament which was only just defeated by the government.

The RP foreign-policy initiatives as voiced by Erbakan were received in many circles as unrealistic given that the existing cooperation schemes, such as the Economic Cooperation Organisation and Islamic Conference Organisation, had achieved very little. Many also argued that his ideas were mostly for domestic political consumption (*Al-Ahram Weekly* 15–19 June 1997). In looking at the strategies of the Erbakan coalition government towards the Middle East, one has to take into account the character of Welfare Party's domestic constituencies. During the tenure of the RP, many foreign-policy initiatives especially toward the Middle East were shaped by a specific segment of the RP electoral support group. Such a target group's electoral support could, however, be obtained by simply being at odds with not only a strong majority of the Turkish electorate but also long-standing Turkish foreign-policy principles and commitments. The use of foreign policy for domestic political gains is not new in Turkey.

The RP initiatives, however, formed an exception to this domestic–foreign policy relationship in the Turkish context. The relationship between public opinion and foreign-policy initiatives is a neglected issue in Turkey. There are, however, some statistics from polls that can be used to analyse developments in 1997. The monthly survey conducted by Strateji/MORI with a nationwide representative sample provides some guidelines about these relationships. When asked about the general foreign-policy stand towards 'Muslims' in general 76 per cent of the respondents seem to support 'solidarity' with them (Strateji/MORI 1997a: 40). Similarly, about 81 per cent of the respondents find the idea of Turkey as having good relations with the Middle Eastern countries as 'important'. However, when faced with a choice between Israel and other Middle Eastern countries only 13 per cent of the respondents seem to favour Israel (Strateji/MORI 1997b: 58–71).[3] There was also only weak support among the Turkish electorate for the 1996 cooperative engagement between Israel and Turkey; only 29 per cent supported cooperation with Israel, whereas 44 per cent was clearly opposed to it (Strateji/MORI 1997a: 40). Taken from this general perspective, the policy principle of the RP towards strengthening the role given to the Middle East countries seemed perfectly in line with the general public attitude. However, there were mixed signals from the public when it came to a choice between Europe and the Middle East. When asked whether Turkey is 'part of a Muslim community of nations' or 'part of Europe', 41 per cent said it is part of a Muslim community of nations, whereas 31 per cent said it is part of Europe, and 16 per cent said it is part of both. Seventy-four per cent of the respondents support Turkey's membership to the EU if an opportunity arises in the next few years, as opposed to only 15 per cent who are against such a development. However, 46 per cent of the same group of respondents said that the likelihood of such a development is not high (Strateji/MORI 1997a: 41–42). It seems that, although Turks feel closer to the Muslim countries, they nevertheless want to be part of Europe at the same time, realistically judging the prospect of such a development to be unlikely.

The exceptional aspect of the RP's use of a foreign-policy initiative for domestic political gains, derives from the fact that, when pushed to its limits, the Turkish electorate seems not to be too supportive of extending relations with the Muslim world at large, especially allying with the radical front of the Muslim countries at the expense of national interests. Erbakan's somewhat scandalous visit to Egypt and Libya in autumn of 1996 is a case in point. After repeated lack of communication on the diplomatic front in Egypt and several misplaced and harsh comments by Muammer Gaddafi in Libya, public opinion seems to have clearly turned against Erbakan. Fifty-two per cent of the population at large said that they did not support Erbakan's visit to these countries, and 55 per cent said its results were not positive (Strateji/MORI 1997a: 43–44). So why did Erbakan take this apparently disastrous step, or was this step really so politically disastrous to Erbakan? Looking at these results from the perspective of RP supporters we see that a clear majority of them were supportive of Erbakan's initiative. From the perspective of Erbakan this visit was a success in sending a clear message to RP constituencies that Turkey's foreign policies were now being re-shaped by RP, giving a clear priority to Muslim solidarity. Here lies a clear danger for a new Turkish foreign policy towards the Middle East. These pro-Islamist constituencies are now one of the strongest groups among the Turkish electorate. To try to exploit these constituencies, however, may not be so beneficial from an electoral point of view, since they have the potential of attracting the reaction of those who shy away from Muslim solidarity in favour of a more advanced cooperative relationship with Europe and thus the West. The developments during the RP/DYP coalition gave signals of an attempt by RP to use domestic polarisation along a secularist versus anti-secularist dimension as a basis for foreign-policy making.

Since its inception as the National Order Party (Milli Nizam Partisi) in the mid-1960s, the RP has always emphasised a rhetoric of national independence, cultural, social, economic and political cooperation with the Islamic world emphasising Islamic values. Such rhetoric has found significant electoral support primarily among small Anatolian merchant communities, uprooted newly urbanised, socially alienated and economically deprived citizens.[4] Without having serious electoral competitors emphasising a similar set of issues, Erbakan found it convenient to manipulate these growing segments of Turkish society in RP's electoral campaigns. Consequently, the RP continually underlined its affinity with the Islamic world and its role both as the protector and promoter of Islamic values in Turkey. On the international scene, the implication of this electoral strategy was to emphasise cooperation with the Muslim countries at large but particularly with the most controversial and radical actors of the Islamic world. Öniş notes that:

> Special emphasis is accorded towards the strengthening of relations with countries of the Middle East, the emerging states of the post-Soviet Central Asia and the highly dynamic second generation NICs of South East Asia which include key countries with predominantly Islamic populations such as Malaysia and Indonesia.
>
> (Öniş 1997: 30)

The cooperative rhetoric of the RP towards select Muslim developing countries is also blended with a serious dose of nationalistic arguments geared towards a self-ascribed leadership within this quite heterogeneous group. The opposition of the RP to any western cooperative mechanism including NATO and the EU is to be seen within this broader context of Islamic developmentalism and international cooperation.

> Turkey, in terms of its economic potential and geographical position, is singled out as the natural candidate for the leadership of the Islamic world. Hence, the recovery of [the] Islamic world from centuries of oblivion and its rise to a position of prominence in the global economy goes hand in hand with the rise of Turkey to the status of a significant power, in the broader context of Islamic cooperation.
>
> (Öniş 1997: 30–31)

The existence of such a constituency behind the RP, which clearly responds positively to the above strategy, can both be an asset as well as a liability. On the positive side, the religiously grounded RP constituencies may be seen as the basis of a dynamic Anatolian entrepreneurial group who might indeed rejuvenate Level II links with the Muslim countries in the Middle East. Largely ignored by most of the centrist parties, RP strategy can indeed be instrumental in creating and mobilising these so-called 'Anatolian tigers' towards the Middle Eastern market. As such, an important domestic constituency behind a new foreign policy emphasising Level II cooperation towards the region can be created. Here we are clearly assuming that a significant portion of RP constituency still resides in peripheral sectors of Turkish society. Although this assumption has been challenged there seems little doubt that the RP does not have a smooth relationship with the economic agents of the centre. In contrast, the RP seems to have gathered together a coalition of electoral support that includes not only the poor, the disadvantaged and the excluded periphery but also

> individuals based in urban areas, who are … extremely well-educated professionals or businessmen well-versed with modern technology … these are clearly people with a modernist orientation who are experiencing a rising status in society, and yet are not fully incorporated into elite status … they are part of a rising, potential or secondary elite who are trying to consolidate their position in society on the basis of Islamic identity.
>
> (Öniş 1997: 15)

There has been much talk on, but little systematic analysis of, this second dimension of the RP support coalition that came to be called the 'Islamic capital' in Turkey. Again, on mostly speculative and/or journalistic accounts there seems to be a rising consensus among Turkish public opinion that significant financial support is obtained by RP leadership from this 'Islamic capital'. Öniş (1997: 37–46) suggests that Anatolian small businessmen, and shopkeepers were transformed into larger and deeper economic entities during the economic liberalisation of the 1980s. Capital flows from German migrant workers as well as substantial capital investment undertaken by the Islamic brotherhood networks (tarikat), combined with a newly arising Anatolian business community, forms the basis of not only electoral support for RP but also one of a financial nature. Although there is no one-to-one correspondence between these Islamic networks and the RP, the observation that the RP is a political manifestation of rising Anatolian business interests attracts very little opposition.

Among these Islamic networks and capital groups one is of particular significance. The Independent Association of Industrialists and Businessmen (MUSIAD), founded in 1990 by a group of very young businessmen, grew fast with about 3,000 members in 1997. In contrast to the Turkish Industrialist and Businessmen Association (TUSIAD), which has about 400 select members, MUSIAD stands as not only representative of interests of the Anatolian capital but also as the largest voluntary business association in the country. Öniş (1997: 40–41) notes that MUSIAD members, with notable exceptions such as the giant KOMBASSAN (a major industrial conglomerate closely associated with RP) of Konya, are predominantly small- to medium-size firms that are spread around the Anatolian provinces. Öniş reports that,

> in October 1996 MUSIAD had a total membership of 2,567. The largest congregations of members included Istanbul (786), Bursa (246), Izmir (205), Konya (184), Kayseri (175), Ankara (169) and Kocaeli (107). Of these only Konya and Kayseri are the traditional RP strongholds in the inner Anatolian region. The rest are major metropolitan centres. It is also interesting that the emerging towns associated with successful industrialisation (the Anatolian Tigers) in recent years namely Çorum, Kahramanmaras, Şanlıurfa, Gaziantep and Denizli have a combined membership of 256 which is also significant.
>
> (Öniş 1997: 40–41)

The so-called Anatolian Tigers are not analysed to any great extent.[5] We should note here that neither the claim that MUSIAD is the sole representative of the small Anatolian business nor the claim that the Anatolian business community is predominantly of pro-Islamist orientation are true. There is a significant community of businesses that are not of a pro-Islamist stand and also some business associations outside of MUSIAD have also been formed. However, a key element in the Anatolian business community does have a pro-Islamist orientation and these are affiliated with MUSIAD. It is imperative here to note that policy stands of MUSIAD do bear a striking resemblance to those of the RP. Besides, with the not-so-surprising demand for support of the small- to medium-size firms by the government, MUSIAD sharply differentiates itself from TUSIAD by propagating the development of ties with the Islamic world and by being against the Customs Union with Europe.

In principle, the dynamism and commitment of small- to medium-size business of the Anatolian provinces could be a fertile ground for developing close Level II cooperative mechanisms with the Middle East. Such Level II cooperation need not solely be restricted to peripheral Anatolian capital interests but must also include those of the centre or traditional business interests of metropolitan areas of Istanbul and Izmir.

On the negative side, Erbakan's constituencies might direct him towards a non-economic agenda emphasising rhetorical and ideological issues. This will certainly please the RP constituency in the short run, but may damage Turkey's long-term interests by alienating not only its Western allies but also most of the moderates in the Middle East. An important dimension of MUSIAD and these new 'Anatolian Tiger' interests might be purely ideological and thus non-economic and non-inclusionary. Yet another dimension might depend on patronage links to the central authority so as to develop their competitive power against more traditional business interests with closer ties to the centre. Any new policy initiative should take these detrimental aspects into account and be geared towards correcting them.

The changes that Erbakan was introducing to Turkish foreign policy engendered mixed reactions in the Middle East. Clearly, Iranian government officials appeared to be delighted by Erbakan's overtures. In Iran there has been a struggle between hard liners who want to protect Iran's revolution from the influence of the outside world, in particular the West, and the pragmatists who are searching for ways to expand Iran's relations with the West and the outside world (Halliday 1994; Hashim 1995). Iran's economy suffered deeply from both the war with Iraq and the inept policies followed by the revolutionary regime. This led to the per capita income being halved between 1979–89 (Hashim 1995: 10). There is growing recognition of the need for western technology and investments to revitalise the Iranian economy (Amuzegar 1992). The recent implicit appeals for a possible dialogue with the US reflect, in some ways, not only a gradual tilt towards moderation within Iranian domestic politics, but also these urgent economic needs.

Erbakan's visit to radical Islamic countries also stood out as a good example of an ideologically motivated foreign-policy initiative. We have noted the domestic political considerations that might have guided RP initiatives. However, international reactions to this initiative were also mixed. Erbakan's visits to Iran and Libya, his close relations with radical and violent Islamic opposition groups such as the Islamic Salvation Front (FIS), Hamas, Hizbullah and the Muslim Brotherhood also explains why Erbakan was not very well received in Cairo at the beginning of his Africa tour in October 1996. Erbakan, during the Egyptian President's visit to Turkey in July 1996 had called on Mubarak to tolerate the Muslim Brotherhood in Egypt. At the time Mubarak had rebuked Erbakan by calling members of the Muslim Brotherhood 'murderers' and told Erbakan that he could have them in Turkey if he liked them so much. In spite of this, Erbakan subsequently held a meeting in Turkey with a leading name of the Muslim Brotherhood, Hassan Al-Benna early in August 1996. The decision to invite representatives of these radical groups to RP's fifth Party Congress held on 13 October 1996 did not help to improve the climate.

Erbakan's policies have also been a source of concern for Palestinian officials who have noted the prominence with which Hamas and Hizbullah representatives were received at the RP's fifth Party Congress. Many officials of RP do not consider the PLO and Yasser Arafat to be representative of the Palestinian people and have criticised the PLO–Israeli peace process. Erbakan and his party's view on Israel is not very positive either. Anti-Israeli and anti-Zionist arguments have become standard in RP political discourse and have been noted to frequently acquire anti-Semitic tones as well (Balı 1996). The fact that the Israeli Prime Minister Binjamin Netanyahu's letter of congratulation and request for a meeting went unanswered was also very much reflective of RP and Erbakan's position on Israel. It is difficult to see how a foreign policy based on expanding relations with radical groups at the cost of offending governments who are, against all odds, attempting to resolve their differences through negotiations, could help security and stability in the Middle East or serve, for that matter, the interests of Turkey.

The new minority government that replaced the RP/DYP coalition government in July 1997 (led by ANAP leader Mesut Yilmaz) has concentrated most of its efforts, once again, in re-establishing the focus of Turkish foreign policy towards the EU and the West. To what extent this new government will bring a new policy towards the Middle East, or how long this government will stay in power to introduce a major overhaul of foreign policy, both remain to be seen. Nevertheless, the foreign-policy experience under the RP/DYP government has marked a risky if not outright dangerous temptation that may gain prominence among the foreign-policy circles of the executive office in the near future. The danger lies in the prominence of pro-Islamist and radical Islamist groups among the Turkish electorate. Even though the RP/DYP coalition has been replaced by a minority government, these groups will not disappear in the near future and are important organisations that can mobilise electoral support for or against any party. It should be noted that the minority government chose to characterise the December 1997 dispute between the EU and Turkey, which stemmed from the EU's refusal to include Turkey on the list of prospective member countries, in terms of exclusion of Muslims from the 'Christian Club'. This is yet another reflection of the persisting attractiveness to ideologise foreign-policy issues so as to appeal to various domestic constituencies. Ideological and hence exclusionary policy-stands of various Islamist groups have most often surfaced in the context of Turkey's foreign policy towards the Middle East. Unless these ideological attitudes are abandoned and replaced with cooperative and inclusionary policy stands that give prominence to 'like-minded' countries rather than those who are pushed to the edges of the international community, Turkish foreign policy cannot be repositioned in a new orbit for the new era of the Middle East.

When talking about some broad policy initiatives that can be taken by Level I actors in Turkey, we cannot overemphasise the need for a conviction and commitment by the Level I leadership of the necessity and the possibility of cooperative, peaceful development in the Middle East based on democratic governance principles. Our two-level-game framework implies that such a conviction and commitment comes about as a function of Level II actors' convictions, commitments and consequent pressures. Accordingly, one is led to search for clues of such dynamics among Level II actors. Perhaps the most direct way to search for clues of such dynamics is by referring to data of public opinion. Despite the fact that we do not have data directly relevant to the question of supporting cooperative foreign-policy initiative concerning the Middle East, we have evidence that suggests that there is support among the public for Turkey's intensified relationships with the region's countries.

Strateji/MORI (1997b: 64–71) reports several interesting sets of answers obtained in their monthly survey completed using a nationwide representative sample. Among the population at large about 69 per cent view Turkey's being in good relations with Middle Eastern countries as important. When the respondents are filtered and only those who consider themselves to be interested in foreign affairs are analysed this ratio rises to 81 per cent. Among different party supporters who consider themselves as being interested in foreign affairs, those who view Turkey's good relations with the Middle East as important are highest among RP supporters: 95 per cent supporting good relations with Middle Eastern countries, excluding Israel. This level of support is relatively lower, though not considerably, among supporters of the Nationalist Action Party (MHP) (68 per cent) and Republican People's Party (CHP) (73 per cent). There seems to be an overwhelming majority of public support for Turkey having good relations with Middle Eastern countries.

In the same survey of Strateji/MORI conducted between 24 May and 6 June 1997, the respondents were asked to judge the degree of benefit from 'good relations' with the Middle Eastern countries in four different areas. The four different areas listed were economic, cultural, religious and political. Those who consider economic relations as beneficial for Turkey are highest among the four areas given for both the sample at large (68 per cent) as well as the group of respondents who consider themselves interested in foreign affairs (81 per cent). Good relations with Middle Eastern countries on religious issues are considered to be beneficial for Turkey only by a minority of about 36 per cent. Similarly, good relations on cultural and political issues are viewed by only about 45 per cent of the people as beneficial. However, those who consider good relations with Middle Eastern countries in cultural and political issues to bring no benefit constitute around 30 per cent of those polled. So, those who believe good relations with Middle Eastern countries to be beneficial are larger in proportion than those who believe this not to be beneficial in all areas except the one concerning religious issues. Only in the case of RP supporters is it true that those who consider good relations with Middle Eastern countries concerning religious issues is larger than those who believe to the contrary. Similar to the pattern that emerged in the previous question, supporters of RP seem to have predominantly positive beneficial expectations about good relations with Middle Eastern countries in all of the four areas. The rate of those with positive expectations declines as one moves from the right end of the ideological spectrum towards the left. Supporters of the Republican People's Party (CHP), for example, have predominantly positive expectations in only the area of economic issues.

Although not part of a comprehensive survey on public opinion concerning foreign-policy issues, the above data give us pointers of at least two important phenomena. The first is that there is a large amount of support for good relations with Middle Eastern countries, especially concerning economic issues. Second, however, we also see that public support follows an ideological pattern in its degree of support for good relations with Middle Eastern countries. RP supporters are typically supportive of good relations with the region's countries to a considerably larger extent compared to other party supporters, especially those on the left of the ideological spectrum.

As noted earlier, a similarly divided picture is obtained on the issue of priority of Israel in Turkey's foreign policy towards the Middle East as well as support for recent military cooperation between Turkey and Israel. Together with the pattern emerging from the above data, this can be taken as an indication that domestic ideological polarisation among the Turkish parties is very much reflected in people's attitudes towards foreign-policy issues. Such a pattern may have important implications if not properly handled by the parties' leadership cadres. If, as noted earlier, the party leadership of the right-wing, and especially that of RP, favours radical constituencies in the region at the expense of the moderates, Turkish foreign policy may be pushed into an infertile vicious circle. The ideological polarisation in the Turkish party system may then be reflected in domestic constituencies that are manipulated to support radical Middle Eastern constituencies and those that see and react to these constituencies on the basis of their domestic political convictions.

Conclusion

Turkey, with its changing ties with the Middle East both internationally and domestically, offers a compelling case study for exploring the role of what we have called 'like-minded' states in the Middle East. There is no doubt that the end of the Cold War has brought about important changes in the region. As a result of these changes, the preference to solve the problems of the Middle East peacefully has gained prominence. So far, progress has been slow and disappointing, especially for the Palestinians. However, there is also a clear recognition by all parties involved that abandoning the peace process would not improve the situation either. As President Mubarak of Egypt noted following the Middle East and North Africa Economic summit held in Cairo in November 1996, the alternative to progress through negotiation would not necessarily be war between states, but violence and terrorism that would engulf the region (*Al-Ahram Weekly* 21–27 November 1996).

As the example of Turkey illustrates, a Middle East that drifts into such violence and instability would adversely affect the interests and security of the 'like-minded' states. In the case of Turkey, the country's security and economic prosperity have become intrinsically tied to developments in the region. On a wide range of issues, from the Kurdish issue to its energy needs, from the water problem to trade, Turkey can reap many benefits from a cooperative and peaceful Middle East.

However, Turkey's relations with the Middle East are not only shaped by international dynamics and the opportunities that they offer, but are intrinsically tied to its domestic changes. As elaborated above, democratisation at home, political changes that came with the Erbakan RP/DYP coalition government followed by the minority Mesut Yılmaz government led by ANAP, coupled with the regional development concerns in the South-East also underline how the domestic dynamics can have important repercussions in the foreign-policy process and its outcome.

Clearly, from the different solutions to the Kurdish question to different opinions on the new rapprochement with Israel, ties with the Middle East are actually highly politicised at the Turkish domestic front. An understanding of how various parties respond to these issues, what various governing coalitions attempt to use foreign-policy issues for their domestic goals, and how political realignments reconfigure priorities and transform the rhetoric of foreign-policy makers, offer insights into the difficulties and possibilities of cooperation in the region.

Exploring such ties between domestic polarisation and foreign-policy outcomes, also demonstrates the utility of the two-level-game framework. Without looking at the strategic and interactive dynamics between such domestic factors at Level II and the ongoing inter-state (Level I) ties in the Middle East, and without a clear understanding the 'Janus-faced' nature of diplomacy in the region, it becomes difficult to discern the otherwise invisible shifts and changes in the foreign policy of these countries. Nor is it possible to note the new opportunities for cooperation and, in effect, use these opportunities efficiently. Clearly a look at this strategic interaction between Level I and Level II actors is not a panacea that will solve all the problems in the Middle East but it clearly offers a better picture as to why governments behave the way they do in the region. As such, it furthers the understanding of the barriers and prospects of cooperation in the region.

Exploring the making of foreign policy in the Middle Eastern countries is particularly important since for the first time in the modern history of the Middle East, there are signs that economic and political cooperation is being thought of as a tool for achieving regional stability and peace. Turkey and the 'like-minded' states are ideally situated to contribute to the making of this new Middle East. Another logical extension of two-level-game framework in foreign policy analysis is a greater emphasis on democratisation and political liberalisation since cooperation is more likely to take place between democratic and open regimes. Such regimes are more likely to be credible in meeting their commitments. For a long time the Middle East was characterised by authoritarian and repressive regimes. It is not surprising that this was also a time that coincided with conflict and instability. Today, the very countries that oppose peace and cooperation in the Middle East are still by and large repressive regimes that are ideological and often dogmatic. Two such countries are Iraq and Syria. It is difficult to see how these countries might change their course unless regime changes occur. In August 1997, Iran swore in a new president promising to take a pragmatic line in domestic policy as well as foreign policy. However, time will show whether Iran will be able to adopt a more cooperative line in its foreign relations.

Advocating and supporting closer ties among a group of 'like-minded' countries in the Middle East – that is, Turkey, Egypt, Jordan, Israel and Palestine – can be the starting point for establishing a 'new' Middle East. These are the countries that appear to be closest to each other and most willing to cooperate. They are also characterised by a greater commitment to economic and political liberalisation. These qualities could be critical in the search for 'democratic peace' in the Middle East. They could come to constitute the first core group of countries that have achieved cooperation and the derived benefits from such cooperation so that this could set an example for others in the region. This core group would be open to all countries of the region as long as they can meet the basic criteria of being democratic, open and market-oriented societies that reject force as a tool of international politics. In Europe, 6 countries started the nucleus of European integration. Today, almost half a century after its inception, this project is evolving towards covering most of Europe. The 5 'like-minded' countries could play a similar role to that the 6 European countries played. A process that would necessarily emulate the European experience and aim towards the same goal of a regional union is not necessarily suggested. Instead, these countries can simply help initiate a process of cooperation and assume a leading role. Where that cooperation eventually could or ought to lead is a different matter. What is important is that it leads to a new Middle East which replaces the one dominated by conflict, violence, destruction and distrust.

Finally, as the two-level-game framework implies, and as the Turkish case demonstrates, establishing political will at Level I is simply insufficient for a lasting peace and cooperation in the region. In this area, Level II actors – organisations, universities, unions, businesses and non-governmental organisations in these 'like-minded' states – will have a very important role to play. This is because, in the final analysis, the success of a 'new' Middle East will, after all, very much depend on whether domestic constituencies in each country support such a 'new' Middle East.

9 Conclusion

This study is based on the premise that economic and political cooperation in the Middle East is not only necessary and urgent but also possible. We have explored the barriers and prospects the region faces in building and fostering cooperation. The end of the Cold War has dramatically changed the dynamics in the region creating an environment more conducive to cooperation. Can Middle Eastern governments make use of this window of opportunity or are these governments doomed to miss the train of globalisation and regionalism in the world economy? At a time when the whole world seems to be acknowledging the need for cooperation and democratisation, will the Middle East remain an exception? Our answer to this question is a conditional no. True, the region is still unique with its oil-dependent, inefficient economies, 'security-minded' state structures, and with its ongoing or prolonged conflicts together with the over-centralisation of power in the hands of state elites. Yet, there is a limit to how long such policies can be maintained.

The time might have indeed come for Middle Eastern governments to undertake political and economic reforms and change their strategies. As oil revenues decline, as the pressures for democratisation both from outside as well as from within mount, as the economic necessities of the region push these states towards cooperation rather than war, the prospects of cooperation in the region are indeed likely to increase. Currently, however, these signs are not all that clear. The general mood in the region shifted from jubilance and support for cooperation, as was the case in the Casablanca conference in 1994, to considerable disappointment and frustration during the course of 1996 and 1997. In a region where issues can change rapidly – for example, security and economic calculations, and uncertainties in terms of balance of power and security threats – our aim in this book has not been to offer a grand design for peace and cooperation in the region. Rather, we aimed to provide an incremental and gradual approach to peace and explore paths and conditions under which cooperation is likely in the region.

Clearly, a scheme of regional integration like that in the EU or even a free trade area is far from being realistic in the Middle East. At a time, where the simplest free trade agreement requires significant harmonisation of domestic policies and coordination, such a model would require a radical overhaul of the regimes and policy patterns in the Middle East and this is highly unlikely. Whichever model is chosen, however, one of the main conclusions of our study is that cooperation in the Middle East cannot be studied unless economic and political factors are simultaneously taken into account. Cooperation in the Middle East is neither a simple cessation of conflicts nor is it signing a free trade agreement. Any analysis in the region will have to explore how the security dynamics of the region shape the economic dynamics and vice versa. From the water conflict to the issue of agricultural self-sufficiency, from energy issues to trade, economic policy-making in the Middle East is essentially a political process. While we suggest that the political barriers and security concerns form the most important impediment to economic cooperation, we also found enough evidence that other factors – i.e., the absence of interdependence among the Middle Eastern economies, limited trade and overemphasis on economies based on inward orientation, and self-sufficiency – also contribute to the existing political hostilities. The region has been caught in a vicious cycle with security concerns overriding concerns of economic efficiency, which in turn perpetuate the existing political regimes and leave the existing state structures intact. Middle Eastern governments have paid the price for their security with waste, overspending on agricultural self-sufficiency, mismanagement of oil rents, and macroeconomic instability and inefficiency.

If the problem of security, which constitutes perhaps the major barrier to cooperation in the region, can be overcome, this vicious cycle can indeed be turned into a virtuous one. A reduction in security concerns and threats would mean an increased peace dividend and more money available for civilian spending. More funds and capital available for development purposes would not only reduce the stronghold of the states over the economy but would also encourage the development of an independent private sector, investment and growth. Increasingly open economies with private sectors would indeed create an environment of freer trade and the establishment of economic rather than political rationale in allocation of resources. Clearly, despite the obvious benefits of such a cooperative environment, the degree to which the Middle East countries can undertake the necessary shift from 'security-minded' policy-making to one based on economic efficiency will fundamentally rely on the resolution of the security issues in the region.

Governments of the Middle East also face another dilemma. With declining oil revenues and the exhaustion of international sources of finance, these governments are increasingly finding themselves in fiscal crisis. These financial concerns are increasingly pushing governments to undertake economic reforms. However, such economic reforms often require transparency and popular support. With a growing young population with increasing demands, how can this support be ensured? How can these reforms be implemented without destabilising the existing regimes, particularly at a time when Islamic fundamentalism appears to be on the rise? The answer to the question implies that with growing fiscal pressures, states are increasingly being pushed towards expanding political participation. Meanwhile, those countries rejecting such reforms risk becoming more and more isolated and marginalised.

The question remains as to how these reforms and democratisation trends can be best introduced? Here too, there are difficult choices to be made. Most analysts agree that reforms must be gradual so as to prevent a social backlash and a basis for resorting to radical solutions such as Islamic fundamentalism. Such a social explosion will not only end all hopes of democratisation in the region but will also undermine all efforts of cooperation for a long time to come. However, gradualism also carries a significant amount of risk. The end of the Cold War, increasing globalisation and regionalisation in the world economy, coupled with fragile steps towards the normalisation of Arab–Israeli relations have created a window of opportunity that may not open for too long. In other words, unless these political and economic reforms are in place immediately, the Middle East might indeed face the risk of permanent isolation and marginalisation in the world economy.

The emphasis on democratisation and on the need for domestic changes throughout this study is also based on the theoretical approach utilised in this book, namely, the two-level-game framework developed by Putnam (1988). The fundamental hypothesis of this game theoretical framework is that in order to understand negotiations between governments, a simultaneous analysis of the negotiators (Level I actors) as well as their interaction with their domestic constituencies (Level II actors) is necessary.

Using the two-level game heuristically as a tool to analyse cooperation in the Middle East offers insights as to how Middle Eastern governments formulate their foreign policies. A simultaneous look at how the statesmen attempt to bargain at Level I, while trying to secure ratification at Level II, helps identify some of the barriers and prospects for regional cooperation. This conception of diplomacy as 'double-edged' (Evans, Jacobson and Putnam 1993) with strategic interaction between the domestic and the international factors goes well beyond the existing explanations of foreign policy which focus either on international dynamics or only the domestic sources.

Putnam's framework suggests, for instance, that the absence of Level II interaction in the Middle East is one of the major barriers to cooperation in the region. The reasons lie primarily in the absence of a sufficiently developed private sector, a civil society and effectively mobilised domestic constituencies that can push for cooperation in the region. Meanwhile, domestic ideological polarisation, the appeal of using the 'security card' at home, the absence of political accountability when promises are not kept, and the abundance of side-payments largely due to the soft-budget constraints (particularly in oil-exporting states) all emerge as fundamental obstacles to regional cooperation.

However, the metaphor of the two-level game also provides clues as to how the dynamics at Level I and Level II can be gradually transformed. Schemes of functional cooperation, particularly on the economic front, can indeed be used to foster such Level II relations. Projects such as water-sharing arrangements that are essential to residents of the region, improved transportation, and energy routes can indeed be effective instruments for peace. Any functional cooperation at Level I, however, has to be accompanied by Level II interaction. A cooperation based on Level I interaction only will not be sufficient.

Similarly, the 'democratic peace' argument is also relevant in the context of the Middle East and follows the logic of the two-level-game framework. Based on the assumption that 'democratic governments are more peaceful and less given to provoking war or inciting violence, (that) they are more likely to support limits on weapons trade, encourage peaceful resolution of disputes and foster trade' (Halperin 1993: 105), we argued that 'the region will continue to suffer from political instability and persistent conflicts until the regimes implement genuine reforms that aim at democratisation and economic development of the region as whole' (Ghosheh 1992: 20).

The dilemma between gradualism and urgency of reforms can also be overcome by simultaneously following two different strategies at two different levels. One is pushing for economic cooperation and reducing security and political barriers to functional cooperation in the region. This Level I project, to use Putnam's terminology, can play a constructive role in bringing the disputing states in the region together and help create a peaceful environment for cooperation. Such a project can start by bringing together a group of countries, which we have called 'like-minded' states in this study. These countries have relatively democratic regimes and open economies. They are also the countries that maintain direct bilateral diplomatic relations and are committed to resolving disputes among themselves peacefully. However, as suggested above, while such efforts at intergovernmental level (Level I) might be very helpful in the short run, a long-term, sustainable peace and cooperation in the region is only possible if the Level II actors – namely, the domestic constituencies, businesses and various interest groups – are also involved in the game. Clearly not all types of Level II interaction will lead to peace and cooperation. What must be underlined, however, is that any analysis of the prospects of peace and cooperation in the region will have to simultaneously take into account Level I and Level II interaction.

Turkey, as one of the 'like-minded' states, offers an insightful case study not only for exploring the intricate ties between the domestic and international factors in the making of foreign policy but also for identifying specifically some of the international, regional and domestic sources of cooperation and conflict in the region. Clearly, Turkey faces an unprecedented opportunity as well as a challenge in the Middle East. A 'new' Middle East can indeed emerge based on cooperation replacing the 'old' Middle East characterised by conflict and hostility. Along with other 'like-minded' states, Turkey's long-term security and economic interests are closely tied to stability and peace in the Middle East. Any chaos, conflict and instability in the region might not only jeopardise the country's access to vital energy resources such as oil and natural gas, but will also form a threat to internal security and regime stability in Turkey. The Kurdish issue and the water problems are only some of the tough issues that Turkey faces in its ties with the Middle East.

However, neglecting the region is no solution. Cooperation among 'like-minded' states such as Turkey, Egypt, Israel, Jordan and Palestine can lead the way towards creating a relatively 'liberal, democratic community' amongst these countries. These countries have much to benefit from such a community through encouraging functional cooperation such as energy-sharing arrangements, electricity grids and pipelines, both bilaterally as well as multilaterally. Such cooperation can also create a spillover effect in the region by creating a model for cooperation.

Although improved government-to-government ties, as outlined above, are indeed a crucial step towards cooperation in the short run, such ties are also not sufficient for long-term stability in the region. Long-term interests of all the 'like-minded' states lie additionally in increased democratisation in the region. If democracy is indeed fundamental in fostering cooperation in the region, then the 'like-minded' states will serve their interests best by supporting and encouraging democratic Level II actors both domestically and amongst other countries in the region. As has become painfully clear from the Arab–Israeli peace process, developing such Level II ties are crucial, since peaceful resolution of conflicts is not likely to have any effect if it is not accompanied by the approval of the respective societies and domestic constituencies. In short, while pushing for a functional approach to peace through various joint projects at the governmental level, both on a bilateral and multilateral basis, these 'like-minded' countries should also target democratisation and Level II interaction in the region. In dealing with states that clearly have different moral principles and regimes, these countries can combine their pragmatic approach with democratic principles. This tough balancing act of trying not to alienate hostile regimes while standing firm on the principles of democratisation, cooperation and economic liberalisation is the fundamental challenge that the 'like-minded' states face in the Middle East.

Finally, an approach in the Middle East aiming for democratic peace also means consolidation of democratic forces at home. The stakes of a foreign-policy failure on the part of 'like-minded' states towards the region are indeed high. Such a failure might not only change the overall balance of power in the region, but might even pose a serious challenge to existing domestic political structures inside these countries. As the two-level-game framework suggests, domestic politics is intimately linked to the foreign-policy-making process and to politics in the Middle East. Long-term interests of the 'like-minded' states are thus fundamentally tied to their ability to strengthen their democracy at home and push for democratisation in other countries in the region.

As Quandt (1996) argues, there are significant prospects for change in the Middle East. This 'new' Middle East, Kramer (1996) proposes, will be 'post-ideological resting on resolute pragmatism'. This can only come about through the concerted efforts of 'like-minded' countries. These states will have to form the core of a joint effort to build a 'new' Middle East for the future.

Precautions and avenues for further research

This book might indeed appear cursory to area specialists, as our concerns were not to give a detailed account of each and every Middle Eastern country but rather to reflect the overall regional dynamics as best as possible. Instead of presenting studies of specific countries, we aimed to establish the possible overall parameters of cooperation and conflict in the region. The strength of this project then is its scope and its ability to combine the economic and political issues in the region. That is why we deliberately chose to focus on the dynamics and issues in the Middle East that have made the region unique rather than dwell on specific differences in each country. Our primary aim has been to identify the political and economic prospects and constraints in the region for cooperation.

There are a number of ways in which this study could be further advanced. One would be a closer analysis of the trade data, which will aid research in terms of determining specific sectors in which potential for trade exists. Given the limited amount of data that was available to us at the time of research, this book has made preliminary remarks on the prospective sectors. A more in-depth analysis on this front would thus be necessary to enrich our argument.

Another potential avenue of research also lies in a more in-depth analysis of Level II actors. Clearly, different kinds of domestic coalitions and their power within the government shape the dynamics of Level I interaction. A further analysis which explores the nature of demonstrative effects of both Level I and Level II cooperation while taking into account the impact the different coalition formations in the Middle East can better underline the role of domestic actors and their links to the foreign-policy process. Focusing on the make-up and behaviour of the coalitions can indeed be useful in understanding regional cooperation in the Middle East.

Furthermore, our aim has not been to provide a list of all the projects of technical and economic cooperation that could be undertaken in the region. What we have done instead is to draw attention to issues and areas in which more democratisation and popular participation is possible. If there has been a selective bias in the choice of the projects, that is because we have used them to demonstrate the importance of domestic actors.

The two-level-game framework is used throughout this book as a heuristic tool to underscore the importance of domestic actors and their interaction with the negotiators. We have not used Putnam (1988) as a model to predict the outcome of the negotiations, neither have we adopted his framework uncritically in its application to the Middle East. We have used this framework largely as a metaphor to underline the dynamic interaction between domestic and international factors in the Middle East. Any attempt to use, the two-level-game framework as a model, therefore, would mean overburdening the approach beyond its original intention.

Finally, the two-level-game framework is also suggestive in terms of exploring the links between domestic public opinion and the foreign-policy-making process. By analysing how party affiliations influence foreign-policy preferences and choices, for instance, the detailed dynamics behind certain policy decisions can be viewed in more detail. A preliminary attempt has been made here in terms of analysing public opinion in respect of Turkish foreign policy. However, further research is clearly needed to analyse the impact of domestic public opinion on foreign policy across various issues as well as in different countries. That, of course, suggests a brand-new research agenda and is well beyond the scope of the current book.

Notes

Chapter 2

1 In April 1995, for instance, a military coup attempt in Paraguay was averted as the foreign ministers of the other MERCOSUR countries came to Asunción, the capital, and threatened complete economic isolation. All the MERCOSUR member presidents promptly agreed that democracy would be a formal condition of membership which explains the lukewarm attitude of Chile toward the agreements with its behind-the-scenes power of Pinochet. For details see 'Mercosur Survey', *The Economist* 12 October 1996: 6.

Chapter 3

1 Major realist works include Aron (1966), Gilpin (1983), Keohane (1986b), Morgenthau and Thompson (1985), Waltz (1959; 1979).
2 For further elaboration on the bargaining tools, see Friman (1993), Lehman (1992), Mayer (1992) and Schoppa (1993).

Chapter 4

1 See also El-Naggar and El-Erian (1993).
2 See Blake, Dewdney and Mitchell (1987: 18) for a detailed exposition of rainfall in the region.
3 See Allan and Mallat (1995), Beschorner (1992), Kut (1993), Lowi (1993), Robins (1991: 87–99), Starr and Stoll (1988), Şen (1993), Turan (1993; 1994) on internationalised water conflict in the Middle East. Clarke (1993), Gruen (1992) and Starr (1991) provide a review of developments concerning water disputes in the world.
4 Economies are divided into groups according to 1994 GNP per capita, calculated using the World Bank Atlas method. These groups are: low income, US$725 or less; lower-middle income, US$726 to US$2,895; upper-middle income, US$2,896 to US$8,955; and high income, US$8,956 or more.
5 A World Bank study of water-management issues notes for example that Algeria, Jordan, Israel, Palestine, Saudi Arabia, Syria, Tunisia and Yemen suffer from water scarcity as of 1991 and Egypt will join the list by the year 2000 (see World Bank 1991).
6 See Richards and Waterbury (1996: 77–102) for a concise discussion of population-related problems in the Middle East.
7 See Richards and Waterbury (1996) and Richards (1995a) for an extensive review of the food-security problem and developments in the agricultural sector.
8 Again using 1987 as the base year but this time using a different data source (exports

and imports of goods and services; (BoP, US$) we see that as of 1995 all countries in the region have increased both their exports as well as their imports from their 1987 level. However, for Algeria, Israel, Morocco, Oman, Tunisia and Turkey, imports have increased more rapidly than exports, whereas for Bahrain, Egypt, Iran, Jordan, Kuwait, Saudi Arabia and Syria, exports increased more than imports (WDI 1997).

9 Using a slightly different definition of the Middle Eastern region (excluding Algeria, Morocco and Yemen and including Cyprus in his definition) Yeats (1995: 5) asserts that mineral fuels that occupy approximately 68 per cent of all regional exports, is 'more than two and one half times higher than energy products' share in the exports of all developing countries combined'.

10 See Richards and Waterbury (1996: 366–389) for a thorough review of labour migration and its impact on the region's economies.

11 This is certainly an unfavourable development for regional cooperation and provides yet more evidence for fears of domination of the less developed economies by the relatively more developed countries of the region, especially Israel and to some extent Turkey.

12 See Summers and Heston (1991) for a discussion of properties of Penn World Table datasets.

Chapter 5

1 See Fernandez and Rodrik (1991) on trade reform from a similar perspective.

2 See Frischtak and Atiyas (1996); Haggard and Webb (1995); Krueger and Buscaglia (1993); Meier (1991); Niblock and Murphy (1993) for recent surveys of difficulties in implementation of structural reforms.

3 See Brander and Spencer (1984) and Krugman (1986) for a detailed exposition of new trade-policy discussions.

4 See also Kalaycıoğlu (1996: 90) for a similar argument about the lack of transportation infrastructure in the region.

5 See Table 4.17.

6 See Fischer (1995) for a concise discussion of the major points in the difficulties to provide an institutional framework for the Middle East development efforts.

7 See Fischer, Rodrik and Tuma (1993).

8 Such fundamental imbalances between forecasted water demand and supply have been the source of many conflicts in the Middle East. See Allan and Mallat (1995), Beschorner (1992), Kut (1993), Lowi (1993), Robins (1991: 87–99), Şen (1993), Starr and Stoll (1988) and Turan (1993, 1994) on internationalised water conflict in the Middle East. Clarke (1993), Gruen (1992) and Starr (1991) provide a review of developments concerning water disputes in the world. Refer also to Clawson (1992), Fischer (1995), Government of Israel (1995), Richardson (1990) and the others mentioned above for a lengthy discussion and comparisons of proposed projects for the resolution of water shortages in the Middle East.

9 Many examples of such shortage-driven pricing mechanisms are available. However, perhaps the most impressive use was the one after the oil-price shock in the Western economies. When oil prices peaked after the OPEC embargo, energy waste due to inefficient use was greatly reduced within a few years. Similar to the water shortage in the Middle East, economists also diagnose that the Californian water shortage is also mainly due to subsidised agricultural water use. As noted above the Israeli government's agricultural subsidies are largely responsible for the excessive use of water in the region, which could easily be curbed by a shortage-driven pricing-policy for water. The Jordanian authorities also use similar agricultural subsidies. Accordingly, 'raising water prices to Israeli and Jordanian farmers is in the interest of the overwhelming majority

of Israelis and Jordanians, and of all Palestinians (who receive no water subsidies)' (Richards 1995b: 333).

10 See Gibbons (1985) for price-elasticity studies as well as Young (1996) for measurement of economic benefits of water investment.

11 See Solingen (1996a) for a similar argument.

12 The relationship between economic and political systems is one of the oldest in social sciences. Our aim here is not to provide a thorough review of the arguments in this literature. The main arguments of this literature can be found in Dahl (1985), Friedman (1962), Hayek (1944), Lindblom (1977) and von Mises (1920).

13 See Luciani (1988) and Richards (1995a: 77) for a similar argument.

14 See Frischtak and Atiyas (1996) and Haggard and Webb (1995) for a lengthy discussion of the politics of policy reform.

15 We should also stress here that an important impediment facing the intensification of intra-regional trade is also the lack of a stable legal environment in many countries of the region.

Chapter 7

1 The participants in the Madrid Framework are:
- Co-Sponsors: United States and Russia
- Regional participants: Israel, Jordan, Palestinians and Egypt
- Arab states: Saudi Arabia, UAE, Oman, Kuwait, Bahrain, Qatar, Yemen, Morocco, Algeria, Tunisia and Mauritania
- Other states: Members of the European Union (15 countries), Canada, Japan, Norway, India, China, Turkey, Switzerland; subsequently, Hungary, Romania and South Korea.

2 It should be noted that technically the DOP was signed not as a result of negotiations under the Madrid Framework but as a result of secret talks held in Norway from January to August 1993.

3 There is a broad literature that empirically supports the notion of 'democratic peace'. Some of this literature can be found in Doyle 1986; Maoz and Russett 1992; Rummel 1983; Russett 1993; Small and Singer 1976; Weede 1984.

4 For the purposes of this paper the areas under the control of the Palestinian Authority are counted as a country even though the final status of this entity is yet to be determined.

Chapter 8

1 For the coverage of the story see the Turkish language weekly *Tempo*, no. 18 1 May 1996.

2 Information obtained from interview held with Serif Egeli, Chairman of the Turkish–Jordanian and Turkish–Pakistan Business Councils and former Chairman of the Foreign Trade Association of Turkey on 11 October 1996.

3 It is important to note here that this particular question pitches Israel against the Middle Eastern countries and not the Muslim countries.

4 Our objective here is not to provide an extensive review of the literature on the development of pro-Islamist political rhetoric, its constituency and electoral base. Extensive discussions of these issues can be found in Ayata (1996); Birtek and Toprak (1993); Heper and Landau (1991); Sayari (1996); Shankland (1996); Sunar and Toprak (1983); Toprak (1981; 1988); White (1995).

5 An extensive exposition of the Anatolian Tigers can be found in a series of articles in the daily, *Milliyet*, July 1996.

Bibliography

Abed, G.T. (1991) 'The Palestinians and the Gulf Crisis,' *Journal of Palestine Studies* 20: 167–214.

Abed, S.B. (1995) 'Islam and Democracy,' in G. Garnham and M. Tessler (eds) *Democracy, War and Peace in the Middle East*, Bloomington, IN: Indiana University Press.

Abu-Amr, Z. (1994) *Islamic Fundamentalism in the West Bank and the Gaza Strip*, Bloomington ,IN: Indiana University Press.

Abu-Amr, Z. (1996) 'Pluralisms and the Palestinians,' *Journal of Democracy* 7, 3: 83–93.

Aggarwal, V.K., Keohane, R.O. and Yoffie, D.B. (1987) 'The Dynamics of Negotiated Protectionism,' *American Political Science Review* 8, 1: 345–366.

Ajami, F. (1979) 'The End of Pan-Arabism,' *Foreign Affairs* 57, 2: 355–373.

Ajami, F. (1991) 'The End of Arab Nationalism,' *The New Republic* 205, 7: 23–27.

Allan, J.A. and Mallat, C. (1995a) 'Introduction,' in J.A. Allan and C. Mallat (eds) (1995b).

Allan, J.A. and Mallat, C. (eds) (1995b) *Water in the Middle East, Legal, Political and Commercial Implications*, London and New York: I.B. Tauris.

Allison, G.T. (1971) *The Essence of Decision: Explaining the Cuban Missile Crisis*, Boston, MA: Little, Brown.

Allison, G.T. and Beschel, R.P. (1992) 'Can the United States Promote Democracy?' *Political Science Quarterly* 107, 1: 81–98.

Amuzegar, J. (1992) 'The Iranian Economy Before and After the Revolution,' *Middle East Journal* 46, 3: 413–426.

Anderson, K. and Blackhurst, R. (eds) (1993) *Regional Integration and the Global Trading System*, London: Harvester.

Anderson, L. (1987) 'State in the Middle East and North Africa,' *Comparative Politics* 20, 1: 1–19.

Anderson, L. (1995) 'Peace and Democracy in the Middle East,' *Journal of International Affairs* 49, 1: 25–45.

Arab Press Service Organisation (1996) 'Turkey's local consumption trends,' 5 June 1996.

Aras, B. (1996) 'The Palestinian–Israeli Peace Process in International Context with a Note on the Consequences for Turkish Foreign Policy,' unpublished MA thesis, Atatürk Institute, Boğaziçi University, Istanbul.

Aras, B. (1997) 'The Place of the Arab–Israeli Peace Process in Turkish Foreign Policy,' *Journal of South Asian and Middle Eastern Studies* 20, 2: 49–72.

Aras, B. (1998) 'Post-Cold War Realities: Israel's Strategy in Azerbaijan and Central Asia,' *Middle East Journal* 5, 4: 1–17.

Arian, A. (1997) 'Israeli Public Opinion on National Security,' *Memorandum* 47, April, Jaffee Center for Strategic Studies, Tel Aviv (www.tau.ac.il/~jcssjb).

Aron, R. (1966) *Peace and War*, Garden City, NY: Doubleday.

Awartani, H. and Awad, S. (1994) 'Palestinian–Israeli Joint Ventures, Constraints and Prospects,' unpublished manuscript, Department of Economics, Center for Palestine Research and Studies, Nablus, West Bank.

Axelrod, R. (1984) *The Evolution of Cooperation*, New York, NY: Basic Books.

Axelrod, R. and Keohane, R. (1985) 'Achieving Cooperation under Anarchy: Strategies and Institutions,' *World Politics* 38: 226–254.

Axline, A. (ed.) (1994) *The Political Economy of Regional Cooperation: Comparative Case Studies*, London: Pinter Publishers.

Ayata, S. (1996) 'Patronage, Party and State: The Politicization of Islam in Turkey,' *Middle East Journal* 50: 40–57.

Aydın, T. and Bekar, O. (1997) *Türkiye'nin Orta ve Uzun Vadeli Ekonomik Çıkarları Açısından Türk-Rus Ilişkileri / Turkish–Russian relations from the perspective of Turkey's medium and long term interests*, Istanbul: Turkish Economic and Social Studies Foundation (TESEV).

Bakour, Y. (1992) 'Planning and Water Management of Water Resources in Syria,' in Le Moigne *et al.* (eds) *Country Experiences with Water Resources Management: Economic, Institutional, Technological and Environment*, Washington DC: World Bank.

Baldwin, R. (1993) 'The new protectionism: A response to shifts in national economic power', in D. Salvatore (ed.) *Protectionism and World Welfare*, Cambridge: Cambridge University Press.

Balı, R. (1996) 'RP ve Türkiye Yahudileri (The Welfare Party and Turkey's Jews),' in Turkish, *Birikim* 91.

Barcelona Declaration (1995) European Document no. 1964, Reuter Textline, Agency Europe, 6 December 1995.

Barkey, H. (1995) 'Can the Middle East Compete?' *Journal of Democracy* 6: 113–127.

Bayart, J. (1994) 'Republican Trajectories in Iran and Turkey: a Tocquevillian Reading,' in G. Salame (ed.) (1994).

Beblawi, H. and Luciani, G. (1987) *The Rentier State*, London, Routledge.

Beschorner, N. (1992a) 'Le Role de l'Eau Dans la Politique Régional de la Turquie,' *Monde Arabe Maghreb Machrek* 138: 48–63.

Beschorner, N. (1992b) 'Water and Instability in the Middle East,' *Adelphi Papers*, International Institute of Strategic Studies, London.

Bhagwati, J.N. (1991) *The World Trading System at Risk*, Princeton, NJ: Princeton University Press.

Bill, J. A. and Springborg, R. (1994) *Politics in the Middle East*, New York: HarperCollins.

Birtek, F. and Toprak, B. (1993) 'The Conflictual Agendas of Neoliberal Reconstruction and the Rise of Islamic Politics in Turkey,' *Praxis International* 13, 2: 192–212.

Biswas, A. (1993) *Middle East Water Issues: From Euphrates to Niles*, Oxford: Oxford University Press.

Blake, G., Dewdney, J. and Mitchell, J. (1987) *The Cambridge Atlas of the Middle East and North Africa*, Cambridge: Cambridge University Press.

BOTAS (1997) Statistics provided by the Head Office, 3 January, 1997.

Boulding, E. (ed.) (1994a) *Building Peace in the Middle East: Challenges for States and Civil Society*, Boulder, CO: Lynne Rienner Publishers.

Boulding, E. (1994b) 'Hope for the Twenty-First Century: NGOs and People's Networks in the Middle East,' in E. Boulding (ed.) (1994a).

Brander, J. and Spencer, B. (1984) 'Export Subsidies and Market Share Rivalry,' *Journal of International Economics* 18: 83–100.

Brookings Institution Project (1995) *Integrating National Economies: Promise and Pitfalls*, Book Series.

Brown, C.L. (1984) *International Politics and the Middle East: Old Rules, Dangerous Games*, Princeton, NJ: Princeton University Press.

Brown, K.D., Deardorff, V.A. and Stern, M.R. (1991) 'A North American Free Trade Agreement: Analytical Issue and a Computational Assessment', discussion paper no. 338, Institute of Public Policy Studies, University of Michigan.

Bruan, A. (1994) 'The Megaproject of Mesopotamia,' *Centrepiece* March–April: 25–30.

Brzezinski Z., Scowcroft, B. and Murphy, R. (1997) 'Differentiated Containment,' *Foreign Affairs* May–June: 20–30.

Bueno de Mesquita, B. (1981) *The War Trap*, New Haven, CT: Yale University Press.

Bueno de Mesquita, B. and Lalman, D. (1992) *War and Reason: Domestic and International Imperatives*, New Haven, CT: Yale University Press.

Cardoso, F.H. and Faletto, E. (1979) *Dependency and Development in Latin America*, Berkeley, CA: University of California Press. Translated by Marjory Mattingly Urquidi.

Çarkoğlu, A. (1997) 'The Turkish General Election of 24 December 1995' *Electoral Studies* 16: 86–95.

Çarkoğlu, A. and Eder, M. (1997) 'Political Economy of Water Conflict: The Case of Euphrates–Tigris,' unpublished working manuscript, Boğaziçi University, Istanbul.

Chan, S. (1984) 'Mirror, mirror on the wall … are freer countries more pacific?' *Journal of Conflict Resolution* 28: 617–648.

Chatelus, M. (1996) 'Economic Cooperation among Southern Mediterranean Countries,' in R. Aliboni, G. Joffe and T. Niblock (eds) *Security Challenges in the Mediterranean Region*, London: Frank Cass.

Chaudhry, K.A. (1989) 'The Price of Wealth: Business and State in Labor Remittance and Oil Economies,' *International Organization* 43, 1: 101–145.

Chaudhry, K.A. (1993) 'Economic Liberalization and Lineages of the Rentier State,' *Comparative Politics* 27: 1–25

Chaudhry, K.A. (1994) 'The Middle East and the Political Economy of Development' *Items* 48: 41–49.

Chaudhry, K.A. (1997) *The Price of Wealth: Economies and Institutions of the Middle East*, Ithaca, NY: Cornell University Press.

Clark, A.M. (1995) 'Non-Governmental Organizations and their Influence on International Society,' *Journal of International Affairs* 48: 507–525.

Clarke, R. (1993) *Water: International Crisis*, Cambridge, MA: MIT Press.

Clawson, P. (1992) 'The Limited Scope for Economic Cooperation in the Contemporary Levant,' in S.L. Spiegel (ed.) *The Arab–Israeli Search for Peace*, Boulder, CO: Lynne Rienner Publishers.

Clawson, P. (1995) 'Practical Prospects for Arab–Israeli Cooperation, in S.L. Spiegel and D.J Pervin (eds) *Practical Peacemaking in the Middle East, Volume II: The Environment, Water, Refugees and Economic Cooperation and Development*, NY: Garland Publishing Inc.

Clawson, P. (1997) 'Prospects for dialogue with Iran: Implications for US policy,' *PolicyWatch*, No. 289, Washington Institute for Near East Policy, 16 December.

Cobban, H. (1990) 'The PLO and the Intifada,' *The Middle East Journal* 44: 207–233.

Cohen, B. (1990) 'The Political Economy of International Trade,' *International Organization* 44, 2: 261–271.

Cohen, S.S. and Zysman, J. (1987) *Manufacturing Matters: The Myth of the Post-Industrial Economy*, New York, NY: Basic Books.

Conybeare, J.A.C. (1983) 'Public Goods, Prisoners' Dilemmas, and the International Political Economy,' *International Studies Quarterly* 28: 5–22.

Craig, Gordon A. and George, A.L. (1990) *Force and State Craft: Diplomatic Problems of Our Time*, New York, NY: Oxford University Press.

Customs Union Agreement (1995) 1/95 Joint council, appendix to Article 16 of the Customs Union Agreement, taken from http://www.turkey.org/cust2.htm

Dahl, R. (1985) *A Preface to Economic Democracy*, Berkeley, CA: University of California Press.

Dahl, R (1989) *Democracy and Its Critics*, New Haven, CT: Yale University Press.

D'Alançon, F. (1994) 'The EC looks to a new Middle East', *Journal of Palestine Studies* 23, 2: 41–51.

Danin, R. (1997) 'An Iraqi–Syrian entente? Prospects and implications,' *Policy Watch* No. 253, Washington Institute for Near East Policy, 11 June.

De Melo, J. and Panagariya, A. (1992) *The New Regionalism in Trade Policy*, Washington DC: World Bank Publications.

De Melo, J. and Panagariya, A. (1995) *New Dimensions in Regional Integration*, Cambridge: Cambridge University Press.

Desch, C. (1996) 'War and Strong States, Peace and Weak States?' *International Organization* 50: 237–267.

Diwan, I. and Papandreou, N. (1993) 'The Peace Process and Economic Reforms in the Middle East,' in S. Fisher, D. Rodrik and E. Tuma (eds) *The Economics of Middle East Peace, Views from the Region*, Cambridge, MA: MIT Press.

Dixon, W.J. (1993) 'Democracy and the Management of International Conflict,' *Journal of Conflict Resolution* 37,1: 42–68.

Doyle, M. (1983) 'Kant, Liberal Legacies, and Foreign Affairs,' *Philosophy and Public Affairs* 12, 3: 205–235.

Doyle, M. (1986) 'Liberalism and World Politics,' *American Political Science Review* 80: 1151–1169.

Dunbar, C. (1992) 'The Unification of Yemen: Process, Politics, and Prospects,' *The Middle East Journal* 46: 456–476.

Duncan, W.R. and Ekedahl, C.M. (1990) *Moscow and the Third World under Gorbachev*, Boulder, CO: Westview Press.

Economist Intelligence Unit (1995) *Country Profile: Jordan 1995–96*, London.

Eder, M. (forthcoming) 'Turkey in Euroasia: Patterns of peripheral integration' in W. Hout and J. Grugel (eds) *New Regionalism and the Semiperiphery*, London: Routledge.

Egeli, S. (1993) *Taktik Balistik Füzeler ve Türkiye* (*Tactical Ballistic Missiles and Turkey*), in Turkish, Ankara: Ministry of Defence, Secretariat for the Turkish Defence Industry.

Eisenstadt, M. (1996) *Iranian Military Power: Capabilities and Intentions*, Washington DC: Washington Institute for Near East Policy.

Eisenstadt, M. (1997) 'Turkish–Israeli military cooperation: An assessment,' *Policy Watch* No. 262, Washington Institute for Near East Policy, 24 July.

Ekeus, R. (1997) 'Dismantling Iraq's weapons of mass destruction: A progress report,' *Policy Watch* No. 235, Washington Institute for Near East Policy, 5 February.

Elekdağ, S. (1997) 'Türk–Israil–Arab Üçgeni (The Turkish–Israel–Arab triangle),' *Milliyet* 30 June.

El-Naggar, S. and El-Erian, S. (1993) 'The Economic Implications of a Comprehensive Peace in the Middle East' in S. Fischer, D. Rodrik and E. Tuma (eds) (1993), 205–225.

Epstein, David, and O'Halloran, S. (1996) 'The Partisan Paradox and the US Tariff, 1877–1934,' *International Organization* 50: 301–323.

Erbakan, N. (1995) 'Türk Dış Politikası Nasil Olmalı?' (How Should Turkish Foreign Policy Be?), in Turkish, *Yeni Türkiye* 1, 3.

Esposito, J. and Piscatori, J.P. (1991) 'Democratization and Islam,' *Middle East Journal* 45: 427–440.

Evans, P. (1992) 'The State as Problem and Solution: Predation, Embedded. Autonomy and Structural Change,' in S. Haggard and R. Kaufman (eds) (1992).

Evans, P., Jacobson, K.H. and Putnam, R. (eds) (1993) *Double Edged Diplomacy: International Bargaining and Domestic Politics*, Berkeley, CA: University of California Press.

Evans, P.B., Rueschemeyer, D. and Skocpol, T. (eds) (1985) *Bringing the State Back In*, Cambridge: Cambridge University Press.

Faria, F. and Vasconcelos, A. (1996) *Security in Northern Africa: Ambiguity and Reality*, Paris, Chaillot Papers 25, Institute for Security Studies, Western European Union.

Ferguson, T. (1984) 'From Normalcy to New Deal,' *International Organization* 38, 1: 41–94.

Fernandez, R. and Rodrik, D. (1991) 'Resistance to Reform: Status Quo Bias in the Presence of Individual-Specific Uncertainty,' *American Economic Review* 81: 1146–1155.

Fischer, S. (1995) 'Prospects for Regional Integration in the Middle East,' in J. De Mello and A. Panagariya (eds) (1995).

Fischer, S., Rodrik, D. and Tuma, E. (1993) *The Economics of Middle East Peace*, Cambridge, MA: MIT Press.

Fishelson, G. (1992) 'Regional Economic Cooperation in the Middle East,' in S.L. Spiegel (ed.) *The Arab–Israeli Search for Peace*, Boulder, CO: Lynne Rienner Publishers.

Flamhaft, Z. (1996) *Israel on the Road to Peace: Accepting the Unacceptable*, Boulder, CO: Westview Press.

Frangi, A. (1983) *The PLO and Palestine*, London: Zed Books.

Frank, A.G. (1967) 'Capitalism and Underdevelopment in Latin America,' *Monthly Review Press*.

Frieden, A.J. (1988a) 'Sectoral Conflict and US Foreign Economic Policy,' *International Organization* 42, 1: 59–90.

Frieden, A.J. (1988b) 'Capital Politics: Creditors and the International Political Economy,' *Journal of Public Policy* 8: 3–4.

Friedman, M. (1962) *Capitalism and Freedom*, Chicago, IL: University of Chicago Press.

Friman, H. R. (1993) 'Side-Payments Versus Security Cards: Domestic Bargaining Tactics in International Economic Negotiations,' *International Organization* 47: 387–410.

Frischtak, L. and Atiyas, I. (eds) (1996) *Governance, Leadership and Communication, Building Constituencies for Economic Reform*, Washington DC: World Bank Publications.

Garnham, G. and Tessler, M. (eds) (1995) *Democracy, War and Peace in the Middle East*, Bloomington, IN: Indiana University Press.

Gaubatz, T.K. (1996) 'Democratic States and Commitment in International Relations,' *International Organization* 50: 109–139.

Ghosheh, B.A. (1992) 'Making Sense of Geopolitics,' *Focus* 42: 1–25.

Gibbons, D. (1985) *The Economic Value of Water*, Washington DC: Resources for the Future.

Gibbs, R. and Michalak, W. (eds) (1994) *Continental Trading Blocs: The Growth of Regionalism in the World Economy*, Chichester: J. Wiley.

Gilpin, R. (1983) *War and Change in World Politics*, New York, NY: Cambridge University Press.

Glasser, B.L. (1995) 'External Capital and Political Liberalizations: A Typology of Middle Eastern Development,' *Journal of International Affairs* 49, 1: 45–73.

Golan, G. (1990) *Soviet Policies in the Middle East: From World War II to Gorbachev*, Cambridge: Cambridge University Press.

Gourevitch, P.A. (1978) 'The Second Image Reversed: The International Source of Domestic Politics,' *International Organization* 32: 881–911.

Gourevitch, P.A. (1986) *Politics in Hard Times: Comparative Responses to International Economic Crisis*, New York, NY: Cornell University Press.

Government of Israel (1996) *Development Options for Cooperation: The Middle East/East Mediterranean Region 1996*, Version IV.

Gowa, J. (1994) *Allies, Adversaries, and International Trade*, Princeton, NJ: Princeton University Press.

Graham, D.F. (1991) *Saudi Arabia Unveiled*, Dubugue, IA: Kendall/Hunt Publishing.

Gresh, A. (1985) *The PLO: The Struggle Within*, London: Zed Books.

Grieco, J. (1988) 'Anarchy and the Limits of Cooperation: A Realist Critique of the Newest Liberal Institutionalism,' *International Organization* 42: 485–505.

Grieco, J. (1990) *Cooperation Among Nations: Europe, America and Non-Tariff Barriers to Trade*, New York, NY: Cornell University Press.

Gruen, G. (1992) *The Water Crisis: The Next Conflict*, Los Angeles, CA: Simon Wiesenthal Center.

Haas, E.B. (1958) *The Uniting of Europe: Political, Economic and Social Forces, 1950–57*, Stanford, CT: Stanford University Press.

Haas, E.B. (1964) *Beyond the Nation-State: Functionalism and International Organization*, Stanford, CT: Stanford University Press.

Haas, E.B. (1968) 'Technology, Pluralism and the New Europe,' in J.S. Nye (ed.) *International Regionalism*, Boston, MA: Little Brown.

Haas, E.B. (1980) 'Why Collaborate? Issue-Linkage and International Regimes,' *World Politics* 45: 357–405.

Haas, M.P. (1989) 'Do Regimes Matter? Epistemic Communities and Mediterranean Pollution Control,' *International Organization* 43: 377–403.

Haas, M.P. (ed.) (1992) 'Knowledge, Power and International Policy Coordination', *International Organization* 46, 1.

Hadar, L.T. (1992) 'The 1992 Electoral Earthquake and the Fall of the "Second Israeli Republic" ', *The Middle East Journal* 46: 594–616.

Haggard, S. and Kaufman, R. (1992) *The Politics of Economic Adjustment: International Constraints, Distributive Conflicts and the State*, Princeton, NJ: Princeton University Press.

Haggard, S. and Webb, S. (1995) *Voting for Reform*. New York, NY: Oxford University Press.

Halliday, F. (1989) *The Making of the Second Cold War*, London: Verso Books.

Halliday, F. (1994) 'An Elusive Normalization: Western Europe and the Iranian Revolution,' *The Middle East Journal* Spring: 309–326.

Halperin, M. (1993) 'Guaranteeing Democracy,' *Foreign Policy* Summer: 105–122.

Hashim, A. (1995) 'The Crisis of the Iranian State,' *Adelphi Papers*, International Institute for Strategic Studies, No. 296.

Hayek, F.A. (1944) *The Road to Serfdom*. Chicago, IL: University of Chicago Press.

Heper, M. and Landau, M. (1991) *Political Parties and Democracy in Turkey*, London: I.B. Tauris.

Heritage Foundation (1995; 1996; 1997) *World Survey of Economic Freedom* published annually, New York, NY: Heritage Foundation.

Herz, J. (1950) 'Idealist Internationalism and the Security Dilemma,' *World Politics* 2: 157–180.

Hinnebusch, R.A. (1993) 'Syria' in T. Niblock and E. Murphy (eds) *Economic and Political Liberalization in the Middle East*, London and New York: British Academic Press.

Hirschman, A. (1981) 'The Rise and Decline of Development Economics,' in M. Gerrsovitz, C. Diaz-Alejandro, G. Ranis, G. Rosenzweig (eds) *The Theory and Experience of Economic Development*, London: Allen and Unwin.

Hoekman, B. (1995) *WTO, European Union and the Arab World*. Washington DC: World Bank Publications.

Hoffmann, S. (ed.) (1960) *Contemporary Theory in International Relations*, New York, NY: Prentice Hall.

Hudson, M. (1996) 'To Play the Hegemon: Fifty Years of US Policy Towards the Middle East,' *Middle East Journal* 50, Summer.

Huntington, S. (1991) *The Third Wave: Democratization in the Late Twentieth Century*, Norman, OK: University of Oklahoma Press.

Huntington, S. P. (1993) *The Third Wave: Democratization in the Late Twentieth Century*, Norman, OK: Oklahoma University Press.

Huntington, S.P. (1996) *The Clash of Civilizations and the Remaking of World*, New York, NY: Simon & Schuster.

Ibrahim S.E. (1995) 'Civil Society and Prospects of Democratization in the Arab World,' in A.R. Norton, *Civil Society in the Middle East Vol. 1*, Leiden, E.J. Brill.

IISS (International Institute for Strategic Studies) (1995) *The Military Balance: 1995/96*, Oxford: Oxford University Press.

Ikenberry, G.J., Mastanduno, M. and Lake, D. (1988) *State and American Foreign Economic Policy*, Ithaca, NY: Cornell University Press.

İnan, Y. (1994) 'Legal Dimensions of International Watercourse,' in A.I. Bağış *Water as an Element of Cooperation in the Middle East*, Ankara: Hacettepe University.

International Monetary Fund (1991; 1997) *Direction of Trade Statistics Yearbook*, Washington DC: IMF.

Ismael, T. (1986) *International Relations of the Contemporary Middle East: A Study in World Politics*, Syracuse, NY: Syracuse University Press.

Istituto Affari Internazionali (1994) 'Cooperation and Stability in the Mediterranean: An Agenda for Partnership,' *The International Spectator* 29, 3.

Jentleson, B. (1996) 'The Middle East Arms Control and Regional Security "ACRF" Talks: Progress, Problems and Prospects,' Policy paper no. 26, University of California Institute on Global Conflict and Cooperation.

Jervis, R. (1988) 'Realism, Game Theory, and Cooperation,' *World Politics* 40: 317–349.

Johnson, B. Holmes, K.R. and Kirkpatrick, M. (1998) *The 1998 Index of Economic Freedom*, Washington DC: The Heritage Foundation and the Wall Street Journal.

Kalaycıoğlu, E. (1993) 'Yeni Demokratikleşme Dalgasi ve Ortadoğu' (New Wave of Democratization and the Middle East) in S. Şen (ed.) *Su Sorunu, Türkiye ve Ortadoğu* (Water Problem, Turkey and the Middle East) in Turkish, Bağlam Publications.

Kalaycıoğlu, S. (1996) 'Regional Economic Cooperation in the Middle East,' *Perceptions* 1: 87–107.

Kaplan, R. (1997) *Freedom in the World: The Annual Survey of Political Rights and Liberties 1995–96*, New York, NY: Freedom House.

Karawan, I.A. (1994) 'Arab Dilemmas in the 1990s: Breaking Taboos and Searching for Signposts,' *Middle East Journal* 48: 433–454.

Katzenstein, J.P. (ed.) (1978) *Between Power and Plenty: Foreign Economic Policies of Advanced Industrialized States*, Madison, WI: University of Wisconsin Press.

Katzenstein, J.P. (1985) *Small States in World Markets: Industrial Policy in Europe*, New York, NY: Cornell University Press.

Kaufman, E. and Abed, S.B. (1993) 'The Relevance of Democracy to Israeli Palestinian Peace' in E. Kaufman, S.B. Abed and R. Rothstein (eds) *Democracy, Peace, and the Israeli–Palestinian Conflict*, Boulder and London: Lynne Rienner Publishers.

Kedourie, E. (1994) *Democracy and Arab Political Culture*, London: Frank Cass.

Keohane, O.R. (1984) *After Hegemony: Cooperation and Discord in the World Political Economy*, Princeton, NJ: Princeton University Press

Keohane, O.R. (1986a) 'Reciprocity in International Relations,' *International Organization* 40: 1–27.

Keohane, O.R. (ed.) (1986b) *Nerorealism and its Critics*, New York, NY: Columbia University Press.

Kerr, M.H. (1975) *The Arab Cold War*, New York, NY: Oxford University Press.

Khalidi, W. (1991) 'The Gulf Crisis: Origins and Consequences,' Washington DC, Institute for Palestine Studies, IPS Papers.

Kienle, E. (1990) *Ba'th vs. Ba'th: The Conflict Between Syria and Iraq 1968–89*, London: I.B. Tauris.

Kindleberger, P.C. (1973) *The World in Depression*, Berkeley, CA: University of California Press.

Kirişci, K. (1986) *The PLO and World Politics: A Study of the Mobilization of Support for the Palestinian Cause*, London: Frances Pinter Publishers.

Kirişci, K. and Winrow, G. (1997) *The Kurdish Question and Turkey*, London: Frank Cass.

Knopf, W.J. (1993) 'Beyond Two Level Games: Domestic-International Interaction in the Intermediate-Range Nuclear Forces Negotiations,' *International Organization* 47: 599–628.

Kolars, J. (1986) 'The Hydro-Imperative of Turkey's Search for Energy,' *The Middle East Journal* 40: 53–67.

Kolars, J. (1994) 'Managing the Impact of Development: The Euphrates and Tigris Rivers and the Ecology of the Arabian Gulf: a Link in Forging Tri-riparian Cooperation,' in A.I. Bagis (ed.) *Water as an Element of Cooperation in the Middle East*, Ankara: Hacettepe University.

Kolars, J. and Mitchell, W. (1991) *The Euphrates River and the Southeast Anatolia Development Project: Water: the Middle East Imperative*, Carbondale, IL: Southern Illinois University Press.

Köksaloğlu, A. (1995) 'The Impact of Domestic Political Opposition on the Launching and the Progress of the Arab–Israeli Peace Process,' unpublished MA thesis, Department of Political Science and International Relations, Boğaziçi University, Istanbul.

Kramer, M. (1996) *Arab Awakening and Islamic Revival*, London: Transaction Publishers.

Krasner, S.D. (1978) 'United States Commercial and Monetary Policy: Unraveling the Paradox of External Strength and Internal Weakness,' in P. Katzenstein (ed.) *Between Power and Plenty*, Madison, WI: University of Wisconsin Press.

Krasner, S.D. (ed.) (1983) *International Regimes*, Ithaca, NY: Cornell University Press.

Krasner, S.D. (1991) 'Global Communications and National Power: Life on the Pareto Frontier,' *World Politics* 43: 336–366.

Krueger, O.A. (1974) 'The Political Economy of Rent-Seeking Society,' *American Economic Review* 64: 292–303.

Krueger O.A. and Buscaglia, E.A. (eds) (1993) *Economic policies at cross purposes*, Washington DC: Brookings Institution.

Krugman, P. (1986) *Strategic Trade Policy and the New International Economics*, Cambridge, MA: MIT Press.

Kut, G. (1993a) 'Ortadoğu su sorunu: Çözüm önerileri (Middle East water problems: Proposals for solutions,' in S. Şen (ed.) (1993).

Kut, G. (1993b) 'Burning Waters: The Hydrolics of the Euphrates and the Tigris,' *New Perspectives on Turkey* 9: 1–17.

Kut, G. and Turan, I. (1997) 'Political-Ideological Constraints on Intra-Basin Cooperation on Transboundary Waters,' *Natural Resources Forum* 21: 139–146.

Laird, S. and Yeats, A. (1990) 'Trends in Nontariff Barriers of Developing Countries, 1966–1986,' *Weltwirtschaftliches Archiv*, 126: 2.

Lake, A.D. (1988) *Power, Protectionism and Free Trade: International Sources of the US Commercial Policy: 1887–1939*, Ithaca, NY: Cornell University Press.

Laqueur, W. and Rubin, B. (1995) *The Israeli–Arab Reader: A Documentary History of the Middle East Conflict*, London: Penguin Books.

Lawrence, R.Z. (1996) *Regionalism, Multilateralism and Deeper Integration*, Washington DC: Brookings Institution.

Lawson, F.H. (1994) 'Domestic Transformation and Foreign Steadfastness in Contemporary Syria,' *The Middle East Journal* 48: 47–64.

Lehman, P.H. (1992) 'The Dynamics of the Two-Level Bargaining Game: The 1988 Brazilian Debt Negotiations,' *World Politics* 44: 600–644.

Lenczowski, G. (1980) *The Middle East in World Affairs*, Ithaca, NY: Cornell University Press.

Lesser, I.O. and Tellis, A.J. (1996) *Strategic Exposure: Proliferation Around the Mediterranean*, Santa Monica, CA: Rand Corporation.

Lewis, B. (1994) *The Shaping of the Modern Middle East*, Oxford: Oxford University Press.

Lindberg, L.N. and Scheingold, S.A. (1970) *Europe's Would-Be Polity*, Englewood Cliffs, NJ: Prentice Hall.

Lindblom, C.E. (1977) *Politics and Markets: The World's Political-Economic Systems*, New York, NY: Basic Books.

Lipsey, G.R. and Dobson, W. (eds) (1987) *Shaping Comparative Advantage*, Policy Study No. 2, Toronto: C.D. Howe Institute.

Lipson, C. (1984) 'International Cooperation in Economic and Security Affairs,' *World Politics* 37: 1–23.

Low, P. and Yeats, A. (1994) 'Nontariff Measures and Developing Countries: Has the Uruguay Round Leveled the Playing Field?,' *World Bank Policy Research Paper*, August.

Lowi, M. (1993) *Water and Power: The Politics of Scarce Resource in the Jordan River Basin*, New York, NY: Cambridge University Press.

Luciani, G. (1988) 'Economic Foundations of Democracy and Authoritarianism: The Arab World in Comparative Perspective,' *Arab Studies Quarterly* 10: 457–475.

Lukacs, Y. (ed.) (1992) *The Israeli–Palestinian Conflict: A Documentary Record 1967–90*, Cambridge: Cambridge University Press.

McGhee, G. (1990) *The US–Turkish–NATO Middle East Connection: How the Truman Doctrine and Turkey's NATO Entry Contained the Soviets*, New York, NY: St Martin's Press.

McKeown, T. (1984) 'Firms and Tariff Regime Change: Explaining the Demand for Protection,' *World Politics* 36: 214–233.

McWilliams, W.C. and Piotrowski, H. (1993) *The World Since 1945*, Boulder, CO: Lynne Rienner Publishers.

Mahdavi, H. (1970) 'The Patterns of Economic Development in Rentier States: The Case of Iran,' in M.A. Cook (ed.) *Studies in the Economic History of the Middle East: from the Rise of Islam to the Present Day*, New York, NY: Oxford University Press.

Mansfield, D.E. (1993) 'Effects of International Politics on International Trade' in K. Anderson and R. Blackhurst (eds) (1993).

Mansfield, D.E. (1994) *Power, Trade and War*, Princeton, NJ: Princeton University Press.

Mansfield, E. and Synder, J. (1995) 'The Dangers of Democratisation,' *International Security* 20, Summer: 5–38.

Maoz, Z. and Russett, B. (1992) 'Alliance, Contiguity, Wealth, and Political Stability: Is the Lack of Conflict between Democracies a Statistical Artifact?' *International Interactions* 17, 3.

Mastanduno, M. (1991) 'Do Relative Gains Matter: America's Response to Japanese Industrial Policy,' *International Security* 16: 73–113.

Mattar, P. (1994) 'The PLO and the Gulf Crisis,' *The Middle East Journal* 48: 31–46.

Mayer, W.F. (1992) 'Managing Domestic Differences in International Negotiations: The Strategic Use of Internal Side-Payments,' *International Organization* 46: 793–818.

Meier, G.M. (ed.) (1991) *Politics and Policy Making in Developing Countries: Perspectives on the New Political Economy*, San Francisco, CA: ICS Press.

Miller, B. and Kagan, K. (1997) 'The Great Powers and Regional Conflicts: Eastern Europe and the Balkans from the Post-Napoleonic Era to the Post-Cold War Era,' *International Studies Quarterly* 41: 51–85.

Milner, H. (1987) 'Resisting the Protectionist Temptation: Industry and the Making of Trade Policy in France and the United States during the 1970s,' *International Organization* 41: 639–665.

Milner, H. (1988) *Resisting Protectionism*, Princeton, NJ: Princeton University Press.

Milner, H. (1992) 'International Theories of Cooperation among Nations' Strengths and Weaknesses,' *World Politics* 44: 466–496.

Milner, H. and Yoffie, B.D. (1989) 'Between Free Trade and Protectionism: Strategic Trade Policy and a Theory of Corporate Trade Demands,' *International Organization* 43: 448–481.

Ministry of Foreign Affairs (1995) *Water Issues Between Turkey, Syria and Iraq*, policy statement booklet, Ankara: Ministry of Foreign Affairs.

Mitrany, D. (1946) *A Working Peace System*, Chicago, IL: Quadrangle Press.

Mitrany, D. (1975) *The Functional Theory of Politics*, London: Martin Robertson.

Monnet, J. (1964) 'A Ferment of Change' in L.B. Krause (ed.) *The Common Market: Progress and Controversy*, Englewood Cliffs, NJ: Prentice Hall.

Moravcsik, A. (1993) 'Introduction: International and domestic theories of bargaining,' in P.B. Evans, H.K. Jacobson and R.D. Putman (eds) *Double-Edged Diplomacy*, Berkeley, CA: University of California Press: 3–43.

Morgenthau, H. and Thompson, K. (1985) *Politics Among Nations*, New York, NY: Knopf.

Morrow, J.D. (1994) *Game Theory for Political Scientists*, Princeton, NJ: Princeton University Press.

Musrey, A. (1969) *An Arab Common Market: A Study in Inter-Arab Trade Relations, 1920–67*, New York, NY: Frederick A. Praeger Publishers.

Mutlu, S. (1996) 'The Southeastern Anatolia Project (GAP) of Turkey: Its Context, Objectives and Prospects,' *Orient* 37: 59–86.

Naff, T. and Matson, R.C. (eds) (1984) *Water in the Middle East: Conflict or Cooperation*, Boulder, CO: Westview Press.

Nakhleh, E.A. (1994) 'The Arab World After the Gulf War: Challenges and Prospects,' in E. Boulding (ed.) (1994a).

Nasser, G.A. (1959) *Philosophy of the Revolution*, Buffalo, NY: Smith, Keynes and Marshall.

Niblock, T. and Murphy, E. (1993) *Economic and Political Liberalization in the Middle East*, London and New York: British Academic Press.

Norton, A.R. (ed.) (1995) *Civil Society in the Middle East Vol. 1*, Leiden: E.J. Brill.

Norton R.A. and Greenberg, M.H. (eds) (1995) *The International Relations of the PLO*, Carbondale and Edwardsville, IL: Southern Illinois University Press.

Norton, R.A. and Wright, R. (1995) 'The Post-Peace Crisis in the Middle East,' *Survival* 36, 4: 7–20.

Olson, M. (1971) *The Logic of Collective Action; Public Goods and the Theory of Groups*, Cambridge, MA: Harvard University Press.

Öniş, Z. (1995) 'Turkey in the Post-Cold War Era in Search of Identity,' *Middle East Journal* 49: 48–68.

Öniş, Z. (1997) 'The Political Economy of Islamic Resurgence in Turkey: The Rise of the Welfare Party in Perspective,' paper presented at the BRISMES International Conference on Middle Eastern Studies held at St Catherine's College, University of Oxford, 6–7 July.

Owen, R. (1988) 'Arab Integration in Historical Perspective: Are There Any Lessons?' *Arab Affairs* 1: 41–53.

Owen, R. (1992) *State, Power and Politics in the Making of the Modern Middle East*, London: Routledge.

Owen, R. (1994) 'Socio-Economic Change and Political Mobilization: the Case of Egypt,' in G. Salame (ed.) (1994b).

Oye, K. (1986) *Cooperation Under Anarchy*, Princeton, NJ: Princeton University Press.

Özbudun, E. (1996) 'Turkey: How far from Consolidation,' *Journal of Democracy* 7: 123–138.

Parson, A. (1985) 'Soviet and American Involvement in the Middle East,' *Journal of Palestine Studies* 14, Summer.

Peretz, D. (1986) 'Israeli Peace Proposals,' in W.A. Beling (ed.) *Middle East Plans*, London: Croom Helm.

Peretz, D. (1994) *The Middle East Today*, Westport, CT: Praeger Publishers.

Perthes, V. (1994) 'The Private Sector, Economic Liberalization, and the Prospects of Democratization: the Case of Syria and Some Other Arab Countries,' in G. Salame (ed.) (1994b).

Peters, J. (1996) *Pathways to Peace, the Multilateral Arab–Israeli Peace Talks*, London: Royal Institute of International Affairs.

Picard, E. (1994) 'Aspects of International Law of the Water Conflict in the Middle East,' in A.I. Bagis (ed.) *Water as an Element of Cooperation in the Middle East*, Ankara: Hacettepe University.

Pipes, D. (1990) *Greater Syria: The History of an Ambition*, Oxford: Oxford University Press.

Plotkin, L. (1997) 'The Doha conference: A post-mortem,' *PeaceWatch* No. 149, Washington Institute for Near East Policy, 24 November.

Poll (1993; 1997) Public Opinion Polls, *Center for Palestine Research and Studies*, (in electronic form at: www.cprs-palestine.org).

Powell, R. (1991) 'Absolute and Relative Gains in International Relations Theory,' *American Political Science Review* 85: 1303–1320.

Przeworski, A., Maravall, J.M. and Pereira, L.C. (1993) *Economic Reforms in New Democracies*, Cambridge: Cambridge University Press.

Putnam, R. (1988) 'Diplomacy and Domestic Politics: The Logic of Two Level Games,' *International Organization* 42, 3: 427–460.

Putnam, R. (1993) *Making Democracies Work*, Princeton, NJ: Princeton University Press.

Quandt, B.W. (1993) *Peace Process: American Diplomacy and the Arab–Israeli Conflict Since 1967*, Berkeley, CA: University of California Press.

Quandt, B.W. (1994) 'The Urge for Democracy,' *Foreign Affairs* 73: 2–7.

Quandt, B.W. (1996) 'The Middle East on the Brink: Prospects for Change in the 21st Century,' *Middle East Journal* 50: 9–17.

Quandt, B.W., Jabber, F. and Lesch, A. (1973) *The Politics of Palestinian Nationalism*, Berkeley, CA: University of California Press.

Ramazani, R.K. (1992) 'Iran's Foreign Policy: Both North and South,' *The Middle East Journal* 46: 393–412.

Rath, K. (1994) 'The Process of Democratization in Jordan,' *Middle Eastern Studies* 30: 530–557.

Reich, B., Dropkin, N. and Wurmser, M. (1993) 'Soviet Jewish Immigration and the 1992 Israeli Knesset Elections,' *The Middle East Journal* 47: 464–478.

Reppert, J. (1989) 'The Soviets and the PLO: The Convenience of Politics,' in A.R. Norton and M.H. Greenberg (eds) *The International Relations of the Palestine Liberation Organisation*, Carbondale and Edwardsville, IL: Southern Illinois University Press.

Richards, A. (1995a). 'Economic Pressures for Accountable Governance in the Middle East and North Africa' in A. R. Norton (ed.) *Civil Society in the Middle East. Volume 1*, Leiden: E.J Brill.

Richards, A. (1995b). 'Strengthening Markets to Build Peace,' in S.L. Spiegel and D.J. Pervin (eds) *Practical Peacemaking in the Middle East Volume II: The Environment, Water, Refugees and Economic Cooperation and Development*, New York, NY: Garland Publishing.

Richards, A. and Waterbury, J. (1990) *A Political Economy of the Middle East: State, Class and Economic Development*, Boulder, CO: Westview Press.

Richards, A. and Waterbury, J. (1996) *A Political Economy of the Middle East: State, Class and Economic Development*, Boulder, CO: Westview Press.

Richardson, J.D. (1990) 'The Political Economy of Strategic Trade Policy,' *International Organization* 44: 107–135.

Roberts, J. (1995) *Visions and Mirages: The Middle East in a New Era*, Edinburgh: Mainstream Publishing.

Robins, P. (1991) *Turkey and the Middle East*, Chatham House Papers, The Royal Institute of International Affairs, London: Pinter Publishers.

Rodrik, D. (1989) 'Promises, Promises: Credible Policy Reform Via Signaling,' *The Economic Journal* 99: 756–772.

Rodrik, D. (1995) 'Comments,' in O.A. Krueger (1995).

Rogowski, R. (1989) *Commerce and Coalitions: How Trade Affects Domestic Political Alignments*, Princeton, NJ: Princeton University Press.

Rothstein, R.L. (1993) 'Democracy and Conflict,' in E. Kaufman, S.B. Abed and R. Rothstein (eds) *Democracy, Peace, and the Israeli-Palestinian Conflict*, Boulder, CO: Lynne Rienner Publishers.

Rothstein, R.L. (1995) 'Democracy in the Third World: Definitional Dilemmas' in G. Garnham and M. Tessler (eds) (1995).

Rowley, G. (1984) *Palestine Into Israel*, London and New York, NY: Mansell.

Rubin, B. (1993) 'The PLO and the Palestinians,' in R.B. Satloff (ed.) (1993).

Rummel, R. (1983) 'Libertarianism and International Violence,' *Journal of Conflict Resolution* 27, March.

Russett, B. (1993) *Grasping the Democratic Peace: Principles for a Post-Cold War World*, Princeton, NJ: Princeton University Press.

Salame, G. (1994a) 'Introduction: Where Are the Democrats?,' in G. Salame (ed.).

Salame, G. (ed.) (1994b) *Democracy Without Democrats?: The Renewal of Politics in the Muslim World*, London and New York: I.B. Tauris.

Saliyeh, E. (1988) *In Search of Leadership*, Washington DC: Brookings Institution.

Satloff, R.B. (ed.) (1993) *The Politics of Change in the Middle East*, Boulder, CO: Westview Press.

Satloff, R. (1997) 'The King is back … And final status may be just around the corner,' *PeaceWatch* No. 150, Washington Institute for Near East Policy, 10 December .

Sayari, S. (1996) 'Turkey's Islamist Challenge,' *The Middle East Quarterly* 3, 3: 35–43.

Schelling, C.T. (1960) *The Strategy of Conflict*, Cambridge, MA: Harvard University Press.

Schiff, I. and Ya'ari, E. (1989) *Intifadah: The Inside Story of the Palestinian Uprising that Changed the Middle East Question*, New York, NY: Simon and Schuster.

Schindler, C. (1991) *Ploughshares Into Swords?: Israelis and Jews in the Shadow of the Intifada*, London: I.B. Tauris.

Schoppa, L. (1993) 'Two-Level Games and Bargaining Outcomes: Why "Gaiatsu" Succeeds?' *International Organization* 47: 353–386.

Şen, S. (1993) *Su Sorunu, Türkiye ve Ortadoğu* (*Water Problem, Turkey and the Middle East*) in Turkish, Istanbul: Bağlam Publications.

Sezer, D. (1992) 'Turkey's Grand Strategy Facing a Dilemma,' *The International Spectator* 27, January–March.

Shankland, D. (1996) 'The Demise of the Republican Turkey's Social Contract,' *Government and Opposition* 31, 3: 304–332.

Shapland, G (1995) 'Policy Options for Downstream States in the Middle East,' in J.A. Allan and C. Mallat (eds) (1995b).

Sicherman, H. (1997) 'The Strange Death of Dual Containment,' *Orbis* 41, Spring: 223–240.

Singer, D. (1961) 'The Level of Anaysis Problem in International Relations,' *World Politics* 14: 77–92.

Siverson, M.R. and Emmons, J. (1991) 'Birds of a Feather Democratic Political Systems and Alliance Choices in the Twentieth Century,' *Journal of Conflict Resolution* 35: 285–306.

Small, M. and Singer, D. (1976) 'The War-Proneness of Democratic Regimes,' *Jerusalem Journal of International Relations* 1, 4: 50–69.

Smith, C. (1992) *Palestine and the Arab–Israeli Conflict*, New York, NY: St Martin's Press.

Snidal, D. (1991a) 'International Cooperation Among Relative Gains Maximizers,' *International Studies Quarterly* 35: 387–402.

Snidal, D. (1991b) 'Relative Gains and The Patterns of International Cooperation,' *American Political Science Review* 85: 701–726.

Solingen, E. (1996a) 'Democracy, Economic Reform and Regional Cooperation,' *Journal of Theoretical Politics* 8: 79–114.

Solingen, E. (1996b) 'Quandaries of the Peace Process,' *Journal of Democracy* 7: 139–153.

Sprinborg, R. (1989) *Mubarak's Egypt: Fragmentation of a Political Order*, Boulder, CO: Westview.

Stallings, B. (ed.) (1995) *Global Change, Regional Response: The New International Context of Development*, Cambridge: Cambridge University Press.

Starr, J. (1991) 'Water Wars,' *Foreign Policy* 82: 17–36.

Starr, J. and Stoll, D. (eds) (1988) *The Politics of Scarcity: Water in the Middle East*, Boulder, CO: Westview Press.

State Institute of Statistics (1995) *SEAP Provincial Statistics*, Ankara: SIS.

State Institute of Statistics (1996) *GAP Statistics*, Ankara: SIS.

Stein, A.A. (1982) 'Coordination and Collaboration: Regimes in an Anarchic World,' *International Organization* 36: 299–323.

Strateji/MORI (1997a). 'Türkiyenin Nabzı, Aylık Siyasi ve Ekonomik İndikatörler Arastırması 1996 Derlemesi (The Pulse of Turkey, Monthly Political and Economic Indicators, 1996 Collection),' in Turkish, distributed by Strateji/MORI, Istanbul.

Strateji/MORI (1997b). 'Türkiyenin Nabzı, Aylık Siyasi ve Ekonomik İndikatörler Arastırması Haziran 1997 (The Pulse of Turkey, Monthly Political and Economic Indicators, June 1997),' in Turkish, distributed by Strateji/MORI, Istanbul.

Summers, R. and Heston, A. (1991) 'The Penn World Table (Mark 5): An Expanded Set of International Comparisons, 1950–88' *Quarterly Journal of Economics* 106, 2: 327–368.

Sunar, I. and Toprak, B. (1983) 'Islam in Politics: The Case of Turkey,' *Government and Opposition* 18: 421–441.

T.C. Petrol Işleri Genel Müdürlügü Dergisi (Journal of Turkish General Directorate of Petroleum Affairs) (1997) 39: 60.

Tessler, M. and Grobschmidt, G. (1995) 'Democracy in the Arab World and the Arab–Israeli Conflict,' G. Garnham and M. Tessler (eds) (1995).

Thompson, R. W. (1996) 'Democracy and Peace: Putting the Cart Before the Horse?' *International Organization* 50: 141–174.

Thucydides (trans. 1954) *History of the Peloponnesian Wars*, translated with an introduction by Rex Warner. Melbourne, Baltimore, MD: Penguin Books

Tibi, B. (1993) *Conflict and War in the Middle East*, New York, NY: St Martin's Press.

Toprak, B. (1981) *Islam and Political Development in Turkey*, Leiden: E.J. Brill.

Toprak, B. (1988) 'The State Politics and Religion in Turkey,' in M. Heper and A. Evin (eds) *State, Democracy and the Military in Turkey in the 1980s*, Berlin: W. de Gruyter.

Tsebelis, G. (1990) *Nested Games: Rational Choice in Comparative Politics*, Berkeley, CA: University of California Press.

Tuma, E.H. (1995) 'Economic Cooperation and,Middle East Regional Stability,' in S.L. Spiegel and D.J. Pervin (eds) *Practical Peacemaking in the Middle East Volume II The Environment, Water, Refugees and Economic Cooperation and Development*, New York: Garland Publishing.

Turan, I. (1993) 'Turkey and the Middle East: Problems and Solutions,' *Water International* 18: 23–29.

Turan, I. (1994) 'The Water Conflict and the Role of the UN,' unpublished manuscript, Koç University, Turkey.

TÜSIAD (1996) *Turkish Economy 1996*, Publication No. T/96, 201, Istanbul.

UNCTAD (1986) *Protectionism and Structural Adjustment*, New York: United Nations.

USACDA (US Arms Control and Disarmament Agency) (1994) *World Military Expenditures and Arms Transfers 1991–92*, Washington DC: US Government Printing Office.

US Department of State (1996) *Country Reports on Human Rights*, Washington DC, US Government Printing Office.

Undersecretariat of Foreign Trade (1996a) Interviews with policy-makers conducted on 9–10 July 1996.

Undersecretariat of Foreign Trade (1996b) Research Department Unpublished Information Note.

Vaitsos, V.C. (1978) 'Crisis in Regional Economic Cooperation Integration. Among Developing Countries: A Survey,' *World Development* 6: 747–750.

Viner, J. (1987) 'Power versus Plenty as Objectives of Foreign Policy in the Seventeenth and Eighteenth Centuries,' (originally published in 1948) in J. Frieden and D.A. Lake, *International Political economy: Perspectives on Global Wealth and Power*, New York, NY: St Martin's Press.

von Mises, L. (1920) 'Economic Calculation in a Socialist Commonwealth,' in F.A. Hayek (ed.) *Collective Economic Planning*, London: Routledge and Kegan Paul (1935).

Wallerstein, I.M. (1983) *Historical Capitalism*, London: Verso.

Walton, R.E and McKersie, R.B. (eds) (1965) *The Behavioral Theory of Labor Negotiations: An Analysis of Social Interaction System*, New York, NY: McGraw Hill.

Waltz, K. (1959) *Man the State and War*, New York, NY: Columbia University Press.

Weede, E. (1984) 'Democracy and War Involvement,' *Journal of Conflict Resolution* 28, December: 649–664.

White, J.B. (1995) 'Islam and Democracy: The Turkish Experience,' *Current History* 94, 588: 7–12.

Wolfers, A. (1962) *Discord and Collaboration*, Baltimore, MD: Johns Hopkins University Press.

World Bank (1991) 'Water Resources Management Study,' EMENA Issues paper, Washington DC: World Bank Publications.

World Bank (1995) *World Tables*, Baltimore, MD: Johns Hopkins University Press.

World Bank (1988; 1989; 1990; 1992; 1994; 1996) *World Development Reports*, Oxford: Oxford University Press.

World Bank (1995) *Global Economic Prospects and the Developing Countries*, Washington DC.

World Bank (1997) *World Development Indicators*, Washington DC.

World Development Report (1996) *From Plan to Market*, Oxford: Oxford University Press.

World Resources Institute, the United Nations Environment Programme, The United Nations Development Programme and the World Bank (1997) *World Resources, A Guide to the Global Environment, The Urban Environment, 1996–97*, Oxford: Oxford University Press.

Wright, Q. (1942) *A Study of War*, Chicago, IL: University of Chicago Press.

Yeats, J.A. (1995) 'Export Prospects of Middle Eastern Countries: A Post-Uruguay Round Analysis. International Trade Division,' *The World Bank*, 1–43.

Young, R.A. (1996) 'Measuring Economic Benefits for Water Investments and Policies,' World Bank Technical Paper no. 338, Washington DC: World Bank Publications.

Zysman, J. (1977) *Political Strategies for Industrial Order: State, Market, and Industry in France*, Berkeley, CA: University of California Press.

Bibliography of journals and newspapers

Al-Ahram, Cairo and New York, NY. Weekly newspaper in Arabic; North American edition in English.

Cumhuriyet, Istanbul. Daily newspaper in Turkish.

CNN (Cable News Network), Atlanta, GA. Cable-television news service in English.

The Economist, London: The Economist Newspaper Ltd. Weekly international magazine in English.

Hürriyet, Istanbul. Daily newspaper in Turkish

Jerusalem Post, Jerusalem. Daily newspaper in English.

Milliyet, Istanbul. Daily newspaper in Turkish.

New York Times, New York, NY: New York Times Company. Daily newspaper in English.

Palestine Report, Jerusalem: Jerusalem Media and Communication Center. Weekly news digest.

Reuter News, London. Global electronic news service in English.

Sabah, Istanbul. Daily newspaper in Turkish.

Tempo, Istanbul. Weekly magazine in Turkish.

Turkish Daily News, Istanbul. Daily newspaper in English.

Wall Street Journal, New York, NY and Brussels, Dow Jones & Company. Daily newspaper in English.

Yeni Yüzyil, Istanbul. Daily newspaper in Turkish.

Index

Abdullah Ibn Hussein, king of Jordan 157
Abed, S. B. 180
ACM (Arab Common Market) 18, 21, 151, 152, 188
Afghanistan 7, 28, 124, 213; Soviet invasion (1979) 141; Soviet withdrawal (1988) 143, 144
Africa 22, 84, 221; Brazzaville and Casablanca groups 139; opening-up of markets 28; *see also* North Africa; *also under various country names*
African Development Bank 131
agriculture 35, 61, 63, 65, 103, 137, 200; barriers to development 56; creating and sustaining fertile land 130; efficiency seeking regulations 132; labour force 63, 84; lack of natural resources for 112; more efficient 209; policies 66; processing products 120–1; production 56, 57, 67, 120, 208; productivity 209; self-sufficiency 61, 113; subsidies 41, 130, 132; unirrigated 57; water for 69, 70, 129, 130
Ahmed, Ghezi 183
aid 121, 202; food 67, 68
Ajami, F. 154
Albania 124
Al-Benna, Hassan 221
Albright, Madeleine 167
Alexandria 140
Algeria 145, 193; classified lower-middle-income country 103; domestic armed conflict 102; exports 75, 81, 83, 204; imports 78, 82, 83; inflation 107; intra-regional trade share 86; labour force 62, 63, 79; Pan-Arab regime 149, 150; rain 57; Soviet connections 140
Algiers 160, 161; Treaty (1975) 148, 149
Allan, J. A. 129
Allende (Gossens), Salvador 25
alliances 48, 202; 'grassroots' 173; *see also* détente; entente; *also under various institutions, e.g.* APEC; ASEAN; CENTO; EFTA; EU; NAFTA; NATO; WEU
Allison, G. T. 40, 190
allocation of resources 31, 116, 117; inefficient 103; water 132, 206
Amman 170, 171, 203
Anatolia 102, 199, 200, 218, 219–20; *see also* GAP
Andean Group 23, 25
Anderson, L. 33, 53
Angola 28
Ankara 207, 220
anti-Semitism 221
ANZCERTA (Australia-New Zealand Closer Economic Relations Trade Agreement) 17
AOPEC (Arab Organisation of Petroleum Exporting Countries) 151
APEC (Asia-Pacific Economic Cooperation) Group 16, 17
Aqaba 134; Gulf of 170
'Arab Cold War' 140, 148
Arab–Israeli affairs 2, 5, 8, 34, 57, 99, 102, 112; breakdown in talks 169; Cold War and 141, 143; conflict (1973) 50; exploitation of conflict 156; first war 149; important factor that exacerbated 155; major threshold crossed 160; multilateral talks 189; US credibility and 145
Arab–Israeli peace process 52, 142, 145, 146, 171–4 *passim*, 176, 180; criticised 221; dynamics changed by 195; important consequence of 194; Interim Agreement (1995) 182, 191; PLO

agreements 202; product of problems of 203; relatively recent accomplishments 192; religious nationalists and 182; treaty with Egypt (1979) 142, 150, 152–3, 191
Arab League 149–53, 160, 169
Arab Union 152
Arafat, Yasser 144, 157–61 *passim*, 166, 180, 183, 221
Argentina 18, 23, 25
arms 10, 99, 112, 165; wasteful spending on 5; *see also* military sector; weapons
ASEAN (Association of South-East Asian Nations) 17, 24
Ashkelon 134
Asi river 131
Assad, Hafiz 163, 169, 180
Australia 98
authoritarianism 3, 4, 7, 10, 20, 177, 182; countries in transition from 181; emphasis on 156; regimes characterised by 200
Awad, Samir 122–3, 124, 125, 128
Awartani, Hisham 122–3, 124, 125, 128
Axelrod, R. 38
Axline, A. 24
Azerbaijan 124

Baghdad 196; Pact (1955) 140
Bahrain: classified upper-middle-income country 103; comparative advantage 88, 89; Environmental Code of Conduct for the Middle East 170; exports 75, 81; imports 73, 82, 84, 86; Israeli contact with 124; labour-force importing 79; population density 57
Balfour Declaration (1917) 191
Bandung Summit (1955) 139
Bangladesh 124, 216
banks: development 170, 171; regional 203; *see also* African Development Bank; European Development Bank; MEBRD; World Bank
Barcelona Declaration (1995) 147, 148, 190, 211–12
bargaining 42, 43, 49, 54, 167–8, 184, 195
Barkey, H. 190
barriers 2, 3, 5, 23, 25, 50, 52, 125, 138; absence of peace explains 32; agricultural development 56; communication 38; ideological 20, 208; informational 38; institutional 33; investment 34; liberalisation 10, 34, 72; market logic 31; non-economic, political will to abolish 128; political 208; trade 17, 98, 119, 120, 122
Bayart, J. 182
Begin, Menachem 158
Beirut 140, 144, 159
Belgium 18
Benelux countries 21; *see also* Belgium; Luxembourg; Netherlands
Berlin Wall 143
Beschel, R. P. 190
Bhagwati, J. N. 26
Bhutan 124
Black Sea 7, 57, 194
Bolivia 23
Bosnia 19, 27
Boulding, E. 189
Brandt, Willy 19
Brazil 18, 23, 25
Britain 19, 57, 140, 148; Commonwealth 16
budgets 52; deficits 34; 'soft' constraints 33, 53
bureaucracy 5, 29, 116, 177; complex 156; corrupt 34; rigid 192
Bursa 220
Burundi 207
Bush, George 24, 144–5

CACM (Central American Common Market) 18, 23
Cairo 150, 167, 170, 171, 172, 203
Camp David peace treaty (1979) *see* Arab–Israeli affairs (peace treaty with Egypt)
Canada 84, 98; *see also* NAFTA
canals 129, 140, 149, 206
capital 29, 120, 128, 132, 220; abundant 121; access to 31; flows from migrant workers 219; foreign 32; free movement 18; human 102, 126; inflow into oil exporters 33; mobility 28, 121; non-residential stock 126; scarce 121; social 103
Caribbean Basin Initiative 24
CARICOM (Caribbean Community) 18, 23, 24, 25
CARIFTA (Caribbean Free Trade Area) 17, 21, 23
Çarkoğlu, A. 210, 216
Carter Doctrine (1980) 141
Casablanca summits (1989/1994) 160, 170, 171, 202–3
Caspian Sea 7, 58, 203
Castro, Fidel 139
Caucasus 7, 194

CEAO (Economic Community of West Africa) 18
CENTO (Central Treaty Organisation) 20
Central Asia 7, 194, 196; newly independent states 112, 218; oil and natural gas 8; Turkish–Israeli investment in 214
centralisation 11, 40, 135
Centre for Palestine Research and Studies 122
cereals 32, 67, 84, 89, 95
Chamberlain, Neville 19
Chan, S. 179–80
Chatelus, M. 115, 116, 128, 131, 134
Chaudhry, K. A. 2
cheating 38, 53, 54
chemicals 88, 96, 120
Chile 23
China 57, 124, 139, 207
Christian militias 169
Churchill, Sir Winston 139, 143
Çiller, Tansu 214
civil society 3, 10, 11, 34, 138, 187–8, 213; commitment to promote 190; expansion of 186, 190; growing demands for democratisation 185; none to speak of 180; strengthening 189; weak 184
Claes, Willy 147
Clawson, P. 56, 67, 114, 174
climatic characteristics 57–60, 66, 126; temperatures 130
Clinton, Bill 167
coalitions 42, 115, 158, 185, 193, 199, 215–16, 219, 221; advancing economic liberalisation 187; military 175; nationalist populist 116
Cohen, B. 47
Colbert, J. B. 16
Cold War 7, 28, 31, 50, 146, 194–5; divisions driven by 139–43; one of the major consequences 139; start 21; US-Soviet relations 19, 50, 140–1, 163
Cold War end/aftermath 2, 6, 8, 11, 26, 27, 32, 154; challenges 12; difficulties experienced by western democracies 118; effects of 143–8, 192; geopolitical and strategic dynamics 16; instability and threats 29; militarised confict 112; prospects 28; Turkey and 194, 202
Colombia 23
COMECON (Council for Mutual Economic Assistance) 21
communism 141, 145, 213
comparative advantage 87–97, 103, 120, 200
competition 22–3, 178; electoral 199; global 26, 28; harmonising rules 30; inner 88
competitiveness 96, 119, 123
complementarity 2, 24, 33, 35, 96, 119–21 *passim*, 128, 133; conspicuous lack of 151; energy supply 133
compromise 54, 125, 128, 206
concessions 44, 47, 54
Congo 28, 139
Copenhagen Declaration (1997) 173
Çorum 220
costs: adjustment 30; benefits and 48; labour 125; lowering 18; military 112, 155; national self-reliance 38; political 53, 160; transportation 21, 134
credit 132, 202
cross-border trade 202
cross-level processes 48, 49
CSCE (Conference on Security and Cooperation in Europe) 147, 170
Cuba 139
currency 24, 105
customs union 17, 25; Turkey–EU (1995) 196, 210–14, 220; Zollverein 16, 18

D-8 group 216
Dahl, R. 177
dams 205–6, 208, 131
debt 40, 155
debt crisis 40; foreign debt 155
decentralisation 11
decision-making 40, 42, 43, 115, 189; domestic apparatus 116; economic rationale in 137; governmental, check on 184; political and nationalistic 121
defence 19, 52, 151
demand(s) 47, 53, 117, 119, 121; agricultural 208; electricity 133, 208; food 66, 67, 68; industrial 208; labour market regulations 79; oil 204; water 103, 130, 132
demilitarisation 117, 118, 135
Demirel, Suleyman 199, 210
Democratic Front for the Liberation of Palestine 184
democratic peace 2–3, 6, 51, 53, 176–91
democratisation/democracy 10–11, 25, 29, 51, 135, 147, 193, 198; convergence based on 52; countries far from being committed to 188; coupled with serious economic liberalisation

reforms 125; danger/threat to 182, 183; dependence on 68; domestic coalitions and 115; elites apparently committed to 187; emphasis on 212; environment that can sustain and consolidate 200; factors that make it precarious and unstable 181; forceful 118; governability 117; help to promote 190; 'incipient' 178, 185, 186; leaders 177; not enough evidence of 186; one important outcome 189; only Muslim country where it has taken some root 182; preference for 180; pressures for 3, 145, 187; promises of 179; pushing for 6; recent waves 191; schemes crucial for 138; support for 33, 179; 'third wave of' 145
demography 9, 146
'demonstration effect' 145, 184, 186
Denizli 220
Denmark 173
desalination research 170
détente 19, 20, 21, 50
diplomacy 142, 159, 167, 172, 187; 'double-edged' 6
distribution: benefits 35; gains 42, 48; income 105, 184; labour force 63; land 208; power 39, 40; resource, through subsidies 33; trade 84; water 61, 132, 207
diversification 24, 67, 120, 137, 188
Diwan, I. 32
Dixon, W.J. 176
Doha 169, 171, 172
Dörtyol 134
Doyle, M. 176, 186

East Asia 9, 24, 25, 72
Eastern Europe 10, 21, 72, 213; markets 28, 102, 112; Partnership-for-Peace programme 147; political revolutions 29
EC (European Community) 26, 38, 146
ECLA (Economic Commission for Latin America) 23
Economic Cooperation Organisation 216
economic growth 3, 4, 118; export-led 28; long-term 11; negative 9, 105; policies not viable to manage 185–6; positive 105; potential for 8; private sector-led 28; rapid, unprecedented 26; slow 1; textiles 84
economic integration 18–19, 118, 172; 'deep(er)' 29–31, 32, 50, 52; equal distribution of benefits 23; full 20; no realistic prospect 35; political and 188
economic liberalisation 5–7 *passim*, 11, 33, 148, 186, 193, 219; barriers to 10, 34; coalitions that favour 116, 187; convergence based on 52; democratisation without 3; factor that complicates 185; greater 181, 188; groups against 115–16; growing importance attributed to 171; more market-oriented 56; opening-up of 136; pressure for 145, 178; regimes that support 176; serious reforms 125; significance 190; social forces and 34; trends towards 28–9, 34; unprecedented rise of 118
economic reforms 10–11, 32–4 *passim*, 53, 56, 115; consolidation of 117; necessary 129, 135, 179; need for 118
economic unions 18–19; failed 35
economies of scale 42, 119, 125
ECOWAS (Economic Community of West African States) 18, 23
ECSC (European Coal and Steel Community) 17, 21
Ecuador 23
Eder, M. 210, 214
education 61, 66, 208, 212
EEC (European Economic Community) 18, 21, 35, 151; *see also* EC; EU
efficiency 119, 120, 132, 133; losses 131
EFTA (European Free Trade Area) 17, 21, 98, 214
Egeli, Serif 213
Egypt 2, 4, 7, 52, 84, 166, 193, 213, 215–18 *passim*; agriculture 69; Arab Socialist Union 178–9; call to tolerate Muslim Brotherhood 221; Camp David peace treaty (1979) 142; cereal aid to 67; cheap manpower from 126; classified low-income country 103; comparative advantage 88, 89, 96; conservative regime 156; diplomatic ties with Israel 124; economic liberalisation and peace process 187; electrical grid 133, 204; exports 75, 81, 83, 96, 97, 204; financial assistance 151; foreign policy 145; GNP per capita 105; ideological conflict with Libya 148; imports 82, 83, 86; 'incipient democratisation' 178; *infitah* 10; inflation 107; intra-regional trade share 86; involvement in civil war in Yemen 148; labour force 61–2, 63, 79;

National Democratic Party 179; natural gas 134; need to bring back into mainstream Arab politics 152; nuclear weapons 170; Pan-Arab regime 140, 141, 149, 157; People's Assembly 179; policies towards Israel 158; political system 182; population dynamics 57, 61; radical Islam 153; rain 57; recognition of peace agreement with Israel 152–3; remittances 79; sanitation 65; tourists 173; Turkey and 202; union with Syria 140, 150, 157; water 129; *see also* ACM; Alexandria; Cairo; Mubarak; Nasser; Sadat
Eilat 170
Eisenhower Doctrine (1958) 140–1
Ekeus, Rolf 176
elections 166, 178, 179, 182, 183, 185, 215; closely controlled 180; free and fair 177; low degree of competition 199
electricity 103, 134; demands for 133, 208; grids 133, 170, 204; need for 205
El-Erian, S. 102, 117
elites 10, 188; agricultural 42; apparently committed to democratisation 187; economic 185; PanArab 156; political 69, 156, 180, 185
El-Naggar, S. 102, 117
El Salvador 23, 140
embargoes 144, 175, 201
'embedded autonomy' 117
emigration *see* migration
employment 18, 208; little prospects of 146; sluggish creation 78
energy 35, 135–7, 208; alternative sources 204; dependence on external sources 203; grid networking 103; need for 205; sharing arrangements 129, 133–4; *see also* coal; crude materials; electricity; gas; oil
entente 19, 50
environmental issues 30, 58, 137, 170
epistemic communities 38, 39
Epstein, D. 41
Erbakan, N. 215, 216, 217–18, 220–1
Esposito, J. 182
EU (European Union) 16, 18–19, 25, 148, 171–2, 192, 218; Euro-Med initiative (195) 147, 190, 211; Libyan trade 87; Med-Campus project 189; Morocco, Tunisia and 188; regional funds 23; Turkey and 87, 196, 197, 210–14, 222; *see also* WEU
Euphrates–Tigris system 9, 12, 58, 175, 205–10
Euro-Arab Dialogue 146
European Central Bank/European Monetary Institute 18
European Commission 19
European Customs Union 18
European Development Bank 131
European Parliament 19
Evans, P. 31, 117
expansionism 20, 140, 174
exports 3, 9, 28, 78, 81, 83, 86–8 *passim*, 95, 200; affected by UR arrangements 98; cheap inputs for 130; competitiveness in 96; earnings from 120; fuel 75; growth in 120; huge increases 73; increased opportunities 121; labour-force 79; oil 33, 34, 35, 53, 80, 84, 175, 201; political conflicts preclude 134; preferences that cannot be met by those who need 121
externalities 27, 39; positive 118
extremists: Jewish 182; Muslim 162, 169, 175

factor mobility/endowments 18, 121, 128; *see also* capital; labour
Fahd, king of Saudi Arabia 153, 163
Fahd Plan (1981) 153
Fashoda War (1898) 19
Fatah group 159
fertilisers 67, 96
Fez Plan (1982) 153
financial assistance 29, 141, 151–2, 155
FIS (Islamic Salvation Front) 221
Fischer, S. 9, 102, 105, 116, 119, 121, 122, 128
food 88, 89, 95–6, 97, 98, 128; cheaper, access to 42; dependency on others for supplies 56, 57, 67, 96; imported 57, 66–7, 98, 113, 120; relatively efficient industries 120; 'security' 10, 66–70, 209; self-sufficiency 10, 66, 67, 68, 103, 209
foreign exchange 130
foreign policy 25, 37, 52; aggressive 20; bureaucratic interests in 40; common 19; economic 41; Egyptian 145; expansionist 20; international explanations of 5–6; Iranian 173; linkage between public opinion and 55, 217; making 51, 54; Middle-Eastern, in Turkey 214–24; Soviet 144, 145; Turkish 12, 194–7 *passim*, 214–22 *passim*; US 11

forest 58
France 16, 19, 24, 25, 140; terrorism (1995) 146; trade negotiations with US 41–2; Treaty of Rome signing 21
free-riders 23, 26, 195
free trade 121, 213–14; agreements 17, 21, 27, 35; international 39; rising cost of system 26; *see also* CARIFTA; EFTA
freedom 177; press 156, 178, 179
fuels exports/imports 75, 78, 80–1; refined 88, 89
functionalists 22, 37
fundamentalism: Islamic 1, 3, 29, 146, 147, 163, 182, 196; Jewish 182, 183

Gaddafi, Col. Muammar 150, 216, 217
gains 38, 98, 217; distribution of 48; economic, mutual 119; improved trade 118; joint 42; long-term 126; microeconomic 114; political 217; relative 23, 48, 50, 125
Gambia 124
game theory 38, 41, 51; *see also* prisoner's dilemma; subgame perfection principle; three-level games; two-level games; zero-sum game
GAP (South-Eastern Anatolia Development Project) 12, 131, 175, 202, 206–10 *passim*
gas 96; natural 8, 133, 134, 203–4, 216
GATT (General Agreement of Tariffs and Trade) 16, 17, 25, 26, 97–8, 192; establishment of 70; most-favoured nation clause 211
Gaza-Jericho agreement (1994) 165
Gaza Strip 159, 165, 166, 167; democracy 180; Hamas dominated areas 183
Gaziantep 208, 220
GCC (Gulf Cooperation Council) 119, 151,188
GDP (gross domestic product) 23, 205, 208; growth forecast 70; per capita income 9, 105; share of consumption in 107; share of military expenditure in 99, 102
Georgia 204
Germany 18, 24, 25; Turkish migrant workers 79
glass(ware) 97, 120, 128
global economy: changing 26–7; emerging dynamics of regionalism 16; integration 193; recent trends 2; transformation 51
globalisation 28, 38, 139, 189
GNP (gross national product) 9, 99, 105, 119
Golan, G. 140
Golan Heights 150, 169
goods 29, 30, 119; free trade 121, 214; Israeli, Arabs opposed to buying 122; manufactured 75, 80, 89, 97, 120; mobility of 18, 28
Gorbachev, Mikhail S. 143, 144; efforts to reform 145; moderating Soviet policies in Middle East 159–60
Gourevitch, P.A. 40, 52–3
governments 10, 31–2, 189, 190; accountability 185; bogged down with security issues 192; closed 33; coalition 215–16, 221; condemned internationally 174; conservative 152, 160, 163; EU 197; expenditure 107; external threats at home 51; forced to resign 178; ineffective 10, 34; international level interactions 37; international pressure on 148; intervention 27, 28, 34, 117; legitimacy 53; loss of control of economy 185; minority 221; more representative 145; personalised power 180; pro-Western 154; reconciled to accepting US dominance 154; reconciliation of differences 187; restrictions imposed by 121; revenues 33, 53; right-wing 144, 145, 158, 159, 161, 162, 168; strong, active 116; unresponsive 181; *see also* military sector
Gowa, J. 26, 27, 39
Graham, D. F. 67
Great Depression 40
Greece 23, 30
'grey-area measures' 26
GSP (Generalised System of Preferences, EU 1971) 211, 213
Guatemala 23, 140
Gulf crisis (1990–91) 148, 175, 180, 194, 195; acceptance of US role in ending 154; Egypt's importance enhanced by 162; Palestinian support 160
Gulf War (1991) 1, 8, 11, 84, 133, 192; consequences of 194, 200

Haas, E. B. 22, 38
Hadar, L. T. 145–6, 162
Hamas 158, 168, 169, 182, 183–4, 197, 221
health 4, 61, 66, 129

Hebron 166, 167, 180, 183, 187
Herz, John 20
Hitler, Adolf 19
Hizbullah 158, 169, 221
Hoekman, B. 212
Hoffmann, Stanley 51
Human Development Index 105
human rights 4, 5, 29
Huntington, S. P. 29, 145, 186
Hussein ibn Talal, king of Jordan 141, 168–9, 179
hydroelectrics 208, 209

Ibrahim, S. E. 184
identity: Arab 49; collective 5; European 214; Islamic 219; Turkish 198
IMF (International Monetary Fund) 29, 31
immigration *see* migration
imports 42, 82, 83, 84, 86; arms 99, 102; countries unable to afford 121; food 57, 66–7, 98, 113, 120; fuel 78; increased 73; labour-force 79; manufactured 75–8, 80; natural gas 134; oil 203; *see also* substitution
INC (Iraqi National Congess) 196
incentives 27, 31; administrative 103; conflicting 37; cooperative 113; economic 114; interest groups 118; lack of 128; military 102, 115; not to emigrate to cities 130; political 102
income 23, 58, 61, 63, 221; country classifications 103–5; distribution 105, 184; export 79; GDP per capita 9, 72; inequalities 112, 184; overall increases in 105–7
independence 5, 139, 160, 178, 216
India 124
Indonesia 216, 218
industrial sector 63
industrialisation 116, 118
inefficiency 10, 42, 125, 131, 137
infant industries 23
infitah 10, 34, 57
inflation 107–10
infrastructure 35, 57, 66, 102, 103; insufficient 112; investment in 131; transportation 120
instability 4, 29, 32, 162, 167, 181; environment characterised by 188
intellectual property 18
interdependence 23, 38, 41–7, 50
interest groups 10, 34, 40–1, 114, 117, 159; coalition forming among 185; domestic interests 155; entrenched 135; incentives 118; interaction 192
International Law Association 206–7
International Law Institute 206
international monetary institutions *see* IMF; World Bank
international realist perspective 37, 50
international relations 19, 29, 36, 38; bureaucratic-politics approach 40; Soviet Union's approach 143; system-level theories 39
International Supervision Force 187
international/world markets 88, 98, 116; disadvantageous trend in 78; former Soviet republics 2, 32; impinging developments in 37; importing supplies from 66; improved competitiveness 119; oil reserves and 56; transfer of rents from 118; valuable funds from 122
intifada 158, 159, 160
investment: access to 31; average share in GDP 107; barriers to 34; capital 120, 219; discouraged 30; financial, for water 130–1; foreign direct 9, 28, 34, 162; high risk for 103; inefficient projects 112; joint Turkish-Israeli 214; natural gas 134; social-sector 102; trade related 98; unproductive 117
Iran 1, 7, 8, 178, 180, 193, 213, 215, 216; African trade 84; attacks on Kuwaiti shipping 144; average tariffs 119; capital stock per worker 126; cereal production 67; classified lowermiddle-income country 103; comparative advantage 88, 89, 96; exports 75, 81, 96; foreign policy 173; GSP status 211; hard-liners 174, 180, 221; imports 73, 82; inflation 107; labour force 61–2; natural gas 204; oil reserves 9; political and economic liberalisation 188; population density/dynamics 61, 105; radical Islam 153, 195; revolution (1979) 141, 151, 153, 158, 221; sovereignty expanded 149; support for PKK 12, 216; trade with OECD countries 98; US dual-containment policy 196; weapons of mass destruction 174; *see also* Iran-Iraq War; Khameini; Khatami; Khomeini; Pahlavi; Rafsanjani; Tehran
Iran–Iraq War (1980–88) 148–9, 158, 162, 221; Arab governments' preoccupation with 159; cost of 155;

GCC and 151; Iraq's retreat 152; Syria's support for Iran 175
Iraq 10, 34, 58, 193, 201; agriculture 69; Ba'th party 180; classified lower-middle-income country 103; compliance with UN Resolutions 199; conservative regime 140, 156; economic opening 57; elections closely controlled 180–1; electrical grid 133, 204; embargoes on 144; exports 81; GSP status 211; imports 82; inflation 107, 110; labour-force importing 79; missiles 154, 161, 176; offensive military capabilities 173, 198; oil pipeline links 134; Pan-Arab regime 149, 150, 163, 175; population density/dynamics 105; post-Gulf War crisis 84; power games between Syria, Turkey and 206; radical Arab regime 141; river dispute 9, 12; sanctions 196, 200, 201; sanitation 65; serious problems with Syria 175; Soviet Pan-Arab regime 140; Tharthal Canal project 206; US dual-containment policy 196; water 206, 207, 208, 210; weapons of mass destruction 174; *see also* ACM; Baghdad; Gulf crisis; Gulf War; Iran–Iraq War; Kurds; Saddam Hussein
iron and steel 97, 120, 128
irredentism 187
irrigation 61, 69, 206, 208, 209
Islam 7, 181, 194, 197, 217, 220; common market 215; developmentalism 218; extremists 162, 169, 175; fundamentalist 1, 3, 29, 146, 147, 163, 182, 196; networks 219; radical 153, 161, 163, 173, 180, 195, 216; Shari'a 182; Shi'a 180; values 218; *see also* Democratic Front; FIS; Hamas; Hizbullah; *intifada*; Islamic Jihad; Muslim Brotherhood; Pan-Arabism
Islamic Conference Organisation 169, 173–4, 216
Islamic Jihad 158, 182
Ismael, T. 153
Israel 51, 213; Arab boycott of 114, 122, 124, 150–1, 169, 171, 202; business and economic deals 171; capital stock per worker 126; classified high-income country 103; comparative disadvantage/advantage 88, 89, 95, 96, 97; creation of 149, 151, 156; democratic politics and economic growth 4; destruction of 154, 156, 166, 182; diplomatic missions and other links 124; economic domination 128, 214; economic liberalisation and peace process 187; exports 75, 81, 83, 84, 96; farming interests 68; GNP per capita 105; growth rates 105; imports 73, 82, 83, 204; income 105; inflation 107; International Supervision Force 187; intra-regional trade share 86; invasions of Lebanon 148; Japanese trade 87, 114; joint ventures 123, 128; labour force 62, 63; Labour government/party 158, 161, 162, 169; national ideology 130; natural gas 134; negligible regional trade 84; 'no peace with' 150; normalisation of relations between Arabs and 113, 123, 172, 173, 186; nuclear weapons 170, 174; Operation Grapes of Wrath (1996) 215; peace treaty with Jordan (1994) 191; potentially dominant position of economy 125; relatively efficient food industries 120; right-wing (Likud) government 144, 145, 158, 159, 161, 162, 168; security 146, 195; Soviet Jewish emigration to 144, 145, 161; Syria's and PLO's ability to confront 152; terms of trade 78; trade offices 166; trade with OECD countries 87, 98; Turkey and 124, 199, 202, 213–14, 215, 216, 221; two-model democracy 177; water 9, 129, 131, 132; Zionist regime 174; *see also* Arab–Israeli peace process; Begin; Eilat; fundamentalism; Jerusalem; Netanyahu; Palestine; Rabin; Weizman
Istanbul 194, 214, 220
Italy 18, 21, 147, 189
Izmir 220

Jamaica 25
Japan 24, 87, 114, 140
Jerusalem 150, 158, 166, 167, 172, 180
joint ventures 122, 123, 128
Jordan 2, 52, 103, 161, 163, 166; African trade 84; Arafat's efforts to negotiate a confederation with 159; bilateral negotiations with Israel 168; British support for royalist regime 141; business and economic deals 171; civil war (1970–71) 141, 178; classified lower-middle-income country 103; comparative advantage/disadvantage

88, 89, 96; conservative regime 140, 156; democratic politics and economic growth 4; diplomatic ties with Israel 124; economic liberalisation and peace process 187; elections 178, 179; electrical grid 133, 204; exports 75, 81, 86; financial assistance 151; imports 73; labour force 62, 63, 79; liberalisation 178; Lomé, Convention status 211; National Charter 179; Palestinians compelled to leave to 160; peace treaty with Israel (1994) 191; political elites 69; political system 182; pressure of less financial support 155; RCA 88; remittances 79; riots 179; sanitation 65; Syrian invasion 148; terms of trade 78; threatened by PLO 156–7; tourists 173; trade with OECD countries 98; Turkey and 202; water 9, 129, 131; *see also* Abdullah; ACM; Amman; Hussein
Judea 158

Kagan, K. 190
Kahramanmaras 220
Kalaycioğlu, E. 178
Kalaycioğlu, S. 234
Kant, Immanuel 176
Kaplan, R. 177, 178
Kaufman, E. 180
Kayseri 220
Kazakhstan 124
Kedourie, E. 178
Kerr, M. H. 140, 141, 148
Khamenei, Ayatollah 174, 180, 181
Khartoum summit (1967) 150, 151, 153
Khatami, Ayatollah Mohammed 173, 181
Khomeini, Ayatollah Ruhollah 8, 153, 180
Knopf, W. J. 48–9
know-how 24, 126
Kocaeli 220
KOMBASSAN (Turkish conglomerate) 220
Kramer, M. 182
Krasner, S. D. 43
Krueger, O. A. 30
Kurds 148–9, 196–201 *passim*, 208, 210; independence 216; rival groups 175; *see also* PKK
Kuwait 63, 144, 163; African trade 84; classified high-income country 103; elections 178; exports 75, 81, 134; GNP per capita 105; imports 82; intra-regional trade share 86; labour-force importing 79; population density/ dynamics 105; press freedom 156; *see also* Gulf crisis; Gulf War
Kyrgyzstan 124

labour 128; abundance of 121; capacity for extra supply 118; common standards 30; costs of 125; free movement 18; mobility 121; rural 84
labour force 61–3; agricultural 63, 84; importing countries 79; major exporting countries 79
labour market: regulations 79; stronger economy 125
LAFTA (Latin American Free Trade Area) 17, 21, 23
Lampuseda 147
Laqueur, W. 152, 161, 182
Latin America 10, 22, 102; divisions driven by Cold War 139–40; opening-up/reforms of markets 28, 112; re-democratisation 29; *see also under various country names*
Lattakia 140
law(s) 29, 30, 184, 185, 187; commercial 18, 211; international 206–7
League of Arab States 35
Lebanon 63, 134, 141, 170, 188; classified lower-middle-income country 103; comparative disadvantage/advantage 88, 89, 95, 96, 97; conservative, relatively pro-Western regime 140; democratic politics and economic growth 4; exports 75, 81, 84, 86, 96–7; imports 73, 78, 82; income 105; invasions of 148, 150, 174; labour-force exporting 79; Litani River 58, 61; Lomé Convention status 211; multi-party democracy after independence 178; political system 156; population density 57; pro-Nasserites 140; radical Islam 153; RCA 88; relatively efficient food industries 120; Syrian invasion/ presence 148, 169, 174; trade with OECD countries 98
left-wing groups 157, 159, 160, 161, 184
Lenczowski, George 149
level-of-analysis problem 39–41
Lewis, B. 7, 140
liberalisation *see* economic liberalisation; political liberalisation; trade liberalisation
Libya 193, 216; average tariffs 119; classified upper-middle-income country 103; comparative advantage 88, 89;

Erbakan's scandalous visit to 217–18; exports 73, 75, 81, 83, 97; ideological conflict with Egypt 148; imports 82, 83; investments on human capital 102; labour force 62, 63, 79; long-standing animosities with West 102; missile attack on Italian island 147; navaland military-base facilities 142; Pan-Arab regime 149, 150; population density 57; radical Arab regime 141; rain 57; Soviet connections 140; support of terrorism 173; trade with OECD countries 87, 98; weapons of mass destruction 174
'like-minded' states 30, 176, 189, 190, 191, 192–226; *see also* Egypt; Israel; Jordan; Palestine; Turkey
Lindberg, L. N. 22
living standards 160
loans 30, 145
Lomé Convention 211
Lukacs, Y. 150, 151, 160
Luxembourg 18; conference (1997) 196, 197

Maastricht Treaty (1992) 18, 19
McKersie, R. B. 48
macroeconomics 35, 98–110
Madrid conference (1991) 123–4, 144, 160–3 *passim*, 163, 168, 169; assassination threat 174; boycotted 172; Turkey and 187, 202
Madrid Declaration (1911) 206
Malaysia 216, 218
Mallat, C. 129
Malta 212
Manley, Michael 25
Mansfield, D. E. 27, 39
manufacturing industries 120
markets 87, 219; access to 26, 30, 31, 70, 73, 98, 125, 126; agricultural 67; barriers to logic 31; beneficial future for 116; common 21–2, 215; credit 132; distortion 31, 117; dynamic 102; efficient functioning 136; enlarged 119; European 72, 73, 84, 98; expanding 32, 118, 134; food 96; import 83; important opportunities 121; inefficiency 31; integration of 72, 73; logic and signals 117; new 102, 116; North American 73; OECD 98; oil 73; opening-up of 28; protection of 116; reforms 112, 115; rent-seeking effects on 41; single 18; textiles and clothing 98; well-functioning 135; *see also* international/ world markets
Marxist-Leninists 141
Mattar, P. 160
Mauritania 124, 166
MEBRD (Middle Eastern Bank for Reconstruction and Development) 122
Mediterranean 133, 134, 140; EU policy 213; partnerships 211, 212; security and stability 146, 147, 190; universities 189
MENA (Middle East North Africa) summits 167, 169, 170–1, 189, 202–3, 212
MERCOSUR (Southern Cone Common Market) 16, 18, 23, 25
Mesopotamia 206
Mexico 30, 207; *see also* NAFTA
MFA (Multi-Fibre Arrangement) 98
migration 130, 161; illegal 146; internal 192; large-scale 146; Soviet Jewish, to Israel 144, 145, 161; workers 78–9, 80, 219
military sector 103, 112, 114, 140, 141–2, 144, 162; Christian militias 169; complex 156; consequences of actions 122; cost of converting installations 118; democratic systems swept away by 178; expenditures 8–9, 32, 34, 57, 99–102; fighter planes 216; impossible to justify out-lays 116; Iraq's offensive capabilities 173, 198; Israel-Jordan bilateral negotiations 168; Israel-Turkey cooperation agreement (1996) 215; lobbies that profit 117; policy 195; security forces 166; strategic incentives 115; threat or use of force 176; trade 192; US use of Turkish NATO bases 154; *see also* demilitarisation
Miller, B. 190
Milner, H. 38
minerals 72, 121
missiles 147, 154, 161, 175, 176, 199; ballistic 146, 174
Mitrany, D. 22, 189
Monnet, J. 22
Moravcsik, A. 6
Morocco 7, 57, 58, 166, 188, 213; capital stock per worker 126; cereal aid/ production 67; classified lower-middle-income country 103; exports 81; imports 73, 82; Israeli liaison office in 124; labour force 61–2, 63, 79; multi-party democracy after independence

178; sanitation 65; terms of trade 78; *see also* Casablanca
Moscow 202
Mubarak, Hosni 162, 167, 169, 172, 179, 221
Muscat 170
MUSIAD (Turkish Industrialist and Businessmen Association) 219–20
Muslim Brotherhood Society 158, 179, 221
Muslims *see* Islam
Musrey, A. 151

Nablus 168
NAFTA (North American Free Trade Agreement) 17, 23, 25, 27, 28, 35, 72, 192
Nasser, Gamal Abdel 140, 142, 149, 150, 162, 178
Nasserites 140
Nateq-Nouri, Ali Akbar 181
national interest 6, 217
nationalisation 151, 156
nationalism 3, 115, 116, 121, 218; Palestinian 156, 157, 158, 159; religious 182–3; weakening the destructive hold of 189
NATO (North Atlantic Treaty Organisation) 19, 20, 147, 154, 218; expansion 27; strategic concept (1991) 146
natural resources 8, 112, 126; locally available 120; *see also* climatic characteristics; crude materials; energy; food; water
neo-functionalists 22, 37–8
neo-institutionalists 38, 40
neo-liberals 38, 117
Netanyahu, Binyamin 167, 169, 172, 221
Netherlands 18
'new world order' 28, 115, 144, 161
New Zealand 98
NGOs (non-governmental organisations) 184, 189, 190
Nicaragua 139
NICs (newly-industrialising countries) 218
Nigeria 124, 216
normalisation 113, 123, 172, 173
North Africa 5, 7, 8, 9; *see also* Algeria; Egypt; Libya; Morocco; Tunisia
North Korea 124, 139
Northern Watch (Operation Provide Comfort) 175, 196
Norton, R. A. 3, 51–2, 177
Norway 161
NTMs (non-tariff measures) 97, 98

OECD countries 87, 98, 120
O'Halloran, S. 41
oil 12, 119, 121, 131, 192; alternative resources 32; Central Asian 8, 112, 203; crisis (1973) 146; exporting states oil 33–5 *passim*, 53, 80, 84, 102, 175, 201, 204; nationalisation of production 151; prices 2, 9, 134, 151, 204; safeguarding supply to the West 195; spill emergency centres 170; transporting 134
oil reserves 1, 9, 56, 96, 112; former Soviet republics 32; largest 140
oil revenues 33, 99; declining 10, 32, 67, 112; drastic fall 154–5; drying up of 7; economies cannot rely on 9; huge 56–7, 101; lost 200
oil seeds 121
Oman 166; African trade 84; cereal production 67; classified upper-middle-income country 103; comparative advantage 88, 89, 96; exports 81, 84, 86, 87; imports 79, 82, 84, 86; Israeli trade office in 124; rain 57; *see also* Muscat
Öniş, Z. 218, 219–20
OPEC (Organisation of Petroleum Exporting Countries) Fund 121
Organisation of African Unity 139
Oslo Accords (1993) 172
Ostpolitik 19
Ottoman Empire 178
Ouchy Agreement (1932) 18
output 70–2
Owen, R. 155–6, 178, 179, 180
Özal, Turgut 210
Özbudun, E. 177

Pahlavi, Mohammad Reza, shah of Persia 148
Pakistan 7, 124, 213, 216
Palestine 2, 52, 122, 129, 133, 154, 159; aid and credit to 202; boycott of Jewish goods 150–1; British mandate 148; democratic politics and economic growth 4; democratisation process 179, 190; economic liberalisation and peace process 187; elections 166, 182; independent 160; joint ventures 123, 128; Legislative Council 179; loss of 149, 152; nationalism 156–7; occupied

territories/Jewish settlements 153, 158–61 *passim*, 165, 166, 183, 184; political system 182; refugees 166; self-government 165; support for peace process 168; threat to Jordan 141; water 132; *see also* PLO; PNC
Pan-Africanism 139
Pan-Arabism 2, 140, 141, 149, 150, 152, 159; call for unification 157; challenged 153; loss of legitimacy 163; regimes basing legitimacy on 156; Soviet relations with 155
Papandreou, N. 32
Paraguay 18, 23
paramilitary forces 99
'Pareto frontier' 43
Paris Treaty (1951) 21
patronage 33, 199, 200, 220
pay-offs 23, 26, 46n, 47, 48
peace *see* democratic peace
Penn World Table 105, 107
Peretz, D. 7
Persian Gulf 7, 124, 206; *see also* Gulf crisis; Gulf War
Perthes, V. 179, 180
Peru 23
Peters, J. 189–90
petroleum 72, 96, 120
Pinochet Ugarte, Augusto 25
Piscatori, J. P. 182
PKK (Workers' Party of Kurdistan) 174–5, 196, 197–8, 199, 208; Iran's support for 12, 216
planned economies 140, 147
PLO (Palestine Liberation Organisation) 124, 141, 142, 145, 150, 162; accepted as Israel's partner 166; challenged by radical Islamic groups 153; commitment to Arab cause 152; Declaration of Principles (DOP) with Israel 161, 165, 166, 168; elections 179; financial assistance 151, 152, 155, 160; forced evacuation from Beirut 143–4; Jordan threatened by 156–7; negotiations with Israel sabotaged 182; not considered representative of Palestinians 221; peace process agreements with Israel 202; pluralism 158; radical left-wing groups within 157, 160, 161; Soviet support for 160; *see also* Arafat
PNC (Palestine National Council) 144, 157, 158, 160, 161
policies 24, 29, 33, 53, 124, 147, 187; agricultural 66, 67, 69, 132; commercial 18, 214; coordinated 38; credit 132; defence 19; distorted 113; domestic factors and 40; dual-containment 196; economic restructuring 184; Euro-Med 147, 190, 213; evolving 148; failed 105; fiscal 17, 18; import substitution 25, 28; ineffective 34; inept 221; institutions that manage disputes 52; military 195; moderating 159–60; monetary 17, 18; Nasserite 140, 162; nationalistic 115; non-economic incentives 103; non-involvement 195; not viable 185–6; protectionist 35; reluctance to moderate 158; security 107, 194; social 113; structural reform 136; trade 17, 18, 26, 118; water 69, 70, 131; *see also* foreign policy; policy-making
policy making 40, 53, 57, 98–110, 199; ineffective and economically irrational 32; socio-economic 112; 'war-minded' 67, 68, 102, 113, 132
political liberalisation 118, 148, 179; barriers to 34; cautious 163; combining economic restructuring policies with 184; commitment to 179, 188; factor that complicates 185; greater 181, 188; regimes that support 176; social forces and 34; trends towards 28–9, 34
political union 19, 20, 21; failed 35
politics 8, 36, 188, 192–3; Arab, gradual evolution of 152; bureaucratic 40; changing international scene 27–8; cleavages and rivalries 121; comparative 43; cooperation 3, 165–76; democratic 4; dispute settlement 135; domestic 40, 41, 43, 49, 51, 152, 221; dynamics of change 139–54; great-power 39; intense confrontation 140; international/world 37, 38, 145, 172, 189, 193, 195; liberalisation in developing world 28–9; 'low'/'high' 22; militarised conflict 114; one-party 147; opposition to change 4; power 198, 199; preferences of the masses 122; reforms 11, 29; repressive regimes 135; Turkey's role 182, 194; water 70, 130, 205–10; *see also* security; stability; also headings above prefixed 'political'
population density/dynamics 9, 56, 57, 61–6, 78, 105, 112, 192; massive growth 146

Portugal 23, 30
poverty 3, 4, 63, 65, 66, 126; rural 84, 208
power: balance of 6, 146, 148, 199, 206; bargaining 49, 195; competitive 220; economic 50, 151; farmers 42; fragmentation of 40; hegemonic 39; international distribution of 39, 40; maintaining 37; monopoly of 163; Pan-Arabist 149; personalised 180; political 39, 50, 198, 199; positional 38; pursuit of 22
pragmatism 159, 160, 221
Prebisch, Raoul 23
precipitation *see* rain
'predatory' states 31, 34
Preferential Trade Area for Eastern and Southern Africa 17
press: censorship 163; freedom 156, 178, 179
pressure groups 184
prices: agricultural 42, 72; common set of 105; controlling 116; export/import 78, 98; food 98; international, human capital 126; metals 72; minerals 72; oil 2, 9, 134, 151, 204; petroleum 72; relative 78; setting 2; water 132
Primakov, Yevgeny 196
prisoner's dilemma 38
private sector 2, 28, 34, 171, 185; alternative 10
privatisation 28
production: agricultural 56, 57, 67, 120, 208; changing paradigms 27; electricity 205; factors of 103, 119, 121; food 66, 67; hydro-energy 210; large-scale 119; oil 151, 155; regional systems 118
productivity 113, 209
profits 27, 102
prosperity 5, 8, 149, 166, 172, 194; long-run 30
protectionism 35, 84
Przeworski, A. 117
PTP (Preferential Tariff Protocol) 213
public opinion 124, 154, 168, 180, 219; linkage between foreign policy and 55, 217
Putnam, R. 5, 37, 40–3 *passim*, 51, 148, 184, 193

Qatar 63, 134, 169; African trade 84; business and economic deals 171; classified high-income country 103; comparative advantage 88, 89; exports 73, 75, 81, 97; GNP per capita 105; imports 78, 82; Israeli contact with 124; labour-force importing 79; natural gas 134; population density/dynamics 105; rain 57; *see also* Doha
Quandt, B. W. 4–5, 145, 190

Rabin, Yitzhak 162, 168, 169; assassination 183
Rafsanjani, Hashemi 216
rain/precipitation 9, 57–8, 130
rapprochement 19, 50, 197
Rath, K. 178, 179
RCA (revealed comparative advantage) index 87–8, 89
realism/realists 37, 38, 50
reconstruction: large-scale 116; need for 110–11
Red Sea 7
reforms: democratic 187; fiscal 10; institutional 30, 137, 212; large-scale 116; liberal(isation) 31, 70, 115, 125; market 112, 115, 138; opposed 117; political 11, 29, 33, 53, 136; structural 110–11, 117, 118, 135, 136; technocratic approach to 117; *see also* economic reforms
refugees: Kurdish 198; Palestinian 166
regimes: authoritarian 3, 4, 7, 10, 20, 182, 200; communist 145; conservative 1, 140–5 *passim*, 149, 153, 155, 156–8 *passim*; democratic 25, 180, 200; dictatorial 34; international security 50; 'laissez-faire' 2; moderate 195, 196; nationalist 3; Pan-Arab 140, 149, 150, 152, 153, 155, 157, 163, 175; pro-Soviet Arab 146; racist, terrorist, expansionist 174; radical 1, 142–5 *passim*, 149, 150, 156, 157, 163, 173, 195, 196; relatively pro-Western 140; repressive 135, 156, 157, 158, 163; royalist 141, 149, 150, 156; secular 158; single-party 156; socialist 2, 25, 149; Zionist 174
regionalism 25–6; changing global economy 26; changing international political scene 27–8; development of 21–3; dynamics of political change 148–55; economic cooperation, potential for 112–38; exploring prospects and restraints 31–5; political cooperation, potential for 165–91; relative failure in developing world 23–5; towards a model of political

economy 36–55; what is 'new' in 29–31
remittances 79, 121, 160
rent-seeking behaviour 2, 30, 41, 117, 137
rents 116; exogenous 33; oil 53; transfer from international markets 118
repression 135, 142, 156–8 *passim*, 163, 184; complete 180
resources *see* allocation of resources; natural resources; underwater resources
restructuring 29, 31, 117, 125, 178; barriers to 2; policies 184; political 11, 136; urgency increases 185
reunification 143, 144
Richards, A. 9, 56, 57, 67, 68, 131–2, 135, 136, 184–5
right-wing governments/groups 144, 145, 158, 161, 162, 168, 180
rights 28; migrant workers 79; minority 200; property 132, 136; riparian 12, 206, 207; sovereign 152, 206; *see also* human rights
risk 73, 102, 103, 116
rivers/riparian issues 9, 12, 58, 61, 131, 205–10
Roberts, J. 1, 155, 177, 180
Rodrik, D. 30
Rome, Treaty of (1957) 18, 21
Rothstein, R. L. 177, 178, 190
Rowley, G. 7
Rubin, B. 152, 159, 161, 182
rural areas 65, 66, 84
Russett, B. 176, 177, 181
Russia 196, 197, 204, 213

SACU (Southern African Customs Union) 18
Sadat, Anwar 142, 150, 157, 178; assassination 162
Saddam Hussein 144, 152, 154, 160, 162, 175; leadership consolidated 180; opponents in Iraq 196
Salame, G. 178, 182, 185
Salinas, Carlos 30
Samaria 158
sanctions 196, 200, 201
Sandanistas 139
sanitation services 65
Şanlıurfa 220
Saudi Arabia 32, 34, 141, 157, 193; African trade 84; cereal production 67; classified upper-middle-income country 103; comparative advantage 88; conservative regime 140, 158; exports 73, 75, 81, 84, 134, 203; foreign debts 155; GSP status 211; imports 82, 84, 99, 200, 204; investments on human capital 102; labour force 61–2, 79; military expenditure 99; monopoly of power 163; North American trade 87; oil reserves 9, 134; population density/dynamics 105; rain 57; *see also* Fahd; Gulf crisis; Gulf War
savings: voluntary external 103; water 132
Scheingold, S. A. 22
Schelling, C. T. 49, 53
Seaga, Edward 25
secularism 158, 159, 182, 213, 215, 218
security 4, 8, 10, 31, 51, 54, 137, 149, 169, 170; advantages associated with 176; budgets 52; 'cord' 54; common 151; countries with constructive role to play in 154; dilemma 50; economic 194; emphasis on 156; externalities 39; food 10, 66–70, 209; government apparatus bogged down with 192; Gulf region/US 141; how best achieved 189; international regime, absence of 50; inter-state conflicts and 148; Israel 146, 195; lasting 191; Mediterranean 146, 147, 190; military concerns about 198; national 199, 200, 209; need to seek 153; overcoming the dilemma 20; policy-making and 57; regional cooperation conducive to 113; threats 29, 32, 53; undermining one's own 50
self-sufficiency: agricultural 32, 61, 113; food 10, 66–70, 103, 209
Shapland, G. 69–70, 130, 131
Shattul-Arab 149
signalling 30, 31
Sinai (Sharim El-Sheikh) 169
Singapore 68
Single European Act (1985) 17, 18
SITC (Standard International Trade Classification) 88
socialism 2, 25, 140, 149, 155, 156, 200
Solingen, E. 3–4, 11, 31, 115, 116, 177, 182–3, 185, 187
South-East Asia 139; *see also* ASEAN; Indonesia; Malaysia; Singapore
South Korea 68, 139
South Pacific Forum 24
sovereignty: economic 125; national 132, 148–9, 175; 'popular' 182; water 206, 207
Soviet Union 20, 102, 139, 162, 165, 195; Cold War relations 19, 50, 140–3, 146,

163; collapse/disintegration 28, 143, 145; expansionism 140; foreign policy 144, 145; former republics 2, 29, 32, 213; Jewish emigration to Israel 144, 145, 161; market reforms 112; Pan-Arab relations with 155; political revolutions 29; Turkey's strategic importance 195; *see also* Azerbaijan; Georgia; Gorbachev; Kazakhstan; Kyrgystan; Russia; Tajikistan; Turkmenistan; Uzbekistan
Spain 23, 30, 147
Sparta 20
'spillover effects' 22, 176, 186
Springborg, R. 179
stabilisation measures 117, 136
stability 2, 3, 8, 25, 146, 147, 149, 194, 196; advantages associated with 176; consolidation of 11; constructive step towards 19; countries critical to 180; countries with constructive role to play in 154; hegemonic theory 39; how best achieved 189; important dynamic in favour of 187; international 29; inter-state conflicts and 148; lasting 191; long-run 30; macroeconomic 35; Mediterranean 147, 190; potential sources of 181; threat to 173, 174; two countries critical to 180; *see also* instability
Strateji/MORI polls 217, 222, 223
structural adjustment programs 135, 136
subgame perfection principle 44–5, 46–7
subsidies 30, 33, 98; agricultural 41, 130, 132; food 70; water 103
substitution 22, 25, 28, 116
Sudan 7, 69, 140, 150, 216
Sudetenland 19
Suez Canal crisis (1956) 140, 149
supply: energy 133, 134; food 56, 57, 67, 68, 70, 96; labour 118; oil 140, 195, 204; water 69, 103, 130, 132, 137
supranational institutions 18, 38
Syria 4, 58, 97, 98, 144, 145, 170, 193, 198–9; agriculture 69; Arab League office in 150–1; arable land 208–9; average tariffs 119; Ba'th party 180; capital stock per worker 126; classified lower-middle-income country 103; comparative advantage 88, 89, 95, 96; conservative regime 140, 156; decision to support Iran against Iraq 152; demand for Israel's withdrawal from Golan Heights 169; electrical grid 133, 204; exports 75, 96; financial assistance 151, 152; imports 82; *infitah* 10; inflation 107; invasions of Lebanon 148, 174; labour-force exporting 79; Lomé Convention status 211; naval- and military-base facilities 142; Pan-Arab regime 140, 141, 149, 150, 157, 163, 175; power games between Iraq, Turkey and 206; radical Islam 153; relatively efficient food industries 120; remittances 79; sanitation 65; serious problems with Iraq 175; support for PKK 12, 174–5; support for secular left-wing groups 159; territorial expansionism 174; Turkey and 201–2, 215; union with Egypt 140, 150, 157; water 9, 12, 129, 131, 206, 207, 208, 210; weapons of mass destruction 174; *see also* ACM; Assad
system-level theories 39, 41, 51

Taif agreements (1989) 174
Tajikistan 124
tariffs 25, 29; average 119; common customs 17, 211; common external 17; elimination of 18, 29; optimal levels 39; reductions 17, 97, 98; zero 214; *see also* GATT; PTP
taxation 33, 103
Tbilisi 204
technology 97, 99, 125, 128, 131, 219; access to 31; advanced 24; desalination 170; dualities or major gaps 126; electronics 114; labour-intensive 120; rapidly changing 10; water-saving 132; western, need for 221
Tehran 169, 173–4; Conference (1997) 199
telecommunications 97, 120, 128, 129
terrorism 148, 160, 166, 167, 169, 182; fundamentalist 146, 147; state that supports 173
textiles 84, 96, 97, 98, 121
Thompson, R. W. 20
three-level games 48
Thucydides 20
Tigris river *see* Euphrates-Tigris system
TII (trade intensity index) 86–7
'tit-for-tat' 12, 38
tobacco 88, 121
tourism 129, 137, 171, 173, 189
trade 30, 99, 128, 213; arms 112; barriers to 17, 98, 119, 120, 122; Black Sea 194; cross-border 202; curtailed

relations 114; embargo 175; extra-regional/international 21; food 68; foreign 151; fuel 80–1; global 25, 86; impediment to 125; increased 54, 120, 202; intra-ACM 151; intra-industry 24; intra-regional 21, 24, 72, 79, 80–1, 84, 86–97, 188; limited ability 114; loss of 200; low potential 24; 'managed' 27; military 142, 192; need to reduce ties with advanced industrial countries 23; oil 192; partnerships 50, 99; policy 17, 18, 26; preferential agreements 211; regulations 119, 121; security and 50; strategic theories 27; terms of 23, 78; volume 211; world 9, 70–98, 102; *see also* free trade; trade liberalisation
trade liberalisation 16, 22, 23, 26, 70, 214; agricultural 41–2; multilateral 25; mutual 29, 118; policies that encourage 187
transnational issues 3, 43, 48–9, 129, 148, 184, 198, 199; developing 189
transportation 21, 35, 120, 126; oil 134
Truman Doctrine (1958) 140
Tsebelis, G. 42, 43, 48
Tuma, E. H. 124, 126
Tunis 150, 159, 171
Tunisia 166, 188, 213; cereal aid/production 67; classified lower-middle-income country 103; exports 75, 81, 83; failed attempt at union with Libya 150; imports 82, 83; Israeli interest office in 124; labour force 62, 63; poverty 65
Turkey 2, 52; annual precipitation 57; Arab countries in proximity to 7, 8; average tariffs 119; capital stock per worker 126; cereal aid/production 67; classified lower-middle-income country 103; comparative disadvantage/advantage 88, 89, 95, 96, 97, 200; conflict 102; economic liberalisation and peace process 187; electrical grid 133, 204; energy needs 203–4; EU trade 87, 214; exports 75, 81, 83, 84, 86, 87, 95, 96–7, 200; foreign policy 12, 194–7 *passim*, 214–22 *passim*; imports 73, 82, 83, 84, 86, 203; improved governance 5; inflation 107; International Supervision Force 187; Israel and 124, 213–14, 215, 216, 221; labour force 62, 63, 79; natural gas use 134, 203, 204; oil pipeline links 134; outside of Middle-Eastern politics 154; political parties 200, 205, 214–20; population density/dynamics 57, 61; RCA 88; role in Middle East 1, 4, 11–13; secularism 182, 213, 215, 218; Syrian assistance to PKK against 174–5; terms of trade 78; trade with OECD countries 98; two-level game perspective 192–226; two-model democracy 177; US use of NATO military bases 154; water 9, 12, 126, 131, 175, 205–10; *see also* Anatolia; Ankara; Balkans; Bursa; Ciller; Çorum; Demirel; Denizli; Erbakan; Gaziantep; Istanbul; Izmir; Kahramanmaras; Kayseri; Kocaeli; Konya; Ottoman Empire; Özal; Şanlıurfa; Yilmaz
Turkey Association Council 213
Turkic communities 194
Turkmenistan 124, 205
TUSIAD (Independent Association of Industrialists and Businessmen, Turkey) 219, 220
two-level games 5, 6, 56, 114, 122, 128–9, 138, 155, 192–226; basic tenets 37; coalitions 116; conceptual and theoretical problems 47–9; energy issues 135–7; governments involved in 184; interaction 119, 121; migrant workers 80; resistance 124; theory of interdependence between domestic and international forces 41–7; use of 50–5; water issues 132–3, 135–7

UAE (United Arab Emirates) 57, 63; agriculture 67; classified high-income country 103; comparative advantage 88, 89, 95, 96; exports 75, 81, 84, 88; GNP per capita 105; imports 73, 82; labour importing 79; population density/dynamics 105; rain 57
UDEAC (Central African Customs and Economic Union) 18
underwater resources 32
unemployment 9, 34
United Arab Republic 150
United Kingdom *see* Britain
United Nations 23, 149, 154, 196, 210; General Assembly 143, 160; International Law Commission 207; Security Council 144, 158, 173, 175, 199, 201; UNCTAD (UN Conference on Trade and Development) 119; UNICEF (UN Children's Fund) 37; UNSCOM (UN Special Commissioner) 175–6

United States 24, 40, 158, 165, 171, 190, 210, 213; African trade 84; Cold War relations 19, 50, 140–1; conservative regimes seeking security from 153–4, 163; diplomacy 167; dominance in global economy 26; double standards 160; dual-containment policy 196; foreign policy 11, 41; Palestinians acceptable to 161; peace process 142, 145–6; PLO and 144; population density 57; pressure on Israel's Likud government 162; shift towards regionalism 27; speech criticising 174; supremacy challenged 139; trade negotiations with France 41–2; Turkey and 195, 196–7, 205, 214; water 132, 207; *see also* NAFTA
urbanisation 63, 130, 218; rapid 9, 34
Uruguay 18, 23
Uruguay Round 97–8
use of force 176
Uzbekistan 124

Vatican 124

wages 2, 116
Walton, R. E. 48
Waltz, K. 40
'war capitalism' 57
war-minded policy making 68, 132
Washington Declaration (1994) 168
water 9, 12, 126, 129–33, 135–7; conflict over 175; distribution 61, 132, 207; drinking, safe 66; lack/scarcity of 57, 58, 103; politics of 69, 70, 130, 205–10; sharing 61, 175, 205, 206; saving technology 132; surplus 58
Waterbury, J. 9, 56, 57
wealth 208; redistribution 156
weapons 155; biological 176; chemical 8, 176; expenditure on 8–9; non-proliferation treaty 174; nuclear 8, 29, 141, 142, 170, 174; of mass destruction 4, 146, 174, 175, 199; proliferation 146; *see also* missiles
Weizman, Ezer 168
welfare 105, 121
West Bank 129, 158, 159, 161, 166, 172, 183; democracy 180; Interim Agreement on 165
WEU (Western European Union) 19, 147
WHO (World Health Organisation) 37
'win sets' 42, 43, 51, 53
Wolfers, A. 19
Working Groups 170, 190, 202, 212
World Bank 29, 31, 61, 103, 107, 131, 171
World Trade Organisation 26
Wright, Quincy 177
Wright, R. 3, 51–2, 177, 181

Yassin, Sheikh Ahmad 183–4
Yeats, J. A. 84, 86–9 *passim*, 97–8, 119–21 *passim*
Yemen 34, 58, 63; classified low-income country 103; conflict 102, 141; conservative regime 155; Egyptian involvement in civil war 148; exports 81, 204; GNP per capita 105; imports 82; Pan-Arab regime 149, 150; remittances 79; Soviet connections 140, 144; unification 155
Yılmaz, Mesut 196–7, 205, 221

zero-sum game 20, 132, 206
Zionists 174, 221
Zollverein 16, 18